CATHOLIC EUROPE, 1592–1648

Catholic Europe, 1592–1648

Centre and Peripheries

TADHG Ó hANNRACHÁIN

OXFORD

UNIVERSITY PRESS

OXFORD
UNIVERSITY PRESS

Great Clarendon Street, Oxford, OX2 6DP,
United Kingdom

Oxford University Press is a department of the University of Oxford.
It furthers the University's objective of excellence in research, scholarship,
and education by publishing worldwide. Oxford is a registered trade mark of
Oxford University Press in the UK and in certain other countries

© Tadhg Ó hAnnracháin 2015

The moral rights of the author have been asserted

First Edition published in 2015

Impression: 2

Published in the United States of America by Oxford University Press
198 Madison Avenue, New York, NY 10016, United States of America

British Library Cataloguing in Publication Data
Data available

Library of Congress Control Number: 2015933907

ISBN 978–0–19–927272–3

Printed and bound by
CPI Group (UK) Ltd, Croydon, CR0 4YY

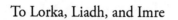
To Lorka, Liadh, and Imre

Acknowledgements

This book would not have been possible without the fellowship provided by the Irish Research Council or the presidential fellowship from University College Dublin and I gratefully acknowledge the support of both institutions. I was fortunate also to be the joint Principal Investigator in an Irish Research Council Thematic Grant entitled 'Insular Christianities' in the course of writing of the book and the opportunities which this gave me to meet and consult with scholars working in this field was an inestimable advantage. The staff of numerous libraries and archives accorded me assistance and I would note with special gratitude the archivists at the Archivio Storico 'De Propaganda Fide' and at the Magyar Országos Levéltár. Thanks also to all the staff at Oxford University Press for their patience and professionalism. I would like to acknowledge also the support of my school and record my thanks to Michael Laffan, Edward James, and John McCafferty, for their patience as my predecessors as Heads.

Many of my colleagues and friends in UCD have been extremely helpful to me. Judith Devlin, Eddie Coleman, Lindsey Earner-Byrne (and Georg), Catherine Cox, Ivar McGrath, and Paul Rouse have assisted and encouraged me in so many various ways. At a time when I had great doubts about ever writing the book Alvin Jackson helped to preserve my confidence in a dinner conversation which he may have forgotten but I have not. I have also been fortunate in being able to share some of my ideas and gain valuable suggestions for improving my work from a number of outstanding scholars such as Alex Walsham, Simon Ditchfield, and Robert Armstrong. Needless to say, the remaining errors in the book are entirely my own. Robert's friendship, like that of Dick Sheil, Michael Murphy, Tom Finnegan, Ildi and Toni, and Bríd McGrath, means an enormous amount to me.

I owe a very great debt to my Irish and Hungarian families. My late father, who passed away while I was writing this book, never allowed his own outstanding scholarship to prevent him from taking an intense and encouraging interest in my work. I miss him every day. To my mother, Deirdre, to Máire, Gar, Donncha, and Mairéad I can only say how utterly grateful I am for all your support. Sincere thanks too to all the other 'Belfasts', 'Strawberries', 'Galways', and 'Oxfords'. Thank you also, Gergö, Klára, and Anna, and my gratitude and love Borcsa, *a sivatagban is*, for everything you have done for me. My children, Lorka, Liadh, and Imre are the light of my life, *bun agus barr mo scéil*, and I dedicate this book to them. *Mo ghrá go deo sibh.*

Contents

1

Introduction—The Periodization of Catholic Renewal

In the conventional canon of the historiography of Catholic renewal, 1592 might seem an unusual date to commence a study. This is not merely because of the obvious accusation of arbitrariness which can be levelled at the choice of any one date in dealing with such a subject, but also because, if a specific date was to be selected, then 1517, the date of Luther's breach with Rome, or 1545, the year of the first assembly of the Council of Trent, or 1563, the year of its close, might appear instantly more logical. By 1592 so many of the vital events and processes which helped to shape the currents of Catholic renewal had already occurred. Not only had the Council of Trent closed almost three decades previously, after almost twenty years of intermittent sittings, but the Society of Jesus, the very model of the new spirituality and organization of the revivified regular orders, was entering into the second half century of its existence. The Capuchins, the Counter-Reformation flagship of the family of St Francis, were similarly long established south of the Alps and had received, as it transpired, the vitally important dispensation to spread into northern Europe by 1570, while the spirituality of the Oratory had already made a significant mark. In Rome the recently deceased pontiff, Sixtus V, had overseen a major rehaul of the Roman Curia and is often depicted as the last of the great reforming popes who had abandoned the historic papal mission of frustration of reform to take on the challenge of leadership of the renewal of the post-Tridentine church. In political terms, the great warrior of the Counter-Reformation, Philip II, was entering into the last decade of his life, his greatest push at the combined enemy of his Dutch rebels and heretical English former sister-in-law having failed in 1588.

The importance of events such as Trent, or of figures of the stamp of Ignatius Loyola, or Filippo Neri, or Philip II, is incontestable yet one of the purposes of this book is to re-emphasize the degree to which the processes of late sixteenth- and seventeenth-century Catholic reform shaped themselves in response to contemporary conditions. It is now largely accepted that the Early Modern evolution of the Catholic world was the result of a number of processes which ran through several centuries.[1] Yet, paradoxically, this focus on the long duration has done

---

[1] This central insight of scholars such as Jean Delumeau, John Bossy, Wolfgang Reinhard, Marc Forster, and A.D. Wright is reflected in the general overviews of Catholic reform: see for instance R. Po-chia Hsia, *The World of Catholic Renewal, 1540–1770* (Cambridge: Cambridge University Press, 1998); Robert Bireley, *The Refashioning of European Catholicism: A Reassessment of the Counter Reformation*

curiously little to offer a new perspective on the last decades of the sixteenth and the first half of the seventeenth centuries. Rather, the older tradition of dealing with the events of the mid-sixteenth century as the era in which the template of Catholic renewal was created, with the succeeding decades as something of a passive backdrop, continues to exert a powerful gravitational influence.[2] This carries the risk of underplaying the contingency of much of the developments which occurred in Catholicism several decades after the close of the Council of Trent.

Recent work on the issue of censorship in Italy, for instance, has operated to revise a traditional narrative of the steadily increasing rigidity of a repressive apparatus emerging in the aftermath of Trent and reaching a crescendo in the Clementine index of 1596. At least until the end of the sixteenth century, significant disagreements and sometimes heated conflicts existed between different individuals, institutions, and tendencies within the church, resulting in revisions and moderations of previous positions on occasion. Moreover, the failure of the Congregation of the Index to establish workable local congregations in the late sixteenth century meant that the task of seizing prohibited books devolved to the local tribunal of the Holy Office. This did not notably impede the process of repression but it undermined the implementation of expurgatory policy which devolved to the centre with the result that incalculable numbers of books were simply removed from circulation and never restored in a 'purified' form. The vast nature of the projected exercise which related not merely to vernacular scriptural, doctrinal, and theological works, but extended to law, cultural treatises, literature, science, indeed practically all aspects of human knowledge, meant that it could not be efficiently implemented, but this very failure created unforeseen knock-on effects which were to ripple through Italian culture for centuries. While it would be false to assign one particular date as the hinge-point in this complex process, it seems clear that the complex manoeuvres between the Holy Office and the Congregation of the Index in the issuing of the Clementine index of the 1590s was at least as significant as the original decision to entrust the revision of the 1559 Pauline index to the bishops at Trent.[3] Thus, rather than the working on of a clockwork engine wound up by the Spiritual Exercises and Trent, in much of Europe the process of Catholic renewal was in temporal terms a phenomenon of the seventeenth century. Moreover it occurred in fits and starts

---

(Washington D.C.: The Catholic University of America Press, 1999), and John O'Malley's wide-ranging historiographical essay *Trent and All That: Renaming Catholicism in the Early Modern Era* (Harvard: Harvard University Press, 2000), which all emphasize the idea of a long and continually evolving series of developments over a wide chronological span.

[2] O'Malley's stimulating essay, for instance, whose subject is the need to interrogate categories and assumptions with care, concludes on precisely this note, that it is in the sixteenth century that the kernel of importance resides. For his part, even the historian of Lamormaini, Bireley, although less subject to this tendency, in his chapter on the papacy, significantly coupled with the Council of Trent, devotes less than two pages to the pontiffs who succeeded Sixtus V.

[3] Gigliola Fragnito, 'Introduction' and 'The Central and Peripheral Organization of Censorship' in idem, *Church, Censorship and Culture in Early Modern Italy* (Cambridge: Cambridge University Press, 2001), pp. 1–12 and 13–49.

rather than in a smoothly linear fashion and involved an active adaptation of the sixteenth-century inheritance.[4]

Even with regard to the council itself, the reification of the Tridentine legacy in the latter part of the sixteenth century, when the bishops and theologians who had actually attended the council, and who were acutely aware of its compromises, inadequacies, and provisionality, were dying and dead, significantly altered the perception of the council's decrees within the Catholic world. The church which formulated itself on the basis of Tridentine norms was notably different to the church which formulated them and, as Guiseppe Alberigo's classical analysis demonstrated, this owed as much to the later process of interpretation as to the content of the council's decisions.[5] The publication of the decrees but not the rich surrounding material accentuated the transmutation of the council from an event to a static body of doctrinal and disciplinary norms, especially because Tridentine decisions frequently did not reflect the ideas brought to light during the debates.[6]

In the period under review in this study, the decrees of the council thus acquired an almost mythical status. The nuncio to Venice, Luigi Taverna, for instance, in 1592 was urged to ensure that the decrees of the council were executed throughout his area of responsibility as this constituted the essence of reform.[7] The importance of Trent in Spain was emphasized in even stronger terms:

> Everybody knows that the greatest benefit which the church of God has received for many years since was the celebration of the Council of Trent and the observation of its decrees. For this reason, Your Lordship will always keep his eye that in all the parts of his nunciature they should be precisely observed and particularly in your Chancellory, on every occasion exhorting all the bishops, prelates, chapters and clergy, both secular and regular to not omit an iota of that which with such great effort and expense from the Holy Spirit through the mouths of so many worthy prelates was decreed in that Holy Council, and doing this, reform without difficulty will succeed and ecclesiastical discipline will be conserved and augmented.[8]

[4] Wolfgang Reinhard, 'Il Concilio di Trento e la modernizzazione della Chiesa' in Paolo Prodi and Wolfgang Reinhard (eds), *Il concilio di Trento e il moderno* (Bologna: Il Mulino, 1996), pp. 27–53, at 39.

[5] See Guiseppe Alberigo, 'Studi e problem relative all'applicazione del concilio di Trento in Italia', *Rivista Storica Italiana* 70 (1958), 239–98, at 297 which emphasizes the importance of the period between 1590 and the first years of the seventeenth century as a critical period of transformation in Italian religious history. An English synopsis of some of his key arguments, where he emphasizes the pontificate of Sixtus V rather than that of Clement VIII as a critical turning point, can be found in Guiseppe Alberigo, 'From the Council of Trent to "Tridentinism"' in Raymond Bulman and Frederick Parella (eds), *From Trent to Vatican II: Historical and Theological Investigations* (Oxford: Oxford University Press, 2006), pp. 19–38.

[6] Alberigo, 'Council of Trent', p. 30; Joseph Bergin, 'The Counter-Reformation Church and its Bishops', *Past & Present* 165 (1999), 30–73, at 34.

[7] Instructions to Luigi Taverna 25 February 1592 (Klaus Jaitner (ed.), *Die Hauptinstruktionen Clemens' VIII., für die Nuntien und Legaten an den europäischen Fürstenhöfen, 1592–1605* (two vols, Tübingen: Max Niemayer Verlag, 1984), 1, pp. 1–5, at 5); see also the Instructions to the nuncio to Florence, Marino Zorzi, 25 February 1592 (ibid., pp. 6–7).

[8] 'Il maggior beneficio che ha ricevuto la chiesa di Dio da molti anni in qua, ognun sa che è stata la celebratione del Concilio di Trento et la osservatione de li suoi decreti. Per questo respetto V.S. haverà sempre l'occhio che per tutte le parti de la sua nuntiatura siano osservati essattamente et massimamente ne la sua Cancellaria, esortando per ogni occasione tutti li vescovi, prelati, capitoli et clero, tanto secolare, quanto regolare, a non preterire di un iota quello che con tanta fatica et spesa da lo

The reconciliation of Henri IV in the pontificate of Clement VIII prompted a long-running series of attempts to secure the promulgation of the Tridentine decrees in France which, almost in themselves, were portrayed as the magic bullet for the kingdom's ills. In 1601, for instance, the new nuncio to the kingdom, Innocenzo del Bufalo, was urged in the strongest possible terms to prevail upon the King to fulfil his long-postponed promise to introduce the council which 'all universally believed should be the only means of reform in France, . . . to take away the ignorance and abuses of the clergy, to introduce the reform of customs and to extirpate heresies'.[9] Del Bufalo was enjoined never to abandon this matter but to attempt every avenue with the King, his ministers, the royal council and the *Parlement* to overcome the difficulties and to demonstrate to the monarch the bad impression created by the refusal of a king reputed the defender of the church to endorse a universal council accepted in the rest of the world and of such great utility to the church.

The fact that the French kingdom, although not the French church, continued to resist the promulgation of Trent precisely during the era when it was becoming the centre of gravity of Catholic spirituality and renewal indicates that the mythical status accorded to the council by its papal proponents also served wider purposes. One of the vital factors underpinning the papal endorsement of Trent was in fact an emphasis on Tridentine endorsement of papal power. In his jurisdictional conflicts with the Spanish monarchy, Clement VIII was eager for the King "to remember with what an attendance of bishops, theologians, and canonists was celebrated the Holy Council of Trent, where his ambassadors participated and prelates of that doctrine and value which he knows, the discussion which was held of all matters of controversy and finally how the superiority of the Apostolic See was recognized and left intact in its supreme position".[10]

The degree to which the decrees of the council had become tied up with issues of papal prestige and leadership was also demonstrated by Clement VIII's furious reaction to the edict of Nantes. The Pope believed that Henri IV's action had made the papacy the laughing stock of the world, not least because of the signal contrast between the French King's willingness to validate the edict and his failure to fulfil his promises concerning the promulgation of the council. And in a particularly turbulent interview with the French ecclesiastical leadership in Rome he made it

---

Spirito Santo per bocca di tanti degni prelate è stato ordinato in quell Sacro Concilio, et facendo questo, si verrà a far la riforma senza travaglio, et la disciplina ecclesiastica si conservarà et augmentarà': Instructions for Camillo Borghese, 27 October, 1592 (ibid., pp. 95–6).

[9] 'lo crede universalmente ognuno, che debba esser l'unico mezzo della riforma della Francia, che sia per tirar via gli abusi et l'ignoranza nel clero, introdurre la riforma dei costume et estirpare l'heresie': Instructions for Innocenzo del Bufalo, July 1601 (Bernard Barbiche, *Correspondance du nonce en France Innocenzo del Bufalo évéque de camerino (1601–1604)* (Rome and Paris: Presses de l'Université Grégorienne/Editions E. de Boccard, 1964), pp. 149–50).

[10] 'ricordarsi con quanta frequenza de'vescovi, theologi et canonisti fu celebrato il Sacro Concilio di Trento, dove intervennero i suoi ambasciatori e prelate di quella dottrina et valore che lei sa, la discussione che fu fatta di tutte le materie controverse, et finalmente come la superiorità della Sede Ap.a fu riconosciuta et lasciata intatta nel luogo suo supremo': Second Instruction for Camillo Borghese, 28 October 1593 (*Die Hauptinstrucktionen Clemens' VIII.*, I, pp. 172–3).

clear that he believed the immediate promulgation of Trent would represent the only acceptable *quid pro quo* for the insult which he had suffered.[11]

Papal assumption of authority over the interpretation of the Tridentine legacy was a critical aspect of the council's reputation. Rome did not merely see the promotion of the decrees of Trent as an essential aspect of its role but it also considered the Apostolic See as their only fit interpreter. This had been emphasized since the conclusion of the council with the publication of the bull *Benedictus Deus* in 1564, which had pointedly failed to take up the council's suggestion of conciliar or consultative assistance to the papacy in addressing any problems which might arise concerning the reception of the decrees, and had arrogated to the papacy complete jurisdiction over the interpretation of the council.[12]

Central to the diplomatic offensive mounted by Rome concerning the centrality of Trent was an insistence on the organic connection between religious and political stability. Not only would religion prosper more in times of peace and tranquillity[13] but reform, in particular of the clergy through the acceptance of the Tridentine decrees, was seen as the key to political order.[14] Thus in 1607 Paul V's new nuncio to Poland, Francesco Simonetta, was informed:

> The conservation of the political state depends on good spiritual government, because secular people, allowing themselves to be influenced more by good ecclesiastics in everything which pertains to the salvation of souls, they are easily induced to offices of charity, through which public tranquillity is maintained and divine worship increases. Your Lordship should therefore principally exhort the bishops to hold the clergy in good discipline and to delegate the care of souls to pious and intelligent persons so as to give good example through words and through actions.[15]

Critical to this whole process was the Council of Trent which, the new nuncio was informed, 'would supply the true remedy to remove abuses and to conserve fear of the Lord God in the people'.[16] Twenty-eight years later, the need for more exact

[11] Arnold d'Ossat to Henri IV, 28 March 1599 (*Lettres de l'Illustrissime et Révérendissime Cardinal d'Ossat, éveque de Bayeux au roy Henry le Grand et à Monsieur Villeroy* (Paris, 1627), book 5, pp. 33–41).

[12] Guiseppe Alberigo, 'From the Council of Trent to "Tridentinism"' in Raymond Bulman (ed.), *From Trent to Vatican II: Historical and Theological Investigations* (Oxford: Oxford University Press, 2006), pp. 19–38, at 20–1; Umberto Mazzone, 'I dibattiti tridentini: techniche di assemblea e di controllo' in Paolo Prodi and Wolfgang Reinhard (eds), *Il Concilio di Trento e il moderno: Annali dell'Istituto Storico Italo-Germanico Quaderno 45* (Bologna: Il Mulino, 1996), pp. 101–36, at 117.

[13] 'Theresia cresce nelle guerre e si distrugge nella pace Christiana': Instructions for Ottavio Corsini, 4 April 1621 (Klaus Jaitner (ed.), *Die Hauptinstrucktionen Gregors XV für di Nuntien und Gesandten an den Europäischen Fürstenhöfen 1621–1623* (two vols, Tübingen: Max Niemeyer Verlag, 1997), 2, p. 539).

[14] Ibid.; Instructions for Innocenzo del Bufalo, July 1601 (Barbiche, *Correspondance du nonce Innocenzo del Bufalo*, pp. 150–1).

[15] 'Dal buon governo spirituale dipende la conservatione de lo stato politico, poiché lasciandosi persuader per lo più li secolari da buoni ecclesiastici tutto quell che appartiene a la salute de l'anima, s'inducono facilmente a li offitii di carità, con la quale si mantiene la quiete publica et s'accresce il culto divino. Dovrà perciò V.ra Signoria esortar principalmente i Vescovi a tenere in buona disciplina il clero, et deputare a la cura de l'anime persone pie et intelligente a dar buon'esempio con le parole et con le attioni.' (Adalbertus Tygielski, *Acta Nuntiaturae Poloniae Tomus XVIII Volumen 1 Franciscus Simonetta* 21 VI 1606–30 IX 1607 (Rome: Institutum Historicum Polonicum Romae, 1990), p. 21).

[16] 'Il Sacro Concilio di Trento somministra il vero remedio per levar gl'abusi et conserver ne'popoli il timore del Signor Dio.' (ibid.).

observance of Tridentine decrees in the Polish-Lithuanian commonwealth, particularly with regard to visitation, residence, and quality control concerning ordinands, continued to be emphasized to the new nuncio, Mario Filonardi.[17]

Identical emphases can be seen in the papacy of Gregory XV, a pontificate deservedly seen as supplementing the Tridentine legacy with a concern for missionary expansion of Catholicism, but which nevertheless like its predecessors continued to emphasize the central importance of the Tridentine decrees. The instructions of Gregory's administration to its first nuncios in 1621 provide a revealing insight into this mental universe. The acceptance of the Council of Trent was advanced as the best remedy to all the many ecclesiastical ills of Germany. Indeed, the appalling state of ecclesiastical discipline was seen as contributory to the origin and spread of heresy.[18] An identical analysis was applied to France. In the instructions to the French nuncio, Ottavio Corsini, the collapse of France into heresy and its continued suffering in this respect was presented as centrally linked to the lack of willingness within the kingdom to embrace the path of reform according to papal and Tridentine principles, which were considered more or less synonymous. While God had originally punished the French people with the affliction of heresy because of their lack of respect for papal superiority and the licence and arrogance of their clergy, 'it was the repugnance to give place to the reforms of the Council of Trent and the Apostolic Constitutions' which had opened the way to France's practical destruction.[19] In turn the reconstruction of the kingdom and the remedy of its ills was seen as effectively reducible to 'the observance of the Council of Trent'. On the acceptance and observance of the council's decrees 'depended in large part the conservation of religion and ecclesiastical discipline'.[20] The 'effects of holy ecclesiastical discipline from the observance of the Council and put into action by the bishops and clergy' would of itself thus eventually result in the extinction of heresy in the kingdom.[21] The same theme continued to be echoed during the long pontificate of Urban VIII.[22]

This emphasis on first the acceptance and then the observance of the decrees of Trent was, therefore, seen as a cardinal element of papal leadership of the Catholic world and an integral aspect of the diplomatic relationship between Rome and the Catholic powers of Europe. Thus, towards the end of the period under review in the 1640s, when the collapse of the Stuart multiple monarchy into civil wars

---

[17] Instructions to Mario Filonardi, 19 July 1635 (Theresia Chynczewska-Hennel (ed.), *Acta Nuntiaturae Poloniae Tomus XXV Volumen 1 Marius Filonardi (1635–43) Volumen 1* (Cracoviae: Academia Scientiarum et Litterarum Polona, 2003), pp. 16–50, at 25).

[18] Instructions for Carlo Carafa, 12 April 1621 (*Die Hauptinstruktionen Gregors XV*, 2, pp. 625, 629).

[19] 'la repugnanza nel dar luogo alle riforme del Conclio di Trento e delle Costitutioni Apostoliche': Instructions for Ottavio Corsini, 4 April 1621 (ibid., pp. 535–74, at 538).

[20] 'l'osservanza del Concilio di Trento', 'dipende in gran parte la conservation della religion (sic) cattolica e disciplina ecclesiastica' (ibid., p. 547).

[21] 'Gli effetti della santa disciplina ecclesiastica dal'osservanza del Concilio e dai vescovi e cleri operati estingueranno ben l'heresia nella Francia' (ibid., p. 549).

[22] See the Instructions to Ranuccio Scotti, 21 May 1639 (Pierre Blet (ed.), *Correspondance du Nonce en France Ranuccio Scotti (1639–41)* (Paris and Rome: E. de Boccard, 1965), pp. 91–9, at 94).

allowed the emergence of a short-lived Catholic state in Ireland, the instructions prepared in the early days of the papacy of Innocent X for its first and, as it transpired, only nuncio, GianBattista Rinuccini, once again placed a primary emphasis on Trent. The promulgation of its decrees was something which he was to push 'with extraordinary diligence' because on these 'was based the reform of relaxed ecclesiastical discipline' which once accomplished would lead to many happy outcomes.[23]

As noted previously, this reification of the Tridentine legacy was a product of an era when the personnel who had actually attended the council were gradually departing the scene. Its dominance was accentuated by the apparent possibilities of success which systematization and bureaucratization of administrative procedures seemed to offer. 'Tridentinism' offered the prospect that the problems of both ignorance and superstition, on the one hand, and heresy, on the other, could be confronted by careful planning and adherence to a particular template. It offered the emotional satisfactions of what might be described as a controlled culpability: its exponents were required both to make good the sins and omissions of their predecessors while confronting the temptations to indulge in the same mistakes of carelessness and disorder. And in certain instances, 'Tridentinism' actually involved the quiet jettisoning of some aspects of Trent and the adoption of new models and behaviours. While the example of censorship indicates that even in Italy the process of evolution continued unabated into the late sixteenth century and beyond, this becomes particularly evident when the perspective adopted is from the periphery of Europe, rather than what might be described as the Mediterranean heartland of Catholicism in the Italian and Iberian peninsulae.

In addition to its starting date, the focus on Europe in this book is also perhaps somewhat unfashionable. Much of the best recent work on Catholicism has in fact attempted to provincialize the European experience. But rather than running counter to this trend, the current study seeks to demonstrate that European Catholicism itself was a house of many mansions where the religion adapted to many varied societal conditions. The Catholicism of Ireland became rooted in an environment very different from that of England or the Netherlands, let alone Bohemia or Hungary, and examining these specificities on the periphery offers new perspectives on the nature of the confession as a whole.

The choice of the election of Clement VIII as the starting point of this study has been influenced by the desire to emphasize this element of contingency and adaptation in late sixteenth- and seventeenth-century Catholicism, particularly in the peripheral societies of Catholic Europe such as the Habsburg lands of Hungary and Bohemia, the Atlantic archipelago of Britain and Ireland, the Netherlands, Poland, and the Balkan peninsula which represent this book's chief focus of interest. But the Clementine papacy also saw the coming together of a number of features and events which were to exert a critical influence on the future development of

---

[23] 'con straordinaria diligenza', 'si fonda la riforma della rilasciata disciplina ecclesiastica': see the Instructions for GianBattista Rinuccini, 1645 (G.A. Aiazzi (ed.), *Nunziatura in Irlanda di Monsignor Gio. Batista Rinuccini Arcivescovo di Fermo negli anni 1645 a 1649* (Firenze, 1844), p. xlv).

European Catholicism, whether in terms of the developing impact of changes instigated in the previous half century or in the gestation of new processes. It is precisely this period, namely the decades around 1600, which Heinz Schilling has identified as a critical era in the fashioning of European modernity, as the forces of confessionalization reordered political identity and the elaboration of a new international system of power states.[24] While the building blocks for the construction of Europe's major confessional identities, Lutheran, Calvinist/Reformed, Anglican, and Tridentine Catholic, are traditionally located in the sixteenth century, according to such milestones as the Lutheran *Confessio Augustana* (1530) and the Book of Concord (1577), the Reformed *Confessiones Helveticae* of 1536 and 1566, the thirty-nine articles of 1563 and the *Professio fidei Tridentina* of 1564,[25] it is widely acknowledged that it was not until the end of the sixteenth century and into the seventeenth that the confessional unity of church and state was able to impose a new degree of social and religious regulation at a local level.[26] The consequences of this revolution were not only extreme in terms of the internal workings of all Europe's polities as the projected power of the state expanded, provoking social conflict and resistance, but also manifested themselves in the international conflicts of the period.

The 1590s have long been seen as a period of particular crisis, especially studied in terms of the themes of dearth, famine, debt, and economic depression in England, France, Germany, Italy, and the Netherlands, but of particular importance also in other parts of the continent such as the Austrian Habsburg lands, which saw a series of revolts in 1588–92 and 1594–6, in Ireland where the entire structure of the English state was called into question, in Spain where it helped to prompt the General Reformation promoted by Pérez de Herrera, in Hungary, and in the Balkan lands of Transylvania, Moldova, and Wallachia which became embroiled in an intricate series of internecine and anti-Turkish conflicts.[27] The complex conjunction of changes in climate, whose effects became sharply accentuated during the 1590s, and a slowing in inflation and the patterns of demographic growth, inevitably had resonances within the system of European religion which represented the chief explanatory structure available to the Early Modern population to interpret the events through which they were living.[28]

---

[24] Schilling's basic thesis has been elaborated in a host of publications: for a recent and succinct overview of his main ideas see Heinz Schilling, *Early Modern European Civilization and its Political and Cultural Dynamism: The Menahem Stern Jerusalem Lectures* (Hanover and London: University Press of New England, 2008), p. 14.

[25] ibid., p. 19.

[26] Sheilagh C. Ogilvie, 'Germany and the General Crisis', *Historical Journal* 35 (1992), 417–41.

[27] Peter Clark (ed.), *The European Crisis of the 1590s* (London: George Allen and Unwin, 1985); Jon Arrizabalaga, 'Poor Relief in Counter-Reformation Castile: An Overview' in Ole Peter Grell, Andrew Cunningham, and Jon Arrizabalaga (eds), *Health Care and Poor Relief in Counter-Reformation Europe* (London and New York: Routledge, 1999), pp. 151–76, at 168.

[28] With regard to climate change see in particular Geoffrey Parker and L.M. Smith, 'Introduction' in Geoffrey Parker and L.M. Smith (eds), *Europe and the General Crisis* (London and New York: Routledge, 1997), pp. 1–31; see also P.H. Wilson, 'The Causes of the Thirty Years War', *English Historical Review* 123 (2008), 554–86, esp. 571–4.

In this regard, the 1590s were in many respects the crucial period with regard to the fashioning of the continent's confessional map. This was most evident with regard to France. While a sustainable case can be made that already by the 1590s it was clear that an outright Protestant victory, in the sense of a refashioning of the French monarchy as a state with a church of the Reformed tradition, was no longer possible, the role that France would play in the future of Catholicism was very much open to question. The abjuration of heresy by Henri of Navarre and his reconciliation by the French bishops at Saint-Denis in 1593 created new ripples of Gallican tension between the French church and Rome, with the idea of a patriarch of the French church emerging once more. Indeed even in the 1640s anxiety that tensions between the Pamfili papacy and Mazarin's government could prompt a French schism *à l'Anglaise* continued to surface.[29] Clement began his reign with the firm intent of pursuing an inherited policy orientated towards the exclusion of Henri of Navarre from the French throne. However, despite papal support for the *Ligue* and Sixtus V's excommunication of Henri IV, even before his final abjuration the Bourbon King remained the key player in terms of determining France's confessional future, particularly since the death of the Cardinal de Bourbon in 1590 had raised the spectre of the Infanta of Spain as a major candidate. Clement's decision to withstand an extraordinary array of pressures, and in particular to deny the Spanish thesis that a twice-lapsed heretic could not be restored to communion with the church, was of incalculable importance to the confessional future of the continent.[30] In political terms, the effect of this decision was to transform Catholicism from an essentially Habsburg-dominated religion to a new bi-polar political condition, in which the papacy could acquire a fresh capacity for spiritual leadership. While bitterly opposed by Philip II, Clement's actions were of considerable relevance to Spain itself in the context of its long war with the Dutch rebels and England. In the early seventeenth century the Clementine example could be voiced in the Spanish Council of State as a reason why Spain had no obligation for the re-Catholicization of England and that the policy of support for English Catholics which had been followed under Philip II had unwittingly contributed to the religion's persecution rather than its survival.[31] It also ensured that the extraordinary spiritual vitality which was to characterize French Catholicism over the following decades, itself in many respects a result of the workable arrangement between throne and Rome over which Clement had presided, was to be a vivifying influence throughout the entire Catholic church, rather than one confined within Gallican boundaries.

In contrary terms, the 1590s can be seen as the decade when another of the traditional pillars of European Catholicism, namely England, slipped definitively from

[29] Tadhg Ó hAnnracháin, 'Vatican diplomacy and the mission of Rinuccini to Ireland', *Archivium Hibernicum* XLVII (1993), 78–88.

[30] Eric Cochrane, 'Caesar Baronius and the Counter-Reformation', *Catholic Historical Review* 66 (1980), 53–8.

[31] Speech of Juan Fernández de Velasco, Constable of Castile, quoted in Henry Kamen, 'Toleration and Dissent in Sixteenth-Century Spain: The Alternative Tradition', *Sixteenth-Century Journal* 19 (1988), 3–23, at 21–2.

the Catholic world. On Elizabeth's accession in 1558, the vast majority of her subjects were content in adherence to her dead sister's religion. In the Stour valley, the Weald of Kent, and in London, significant numbers of Protestants were to be found yet Mary's aggressive and programmatic restoration of Catholicism had enjoyed remarkable success.[32] On taking the throne Elizabeth was clearly aware of the power of the old religion and was wary about provoking conservative reaction, as were bishops of the stamp of William Downham who did little or nothing to enforce uniformity of practice in the diocese of Chester. Throughout the 1560s the possibility of a Habsburg match also encouraged an emollient approach to the instigation of reform, setting aside the Queen's own idiosyncratic tendencies in religion.[33] For a large portion of Elizabeth's reign, a second restoration of Catholicism remained an active possibility depending on the vagaries of the monarch's health, dynastic succession and the international situation. Yet, as in the Dutch Republic, the existence of real attachment to the old religion was outweighed by unwillingness to oppose legitimate authority on religious grounds.[34] By the 1590s, only a tiny minority of the English population was prepared to risk outright recusancy, although Catholic sympathies were also manifested by a variety of other behaviours, such as infrequent attendance at the religious services of the established church or a reluctance to take its sacraments or the Oath of Supremacy. Within the majority population, however, the odd religious compromises of the Elizabethan settlement had sunk sufficiently deep roots to confirm much of the English people in an identity which was explicitly Protestant and anti-Catholic.[35] However shallow the grasp of the theological principles of the new religion may have been among the general populace, and however much reformers might deplore the survival of popish habits and superstitions, the possibility of a Marian-style restoration with relatively minimal coercion and widespread support had definitively vanished, although even down to the 1640s Rome was to cherish chimerical delusions of the possibility of reintegrating England into the Catholic fold.

Precisely the opposite trajectory can be glimpsed in the dependent English sister kingdom of Ireland. Although no real evidence of native enthusiasm for either the Henrician or Edwardine Reformations has ever been detected in Ireland, the original Elizabethan settlement paradoxically encountered less opposition in the Western kingdom than in England. Whereas the Marian episcopacy in England, despite the loss of Pole's leadership, mounted strong opposition in parliament to

[32] Eamon Duffy, *Fires of Faith: Catholic England under Mary Tudor* (New Haven: Yale University Press, 2009), pp. 113, 161 detail concentrations of Protestants in England during the 1550s.
[33] K.J. Kesselring, *The Northern Rebellion of 1569* (Basingstoke: Palgrave Macmillan, 2010), pp. 18–22; Susan Doran, 'Religion and politics at the Court of Elizabeth: the Habsburg marriage negotiations of 1559–1567', *English Historical Review* 104 (1989), 908–26.
[34] Jo Spaans, 'Catholicism and Resistance to the Reformation in the Netherlands' in Philip Benedict, Guido Marnef, Henk Van Nierop, and Marc Venard (eds), *Reformation, Revolution and Civil War in France and the Netherlands 1555–1585* (Amsterdam: Royal Netherlands Academy of Arts and Sciences, 1999), pp. 149–63.
[35] Jeremy Gregory, 'The making of a Protestant nation: "success" and "failure" in England's Long Reformation' in Nicholas Tyacke (ed.), *England's Long Reformation 1500–1800* (London: UCL Press, 1998), pp. 307–33, at 309–10; Michael Finlayson, *Historians, Puritanism and the English Revolution* (Toronto: University of Toronto Press, 1983).

the Queen's ecclesiastical policies and found widespread support in the lower house of convocation and in the universities of Oxford and Cambridge for their stance, ultimately leading to fourteen bishops and the majority of prebendaries and office holders being deprived for refusal of the Oath of Supremacy, in Ireland only two bishops suffered a similar fate.[36] This contrasting pattern may have reflected the two kingdoms' differing experience of the Henrician and Edwardine Reformations. Whereas the Marian bishops in England had become keenly aware of the power of the Royal Supremacy under the Queen's predecessors, and thus were determined to oppose it, the limited nature of religious change in Ireland under Henry VIII and his son may have helped to dull the sense of urgency within the Irish episcopacy, particularly as Elizabeth's government, alarmed at the extent of English opposition to the settlement, offered some sops to religious conservatism. It is unclear whether the entire Episcopal bench or the prebendaries in Dublin's two cathedrals, for instance, were systematically required to take the Oath of Supremacy. Overt denial of the real presence was avoided in the Act of Uniformity passed in the Irish parliament in 1560, which also lacked offensive references to papal power. The permission for clerics who lacked linguistic competence in English to make use of Latin liturgical forms, and provision for church ornaments and clerical vestments based on the ordinances from the early years of Edward VI's reign, further contributed to a certain sense of continuity with past practice.[37]

For the first decades of Elizabeth's reign little genuinely principled religious opposition raised its head in Ireland. Certainly the political opponents of the growing expansion of the Tudor state were prepared to couch their opposition in religious terms, both in an attempt to appeal to the conservative instincts of the Irish population and in an effort to attract continental Catholic support for resistance, as had already occurred in the 1530s in the rebellion of Silken Thomas FitzGerald and in the Geraldine League's war against Henry VIII. But while little enthusiasm existed for the innovations of the Elizabethan settlement, the driving force behind Irish rebellion was political resentment rather than religious sentiment. As late as 1576 the English governor of Ireland, the lord deputy Sir Henry Sidney, in a scathing report on the weaknesses of the Established church in Ireland, focused on its infrastructural deficiencies rather than any Catholic threat. Even in the diocese of Meath in the heart of the English Pale, the ignorance and poverty of the clergy were identified as key obstacles to the inculcation of religious reform. From Sidney's perspective reform lay in addressing three basic problems: the physical ruin of churches, the lack of adequate ministers, and the insufficient financial support available to support a proper ministry.[38] The following decades, however, added the emergence of a confessional rival to the structural problems of the

---

[36] Duffy, *Fires of Faith*, pp. 193–7; Henry A. Jeffries, *The Irish Church and the Tudor Reformations* (Dublin: Four Courts Press, 2010), pp. 125–7.

[37] Steven G. Ellis, *Ireland in the age of the Tudors 1447–1603* (London: Longman, 1998), pp. 225–6.

[38] Sir Henry Sidney to Elizabeth I, 28 April 1576 (W. Maziere Brady (ed.), *State papers concerning the Irish church in the time of Queen Elizabeth* (London: Longmans, Green, Reader & Dyer, 1868), pp. 15–16).

Established church in Ireland. Within three years of Sidney's report to the Queen, a papally-backed military excursion landed in Ireland. While the leaders of the ensuing rebellion can be located within a traditional pattern of politically-motivated alienation which found expression in the language of religious grievance, a genuine element of confessional conviction can be glimpsed in the invasion's original leader, Sir James FitzMaurice FitzGerald, and even more evidently in the Pale aristocrat, Viscount Baltinglas, and the coterie of Pale gentry in his entourage, who rose the following year in support of the rebellion. Significantly, however, the principal intellectual underpinning of the revolt was provided by the English Catholic priest and author, Nicholas Sanders. It was not until the end of the century that Irish Catholicism was to produce a major intellectual figure, in the person of Peter Lombard, to articulate a coherent religiously-motivated argument concerning the validity of rebellion. This was in sharp contrast to England where the university tradition of Catholic resistance to Elizabeth that had flared up in Oxford and Cambridge on her accession relocated to the continent, where it constituted itself as a significant rival to the intellectual hegemony of the established church.[39]

The 1580s witnessed a steady intensification of the Catholic challenge to the Established church in Ireland and increasing numbers of Irish men going abroad in search of a Catholic education in continental universities but it was the 1590s which in many respects represented the watershed decade in terms of the confessional division of the island. The submergence of the island in massive rebellion gave the opportunity for unpunished recusancy even in the traditionally loyal English community of the Pale and the towns. The Bishop of Cork and Ross, William Lyon, noted in 1596, for instance:

> where I had a thousand or more in a church at sermon, I now have not five; and whereas I have seen 500 communicants or more, now are there not three; and not one woman either at Divine service or communion.

He placed the blame for this change on 'false teachers' who drew the people 'to that palpable and damnable blindness, to obey her Majesty's capital enemy, that Antichrist of Rome'. Chief among these he identified seminary priests who had returned to Ireland and who not only convinced the general population that the ceremonies of the established church represented the 'devil's service' but who convinced many of the serving clergy within the state church to abandon their benefices to become 'massing priests'.[40]

While the ethnically English population of the island did not, as it transpired, rise in bulk in support of a rebellion which they continued to fear as a principally Gaelic insurrection, their loyalty to the crown, as Lyon himself noted bitterly, was significantly compromised. In 1599, the most important magnate defending the crown's presence in Ireland, Thomas Butler, the Earl of Ormond, commented on the 'dangerous impressions' made in the minds of the Queen's traditionally loyal

[39] Marvin O'Connell, *Thomas Stapleton and the Counter Reformation* (New Haven and London: Yale University Press, 1964), pp. 28–30.

[40] William Lyon to Lord Hunsdon, 6 July 1596 (TNA SP/63/182/47).

subjects by the 'pretexts of religion' advanced by the leader of the rebellion, Hugh O'Neill, second Earl of Tyrone. Even more tellingly, he noted that of the two thousand troops who should have come to support the resistance of the royal army to the rebels' incursion into the English Pale hardly two hundred had actually appeared to muster.[41]

The long-term effects of this pallid loyalty were deeply significant. For what became the ruling administrative elite of Ireland in the seventeenth century in the wake of the state's final victory over Hugh O'Neill, the lack of enthusiastic support from the Old English community in Ireland during the great rebellion was never forgiven and was highlighted as a justification for their political marginalization in the decades that followed.[42] The wedge which developed between the two communities was heightened also by an Old English perception of governmental heavy-handedness and understandable resentment of the economic privations that the community had endured during the 1590s, which ensured that they adhered ever more intensely to the recusant positions that had found relatively free expression in that decade. These developments ensured that there was to be little or no input from the traditional colonial community into the state church's attempted evangelization of the Gaelic population during the seventeenth century. This was to be a contributory factor in the spectacular lack of success which the Reformation was to enjoy in Gaelic Ireland, in sharp contrast to the linguistically and culturally similar community of Gaelic Scotland.[43]

For this second ethnic community in Ireland, the 1590s were also a key decade. O'Neill's ardent embracing of Counter-Reformation ideology undoubtedly owed much to the traditional pattern of political expediency but his very success in attracting Spanish support increasingly foregrounded this aspect of the rebellion. His utilization of clerical networks to support his lobbying of Spanish power further intensified a perception of the rebellion as principally motivated by religious issues. The extraordinarily brutal repression of the insurgency, which involved the deliberate destruction of the food sources of the generality of the rebel population, as well as the indiscriminate slaughter of non-combatants, presumably also contributed to the alienation of the Gaelic population from all aspects of English governmental innovation, including its church.[44] For both Irish ethnic communities, a vital component in the future strengthening of their Catholic identity was

---

[41] The Lords Justice Carey and Loftus, the Earl of Ormond and the rest of the Irish Council to the Privy Council of England, 3 December 1599 (*Calendar of the State Papers relating to Ireland Elizabeth I, 1599 April-1600 February*, ed. Ernest George Atkinson (London: Public Record Office, 1899), pp. 289–92).

[42] David Finnegan, 'The influence of the Irish Catholic clergy in shaping the religious and political allegiances of Irish Catholics, 1603–41' in Robert Armstrong and Tadhg Ó hAnnracháin (eds), *Insular Christianity: Alternative models of the Church in Britain and Ireland, c. 1570–1700* (Manchester: Manchester University Press, 2013), pp. 107–28, at 107–8.

[43] Tadhg Ó hAnnracháin, 'Introduction: Religious Acculturation and Affiliation in Early Modern Gaelic Scotland, Gaelic Ireland, Wales and Cornwall' in Tadhg Ó hAnnracháin and Robert Armstrong (eds), *Christianities in the Early Modern Celtic World* (Basingstoke: Palgrave Macmillan, 2014), pp. 1–16.

[44] Tadhg Ó hAnnracháin, 'Guerre de religion ou guerre ethnique? les conflits religieux en Irlande 1500–1650', *Revue Historique* 647 (2009), 65–97.

the development of an educational infrastructure on the territory of Catholic powers on the continent for the provision of educated priests for the Irish church. The first of these colleges, St Patrick's of Salamanca, opened its doors in 1592 and it was to be followed by seventeen more sister institutions by the fifth decade of the seventeenth century.[45] As is examined in more detail in Chapter 2, the 1590s were also a period of critical importance in terms of the organization of Dutch Catholicism with the institution of Vicars Apostolic as the administrative leadership of the *Missio Hollandica*.

Although ultimately it was not to lead to any significant revision of confessional borders, the 1590s also marked a deepening of papal interest in Eastern Europe which was to manifest itself in a series of directions. In 1587 the ardent Catholic Sigismund Vasa ascended the throne of Poland which since the union of Lublin in 1569 represented one of the largest states in Europe. This opened the door to an intensification of the existing dynamic of re-Catholicization in Poland. Dynastic, geographical, and ethnic factors also rendered Poland a potential nodal point for Catholic expansion in three directions, towards the Lutheran Scandinavian north, to the Orthodox East and in an anti-Turkish context to the south, via Transylvania where significant links had been forged through the Zapolya and Báthory families.[46] Clement VIII's personal experience as cardinal-legate in Poland meant that an individual with some genuine understanding of the Polish situation now held the throne of St Peter. The experience of living in and observing a multi-confessional society evidently made an impression on the future pope. In particular the possibilities inherent in the exercise of royal favour to further the expansion of the Catholic religion were borne in upon him and this may have formed part of the package of influences which impelled him to gamble in supporting Navarre as the King of France.[47]

It was during Clement's papacy also that significant efforts were made to evaluate the possibilities of rapprochement and union between the confessionalized Catholicism which derived from Trent and non-Latin Christian churches. The most famous of these was the Union of Brest which created the template for the integration of individuals from the orthodox metropolitanate of Kiev into the church of Rome.[48] As legate in Poland, Aldobrandini had become aware of tentative discussions concerning the subject of union between Ruthenian Orthodox Christians and Roman Catholicism which he encouraged. The aggressive behaviour

[45] For an introduction to this still under-researched phenomenon see T.J. Walsh, *The Irish Continental College Movement: The Colleges at Bordeaux, Toulouse, and Lille* (Dublin and Cork: Golden Eagle Books, 1973).

[46] Jan Slaski, 'Bellarmino e la letteratura della controriforma in Polonia' in Romeo de Maio, Agostino Borromeo, Luigi Gulia, Georg Lutz, and Aldo Mazzacane (eds), *Bellarmino e la Controriforma* (Sora: Centro di Studi Sorani Vincenzo Patriarca, 1990), pp. 521–30, at 521.

[47] Certainly, it was the papal hope that the King would adopt positions towards the favouring of converts from Protestantism on the model of Poland: see the Instructions for Innocenzo del Bufalo, July 1601 (Barbiche, *Correspondence du nonce Innocenzo del Bufalo*, pp. 143–4).

[48] Sophia Senyk, 'The Union of Brest: An Evaluation' in B. Groen (ed.), *Four Hundred Years: Union of Brest 1596–1996* (Leuven: Peeters Publishing House, 1998), pp. 1–16.

and financial demands of Patriarch Jeremiah II of Constantinople in a visit to the Metropolitan province of Kiev in 1588 created deep hostility within the Ruthenian clergy and accentuated their interest in union, which was also favoured by the crown.[49] Clement's subsequent election as Pope also stimulated hopes among the Ruthenian clergy for a more favourable union than had occurred at Florence and in effect they aspired to the replacement of the existing relationship between the metropolitanate of Kiev and Constantinople with an almost identical arrangement between Kiev and Rome.[50]

In the event, Holy Office suspicion of the Orthodox church, a reluctance to accept anything other than the articles of Trent as the basis of union, and a concern that the Union might weaken the buttresses which divided Tridentine Catholicism from contemporary Protestant belief, ensured that the terms of the Union were anything but generous. The bull *Magnus Dominus* of December 1595 permitted the continuation of Greek rites not by right but by apostolic benignity and although a further bull was granted two months later this did not guarantee the acceptors of the union that Rome would not require further concessions.[51] Nor under Sigismund did the Uniate prelates reap the rewards which they had hoped: Uniate bishops were not admitted to the Senate and there was resentment of the perceived Latinizing policy of the royal government. Following several turbulent decades, the royal government recognized the Orthodox hierarchy which resulted in a curial commission in 1636 to discuss the creation of a Kiev patriarchate under Roman jurisdiction. The original Clementine line, however, was reiterated and insistence on direct submission to Rome was again required following discussions of proposals sponsored by the King of Poland within *Propaganda Fide* in 1638 and 1645. Ultimately, therefore, rather than the successful assimilation of the Ruthenian church, the union enjoyed only limited success, largely because the Roman church lacked any capacity to compromise on what it saw as core Tridentine principles.[52] During the same time-frame other initiatives were pursued with different groupings. In 1593 Clement dispatched an envoy, GianBattista Vecchietti, to the Coptic Patriarch in Alexandria in an attempt to bring about the union of the Coptic church with Rome. This was eventually officially promulgated in June 1597, on terms which offered little element of compromise or any sense of equivalent ecclesial validity. In 1593 also Clement oversaw an intensification of Roman interest in the Greek

---

[49] Borys Gudziak, *Crisis and Reform: The Kyivan Metropolitanate, the Patriarchate of Constantinople and the Genesis of the Union of Brest* (Cambridge, MA: Harvard University Press, 1998).

[50] Ambroise Jobert, *De Luther à Mohila: La Pologne dans la crise de la chrétienté, 1517–1648* (Paris: Institut d'Études Slaves, 1974), pp. 332–5; Mikhail V. Dmitriev, 'Western Christianity and Eastern Orthodoxy' in R. Po-Chia Hsia (ed.), *The Cambridge History of Christianity: Reform and Expansion*, (Cambridge: Cambridge University Press, 2007), pp. 321–42.

[51] ibid., p. 339.

[52] ibid., p. 341; Laurent Tatarenko, 'La Naissance de l'Union de Brest: La Curie romaine et le tournant de l'année 1595', *Cahiers du Monde russe* 46: 1/2 (2005), 345–54, at 353–4; Dmitriev, 'Western Christianity'; nevertheless in 1939 the number of Greek Catholics stemming from this Union stood at over four million which marked it as the single most successful realization of union between the Greek and Latin churches: see Wincenty Urban, 'L'oeuvre des missions de l'église catholique en pologne' in Marian Rechowicz (ed.), *Millénaire du Catholicisme en Pologne*, (Lublin: The Scientific Society of the Catholic University in Lublin, 1969), pp. 357–409, at 391.

church in Italy by establishing a congregation for the reformation of its abuses under his trusted administrator, Cardinal Santorio.[53]

From the beginning of his papacy Clement was animated by the desire to use the Catholic polities of Eastern Europe, most notably Poland, as well as the dependent Ottoman satellite states of Transylvania, Moldova, and Wallachia in conjunction with the Christian populations of the Balkans in an attempt to undermine Turkish power in Europe. To achieve this he was prepared to contemplate going himself to Transylvania and as events transpired he was to prove generous with subsidies of money and soldiers in the course of the Hungarian/Balkan wars of his reign.[54]

The 1590s also helped to define the northern border of European Catholicism with significant effects on the future politics of the continent. In 1592 the King of Poland, Sigismund Vasa, ascended to the throne of Sweden on the death of his father King John III, who since the 1570s had flirted with the possibility of reconciliation with Rome and who, in order to safeguard the Polish inheritance, had caused Sigismund to be raised a Catholic. Although constrained by the terms insisted on by the Synod and Diet of Uppsala to do nothing to damage the established Lutheran character of the kingdom, Rome cherished hopes that Sigismund would be able to nurture a Catholic revival in Sweden. The nuncio in Poland was urged to maintain pressure on the King to do all in his power to work for the resurrection of the church.[55] The King was to be informed that the Pope believed that providence had revealed its intentions in allowing him to take possession of the Swedish crown and that his future successes would reflect the degree to which he recognized that his growth in power stemmed from God's assistance and that therefore he should continue to exert himself on behalf of the Catholic faith.[56] Thus, 'he was to hold himself more fortunate in no matter than the commodity of replanting the catholic faith in those kingdoms, in which it was overthrown from the time of his ancestor [Gustav I Vasa] with the perdition of an infinite number of souls'.[57] The hand of providence was also seen in the failure of the previous king to fill the vacant archbishopric of Uppsala. Sigismund should appoint a Catholic to this post and seek confirmation in the fashion of Catholic monarchs from Rome. In this way, with a pleasing symmetry, salvation would emanate from the See which had played a key role in the original lapse of Sweden from Catholicism.[58] The vacant see of Strengnäs, too, could be provided with a Catholic incumbent and, although it was accepted that the King might need time to gradually recatholicize

[53] Preliminary discussions in this regard had been ongoing in the pontificates of Gregory XIII and Sixtus V: see Tatarenko, 'Naissance de l'Union'; since his disillusionment with the prospect of forging links with the Muscovy of Ivan the Terrible, Antonio Possevino had also become an advocate of union.

[54] In this regard see Chapter 4 of the present study.

[55] See Instructions to Bartolomeo Powinski, envoy in Poland, 27 July 1593 (*Die Hauptinstruktionen Clemens' VIII.*, 1, pp. 134–43, at 134).

[56] ibid., p. 136.

[57] 'Laonde di niuna cosa deve tenirsi più venturata che della commodità di ripiantare la fede cattolica in quei Regni, da' quali fin da' tempi dell'avolo suo (Gustave Vasa) ella fu sbandita con la perditione d'un infinito numero d'anime' (ibid.).

[58] ibid., p. 138; the survival of the convent of nuns of St Brigidat Vadstena was seen as another example of this providential pattern.

the episcopal bench, it was believed that he could do so with prudence and zeal. These bishops would take care then to employ preachers and school masters of the Catholic faith.

As part of this blueprint of religious restoral, the papacy provided the King with a list of eminent Swedish Catholics, while warning him that some of the information might be outdated. It was a prime necessity that the King should work to draw together young and zealous Catholics to provide for the future, keeping some of them with him in court, sending others to exemplary Polish Catholic bishops, and maintaining still others in the Jesuit colleges at Riga and Dorpat in Livonia and in Braunsberg in Prussia. Moreover, with the presence of the King it should be possible to institute a Jesuit college in Stockholm which would surely stimulate divine approval.[59] It was considered of importance also to provide suitable religious literature. The King needed to look to bring Catholic texts into the kingdom and have them printed in Swedish 'for the unlearned people so that even the sheep that cannot immediately have preaching and verbal ministry should have some capacity to learn the danger in which they are held with so great prejudice to their souls'.[60]

This careful marriage of providential conviction and programmatic planning was entirely characteristic of papal understanding of its confrontation with Protestantism. It reflected a vision of the Christian religion in which issues of personal salvation and relationship with the divine were subordinated to an ecclesiological vision in which obedience was foregrounded as the critical criterion for entrance into the unique vehicle of salvation represented by the Roman church. The more subtle theological questions of under what conditions the members of this church might fail to attain salvation were relegated to secondary status beside the practically inescapable certainty of damnation for all those outside its ranks. There was thus no contradiction apparent in making use of worldly motives, such as interest in office, to advance the cause of Catholicism. Cognate to the manner in which attrition could open the way for the grace of the Holy Spirit through the sacrament of penance, material interests could possibly provide a providential opening for redemptive grace in the soul of the individual magistrate. Moreover, the adherence of such figures would inevitably prepare the way to possible salvation for others dependent on their leadership, in particular by opening up to them the sacramental conduits of divine grace ministered by the church, especially penance and the Eucharist, which created a mystical unity between the recipient and the Lord.[61] At the very least, magistrates prompted merely by worldly considerations might gain some merit for their role in saving the souls of others.

In the event, the King's attempts to stimulate revival excited a vigorous reaction which culminated in his deposition by his uncle Charles IX. The legacy of these

---

[59] ibid., pp. 138–9.

[60] 'per la gente indotta, accio quelli anco ove non potranno cosi di subito pervenire prediche et ammaestramenti vocali habbiano qualche commodità d'andare conoscendo l'inganno, in che sono stati tenuti con sì grave pregiuditio delle anime loro' (ibid., p. 140).

[61] See for instance Fulvius Androtius, *Certain Devout Considerations of Frequenting the Blessed Sacrament with sundrie other precepts and rule of direction composed for the benefit of such as seek to attaine to the perfection of virtue* (Douai, 1606), pp. 1–13.

events, the irredentism of the Vasa kings of Poland and the fusion of Lutheran and national identity as the underpinning of the ruling branch of the dynasty in Sweden, threw long shadows into the seventeenth century and was to play its part in the elaboration of a religiously-based Swedish Baltic imperialism and the intervention of the Swedes in the Thirty Years War.[62]

If in Sweden the Protestant estates and not the ruler established the juridical and theological basis of a confessional state in the 1590s, the same period saw the gestation of an entirely contrary process in the Habsburg lands of Austria, Bohemia, and Hungary. In these areas, the Clementine papacy represented not so much the clarification and hardening of confessional boundaries as the gestation of crucially important processes of confessional change. Of critical significance in both Austria and Bohemia were the attitude and policies of Ferdinand II who was elected King of Bohemia in 1617 and who became Holy Roman Emperor two years later. But the template for Ferdinand's future behaviour was in many ways established by his earlier governorship of Inner Austria and his aggressive expulsion of Protestant preachers immediately following the end of his cousin's regency in 1595.[63]

Ferdinand II was the product of a Jesuit education and his patronage of the Society and his reliance on his Jesuit Confessor, William Lamormaini, were to be *leitmotifs* of his entire career. The profound importance of the Society as educators can certainly be traced back to the middle decades of the sixteenth century. Although education had not been one of the areas in which Loyola had planned to deploy the members of the Society, the decision to add this to their quiver of responsibilities was made during his generalship. And the importance of Ignatian spirituality and organizational practice on the future course of Jesuit education was certainly profound. Yet the fourth and final redaction of the *Ratio Studiorum*, the fruit of intense discussion over a period of almost twenty years within the Society and the curricular basis of what might be termed the Jesuit revolution in education, to which only limited local adaptation was considered permissible, was not made until 1598 in the generalship of Acquaviva.[64] Even more pertinently, it was not until towards the end of the sixteenth century that the Jesuits possessed the numbers either of reliably-trained personnel or of institutions, tightly woven together by an evolving administrative apparatus, to make a mass impact on the formation of the minds and consciences of a wide swathe of the elite of Catholic Europe. Throughout the sixteenth century Jesuit schools struggled with chronic problems of understaffing: so dire was the situation in 1576 that the General advocated no further institutions be opened until the situation of the existing

[62] Otfried Czaika, 'La Scandinavie' in Wolfgang Kaiser (ed.), *L'Europe en conflits: Les affrontments religieux et la genèse de l'Europe modern vers 1500–1650* (Rennes: Presses Universitaires de Rennes, 2008), pp. 137–68, at 153–4.

[63] Robert Bireley, *Religion and Politics in the Age of the CounterReformation: Emperor Ferdinand II, William Lamormaini, S.J. and the Formation of Imperial Policy* (Chapel Hill: University of North Carolina Press, 1981), p. 14, this topic is covered in much greater detail in Chapter 3 of the current study.

[64] See the introduction in Ladislaus Lukács (ed.), *Monumenta Paedegogica Societatis Iesu 6: Collectanea de ratione studiorum Societatis Iesu*; Sabina Pavone, *I Gesuiti: dalle origini alle soppressione, 1540–1773* (Rome and Bari: Editori Laterza, 2004), p. 58.

ones had stabilized.[65] Despite their extraordinary rate of growth, in 1565 the Society still only boasted 3500 members and the speed at which they opened schools saw a sharp diminution in the numbers per school over the following decade.[66] By 1614, however, the numbers in the Society had practically quadrupled to 13,112. In 1579 the number of colleges stood at 144 but this number had zoomed to 372 a quarter of a century later, which in their various forms served a diversity of constituencies, some acting as teaching centres for the novices of the Society, while other provided day or boarding education for different classes of society, or acted as seminaries for the training of priests.

The impact of these colleges, principally among the noble classes and the educated elite of Catholic Europe and in urban areas, was profound. The remarkable expansion of the order which reached ninety per cent of its maximum geographical extent within its first century of existence, before nearly two centuries of essentially stable configuration of its provinces, was itself testament to the manner in which both the Jesuits and the wider society of the Catholic world perceived the existence of a gap to be filled.[67] Thus Jesuit education can arguably be better identified as one of the complex of interacting and evolving traits which helped to determine the character of European Catholicism in the period under review rather than merely an inheritance of the Ignatian era. Of major importance in this respect was the manner in which the order's educational projects not only represented a programme of cognitive disciplining of the students who attended their numerous colleges but also involved the Jesuits in processes of cultural transmission within the wider society. In this way the order came to enjoy a powerful influence on the attitudes and tastes of the cultural elite of Europe who inhabited the Republic of letters and who acted as aristocratic patrons of the Arts and Sciences.[68] It was under Acquaviva too that a renewed impetus on mission work came to characterize the Society and new organizational outlines were developed which were to prove highly important over the following centuries. His circular letters from 1590–1609 constantly urged mobilization in mission work and his *Instructio XII: pro iis qui ad missions proficiscuntur* and the notion that every suitable Jesuit should undertake annual mission work resulted in an enrichment and systematization of Jesuit missionary activity in the decades that followed.[69]

[65] Christopher Carlsmith, 'Struggling towards success: Jesuit education in Italy, 1540–1600', *History of Education Quarterly* 42 (2002), 215–46.

[66] A. Lynn Martin,'Vocational Crises and the Crisis in Vocations among Jesuits in France during the Sixteenth Century', *Catholic Historical Review* 72 (1986), 201–21, at 209–10.

[67] Steven J. Harris, 'Mapping Jesuit Science: The Role of Travel in the Geography of Knowledge' in Gauvin Alexander Balley, Steven J. Harris, John O'Malley, and T. Frank Kennedy (eds), *The Jesuits: Cultures, Sciences and the Arts, 1540–1773* (Toronto: University of Toronto Press, 1999), pp. 212–40, at 222.

[68] Steven J. Harris, 'Confession Building, Long-Distance Networks and the Organization of Jesuit Science', *Early Science and Medicine* 1 (1996), 287–318, at 292; see also *idem*, 'Transposing the Merton Thesis: Apostolic Spirituality and the Establishment of the Jesuit Scientific Tradition', *Science in Context* 3 (1989), 29–65.

[69] Bernadette Majorana, 'Une pastorale spectaculaire: Missions et missionnaires jésuites en Italie (XVIe-XVIIIe siècle)', *Annales, Histoire, Sciences Sociales* 57 (2002), 297–320; Antal Molnár, *Katolikus missziók a hódolt Magyarországon I 1572–1647* (Budapest: Balassi Kiadó, 2002), pp. 153–4.

It was towards the end of the sixteenth century that with a new sense of confidence the Catholic church started to re-institute official canonization procedures of new saints, suspended for sixty-five years, beginning with Diego of Alcalá,[70] although during that time-frame fourteen non-universal cults had been recognized. Clement's papacy, however, marked a significant moment in the remodelled understanding of sanctity which came to underpin Early Modern Catholicism. For a confession in which saints and their cults represented a vital constitutive element, with constructions of saintliness and heresy acquiring key hermeneutical significance, and functioning in areas of religious diversity as a visible marker of confessional boundaries,[71] it became of increasing importance to ensure that hagiographical tradition corresponded to the official understanding of Tridentine norms. It was under Clement that the curial trend of asserting control over the definition and legitimization of saints came to a climax with the creation of the *Congregazione dei Beati* in 1602.[72] The representation and self-definition of the Roman curia from the end of the sixteenth-century as a *corte santa* can in significant respects be seen as the product of Sixtus V's conscious attempts to remodel the understanding of the papal role, not least through the symbolic acts of Christianization and dislocation of ancient obelisks before the major churches of Rome in 1588 and the crowning of the Trajan column with the statue of the apostle Peter in 1587. Yet it was in Clement's much longer papacy that the motive power of this recuperation and Christianization of the history of ancient Rome became embedded.[73] Important in this process was the increasing importance of the Holy Year which under Clement in 1600 took on a new salience, absorbing and amplifying both the Gregorian and Sixtine inheritance, with half a million pilgrims visiting the city during that year.[74]

The Sixtine revision of the organizational structures of the church also had unforeseen consequences which really began to work through the church in the following decades. As Simon Ditchfield has demonstrated, for instance, the need to establish the legitimacy of traditional expressions of piety, and to justify the continued existence of local saints' cults in the face of the concern of the newly-established Sacred Congregation of Rites and Ceremonies to investigate and regulate local liturgical practice, was responsible for an upsurge in local hagiography and erudition.

[70] Peter Burke, 'How to be a Counter-Reformation Saint' in *idem, The Historical Anthropology of Early Modern Italy* (Cambridge: Cambridge University Press, 1987), pp. 48–62; Simon Ditchfield, 'How not to be a Counter-Reformation Saint: The Attempted Canonization of Pope Gregory X, 1622–25', *Papers of the British School at Rome* 60 (1992), 379–422; Simon Ditchfield, 'Thinking with Saints: Sanctity and Society in the Early Modern World', *Critical Inquiry* 33 (2009), 552–84; Simon Ditchfield, 'Sanctity in Early Modern Italy', *Journal of Ecclesiastical History* 47 (1996), 98–112.
[71] Simon Ditchfield, 'Tridentine Worship and the Cult of Saints' in Po-Chia Hsia (ed.), *The Cambridge History of Christianity* 6, pp. 201–24.
[72] Ruth Noyes, 'On the Fringes of Centre: Disputed Hagiographic Imagery and the Crisis over the *beati moderni* in Rome c. 1600', *Renaissance Quarterly* 64:3 (2011), 800–46.
[73] Maria Antonietta Visceglia, *La Città Rituale: Roma e le sue cerimonie in età moderna* (Rome: Viella, 2002), pp. 101–7.
[74] ibid.; Jack Freiberg, 'The Lateran Patronage of Gregory XIII and the Holy Year 1575', *Zeitschrift für Kunstgeschichte* 54 (1991), 66–87, at 84; Caravale and Caracciolo, *Lo Stato pontificio*, pp. 387–8; Guido Bentivoglio, *Memorie del cardinal Guido Bentivoglio con correzioni e varianti dell'edizione d'Amsterdam del 1648* (Milan: G. Daelli, 1844), pp. 1–9.

These endeavours aimed to provide a historical basis for reformed local religious practice that would meet the standards of a Tridentine template of authenticity,[75] not merely in Italy but in other parts of the Catholic world also. As recent research has demonstrated, Clement himself was also a significant figure in terms of the re-organization of papal government. Alarmed by its strength and ubiquity, the Aldo-brandini Pope strove to limit Spanish influence in the consistory. Power became concentrated into the hands of the Cardinal-nephews, Cinzio and Pietro Aldebran-dini, and other trusted administrators such as Cardinal Santori and Clement relied on different congregations for the execution of business which always required the approval and consent of the pope. In this way he heightened the emphasis on the monarchical power of the papacy.[76]

Aldobrandini's ascent to the papal throne marked the opening of a new chapter in addition in the papal relationship with Christians *in partibus infidelium*. In the immediate aftermath of Trent, Pope Pius V's attempts to set up a Roman institu-tion coordinating the activities of missionaries throughout the world had been largely frustrated by the opposition of Philip II and his concern to defend the ecclesiastical influence of the crown of Spain. Gregory XIII's plans for a similar project were again frustrated by obdurate Spanish opposition and the Pope was restricted to dispatching a series of Apostolic visitors to various European destin-ations. In 1599, however, Clement created the first, short-lived *Sacra Congregatio de Propaganda Fide*. Although it lacked the resources which its successor congrega-tion of the same name enjoyed after its foundation in 1622 by Pope Gregory XV, this established the first template for Roman direction of missionary activity throughout the world. The formidable membership of the congregation under the presidency of Cardinal Santori, who had bitterly resented Sixtus V's neglect of missionary activity, and who was probably a prime mover in the creation of the congregation, included Robert Bellarmine, Cesare Baronius, Federico Borromeo, and the papal nephew. Although Santori's death seems to have more or less sig-nalled the end of the institution's sittings, papal oversight of missions continued with the appointment of two discalced Carmelites, Pedro de la Madre de Dios and, after his death in 1608, Domingo de Jesús Maria, as *superintendens* of missionary activity. Domingo de Jesús Maria was then to serve as the only non-cardinal member of the new Congregation of *Propaganda Fide* when it was founded in 1622.[77] In terms of several of the peripheral Catholicisms of Europe with which this study is chiefly concerned, *Propaganda Fide* was to become arguably the single most important ecclesiastical institution in their development and organization.

Of significant importance to the Clementine papacy also was the heightened role which it conferred on two of the pivotal figures of Early Modern Catholicism, Robert Bellarmine and Cesare Baronius. The two had come to know each well in

[75] Simon Ditchfield, *Liturgy, Sanctity and History in Tridentine Italy: Pietro Maria Campi and the Preservation of the Particular* (Cambridge: Cambridge University Press, 1995), p. 97.
[76] Maria Teresa Fattori, *Clemente VIII e il Sacro Collegio, 1592–1605: Meccanismi istituzionali e accentramento di governo* (Stuttgart: Hiersemann, 2004); see also Reinhard, 'Concilio di Trento', p. 41.
[77] István György Tóth, 'A Propaganda megalapítása és Magyarorszg (1622)', *Történelmi Szemle* 42: 1–2 (2000), 19–68, at 21–9; Molnár, *Katolikus missziók*, pp. 139–42.

1576–7 in the context of Curial preparation to realize a project to oppose the *Centuries of Magdeburg*, the massive thirteen-volume demonstration that *succesio dottrinae* in the Apostolic tradition was the inheritance of the Lutheran camp alone.[78] Their two chief contributions to this enterprise, Bellarmine's *De Controversiae Christianae fidei adversus hujus temporis haereticos*, first published in Ingolstadt between 1586 and 1593, and Baronius's *Annales Ecclesiastici* which were issued in twelve volumes, 1588–1607, represented a major step in the confessional consolidation of post-Tridentine Catholicism. For Bellarmine, in particular, the end of the pontificate of Sixtus V was of great importance. While he had been recognized as a major intellectual figure within the church prior to 1592, the holder of the chair of controversial theology at the Gregorian university of Rome since his return from Louvain in 1576 until 1586, whose theological influence had been vital, for instance, in ensuring the dominance of Thomism in the Jesuit teaching of theology in their schools, he had enjoyed a difficult relationship with the Franciscan Pope. Bellarmine, himself hardly immune to arrogance, had been horrified by Sixtus's approach to the production of a new version of the Vulgate. In his view this would result in a flawed text for use in the Catholic world which reflected the Pope's ignorant and obstinate personal involvement rather than the best of contemporary scholarship, and would in addition give ample ammunition to Protestant apologists to gloat over the inaccuracy of the Catholic bible.[79] Moreover, under Sixtus, hostile scrutiny directed towards his own work had amplified, which culminated in the papal decision to place the first volume of the controversies on the Index on the basis of its insufficiency in the defence of papal authority.[80]

On Clement's accession, however, the reversal of fortune which Bellarmine had begun to enjoy under the short-lived pontificate of Gregory XIV continued. He himself provided the preface to the Clementine edition of the Vulgate, which eliminated the Sixtine errors which had principally preoccupied him while attempting to safeguard the dead Pope's authority by referring to the pontiff's wishes for a new edition free of typographical and other errors. Baronius, Bellarmine's close friend and confidant, was in a position to exercise substantial influence in Rome which he mobilized on Bellarmine's behalf on several occasions, as for instance in early 1597 when he was instrumental in having the Jesuit recalled from Naples to replace the deceased Cardinal Francesco de Toledo as theological advisor to the Pope.[81] Much against his wishes Baronius was created a Cardinal in 1596 and he worked hard to ensure that his equally unwilling friend, Bellarmine, was also raised to the purple in 1599. The overt demonstration of papal approval manifested in

[78] Enrico Norelli, 'The authority attributed to the early church in the *Centuries of Magdeburg* and the *Ecclesiastical Annals* of Caesar Baronius' in Irena Backus (ed.), *The Reception of the Church Fathers in the West from the Carolingians to the Maurists* (two vols, Leiden, New York, Köln: Brill, 1997), 2, pp. 745–74, at 747.

[79] James Broderick, *The Life and Work of Blessed Robert Francis Cardinal Bellarmine, 1542–1621* (two vols, London: Burns, Oates & Washbourne, 1928), 2, p. 59.

[80] Anthony D. Wright, 'Bellarmine, Baronius and Federico Borromeo' in de Maio et al., *Bellarmino e la Controriforma*, pp. 325–70, at 327.

[81] Stefano Zen, 'Bellarmino e Baronio' in de Maio et al., *Bellarmino e la Controriforma*, pp. 279–321, at 279–81.

their elevation to the college of cardinals was part of the process which allowed the two men to acquire particular symbolic importance and spiritual prestige in Rome as representatives of an ecclesiastical ideal, although Bellarmine's criticisms of Pietro Aldobrandini's government of the church contributed to his marginalization from Rome in 1600 as Archbishop of Capua.[82]

In addition to their friendship, their reluctance for ecclesiastical advancement, and widely respected erudition, the two men shared a number of other characteristics. Both genuinely regretted the loss of regular poverty which followed their elevation and were ill at ease with the material pomp and splendour which went with the purple. Baronius's household was significantly smaller than the average for cardinals in Rome while Bellarmine's numbered only about thirty persons when most of his contemporaries possessed entourages of between seventy and one hundred servants and retainers, and as Cardinal his personal life continued in the same sober and restrained manner as before. Both men were also troubled by a sense of personal sinfulness. The fear of damnation which this occasioned heightened their impulse towards sanctity of behaviour, which deeply impressed onlookers in Rome, including Pope Clement himself who was personally affected by his interactions with both. Together with their personal representation of a particular model of post-Tridentine piety, both proved influential in their role as consultors to the Congregation of Rites. They acted as champions for the canonization of recent exemplars of Catholic spirituality and leadership, most notably Carlo Borromeo (cause submitted to the Congregation of Rites in 1604 and canonized in 1610), Filippo Neri (beatified in 1615 and canonized in 1622) and Ignatius Loyola (beatified in 1609 and canonized in 1622), whom they perceived as incarnating a series of virtues and saintly behaviours to which both aspired but which they did not dare to believe that they had personally achieved. The cross-order friendship of the Oratorian, Baronius, and the Jesuit, Bellarmine, proved useful to each other in this respect as Baronius put particular emphasis on the saintly qualifications of the founder of the Jesuits while Bellarmine ardently and publicly championed the cause of Filippo Neri.[83]

Their shared preoccupation with liturgical reform also left its stamp on their era. As has been recently demonstrated this process was of huge significance to the Tridentine project in both its disciplinary and didactic manifestations which aimed to produce a purified and canonical Roman text with universal validity throughout the Catholic world.[84] Neither Baronius nor Bellarmine was content with the 1568 reforms of the Roman Breviary, which they considered riddled with literally hundreds of errors, and in 1592 Clement appointed the former as president and the latter as a member of the commission for its amendment which resulted a decade later in a new version of the text. Bellarmine, in particular, was also an influential protagonist of Catholic censorship, which he saw as an integral weapon in the struggle against religious heterodoxy, and he served both as Consultor to the Holy Office and as a member of the Sacred Congregation of the Index. Despite their

---

[82] Fattori, *Clemente VIII e il Sacro Collegio*, pp. 226–3; Paolo Prodi, *Il sovrano pontefice* (Bologna: Il Mulino, 1982), pp. 213–14.

[83] Zen, 'Bellarmino e Baronio', pp. 284–96.

[84] Ditchfield, 'Tridentine worship', pp. 201–5.

own youthful flirtations with verse, the style of saintliness which he and Baronius espoused had little time for poetry. Bellarmine was prepared to condemn Dante, Petrarch, and Boccaccio because of the manner in which they furnished anti-papal testimony to Protestant authors and his intellectual stature helped to legitimize the campaign which deprived the generality of the Italian population of so many of the jewels of its literature. Both also championed the censorship of what they saw as licentious pictorial art because of its immoral character and the potential ammunition which it might furnish Protestant critics of Catholicism.[85]

Several of the most significant events of Clement's reign, such as the reconciliation of Henri IV, the incorporation of Ferrara within the papal states, and the decision to make no definitive judgement on the Grace controversy, which pitted two of the most influential teaching orders of Catholicism against each other, were directly influenced by the counsel and arguments provided by Bellarmine and Baronius.[86] However influential as papal advisors, nonetheless, it was the massive impact of their literary work which marked the single most important aspect of their careers. Bellarmine's *Controversiae* were the fruit of almost two decades of teaching controversial theology at Louvain and at the Roman college between 1569 and 1586.[87] Following the publication of the first edition at Ingolstadt, a reviewed and corrected complete edition was published in Venice in 1596 and this became the standard for over one hundred subsequent editions, and almost two hundred full-scale Protestant ripostes, which appeared in the following centuries.

The books enjoyed immediate success. In Louvain all copies were purchased on the first day and when the eagerly-awaited second volume appeared at the Frankfurt book fair of 1588 it sold out immediately.[88] The effect on Europe, both Catholic and Protestant, was profound. Bellarmine was certainly not the first Catholic nor the first Jesuit controversialist. Prior to the emergence of his *opus magnus* roughly forty members of the Society had produced controversial tracts.[89] But it was the fragmentary nature of this work which prompted the belief in the need for a comprehensive synthesis of the subjects in dispute between the church of Roma and its various Protestant counterparts. This would provide an essential weapon and teaching tool for Catholic students, teachers, missionaries and members of the Republic of Letters which would also be relatively easily accessible in economic terms.

---

[85] Zen, 'Bellarmino e Baronio', pp. 299–301; Romeo de Maio, 'Introduzione: Bellarmino e la Controriforma' in de Maio et al., *Bellarmino e la Controriforma*, pp. xxi–xxiv.

[86] Zen, 'Bellarmino e Baronio', p. 282.

[87] Gustavo Galeota, 'Genesi, Sviluppo e fortuna delle *Controversiae* di Roberto Bellarmino' in de Maio et al., *Bellarmino e la Controriforma*, pp. 3–48, at 15 notes the importance also of his period as a student in Padova in terms of his intellectual evolution as an independent thinker on the subject of predestination.

[88] Robert Richgels, 'The Pattern of Controversy in a Counter-Reformation Classic: the *Controversies* of Robert Bellarmine', *Sixteenth Century Journal* 11 (2), 1980, 3–15, at 3–4; Pontien Polman, *L'élément historique dans la controverse religieuse du XVIe siècle* (Gembloux: J. Duculot, 1932); Broderick, *Bellarmine*, 75.

[89] Anita Mancia, 'La Controversia con i Protestanti ed i programme degli studi teologici nella Compagnia di Gesù (1547–1599)', *Archivium Historicum Societatis Iesu* 54 (1985), 1–43, 209–264, at 15–17.

Seventeen major topics were confronted in the *Controversiae*. Bellarmine's objective was not originality, although in matters such as, for example, the importance of the evidence of Saint Cyril of Jerusalem concerning the doctrine of the real presence, or the rejection of Pope Gelase as the author of a tract against Eutyches, he introduced a new perspective into Catholic controversy.[90] On questions which were considered to be open by Catholic authors, he was content to present the variety of opinions rather than coming down in favour of one or the other. He relied heavily on other theologians, for instance Hosius, Cano, and Fisher, when treating of the church as the necessary and authentic interpreter of Scripture and the existence of an unwritten Revelation, and on Sanders concerning the government of the church, contenting himself with a compression and reordering of material without substantially adding to the argumentation. The uniform layout of the material across the seventeen controversies which he treated was also intended to allow ease of consultation, passing from a summary of the material treated and the bibliography on the subject to an exposition of the positions of Catholics and their opponents and a presentation of their arguments, culminating in a refutation of the non-Catholic position.[91]

Not only did Bellarmine refer to practically the entire range of Catholic theologians to buttress his arguments but it has been calculated that he made 7135 named citations to eighty-three different individual opponents in the course of the *Controversiae*.[92] The manner in which he did so did not meet with universal favour on the grounds that the presentation of heretical positions, even for refutation, might in fact lead to a diffusion rather than rejection of heterodox opinion. This danger was heightened because Bellarmine was at pains to quote accurately, in general deriving his quotations directly from the works of his adversaries.[93] The single most important opponent with which Bellarmine concerned himself was Calvin, whom he cited directly on 1647 occasions. In second place was Chemnitz, a major figure in the reorganization of sixteenth-century Lutheranism and the co-author of the formula of Concord, a major step in the elaboration of the Lutheran confession, who appeared in 1258 citations, while Luther himself was cited 860 times.[94] Yet while the *Controversiae* provided a comprehensive survey of the points at issue between the Roman church and the Lutheran and Reformed confessions, their coverage extended also through the entire gamut of sixteenth-century Protestant opinion, from Anabaptism and Ubiquitism to the Unitarian theology of Valentin Gentilis, Michael Servet, and Francis Stancarus. Thus, even in areas of relatively less centrality to what Bellarmine saw as the core elements of his refutation of Reformed and Lutheran thought, such as the rejection of anti-Trinitarian views, his influence was significant. In Poland, where Unitarianism represented a significant strand of radical belief, Bellarmine's work was taken up by Jakub Wujek, the translator of the Polish bible with great effect in both Latin and Polish editions which, largely thanks to the almost verbatim translation from volume one of the *Contro-*

---

[90] Polman, *L'Élément Historique dans la Controverse religieuse*, p. 524.
[91] ibid., pp. 515–21.   [92] Richgels, 'Controversies of Bellarmine', p. 5.
[93] Polman, *L'Élément Historique dans la Controverse religieuse*, pp. 519–20.
[94] Richgels, 'Controversies of Bellarmine', p. 6.

versiae, brought a new standard of biblical exegesis to Polish Catholic anti-Unitarian polemic.[95]

Baronius's *Annales Ecclesiastici* were also a major work of synthesis intended to provide the historical basis for the undermining of the enemies of the Roman church by reconstructing the outline of the primitive church and demonstrating its unchanging institutions and doctrines. In particular the traditions of the church, which the centuriators of Magdeburg had attacked for their lack of biblical foundation, were to be protected by the demonstration of their biblical origins, while the doctrines of Protestantism were contextualized as the latest in a long series of heresies opposed and overcome by the true church. The chief means of achieving these aims was through the use of extensive original documentation, to much of which Baronius had privileged access in Rome, and through the critical interrogation of source material in terms of its validity and context. Like Bellarmine's *magnum opus*, the utility of Baronius's *Annales* was immediately perceived by the wider Catholic world. In Poland the fiery preacher Skarga made extensive use of both and published a version of the *Annales* encompassing the first millennium of church history in 1603,[96] and numerous other Latin and vernacular editions and compendia of Baronius's text were produced all over Europe. Several high-profile conversions such as Kasper Schoppe and Giusto Calvin, professor of theology at Heidelberg, were attributed to the influence of Bellarmine's and Baronius's work, which conferred still more prestige on their authors.[97]

Nevertheless, the true importance of these pivotal texts lay more in their perception within their own confession than by opponents. Both filled a vital role in completing the intellectual fortifications of Catholic Europe by providing a comprehensive historical and controversial underpinning to the Tridentine confession of faith. The revelation of an unchanging eternally correct church, depending on a strict appreciation of hierarchy and the unchallengeable spiritual authority of the papacy, was a vital aspect of what became the intellectual tenor of post-Tridentine Catholicism. Dogmatic, intolerant, reliant on censorship and a gathering realization of the potentialities of bureaucratic pressure and educative indoctrination, Catholicism could begin to look again in a new light at the Europe which had been fractured at the Reformation and could once again espy a potential path to its reunification within a single church. While both the Protestant north and the non-Italian Catholic states of Europe had greater resources to combat this tendency, in Italy the deliberate attempt to restrict access to vernacular versions of scripture, thus heightening the dependence of the laity on the clergy as intermediaries, found its fullest expression with very significant cultural results.[98] In this regard, the dangers of leakage to Protestantism, while requiring constant vigilance, were seen as containable.

---

[95] Slaski, 'Bellarmino e Polonia', p. 530.
[96] Jobert, *La Pologne dans la crise de la chrétienté*, pp. 264–6.
[97] Zen, 'Bellarmino e Baronio', pp. 302–4.
[98] Gigliola Fragnito, *Proibito Capire: La Chiesa e il volgare nella prima età moderna* (Bologna: Società Editrice il Mulino, 2005).

To suggest that the Clementine papacy of the 1590s and early seventeenth century marked an abrupt *caesura* in all aspects of the development of Early Modern Catholicism is of course untenable. Very obvious continuities link this period not merely to processes which gestated in the middle of the sixteenth century but to even older currents of renewal within the church of Rome. On the other hand, however, too great an emphasis on the traditional staples of Counter-Reformation historiography, namely Trent, the reforming papacy down to Sixtus V, and the impact of new religious orders, particularly the Jesuits and the Capuchins, carries its own risks of underplaying the contingency of developments within the Catholic world in the late sixteenth century. While the decrees of Trent were of fundamental importance, they did not operate as a thunderclap. In many respects, the impact of Tridentine reforms, particularly in the areas of clerical training and residence, was delayed until the last decades of the sixteenth century when a differently-formed generation of priests began to make their presence felt in the localities, whose function and understanding of their role was critically influenced by the conditions in which they then found themselves operating. Even in Italy itself, where Tridentine proscriptions concerning the education of priests in diocesan seminaries made only minimal impact in the sixteenth century, a number of key processes can be seen as coming together during the Clementine papacy, in terms of the provision of a usable if hardly perfect Vulgate text, an accompanying process of censorship, and the elaboration of clear intellectual fortified points in terms of Catholic self-definition *vis-à-vis* the confessions which had emerged from the Reformation. But this book is concerned above all with societies on the western and eastern peripheries of Europe where the nature of their Catholic identity was hammered out in the crucible of the last decades of the sixteenth and the first half of the seventeenth century. Indeed in areas such as Ireland, the Netherlands, Bohemia and Hungary, the movement of Catholic renewal was acutely limited until the conditions of the 1590s. The objective of the following chapters in part one of this study is to trace the evolution of some central aspects of the movement of Catholic reform in these 'marginal societies'. Chapters 2 and 3 offer a consideration of the evolution of Catholicism in two general areas, the Western territories of Britain, Ireland, and the Netherlands, where a number of different varieties of Catholic identity and practice evolved under the authority of a hostile confessional state, and an arc of territory stretching from Poland through Austria and Bohemia to Hungary where Catholic monarchs presided over societies which had become important centres of indigenous Protestantism of various forms. Part two of the book, through two case studies, then examines a number of themes which preoccupied the Early Modern papacy and exerted significant influence on its relationship with the margins of Catholic Europe. Both Chapters 4 and 5 concentrate on the north of the Balkan peninsula and Hungary, examining two themes which dominated Roman interaction with the area. Chapter 4 investigates the papal attempt to roll back Turkish power in the Balkans in conjunction with the Catholic states of east-central Europe which reached its peak during the Clementine papacy. Chapter 5 offers a case study of mission activity in the northern reaches of the Balkan peninsula in the wake of the frustration of attempts to free the Christian population of the area from Turkish rule. The book concludes with a brief discussion of the significance of the end of the 1640s, not merely in terms of the Peace of Westphalia but for other societies such as Britain, Ireland, and Poland, where the end of that decade also marks a significant watershed, and an assessment of some of the dominant factors which influenced the relationship between Rome and the more peripheral Catholic societies of Europe.

2

The Western Margins

This chapter offers an investigation of the evolution of Catholicism in three societies: Britain, where the emphasis is principally on England; Ireland, the only area of the Atlantic archipelago where Catholicism survived the sixteenth century and beyond as the majority confession within the population; and the Netherlands where a significant Catholic population, reorganized in the course of 1590s and the first decades of the seventeenth century, was in existence at the end of the great Spanish-Dutch conflict in 1648. In addition to their geographical proximity the factor linking these three areas is their shared inheritance of state hostility and the existence of a favoured non-Catholic church establishment which posed a considerable challenge to the possibilities of survival and growth of Catholicism. However, despite this basic commonality, the difference in the self-understanding of the confession favoured by the state and the varying extents of temporal power in enforcing programmes of coercion were critical factors in the differing evolution of Catholicism in the three areas.

BRITAIN

One of the conundrums of the sixteenth century, as Patrick Collinson has observed, is the process whereby one of the most Catholic countries in Europe, namely England, developed into one of the least.[1] Prior to the Henrician break with Rome, the Catholic church in England was in strong working order. The threat to orthodoxy which Lollardy had posed was fairly minimal. By European standards, the English clergy were of a high standard. The combination of an anti-Lutheran monarch, recognized as *Fidei Defensor* by the Pope, a powerful and centralized state, and an efficient system of ecclesiastical courts, meant that the English church was in a strong position to confront and contain the advances of Protestantism. Henry VIII's divorce, however, meant that the latter part of his reign and more particularly the reigns of his two younger children opened the way for the steep decline of English Catholicism. Despite the grudging and reluctant nature of the acquiescence of much of the population to the religious innovations of the Tudors, over the course of three generations, the position of the Catholic church suffered a precipitous collapse in England. This decline was by no means uniform or evenly spaced

---

[1] Patrick Collinson, 'Comment on Eamon Duffy's Neale Lecture and the Colloquium' in Nicholas Tyacke (ed.), *England's Long Reformation 1500–1800* (London: UCL Press, 1998), pp. 71–86, at 75.

throughout the country, still less so in the dependent principality of Wales and in the western kingdom of Ireland which from 1541 became a secondary title of the English monarchs, replacing the medieval lordship which was tainted by its origins in papal donation.

Nevertheless, by the end of the century anti-Catholicism had emerged as a key constituent of the identity of wide swathes of the English population. Such a development, however, did not mean that England lost all importance to Catholic Europe. On the contrary, the island kingdom continued to exercise a whole series of fascinations for Catholics on the continent. In this regard, England constituted a vitally important imaginative space, not least as the locus of martyrdom. Early Modern Catholicism was relatively short of martyrs in Europe, although this deficiency was to a certain extent remedied by stories of the heroism of missionaries in areas like Japan. However, in the central conflict against Protestant heresy in Europe, England occupied a special role in the generation of imaginative horror and sympathy as the result of the state's execution of Catholic clerics. Robert Persons's *De persecutione Anglicana libellous*, first published in Latin in 1582, became a runaway publishing success in continental Europe with fresh editions being prepared in Rome, Paris, and Ingolstadt and translations being undertaken into Italian, German, French, and Spanish.[2] Edmund Campion, who had worked as a missionary in Central Europe, was revered as a martyr in Habsburg territories and a translation of his *Rationes Decem* was published in Graz in 1588.[3]

English exiles played a significant role in shaping the attitudes of other Catholic national identities. The principal architect of the Hungarian Catholic renewal, Péter Pázmány, was undoubtedly influenced by his contacts with English Jesuits while in Rome during the 1590s. In Poland Arthur Faunt helped to mould the confessional attitudes of a generation of influential Polish Catholic activists and intellectuals.[4] Supplementing the personal impact of such exiles was the intellectual effect of the writings of English Catholic intellectuals. In this regard, the published output of Thomas Stapleton was of critical significance. While Bellarmine's work was arguably of more foundational importance for Catholic identity, Stapleton was one of the few controversialists whose work matched that of the Italian Jesuit in terms of its intellectual depth and importance in establishing stable nodal points around which Catholic criticism of heresy could coalesce.[5] In the early seventeenth century, the Stuart monarchs of England also contributed to a process of crystallization of intellectual positions with the furore over the issue of oaths of allegiance which resulted in a personal duel between Bellarmine and James I. In the latter part of the reign of James I and that of his son, Charles I, the issue of a royal marriage to a Catholic

[2] Stefania Tutino, *Law and Conscience: Catholicism in Early Modern England, 1570–1625* (Ashgate: Aldershot, 2007), p. 35.

[3] Regina Pörtner, *The Counter-Reformation in Central Europe: Styria 1580–1630* (Oxford: Clarendon Press, 2001), p. 206.

[4] Ambroise Jobert, *De Luther à Mohila: La Pologne dans la crise de la chrétienté, 1517–1648* (Paris: Institut d'Études slaves, 1974), pp. 264–6.

[5] Stapleton was apparently one of the authors most frequently chosen by Clement VIII to be read to him at his meals: see Marvin O'Connell, *Thomas Stapleton and the Counter Reformation* (New Haven and London: Yale University Press, 1964), p. 23.

princess then brought into focus issues relating to Catholic loyalty and allegiance to a heretical monarch which troubled and complicated the neat divisions between orthodoxy and heresy which generations of Catholic controversialists had assiduously cultivated. These issues eventually proved incapable of resolution during the 1640s with devastating effects both for the King himself and for the Catholic subjects of his Irish kingdom, who laboured in vain to produce a durable treaty with the King, approved by Rome, which would allow them to pool their resources with Protestant royalists to confront the threat of the English parliament.[6]

Perceptions of England were thus vital in shaping attitudes in Rome towards the more important Catholic reservoirs of Ireland. By the 1640s Ireland was the only part of the archipelago where the majority of the population was Catholic, yet even for the Roman pontificate the position of Catholicism in Ireland continued to be viewed through the prism of English centrality. The chimerical hope that Ireland might ultimately prove a springboard for the re-introduction of Catholicism into England was an important factor in the original decision to send GianBattista Rinuccini to Ireland, as evidenced by the ludicrous instructions which were issued to him, which included a glowing account of Wentworth's rule. In the later 1640s, Pope Innocent X was only tempted to consider seriously a major further investment of Roman gold in Ireland if it promised potential advantages for English as well as Irish Catholics.[7] England was more central, not merely because of its traditional importance within the Christian world, but also because the execution of priests under England's ferocious anti-recusant legislation was easier to romanticize than the pettier harassments of the Irish majority, or the murky mingling of religion and politics which figured in Irish rebellions of the later sixteenth century.[8]

Perhaps most importantly of all, the political memory of the English breach with Rome exerted a significant influence over subsequent papal policy. It seems highly probable that Clement VIII's decision to absolve Henri IV of France in the 1590s was influenced by a desire not to emulate Clement VII, whose inability to stand up to Habsburg pressure had led to the alienation of England from the church of Rome. During the 1630s, as pressure mounted on the Barberini papacy of Urban VIII to employ sharp sanctions against Richelieu's support of Protestant anti-Habsburg forces, the example of England was explicitly invoked to justify papal caution in this respect. In 1635, for instance, the Polish nuncio, Marius Filonardi, was informed that Spanish pressure for a censure of France had been rejected by a congregation of cardinals. Among the grounds for this decision was

---

[6] Tadhg Ó hAnnracháin, *Catholic Reformation in Ireland: The Mission of Rinuccini, 1645–49* (Oxford: Oxford University Press, 2002), pp. 123–65, 253–67.

[7] ibid., pp. 129–30; G. Aiazzi, *Nunziatura in Irlanda di Monsignor Gio. Baptista Rinuccini arcivescovo di Fermo negli anni 1645 à 1649* (Florence, 1844), p. xl; Stanislaus Kavanagh (ed.), *Commentarius Rinuccinianus, de sedis apostolicae legatione ad foederatos Hiberniae catholicos per annos 1645–49* (six vols, Dublin: Irish Manuscripts Commission, 1932–49), 2, pp. 118–19.

[8] Thomas O' Connor, 'Hugh O'Neill: free spirit, religious chameleon or ardent Catholic?' in Hiram Morgan (ed.), *The Battle of Kinsale* (Bray: Wordwell, 2004), pp. 59–72; Anthony McCormack, *The Earldom of Desmond, 1463–1583: The Decline and Crisis of a Feudal Lordship* (Dublin: Four Courts Press, 2005), pp. 110–17, 160–2.

the belief that, but for his excommunication, Henry VIII would have renewed the communion with Rome following the execution of Anne Boleyn, while, without Pius V's unfortunate decision to excommunicate Henry's daughter Elizabeth, liberty of conscience would have been available to English Catholics.[9]

If England figured surprisingly large in the continental imagination as a site of religious persecution and as historical warning, this did not necessarily translate into a harder knowledge of English religious affairs. Rinuccini himself was arguably proof of that. It seems probable that one of the reasons why he was originally offered the post of nuncio to the Confederate Catholics of Ireland was because of his enormously successful quasi-novel, *Il Cappucino Scozzeze*, which represented a fictionalized and highly romanticized version of the life and career of George Lesley, a Scottish Capuchin whom he had come to know in Italy. Significantly, even in the version of the text which he revised following his return from Ireland, Rinuccini continued to show little capacity to distinguish between the various strands of British Protestantism. England's history, intellectuals, and potentialities thus cast a surprisingly long shadow into Catholic Europe. Moreover, the corollary to this was also true. As Anthony Milton has demonstrated, despite the restricted numbers of English Catholics, the influence of "Catholic ideas, books, images and people" over the culture of England was by no means negligible.[10]

The long reign of Elizabeth I, from 1558 to 1603, was certainly the watershed in the transformation of England into a country where those prepared to stand outside the state's religious legislation by championing outright recusancy represented only a tiny minority of the population. This was a significant achievement of the Elizabethan regime. As noted in the previous chapter, the evidence suggests that on her accession the majority of the population throughout her dominions, with the exception of small pockets such as the Stour valley, were unenthusiastic, at best, at the prospect of another breach with Rome. Elizabeth had to face significant opposition towards her religious legislation in parliament and was eventually forced to cashier the entirety of the Episcopal bench which she had inherited from her sister, with the exception of the Bishop of Llanduff, an established exponent of trimming his sails to the prevailing political wind.[11] For more than a decade after her accession, religious change was characterized by a high degree of caution on the part of the regime, which reflected the Queen's own idiosyncratic religious consciousness, the demands of external politics and negotiations with the Habsburgs, and an awareness of the depth of conservative opinion within the state.[12]

[9] Instructions to Marius Filonardi, 19 July 1635 (Theresia Chynczewska-Hennel (ed)., *Acta Nuntiaturae Poloniae Tomus XXV Volumen 1 Marius Filonardi (1635–43)* (Cracoviae: Academia Scientiarum et Litterarum Polona, 2000), pp. 16–50, at 38–9.

[10] G.B. Rinuccini, *Il Cappuccino Scozzese* (Roma: per il moneta, 1645), p. 119; Anthony Milton, 'A Qualified Intolerance: the Limits and Ambiguities of Early Stuart Anti-Catholicism' in A. Marotti (ed.), *Catholicism and Anti-Catholicism in Early Modern English Texts* (London: St Martin's Press, 1999), pp. 85–115, at 86.

[11] Eamon Duffy, *Fires of Faith: Catholic England under Mary Tudor* (New Haven: Yale University Press, 2009), pp. 193–7.

[12] Diarmaid McCullough, 'Putting the English Reformation on the map', *Transactions of the Royal Historical Society* 15 (2005), 75–95: Susan Doran, 'Religion and politics at the Court of Elizabeth: the Habsburg marriage negotiations of 1559–1567', *English Historical Review* 104 (1989), 908–26.

The rising of the northern earls in 1569 followed by the excommunication of the Queen by Pius V in 1570, however, sharpened the lines of division between Elizabeth and her Catholic subjects. While many adherents of the old religion continued to proclaim their loyalty to the Queen, the regime had good reason to believe that others wished to replace Elizabeth with a Catholic monarch. Internal changes within Catholicism also contributed to a heightened polarization. Prior to the excommunication, it had been easier to blur the lines between the new and the old religious settlements, particularly in dioceses where emollient bishops, such as William Downham of Cheshire, were cautious in their attempts to inculcate conformity and even those clergy unable to reconcile themselves with the new dispensation were often loath to promote outright resistance to the legally established religion of the state.[13] However, after 1570 Marian survivalist clergy began to be supplemented in increasing numbers by seminary-trained priests from the continent, among whom Jesuits rapidly acquired particular prominence. With increasing urgency after the synod of Southwark in 1580, these newcomers began to emphasize the incompatibility between attendance at the services of the established church and a Catholic identity.[14] For its part, a willingness to conform to the law of the land in matters of religion increasingly became something of a touchstone of loyalty for the state.[15] Elizabeth might not wish to make windows into the souls of her subjects but a refusal to obey the law began to be taken as a transparent indication of dubious allegiance. Not necessarily always at the wishes of the Queen herself, the severity of the anti-recusant legislation increased dramatically across the reign, leading ultimately to the execution of well over one hundred clergy and a lesser but significant number of Catholic laity. Simultaneously, and in sharp contrast with Ireland, the financial penalties to which recusancy exposed the Queen's English subjects were exponentially increased, although naturally the actual implementation of penalties against non-conformity to the established church varied both over time and with regard to region.[16]

In the face of such pressure, and as a response also to the often haphazard and inadequate distribution of clergy, English Catholicism both contracted and splintered. Around a hard core of outright recusants, who were prepared to suffer indictment, developed a wider panoply of church papistry and covert Catholic sympathy. As Walsingham noted in 1587, among the behaviours which distinguished such suspect subjects included occasional conformity, sometimes only by the head of a household. Even if they did enter the doors of the church as the law demanded, a disinclination to take the sacraments of the established church or to swear the Oath of Supremacy betrayed the dubious nature of their allegiance. Even among those who offered all necessary outward signs of submission to the

---

[13] K.J. Kesselring, *The Northern Rebellion of 1569* (Basingstoke: Palgrave, 2010), pp. 18–23.

[14] Tutino, *Catholicism in Early Modern England*, pp. 16–22.

[15] Patrick McGrath, 'Elizabethan Catholicism: a reconsideration', *Journal of Ecclesiastical History* 35 (1984), 414–28.

[16] ibid., p. 422; Michael Questier, *Catholicism and community in early modern England: politics, aristocratic patronage and religion, c. 1550–1640* (Cambridge: Cambridge University Press, 2006), pp. 148–9; Alexandra Walsham, *Church Papists: Catholicism, conformity and confessional polemic in early modern England* (Woodbridge: Boydell Press, 1993), pp. 54–80.

ecclesiastical settlement were some whose other behaviours betrayed strong Catholic sympathies, although it was not necessarily expedient to seek confrontation with them.[17] While it can be difficult to resurrect the precise motivations of those who refused conformity to the state church, it seems probable that the claims of tradition and a deep unwillingness to countenance the idea that previous generations of English men and women had lived in a religion unacceptable to God were important. Beside such sentiments relating to the rooted identity of an English past[18] existed a transnational sense of a wider church from which Protestant England had wilfully cut itself off[19] as 'aliens and strangers from the whole body of Christendom'.[20]

The Catholicism best suited to survive the pressures of the Elizabethan state was among the representatives of the social elite, whose local standing provided a bulwark against the mechanisms of the law. Even as late as 1641, it is estimated that as much as twenty per cent of the English aristocracy may have been Catholic, although not necessarily representative of an unbroken tradition of non-conformity.[21] Rather than a monolithic group, various aristocratic entourages and differing and sometimes conflicting nexuses of kinship, patronage, and political orientation existed within this elite.[22] A more widespread survival of Catholicism was also favoured by geographical distance and inaccessibility from the centres of power. In the north and west of the country, in Lancashire, Durham, Monmouthshire, in Whitby, Lythe, Egton, Fylingdales, and the Tees valley of Yorkshire, significant numbers of adherents to the old religion continued to persist following the death of the Queen in 1603. Relatively more Catholic gentry families could be found in the west than in the east midlands of England while west Sussex, Hampshire, and the adjoining areas of Wiltshire and Dorset contained the largest concentrations of Catholics in the rural south.[23] Non-gentry Catholicism did not entirely disappear, often temporarily and successfully loculating itself across the border of church papistry when necessity demanded.[24] For most of the English population, however,

---

[17] Questier, *Catholicism and community*, p. 47.

[18] A more violent desire to deliver England from its religious servitude seems to have played a part in influencing some of the most influential gunpowder plotters: see Mark Nicholls, 'Strategy and Motivation in the Gunpowder Plot', *Historical Journal* 50 (2007), 787–807, at 797.

[19] Christopher Haigh, *The Plain Man's Pathways to Heaven: Kinds of Christianity in Post-Reformation England, 1570–1640* (Oxford: Oxford University Press, 2007), pp. 184–6.

[20] These are the words of Thomas Stapleton quoted in O'Connell, *Thomas Stapleton*, p. 191. Stapleton also argued that the primacy of the pope, for instance, could 'not be abrogated by the private consent of any one or few realms, no more than the city of London can justly abrogate an Act of Parliament'. Quoted in ibid., p. 170.

[21] Questier, *Catholicism and community*, p. 1.   [22] ibid., *passim*.

[23] Marie Rowlands, 'Hidden people: Catholic Commoners 1558–1625' in Marie Rowlands (ed.), *English Catholics of parish and town* (London: Catholic Record Society, 1999), pp. 10–35; J.A. Hilton, 'The Catholic poor: Vagabonds and paupers 1580–1780' in ibid., pp. 115–28.

[24] John Bossy, *The English Catholic Community 1570–1850* (London: Darton, Longman and Todd, 1975), pp. 78–100; Hugh Aveling, *Northern Catholics: the Catholic recusants of the North Riding of Yorkshire* (London: Geoffrey Chapman, 1966), pp. 129, 171, 178; William Sheils, '"Getting on" and "getting along" in parish and town: Catholics and their neighbours in England' in Benjamin Kaplan, Bob Moore, Henk Van Nierop, and Judith Pollmann (eds), *Catholic Communities in Protestant States: Britain and the Netherlands c. 1570–1720* (Manchester: Manchester University Press, 2009), pp. 67–83, at 69.

the state church proved surprisingly successful in reaching out to mutate practice and alter allegiance, even in many areas where only grudging acquiescence greeted the original settlement.

As Eamon Duffy has noted, the conservative rootedness of the old religion within the localities of England meant that its practitioners generally had little option but to adapt to the demands of conformity. In doing so, the habit of obedience and the past futility of resistance were formidable tools at the regime's disposal. Not insignificant bridges to previous practice, such as parish ales, churching of women and rogation-tide processions, probably helped reconcile parishioners to the new conditions.[25] And the claims of adherents to the Elizabethan settlement that the new dispensation differed from the old only on relatively limited points, not sufficient to warrant separation from the national church, probably helped soothe the consciences of those willing to be convinced.[26] Elizabeth's insistence on the wearing of the surplice by the clergy of her church possibly also had the effect of minimizing the transgressive impact of the new order. The hostility expressed by exponents of a more advanced Protestantism to such a hang-over of popery may well be an indication that the Queen was correct in assuming that it might have a certain emollient effect on religious conservatives.[27] That the practice of the old religion was also substantially inflected by a devotional culture which encoded itself in material expressions such as furnishings and adornments also made it vulnerable to the state's prohibition and confiscation of such objects. Transmutation in pietistic practices was probably enhanced by a natural reluctance to invest in materials which might simply be destroyed or, worse, taken away to enrich the coffers of the regime, and could be justified theologically by a more Protestant emphasis on the importance of charity to one's neighbours over material exhibitions of devotion.[28]

Part of the double bind of English Catholicism was the manner in which it could only be sustained through a wide range of contacts with continental Europe. As Claire Walker has demonstrated, multiple tendrils of English Catholicism stretched, for instance, into the southern Netherlands. Particularly important was the provision of Catholic education to gentry families. Many of these proceeded from establishments such as Douai, St Omer's or Ghent to become missionary priests or to take the veil. But many others were destined to return to England, ultimately to become the spouses and parents of a new generation.[29] In Elizabeth's reign alone in the region of 600 clergy returned to England where, despite casualty rates of over twenty per cent, they made a significant impact on the evolving recusant

---

[25] Eamon Duffy, *The Voices of Morebath: Reformation and Rebellion in an English Village* (New Haven and London: Yale University Press, 2003), pp. 170–83.

[26] For example Edmund Bunny, *A Booke of Christian Exercise, Appertayning to Resolution…and Accompanied Now with a Treatise Tending to Pacification* (London, 1584), p. 164. I am indebted to Michael Questier for this reference.

[27] Alec Ryrie, *The Age of Reformation: The Tudor and Stewart Realms 1485–1603* (Harlow: Pearson Longmann, 2009), p. 269.

[28] Duffy, *Voices of Morebath*, pp. 170–83.

[29] Claire Walker, 'Priests, nuns, presses and prayer: the Southern Netherlands and the contours of English Catholicism' in Kaplan et al. (eds), *Catholic Communities*, pp. 139–55, at 145–6.

community. But, as in Ireland, the effects of dependence on the continent had significant ramifications for the relationship of English Catholics both with the regime and with the wider community. The sharpening anti-Catholicism which became increasingly evident at all levels of English society in the course of the Elizabethan period was stimulated above all by a xenophobic and defensive anxiety about continental threats to the English monarchy. Peaceable recusants living in the localities of England might indeed attract less opprobrium than trouble-making Puritans but the inevitable connection between Catholicism and the continental enemies of the regime, most notably Spain, undoubtedly had deleterious effects on the general perception of the recusant community.[30]

Such effects were inevitably heightened by the transmutative influence of the continental connection on English Catholics themselves. While conservative religious instincts may have underpinned the widespread Catholic sensibility in England at the beginning of Elizabeth's reign, contact with the continent not only brought recusants into open conflict with the laws of the land but exposed them to radicalizing trends in post-Tridentine Catholicism. By the last decade of the century, the internal conflict between more conservative Catholic forces and those radicalized by opposition to the regime became mapped onto a complex clerical rivalry between the Society of Jesus and other clerical groups which resented its influence. The level of tension which developed between supporters of the Jesuits and the English secular clergy was probably accentuated by the fact that, to a much greater extent than across the sea in Ireland where a distinct continuity was maintained with the past, the long-established regular orders of England had suffered a major disruption in terms of personnel and in several cases had effectively to be refounded in the seventeenth century.[31] To a wide swathe of English religious conservatives, these developments within Catholicism were probably alienating. Moreover, the difficulty and expense of accessing the continent for education meant that this option was effectively only open to the wealthier members of society. While the returning missionaries did not devote their time only to gentry households,[32] it can be suggested that a disproportionate amount of their energy did become concentrated on the upper echelons of society, where, in the context of the real danger which Elizabethan England represented for Catholic missionaries, a greater likelihood of protection could be found.

Political considerations also impacted on the distribution of resources. Regime change had already delivered several alterations in the religion of England in the course of the sixteenth century. The possibility of a Catholic succession, whether in the person of the Queen of Scots or through a monarch from the continent displacing the heretical Queen, could not be discounted. The latter decades of the sixteenth, and the first half of the seventeenth, century also furnished ample proof from the Habsburg domains of Austria, Bohemia, and Hungary of the manner in

---

[30] Ryrie, *Age of Reformation*, pp. 247–53, 285–7.

[31] I am grateful to my colleague Professor John McCafferty for bringing this point to my attention.

[32] Michael Mullett, '"So they become contemptible": clergy and laity in a mission territory' in Kaplan et al. (eds), *Catholic Communities*, pp. 33–47, at 36.

which Catholic reform could be inculcated by the exercise of monarchical power and prerogative among a population which had turned from the church of Rome.[33] Certainly Robert Persons in 1596 believed in the possibility of the instigation of a successful programme of re-Catholicization by a new regime centred on the development of an adequate body of properly-led and regulated clergy which could inculcate a revived spirit of devotion in the general population through education, visitation, and pastoral care.[34] Such considerations, therefore, may have influenced Catholic emphasis on the gentry and the less receptive and more dangerous environment of London and the south of England.[35] Many priests of course, such as John Bennett in Wales, Ambrose Barlow in Lancashire, and Nicholas Postgate in Yorkshire, did seize the opportunity to minister to all levels of society in areas relatively amenable to such endeavours. Even in London, where many Catholics of all classes naturally congregated, a figure such as William Whittingham became known as *sacerdos pauperum*.[36] Nevertheless, the probable effect of the pattern of clerical provision was to leave the wider society relatively under-resourced and it was thus a contributory factor to what became the progressive obliteration of the Catholic past.[37] It was arguably within this context that religious conservatism, distaste for innovation and for Puritanism in particular, and commitment to an English church and sovereign, found the opportunity to coalesce around the text and rituals of the Prayer-book, which by the 1640s had evidently become a cherished part of the fabric of religious life for much of the English population.[38]

Ironically something similar may have been occurring in recusant households. The extra-legal character of Catholicism in England created an increased importance for printed material, a tendency which the sometimes intermittent possibilities of contact with priests, and through them with the sacraments, may have accentuated. The circumstances of England also rendered ecclesiastical control over the cult of relics particularly difficult and the bloody circumstances of Elizabeth's reign meant that for those who rejected the legitimacy of the state's activity the cult of relics of martyrs became more intense in England than on the continent of Europe.[39]

The commitment of many English Catholics to forcible regime change seemed closest to fruition after the execution of Mary Queen of Scots in 1587 and the heightening of English support for the rebel Dutch impelled Philip II to make England a major target of Europe's pre-eminent military power. The lucky defeat of the Armada at sea in 1588 effectively closed off the best possibility of any

[33] In this regard see the following chapter.

[34] Alexandra Walsham, 'Translating Trent? English Catholicism and the Counter Reformation', *Historical Research* 78 (2005), 288–310, at 288–9.

[35] Michael Carrafiello, 'English Catholicism and the Jesuit Mission of 1580–81', *Historical Journal* 37 (1994), 761–74.

[36] Walsham, 'Translating Trent?', 300–1; M. Gandy, 'Ordinary Catholics in mid-17th century London' in Rowlands, *English Catholics*, pp. 153–77.

[37] Eamon Duffy, 'The Long Reformation: Catholicism, Protestantism and the multitude' in Tyacke, *England's Long Reformation*, pp. 33–70, at 36.

[38] Judith Maltby, *Prayer Book and People in Elizabethan and Early Stuart England* (Cambridge: Cambridge University Press, 1998).

[39] Alexandra Walsham, ' "Domme Preachers"? Post-Reformation English Catholicism and the culture of print', *Past & Present* 168 (2000), 72–123.

reassertion of Catholicism in England through the force of continental arms, although war and the possibility of intervention rumbled on until the advent of the new king in England and peace with Spain in 1604. As the son of a queen widely considered as a Catholic martyr, the accession of James VI and I to the thrones of England and Ireland in 1603 created widespread optimism among English Catholics that a marked upturn in their status was possible. Indeed, as Michael Questier has argued, the prospects of toleration in the new reign had begun to inflect the conduct of both Catholics and the state in the years prior to the old Queen's death.

In February 1604, however, a proclamation banishing priests followed by the King's speech to parliament in March proved the futility of such optimism.[40] Rather than the uncertainties relating to the succession of an aging queen, Protestantism was now represented by an adult male monarch with guaranteed heirs.[41] The effects of the Gunpowder Plot and continuities with the Elizabethan regime ensured that Catholics continued to face major difficulties in their attempt to renegotiate their status within the English kingdom. Executions, principally of priests, continued in Jacobean England and financial pressure was increased as the state strove to derive increased pecuniary advantage from the extra-legal position of the recusant community. Indeed, there seems to have been something of a peak in conformity by former recusants between 1612 and 1615, probably to avoid the financial penalties which a tightening system of fining was rendering more onerous and threatening.[42] However, while the financial penalties for recusancy were undoubtedly severe, particularly in comparison to the contemporaneous Stuart regime in Ireland, the implementation of the statutes was not designed to push Catholic families into ruin. In the West Riding of Yorkshire, recusancy proceedings did not apparently destroy the financial stability of a single family in the period up to outbreak of the English Civil War in 1642.[43] The second viscount Montague offers another perspective on these processes. Despite his refusal of the Jacobean oath of allegiance, he escaped total forfeiture of his patrimony by compounding for the (admittedly enormous) sum of £6000.[44] Under the personal rule of James's successor, Charles I, the processes whereby recusants could compound for their religious dissidence by payments to recusancy commissioners, already foreshadowed informally during the previous regime, became more officially established. The financial implications of this procedure could be onerous but it freed recusants from harassment by other agencies whose involvement had previously caused them difficulty and insult.[45]

While the total number of Catholics evidently declined significantly by the last years of Elizabeth's reign, and while the following decades witnessed also the gradual weakening of the penumbra of sympathizers with the old religion, as those

---

[40] Nina Taunton and Valerie Hart, '*King Lear*, King James and the gunpowder treason of 1605', *Renaissance Studies* 17 (2003), 695–715.

[41] Nicholls, 'Gunpowder plot', 802.   [42] Haigh, *Plain Man's Pathways*, pp. 190–1.

[43] Caroline Hibbard, 'Early Stuart Catholicism: revisions and re-revisions', *Journal of Modern History* 52 (1980), 1–34, at 20.

[44] Questier, *Catholicism and community*, p. 359.   [45] ibid., pp. 430–1.

with actual memories of its practices died off, the first half of the seventeenth century witnessed a sharp increase in the numbers of clergy. These reached a peak in the 1630s, not merely in absolute terms but with regard to the ratio of priests to the general population.[46] This pattern was most evident within the regular orders whose numbers more than quadrupled in size in the first decades of the new century, with almost 5000 men and women professing vows between 1598 and the outbreak of the English Civil War.[47] While the increase in the secular clergy was less dramatic, total numbers almost doubled within this time-frame. The organization of this latter grouping, however, proved one of the most divisive issues within English Catholic life. Between 1598 and 1621 the English church was regulated by a system of archpriests, who disposed of an authority significantly weaker than the bishops who functioned in Ireland or indeed the vicars apostolic used elsewhere by Rome *in partibus infidelium*, most notably in the Netherlands. From 1621, in a similar fashion to contemporaneous initiatives in the Turkish Balkans, Rome then experimented for a decade with the revival of Episcopal authority by creating two successive titular bishops of Chalcedon. The vicious disputes occasioned by these bishops and their opponents ultimately resulted in the ending of this system when Bishop Richard Smith fled to the continent in 1631. In his absence the vacuum of authority was filled to some extent by a dean and chapter chosen from among the English secular clergy. Not until 1685 and the extensions to England of the system of vicars apostolic was another sustained effort made by Rome to alter the governance of the English Catholic church.[48]

The extra-legal characteristics of English Catholicism naturally posed difficulties for the extension of Tridentine-style reform across the channel.[49] On the one hand, dependence on the gentry and the inability of the clergy to control property in England in a corporate fashion necessarily threatened the freedom of action to discipline and instruct which underpinned the spirit of much Tridentine reform on the continent. Even in London, where the ambassadors' chapels and, following Charles I's marriage, the sumptuous chapels of the Queen allowed for a public, indeed theatrical, manifestation of Catholic worship,[50] the dependency of clergy on lay patrons and protectors was pronounced. On the other hand, however, the exposure of domestic Catholic households to the intense ministrations of highly motivated clergy, actually sharing their residences, offered exceptional opportunities for pastoral care.[51] John Gerrard's autobiography, for instance, gives clear indications of the manner in which a Jesuit could reap significant devotional

[46] Hibbard, 'Early Stuart Catholicism', 11.
[47] J.C.H. Aveling, *The handle and the axe: the Catholic Recusants in England from Reformation to Emancipation* (London: Blond and Briggs, 1976), pp. 98–9; Bossy, *Catholic Community*, pp. 216–23.
[48] Robert Armstrong and Tadhg Ó hAnnracháin, 'Alternative Establishments? Insular Catholicism and Presbyterianism' in Robert Armstrong and Tadhg Ó hAnnracháin (eds), *Insular Christianity: Alternative models of the church in Britain and Ireland c. 1570–1700* (Manchester: Manchester University Press, 2013), pp. 1–27, at 12.
[49] For a discussion on the limitations on Tridentine reform in non-Catholic jurisdictions see Ó hAnnracháin, *Catholic Reformation*, Chapter two; Walsham, 'Translating Trent?', 294.
[50] Frances Dolan, 'Gender and the "Lost" Spaces of Catholicism', *Journal of Interdisciplinary History* 32 (2002), 641–65, at 648–9.
[51] Walsham, 'Translating Trent?', pp. 296–8.

dividends from the peculiar conditions of the English mission.[52] And while matriarchal power could possibly pose a threat to priestly authority, and while the absence of priests might allow women a certain spiritual independence,[53] it also enabled clergy to develop very vital spiritual relationships with women who often eagerly sought to take advantage of such opportunities.[54]

Although seventeenth-century Catholics represented only a small minority of the population, and one, despite the significant proportion of the social elite among their numbers, disproportionately excluded from office, their religion held a surprising saliency in the life of the kingdom of England. During Elizabeth's reign, the challenge presented by Catholic intellectuals was treated with the utmost seriousness, even perhaps to the extent of giving it an oxygen which it might otherwise have lacked.[55] This process continued too in the seventeenth century when King James himself, somewhat unwisely, was prepared to enter the lists against Catholic Europe's foremost intellectual, Robert Bellarmine. As a consequence, a detailed knowledge of Catholic texts and intellectuals was of fundamental importance even to the academics of the established church. The (often unacknowledged) influence of the church of Rome on the devotional literature consumed by English Protestants was also undeniable. Moreover, much of the artistic production of the kingdom was deeply influenced from the Catholic continent.[56]

As Michael Questier has argued, the political impact of English Catholicism should not be underestimated. The level of anti-Popish anxiety which became increasingly evident towards the end of James's reign reflected a realization that the court's pursuit of a Spanish match threatened a profound realignment of English politics. Catholics were intensely aware of the possibilities inherent in this situation. They could not only hope to obtain mere toleration through the negotiation of a dispensation for a Catholic princess's marriage to the Prince of Wales, but could also pose as the natural allies of the crown against invasions of the royal prerogative to determine foreign policy. Simultaneously, the divisions within the Established church between proponents of the beauty of holiness and avant-garde conformity, on the one hand, and those who looked with horror on such manifestations of popishness, on the other, offered an entry point to Catholics who might hope to see in the triumph of the former a repositioning of the Church of England towards ground where the cleavages between Catholics and the religion established by law would be more susceptible to negotiation. Indeed, within this process the internal debates within English Catholicism could be artfully employed to draw parallels between attempts to restrict the freedom of action of the regular orders by the reinstitution of Catholic Episcopal authority and the alleged danger to proper order in worship posed by demagogic Puritans. The anxieties of English Protestantism

[52] Philip Caraman (ed.), *John Gerard, the autobiography of an Elizabethan* (London: Longmans, Green, 1951).

[53] Dolan, 'Gender and the "Lost" Spaces', 652 points out that priests rather than husbands were seen as the proper spiritual guides for Catholic women.

[54] ibid.; Walsham, 'Translating Trent?'.   [55] Ryrie, *Age of Reformation*, pp. 251–3.

[56] See Milton, 'A Qualified Intolerance'; Alison Shell, *Catholicism, Controversy and the English Literary Imagination 1558–1660* (Cambridge: Cambridge University Press, 1999).

were not eased even by the quite severe measures taken against Catholics in the course of the war against Spain and France in the 1620s. During the King's personal rule, the visibility of Catholics at court, including of course the Queen and even worse the papal ministers whom she entertained, ensured that the fear of Popery did not abate, although the lack of a parliament until 1640 deprived it of its most natural forum.

For English Catholics the Civil War offered arguably the last opportunity for a profound renegotiation of their status within the state. An outright victory for the royalist party, which was supported with enthusiasm by gentry English and Welsh Catholics, offered the best hope of such an outcome. In the shorter term, the war offered the possibility for Catholics to serve their monarch in arms, a privilege largely denied to them in the previous decades. Most of the Catholic officers in Royalist forces during the conflict of the 1640s had not previously held office under the Stuarts.[57] On the other hand, parliament's suspicions of Catholics were given concrete expression in 1643 when the Ordinance for sequestering notorious delinquents' estates allowed for the confiscation of two thirds of Catholics' property. Catholics were prominent also in the conspiracies of the 1650s which helped to give focus to the Royalist cause in exile but the national conditions of the Restoration meant that the King's sense of debt and gratitude was necessarily circumscribed by political necessity.[58]

In the Principality of Wales, the English Reformation faced some significant problems not dissimilar to those which it spectacularly failed to surmount in Ireland. Nevertheless, despite the fact that Wales like Ireland contained a majority population for whom English was a foreign tongue, and one which evoked little cultural sympathy within the English state, Welsh Catholicism failed to translate the possibilities of widespread religious conservatism into an ongoing survival at a popular level. Instead, the residues of the old religion became embedded in a complex process of negotiation with the new dispensation in which reverence for saints, the traditional features of the sacred landscape, and credence in spirits continued to figure.[59] Importantly, and largely in contrast to Ireland, the Established church neither spurned the possibilities of making capital out of the Welsh past[60] nor the use of the vernacular language to advance its cause. By 1567 both a New Testament

---

[57] P.R. Newman, 'Roman Catholic Royalists: papist commanders under Charles I and Charles II', *Recusant History* 15 (1981), 396–405, at 402; Questier, *Catholicism and community*, p. 507.

[58] C. Walker, 'Prayer, patronage and political conspiracy: English nuns and the Restoration', *Historical Journal* 43 (2000), 1–23.

[59] Katharine Olson, ' "Slow and cold in the true service of God": Popular Beliefs and Practices, Conformity, and Reformation in Wales, c. 1530–1600' in Tadhg Ó hAnnracháin and Robert Armstrong (eds), *Celtic Christianities in the early modern world* (Basingstoke: Palgrave, 2014), pp. 92–110.

[60] For the success of Welsh Protestants in presenting the Reformation as the restoration of an original Welsh purity of faith see Glanmor Williams, 'Some Protestant Views of the Early British Church' in Glanmor Williams, *Welsh Reformation Essays* (Cardiff: University of Wales Press, 1967), pp. 207–19; Peter Roberts, 'Tudor Wales, National Identity and the British Inheritance' in P. Roberts and B. Bradshaw (eds), *British Consciousness and Identity: The Making of Britain, 1533–1707* (Cambridge: Cambridge University Press, 1998), pp. 8–42; Lloyd Bowen, 'The Battle of Britain: History and Reformation in Early Modern Wales' in Ó hAnnracháin and Armstrong (eds), *Celtic Christianities*, pp. 135–50.

and a Book of Common Prayer was available in Welsh, and a complete bible followed two decades later. By the time of the provision of a relatively affordable five shilling version of the entire biblical text in Welsh in 1630, there was a host of other devotional texts available within the principality's native language.[61] The work of Welsh scholars and antiquaries thus provided a vital bridge towards the reception of the Established church by a conservative population. In contrast, as previously noted with parts of England, it has been suggested that the Catholic missionaries of the Elizabethan era relatively neglected Wales, concentrating greater attention on the less promising south and east of England.[62] The Established church, on the other hand, entrusted Welsh bishoprics to natives of the principality: thirteen of the sixteen Elizabethan bishops in the four sees of Wales were Welsh.[63] By the end of Elizabeth's reign fewer than a thousand recusants were identified within Welsh dioceses[64] although the number of Catholic sympathizers was of course significantly greater. In contrast to England, where clerical numbers expanded dramatically during the first half of the seventeenth century, the numbers of Welsh Catholic clergy declined sharply. Ordinations in the diocese of Llanduff plummeted during the first four decades of the seventeenth century to roughly a quarter of the rate during Elizabeth's reign.[65]

Prior to 1603 Scotland was a separate and independent kingdom under its own ruling dynasty which over the previous centuries had nourished a long tradition of enmity with England and alliance with France. Yet, coterminous with Elizabeth's slow inculcation of disjunction from the church of Rome in England, an extraordinary collapse of Scottish Catholicism occurred which prepared the way for the way for an alliance of two Protestant regimes and then the tense but ultimately surprisingly successful union of the two kingdoms under the Stuarts in 1603. By this stage, except for some pockets in the North-East and inaccessible largely Gaelic-speaking regions of the Highlands, Scottish Catholicism had largely been obliterated by a highly active new church establishment, centred on consistories or 'kirk sessions' which rapidly established a formidable preaching ministry that disposed of real moral authority over the Scottish population.[66] In sharp contrast to Ireland, where the impact of the Reformed religion on the Gaelic-speaking population was minimal, the kirk adopted early and proactive measures to ensure that the Highlands became subject to an evangelical project which in many respects

[61] Glanmor Williams, 'Some Protestant Views of the Early British Church', pp. 207–19; Roberts, 'Tudor Wales, National Identity', *passim*; Glanmor William, *Renewal and Reformation: Wales c. 1415–1642* (Oxford: Oxford University Press, 1993), p. 476.

[62] Christopher Haigh, 'From Monopoly to Minority: Catholicism in Early Modern England', *Transactions of the Royal Historical Society* fifth series 31 (1981), 129–47.

[63] Philip Jenkins, 'The Anglican Church and the unity of Britain: the Welsh experience, 1560–1714' in Steven Ellis and Sarah Barber (eds) *Conquest and Union: Fashioning a British state 1485–1725* (Harlow: Longman, 1995), pp. 115–38.

[64] Glanmor Williams, *Recovery, reorientation and Reformation: Wales c. 1415–1642* (Oxford: Oxford University Press, 1987), p. 328.

[65] Tadhg Ó hAnnracháin, 'An alternative establishment: the evolution of the Irish Catholic hierarchy, 1600–49' in Armstrong and ÓhAnnracháin, *Insular Christianity*, pp. 190–206.

[66] Ryrie, *Age of Reformation*, pp. 229–30, 255–64, 303–5.

mirrored that of the Lowlands.[67] Critical in this regard was the role of Clan Campbell. The major magnate family of Early Modern Scotland effectively acted as the midwives of the Reformation in the Scottish Gàidhealtachd, although ironically the confessional choices of the minority of Gaelic aristocratic families who did persist in allegiance to Rome was probably heavily influenced by rivalry with the Campbells.[68] In the course of the seventeenth century, Scottish Catholics numbered hardly more than two per cent of the population. While a certain shoring up of Gaelic Catholicism in the Hebrides occurred as a result of a somewhat reluctant mission undertaken by Gaelic Irish Franciscans in the seventeenth century,[69] Catholicism in Scotland overall suffered a significant penury of priests, particularly seculars. It was estimated to *Propaganda Fide* in the 1620s that only thirteen secular priests were ministering in Scotland and by the 1650s this number had more than halved to a mere five.[70]

IRELAND

Across the Western sea in Ireland, Catholicism developed according to a completely different trajectory. While from both a papal and an English perspective late medieval Ireland was a territory of very limited importance, the surprising religious developments in Ireland were to have genuinely critical repercussions. The consolidation of a Catholic identity in Early Modern Ireland ensured that the nascent British empire did not evolve as an exclusive bastion of Protestantism. Rather, contiguous to its very centre, there developed a significant Catholic English-speaking population which in the course of the nineteenth and twentieth centuries spread throughout the empire. Irish emigration provided the core of the Catholic communities which developed not merely in areas such as Australia and New Zealand but also within Britain itself, with the greatest impact in Scotland, where Catholics, overwhelmingly of Irish origin, came to represent about seventeen per cent of the Scottish population. Even more crucially, extensive Irish immigration to America created a vital stratum within Catholicism in the USA.

The evolution of the Irish population towards a strong Catholic majority is in a sense the opposite of the conundrum of the transmutation of Catholic England in the course of the sixteenth century. In 1500, particularly in the majority of the

[67] James Kirk, 'The Kirk and the Highlands at the Reformation' in James Kirk, *Patterns of Reform: Continuity and Change in the Reformation Kirk* (Edinburgh: T. & T. Clark, 1989), pp. 305–33; *idem*, 'The Jacobean Church in the Highlands, 1567–1625', ibid., pp. 449–87; Jane Dawson, 'Calvinism and the Gaidhealtachd in Scotland' in Andrew Pettegree, Alastair Duke, and Gillian Lewis (eds), *Calvinism in Europe 1540–1620* (Cambridge: Cambridge University Press, 1994), pp. 231–53.

[68] R. Scott Spurlock, 'The Laity and the Structure of the Catholic Church in early modern Scotland' in Armstrong and Ó hAnnracháin, *Insular Christianity*, pp. 231–51.

[69] Cathaldus Giblin (ed.), *Irish Franciscan Mission to Scotland, 1619–46* (Dublin: Assisi Press, 1964).

[70] J. Durkan, 'Early letter of John Brown, Minim and report to *Propaganda Fide*, 1623, by Scots Minims', *Innes Review* 52 (2001), 75–6; A. Macinnes, 'Catholic recusancy and the penal laws, 1603–1707', *Records of the Scottish Church History Society* 23 (1987), 27–63; Daniel Szechi, 'Defending the True Faith: Kirk, state and Catholic missioners in Scotland, 1653–1755', *Catholic Historical Review* 82 (1996), 397–411.

island largely outside the control of the English monarchs and dominated by warring Gaelic and Gaelicized lords, Irish Catholicism represented arguably one of the most anomalous strands of the late medieval church. Prior to the creation of a regular organization of dioceses and parishes in the twelfth century, the church in Ireland had primarily been structured around monasteries. Deriving from this, most ecclesiastical land in Gaelic areas was in the hands of clerical families whose duties included the maintenance of parish churches, the payment of rent to the bishop and the provision of hospitality for the Episcopal household in its circuits through the diocese.[71] Within this *ecclesia inter hibernicos*, most notably in the thirteen dioceses to which a Gaelic Irish bishop was invariably appointed, church canons on clerical celibacy were routinely ignored. Not only clerical marriage but the succession of sons of clerics to church positions had become routine. Since Gaelic Ireland produced little urban development, the church was both profoundly rural, with large, sprawling parishes, and very poor by contemporary English and European standards. Clergy not infrequently participated in the endemic violence which characterized the world of the Gaelic lordships. In 1522, for instance, the Bishop of Leighlin, Maurice Doran, was murdered by Maurice Kavanagh, an archdeacon (and son of a Cistercian abbot), who resented his rebukes.[72]

Since the twelfth century, the lordship of Ireland had been appended to the kingdom of England. While the monarchs of England could assert a claim to Ireland on the basis of the (extensive but incomplete) Norman conquest and prescriptive rights, their claim was validated also by the papal bull *Laudabiliter,* according to which the English pope Adrian granted permission to Henry II to intervene in Ireland. Down to the Henrician schism, there was relatively little tension between these alternative sources of legitimization as English kings by and large enjoyed good relations in Rome and managed to have favoured nominees appointed as bishops to the dioceses in the parts of the island actually under their control. *Laudabiliter* and the *mission civilitrice* of the English colony in Ireland became especially important to the 'English by blood', the descendants of the Anglo-Norman invaders of the twelfth century, who validated their sense of cultural superiority over the Gaelic Irish of the island with particular reference to their greater adherence to the canonical norms of the late medieval church.[73] Henry VIII's break with Rome led indirectly in 1541 to the elevation of Ireland to the status of kingdom and the vindication of the monarch's title to the island according to parliamentary statute rather than papal donation.

But the Henrician Reformation left little mark on Ireland. Under the more radical regime which took power under his son, Edward VI, elements of the Irish ecclesiastical elite demonstrated bitter hostility to both clerical marriage and the

---

[71] Steven G. Ellis, *Ireland in the Age of the Tudors 1447–1603: English Expansion and the End of Gaelic Rule* (London: Longman, 1998), pp. 193–5.

[72] Patrick Corish, *The Irish Catholic Experience: a historical survey* (Dublin: Gill and MacMillan, 1985), p. 55.

[73] James Murray, 'The diocese of Dublin in the sixteenth century: clerical opposition and the failure of the reformation' in James Kelly and Daire Keogh (eds), *History of the Catholic Diocese of Dublin* (Dublin: Four Courts Press, 2000), pp. 92–111.

denial of transubstantiation in the sacrament of the Eucharist, while a strong attachment to the traditional form of the mass was evident at a popular level.[74] Bishops who had supported the Royal Supremacy reported the unease of the people in the face of the Edwardine reforms. In contrast to England, there was remarkably little opposition to the re-instigation of Marian Catholicism. The lesser impact of her father's and brother's reforms in Ireland may explain why Elizabeth initially encountered less overt opposition in the western island to the church settlement, modelled on the English statutes, which was introduced in the Irish parliament in 1560. As noted in the previous chapter, the regime took certain measures to reassure Irish religious conservatism. The Irish Act of Uniformity did not explicitly deny the real presence[75] and ordained that 'in every such church or place, where the common minister or priest hath not the use of the English tongue it shall be lawful... to say the mattens, even-song, and the celebration of the Lord's Supper, and administration of each of the sacraments, and all their common and open prayer in the Latin tongue'.[76]

However, in contrast to the practically unanimous opposition to the religious settlement on the part of the English hierarchy, the lack of overt resistance on the part of the Irish bishops was somewhat remarkable. At least two archbishops and five Irish bishops proved willing to take the Oath of Supremacy while only two were deprived of their sees for an overt denial of the Queen's supreme governorship.[77] In contrast to England, therefore, the acquiescence of religious conservatives to the Elizabethan settlement removed the necessity of wholesale remodelling of the island's religious leadership. In practical terms, this may have proved disadvantageous to the instigation of real religious change by creating a potential fifth column within the Irish church, although the suggestion that this corresponded to something of a planned strategy on the part of Irish clergymen seems unlikely.[78] More probably, the Irish bishops lacked the visceral fear of the Royal Supremacy which had been learned by their English counterparts for the simple reason that, unlike England, the Edwardine Supremacy had actually impacted relatively little on the western island.

Despite parliamentary and episcopal acquiescence, the new church settlement faced formidable obstacles in embedding itself in Ireland. Poverty was certainly a massive problem. Prior to the Henrician breach with Rome even the richest Irish dioceses could not compare with their English counterparts[79] and this situation did not improve. Although the dissolution of the monasteries released significant

[74] James Murray and Ciaran Brady, 'Sir Henry Sidney and the Reformation in Ireland' in Elizabethanne Boran and Crawford Gribben (eds), *Enforcing Reformation in Ireland and Scotland, 1550–1700* (Aldershot: Ashgate Publishing, 2006), pp. 14–39, at 27–9.

[75] Ellis, *Age of the Tudors*, pp. 221, 225–6.

[76] Quoted in Richard Mant, *History of the Church of Ireland, from the Reformation to the Revolution* (London: J.W. Parker, 1840), p. 260.

[77] Henry A. Jeffries, *The Irish Church and the Tudor Reformations* (Dublin: Four Courts Press, 2010), pp. 125–7.

[78] James Murray, *Enforcing the English Reformation in Ireland: clerical resistance and political conflict in the Diocese of Dublin, 1534–1590* (Cambridge: Cambridge University Press, 2009), pp. 256–7.

[79] S.G. Ellis, 'Economic Problems of the Church: why the reformation failed in Ireland', *Journal of Ecclesiastical History* 41 (1990), 239–65, at 248–9.

resources these were not used to build up the evangelical capacities of the church but were utilized to buy support from local lay elites and to fund expenditure by the government. By the mid 1570s, the English governor of Ireland, Sir Henry Sidney, painted a devastating picture of Meath, the richest and among the most anglicized dioceses in Ireland, with ruined churches, inadequate clergy, and utterly insufficient resources to support a better ministry. Other areas were presumably in a worse case, as he noted:

> If this be the state of the church in the best peopled diocese and best governed country of this your Realm (as in truth it is), easy it is for your Majesty to conjecture in what case the rest is, where little or no reformation, either of religion or manners, hath yet been planted and continued among them; yea, so profane and heathenish are some parts of this your country become, as it hath been preached publicly before me that the sacrament of baptism is not used among them, and truly I believe it.[80]

One of the key deficiencies of the Elizabethan church in Ireland was the lack of a university to form a preaching ministry committed to the new settlement. Despite a number of schemes, such an institution was not created until 1592. By that stage, however, the problems confronting the new church establishment had become significantly greater than mere conservatism and lack of resources. A number of processes evidently came together to transform what had not initially appeared as terminal hostility towards religious change into an increasingly ardent and deter- mined self-fashioning of the island's disparate ethnic communities as Catholic.

The Old English of Ireland, the descendants of the initial Anglo-Norman con- quest and colonization of the island, should logically have acted as the spearhead for the embedding of the Elizabethan form of Protestantism in Ireland. But the alienation of this grouping from the state in the course of Elizabeth's reign was severe. A significant portion of Old English hostility towards the Irish government was economically motivated. The gradual unravelling of Tudor policies of assimi- lation of the Gaelic Irish population in the latter decades of the century meant that the English governors of Ireland were forced to make unparalleled exactions on local English resources to help fund what ultimately became a war of conquest. Bitter resentment of constitutional innovation on the part of the government evidently assisted the development of a kind of ecclesiastical patriotism which resented attempts to change cherished traditional structures, whether ecclesiastical or lay. The fact that much of the Old English clerical elite vested a notion of English cultural superiority over Gaelic Ireland in the very corpus of late medieval Catholic practice and identity which the Elizabethan church was committed to transforming probably helped ensure that resentment of the state's intrusiveness and innovation easily found expression in religious dissidence.[81]

Not only did the state lack the financial resources to mount any aggressive pro- gramme of evangelization but its coercive machinery was limited as well. The

---

[80] Sir Henry Sidney to Elizabeth I, 28 April 1576 (W. Maziere Brady (ed.), *State papers concerning the Irish church in the time of Queen Elizabeth* (London: Longmans, Green, Reader & Dyer, 1868), pp. 15–16).

[81] Murray, 'The diocese of Dublin', pp. 92–111.

administrative procedures to deal with refusal of the Oath of Supremacy were highly cumbersome while the Commission of Ecclesiastical Causes proved largely ineffective as a tool for enforcing lay conformity because local juries were notably unwilling to cooperate with it.[82] In sharp contrast to England, where by the end of Elizabeth's reign the state disposed of a truly formidable collection of anti-Catholic legislation,[83] there was to be no updating of the parliamentary statutes of the original settlement in Ireland until the Commonwealth regime of the 1650s.[84] However, the late sixteenth century saw an increasing number of what came to be termed 'New English' settlers in Ireland. Some of these were the products of direct governmental schemes of plantation, particularly in Munster and west Leinster, others were officers in the expanding Elizabethan military establishment in Ireland, while others served as office-holders, increasingly at the expense of local candidates for such positions, in both the central administration in Dublin and the devolved provincial presidencies in Munster and Connacht. While the English colony in Ireland had a tradition of assimilating English immigrants dating back to the original medieval settlement, towards the end of the sixteenth century this began to falter. In particular, a religious fault line developed according to which Protestants were far less likely to merge with the existing colony, a process accentuated by the sharp divisions between the state and the Old English population on economic, religious, and political grounds.[85]

As noted in Chapter 1, the 1590s were in many respects the fulcrum decade in terms of the hardening of confessional boundaries with regard to the Old English of Ireland. While reluctant to support wholeheartedly the rebellion of the Gaelic dynast, Hugh O'Neill, the fact that the state was so hard pressed to maintain an English foothold in the island allowed for an increasingly confident assertion of Catholic identity. Of significance in this respect was the increasing influence of clerics returning from a continental education. This process was already evident in the 1570s as Irish men in increasing numbers began to abandon the universities of Oxford and Cambridge in search of an education more in tune with conservative religious sentiments in continental institutions. By 1582, a small Irish residence had been set up in Vallodolid while in Lisbon in 1592 twenty-four Irish were crammed together in facilities barely adequate for twelve students.[86] The effect

---

[82] Aidan Clarke, 'Varieties of Uniformity: The First Century of the Church of Ireland' in W.J. Sheils and Diana Wood (eds), *The Churches, Ireland and the Irish: Studies in Church History 25* (1989), 105–22, at 112–14.

[83] A. Morey, *The Catholic Subjects of Elizabeth I* (London: George Allen and Unwin, 1978), pp. 45–71.

[84] T.C. Barnard, 'Conclusion: Settling and Unsettling Ireland: The Cromwellian and Williamite Revolutions' in Jane Ohlmeyer (ed.), *Ireland from Independence to Occupation, 1641–60* (Cambridge: Cambridge University Press, 1995), pp. 265–91, at 283.

[85] English Catholics coming to Ireland however apparently continued to integrate to a high degree: see David Edwards, 'A haven of popery: English Catholic migration to Ireland in the age of plantations' in Alan Ford and John McCafferty (eds), *The origins of sectarianism in early modern Ireland* (Cambridge: Cambridge University Press, 2005), pp. 95–126.

[86] Thomas M. McCoog, '"Replant the uprooted trunk of the tree of faith": the Society of Jesus and the continental colleges for religious exiles' in Armstrong and Ó hAnnracháin, *Insular Christianity*, pp. 28–48, at 32–4.

of attendance at such universities was profound. Evidently continentally-trained priests were to the fore in demanding outright recusancy rather than occasional conformity from the Irish population. By the 1590s the level of Irish engagement with foreign education abroad had developed to such an extent that an Irish college was founded at Salamanca in 1592, the first of eighteen such institutions which developed before 1640. Over the next five decades, Salamanca and its sister institutions scattered all over Europe successfully outperformed the state seminary at Trinity College, also founded in 1592, in terms of providing educated clerical personnel to staff the parishes of Irish Catholicism.[87] Multiple Irish trading links with the Catholic states of Europe both facilitated the original outflow and the journey back to Ireland by graduates of the colleges, although that trip could be fraught with anxiety.[88]

The effects of what became the Tudor conquest of Ireland appear also to have been the chief cause of the almost total failure of any form of Protestantism to take root in Gaelic Ireland.[89] In sharp contrast to the Gaelic-speaking population of Scotland, or to largely Welsh-speaking Wales, Gaelic Ireland suffered from a potent combination of native indifference, if not outright hostility, to the Reformed religion and an almost complete neglect of any positive programme of evangelization on the part of any Tudor government. The lack of provision of Gaelic texts has traditionally been highlighted as a telling indication of the low priority placed by the state on the inculcation of religious change in the non-English-speaking population of the island.[90] Neither a New Testament nor a Book of Common Prayer was available in the Irish language until the early seventeenth century. The Scottish parallel suggests that the lack of an educational institution to form a Gaelic-speaking ministry was even more crucial. When Trinity was founded in the 1590s a greater number of Gaelic students than Old English students did attend the institution but the tide was already running against the new religion. A key actor in this regard was the Franciscan order. Interestingly, in contrast to Gaelic Scotland, Gaelic Ireland had witnessed an efflorescence of Franciscan Observancy in the late medieval period. This led to the establishment of new Observant convents as well as the conversion of older establishments and a dramatic expansion of the Franciscan Third Order Regular, with the foundation of over forty houses.[91] The mendicant friars enjoyed a high reputation in Gaelic Ireland and they rapidly emerged as fierce opponents of the Reformed religion, as was noted, for instance, in 1567 by

[87] T.J. Walsh, *The Irish Continental College Movement: The Colleges at Bordeaux, Toulouse, and Lille* (Dublin and Cork: Golden Eagle Books, 1973).

[88] See for example the letter of the Archbishop of Cashel, Thomas Walsh, to Luke Wadding, 1 September 1628 (Brendan Jennings (ed.), *Wadding Papers* (Dublin: Irish Manuscripts Commission, 1953), pp. 269–73).

[89] The trajectory of religious change in the 'Celtic Fringe' of Early Modern Britain and Ireland is explored in Tadhg Ó hAnnracháin, 'Religious acculturation and affiliation in Early Modern Gaelic Scotland, Gaelic Ireland, Wales and Cornwall' in Ó hAnnracháin and Armstrong (eds), *Celtic Christianities*, pp. 1–16.

[90] In this regard see Tadhg Ó hAnnracháin, 'Bridging the Ethnic Divide: Creating a Catholic Identity in Early Modern Ireland' in Rita Librandi and Maria D'Anzi (eds) *Lingua e testi delle riforme cattoliche in Europa e nelle Americhe* (Firenze: Cesati, 2013), pp. 265–79.

[91] Corish, *Irish Catholic Experience*, p. 57.

the Gaelic Scottish reformer, Seon Carsuel.[92] The Gaelic polemic of friars such as Eoghan Ó Dubhthaigh in the sixteenth or Aodh Mac Aingil in the seventeenth century placed a heavy emphasis on the fleshly indulgence of the chief reformers and their followers which was contrasted with a traditional Gaelic Catholic asceticism, as exemplified in the hagiography of medieval Irish saints which became a major trope of Early Modern Gaelic literary endeavour.[93]

Gaelic antagonism towards the new religion was evidently heightened by the effects of the extraordinarily brutal wars of conquest waged by the English state during Elizabeth's reign. Faced with an escalating series of rebellions by Gaelic and Gaelicized dynasts, who resented the increased intrusiveness of English government, governors and military captains responded with campaigns of violence which had no parallel in contemporary Western Europe. In Munster during the 1580s and in Ulster during the 1590s, in particular, ruthless campaigns were waged which prioritized the indiscriminate destruction of foodstuffs leading to general starvation as well as organized killing of non-combatant populations. One natural strategy for the Gaelic elites who resisted the crown was to appeal for assistance to continental forces opposed to Elizabeth's regime. Inevitably this led them to heighten the importance of the religious dimension of their conflict. Rejection of the heretical Queen in the interests of the Catholic religion was already declared as a principal objective in the great rebellion which swept southern Ireland in the late 1570s and 1580s, which attracted the support of a formidable English Catholic intellectual, Nicholas Sanders, whose own opposition to the Queen had nothing to do with the issues of local politics in Munster that gave the rebellion much of its impetus.[94] The religious card was again played in the 1590s by Hugh O'Neill, the second Earl of Tyrone, who masterminded a formidable coalition of Gaelic forces that came close to shaking English dominion over the island and which attracted Spanish support.

A by-product of this ultimately unsuccessful opposition to the crown was the creation of Gaelic communities in exile on the continent, who naturally continued to emphasize the centrality of religion as the cause of their woes. Such exiles fused naturally with the growing number of Gaelic clerics who sought education on the continent, particularly in Flanders where regiments of Irish mercenaries were organized in Spanish service. Ultimately these continental enclaves became the centre of a major intellectual reinterpetation of Irish history, which emphasized the centrality of Catholicism in Gaelic identity and which offered a narrative of the conflicts within sixteenth-century Ireland as primarily a war of defence of religion against the attempts of the heretical English state to overthrow it. Of critical importance in what became a successful movement of Catholic reformation in Gaelic Ireland was the support of traditional elites. In sharp contrast to Gaelic Scotland,

[92] Mícheál Mac Craith, 'Collegium S. Antonii Lovanii, quod Collegium est unicum remedium ad conservandam Provinciam' in Edel Bhreathnach, Joseph MacMahon, and John McCafferty (eds), *The Irish Franciscans, 1534–1990* (Dublin: Four Courts Press, 2009), pp. 233–59, at 246.
[93] ibid.; Mícheál Mac Craith, 'The political and religious thought of Florence Conry and Hugh McCaughwell' in Ford and McCafferty (eds), *Sectarianism*, pp. 183–202, at 194–202.
[94] McCormack, *The Earldom of Desmond*, pp. 110–17, 160–2, 193–4.

where the Reformed church was able to recruit both from the native aristocracy and from the traditional learned families into its ministry, in Gaelic Ireland these groups increasingly emerged in leadership positions within the Catholic clergy.[95]

The failure of the Old English community in Ireland to throw in its lot with Hugh O'Neill, despite his insistence after 1596 that he was in arms for 'conscience and the defence of the catholic religion',[96] was a critical factor in the eventual success of the Elizabethan regime in crushing his rebellion in 1603. The final negotiated settlement coincided almost exactly with the demise of the Queen herself. Optimism that her successor James would offer at least freedom of worship was an important factor in the recusant revolt in various urban centres at the beginning of the new reign, which reconsecrated churches for Catholic use with highly public demonstrations of support for Catholic clergy and independence from local governmental institutions.[97] The sharp repression of this movement was an indication, however, that hopes of a new era were ill-founded. The contention that Old English constancy during the war against O'Neill deserved reward and acceptance by the government of their solid loyalty in temporal matters was to become a central plank of Old English identity in the following decades. Yet not only was the King personally dubious about the allegiance of what he termed half-subjects but the Irish government was bitterly hostile to this notion. With some justification they believed that the lukewarm nature of Old English support for the state had greatly impeded the repression of the rebellion and influential figures within the administration argued that the religious dissidence of Catholics was a sufficient reason for their exclusion from office on the grounds of untrustworthiness.[98] Over the next four decades the expanding New English population was to act as a major destabilizing influence on Irish politics. A largely immigrant community, between 1580 and 1640 it has been estimated that roughly one hundred thousand people settled in Ireland from Britain, they portrayed themselves as the only genuinely loyal segment of the Irish population. The subject of considerable governmental support on the grounds of both ethnicity and conformity in religion, they enjoyed substantial economic success in the period of peace following the ending of major warfare in 1603, much of it at the expense of native landed proprietors.[99]

Although the early Stuart era witnessed a spectacular growth in an immigrant Protestant community, and the effective foundation of an Irish Protestant church, there was little successful evangelization of either the Gaelic or Old English

[95] Tadhg Ó hAnnracháin, 'Guerre de religion ou guerre ethnique? les conflits religieux en Irlande 1500–1650', *Revue Historique* 647 (2009), 65–97.

[96] The Lords Justice Carey and Loftus, the Earl of Ormond and the rest of the Irish Council to the Privy Council of England, 3 December 1599 (*Calendar of the State Papers relating to Ireland Elizabeth I, 1599 April–1600 February*, ed. Ernest George Atkinson (London: Public Record Office, 1899), p. 290).

[97] Anthony Sheehan, 'The Recusancy Revolt of 1603: A reinterpretation', *Archivium Hibernicum* 38 (1983), 3–13.

[98] David Finnegan, 'The influence of the Irish Catholic clergy in shaping the religious and political allegiances of Irish Catholics, 1603–41' in Armstrong and Ó hAnnracháin, *Insular Christianity*, pp. 107–28, at 107–8.

[99] The most comprehensive study of New English settlement and political culture is Nicholas Canny, *Making Ireland British* (Oxford: Oxford University Press, 2002).

populations. Instead a linked and parallel process of Catholic reformation intensified in both groupings.[100] The pronounced Anglocentric focus of the Established
church in Ireland continued to ensure that little effort was made to evangelize
in the Gaelic language. By the 1630s, the Protestant Bishop of Kilmore, William
Bedell, stood out as a major exception within the state church because of the
emphasis which he placed on trying to equip his ministers with the linguistic capacity to reach out to the Irish-speaking population, even to the extent of privileging
for benefices less qualified clergy who possessed the requisite fluency in the Irish
language.[101] As a result, even in Ulster, where large-scale confiscation of land had
created a potentially strong infrastructure for the state church,[102] and where initially
a considerable portion of the native clergy had been prepared to offer a certain
conformity, the second and third decades of the seventeenth century witnessed a
solidification of Catholic identity among the Gaelic population.[103]

In the case of the Old English community of Ireland, evangelization was not
dependent on any prior process of Anglicization. Nevertheless even with this older
colonial community the efforts of the state church in inculcating conformity with
the religion established by law were highly unsuccessful. From the perspective of
many state officials and Protestant clerics, a fundamental reason for this state of
affairs was the inadequate level of pressure to which the Old English were subjected. Although largely excluded from office-holding in the central administrative
apparatus, and although a massive creation of boroughs allowed the government
to engineer a Protestant majority in the Irish parliament, the state shrank from a
programme of anti-recusancy action of the kind which had been instituted in
Elizabethan England. Recusancy fines were something of a pittance compared to
their English equivalents and their levying was intermittent. A restraining influence on the Irish government was the English Privy Council which was reluctant
to contemplate the eruption of renewed and expensive rebellion on account of
religion in Ireland. One result of this was a substantial influx of English Catholics
to Ireland in the later Elizabethan and early Stuart periods.[104] The effect of these
English exiles on the wider Catholic culture is somewhat difficult to assess. It seems
probable that they brought with them a stronger ideological opposition to any
participation in the state church and they may have had an effect in helping to
polarize attitudes in Ireland.[105] Certainly this was the impression of William Lyon,

---

[100] The period 1603–32 has been described as an era of confessionalization 'within' Irish society
which was critical both to the evolution of the state church and to its Catholic counterpart: see Ute
Lotz-Heumann, 'Confessionalisation in Ireland: periodisation and character, 1534–1649' in Ford and
McCafferty (eds), *Sectarianism*, pp. 24–53, at 46–50.
[101] E. Shuckburgh, *Two biographies of William Bedell, Bishop of Kilmore: with a selection of his letters
and an unpublished treatise* (Cambridge: Cambridge University Press, 1902), pp. 40–2.
[102] Philip Robinson, *The Plantation of Ulster: British Settlement in an Irish Landscape 1600–1670*
(2nd edition, Belfast: Ulster Historical Foundation, 1994), pp. 69–70.
[103] Brian Mac Cuarta, *Catholic Revival in the North of Ireland, 1603–41* (Dublin: Four Courts
Press, 2007), pp. 46–8; Alan Ford, *The Protestant Reformation in Ireland, 1590–1641* (2nd edition,
Dublin: Four Courts Press, 1997), pp. 38–49.
[104] Edwards, 'A haven of popery', pp. 95–126.
[105] *Calendar of Carew Papers in the Lambeth Palace Library*, ed. J.S. Brewer and W. Bullen (London:
Kraus-Thomson, 1873), p. 376.

the Bishop of Cork, in the 1590s, who saw the influence of English recusants in Irish urban communities as particularly malignant.[106]

For the first decades of Elizabeth's reign the chief intellectual critics of her church were certainly English rather than Irish. This was hardly surprising since her accession had resulted in the exile of a large community of English university academics. Not until Peter Lombard late in the century did Irish Catholicism produce an intellectual of the standing of figures such as Nicholas Sanders, Thomas Stapleton, and Robert Persons. Political, economic, and ethnic issues, and simple religious conservatism, were evidently more salient in shaping opposition to the state church in Ireland than in England, although of course the lines of religious division in England too were never drawn simply on intellectual grounds. In the seventeenth century, the existence of multiple links with English Catholicism probably also had an effect on the political stance adopted by Old English.

From a purely Irish perspective, the political attitudes of the Old English of Ireland can smack of a certain political naivety. Given the bitter hostility of the Irish government to Catholicism, and the dominance of confiscatory plantation as an administrative weapon in the first half of the seventeenth century, the persistent belief of the Old English Catholic leadership in the possibility of a negotiated settlement with the crown which would protect and confirm their established position can appear difficult to explain. Yet such attitudes become more comprehensible when account is taken of contemporaneous developments in England and the *de facto* state acceptance of gentry English Catholicism through processes of compounding, and the consistent attempts of English Catholics to make use of the shifting international and ecclesiastical politics of the later Jacobean and Caroline state to argue the case for their reinsertion into the political nation.[107]

During James VI and I's reign in Ireland, the Old English community benefited in a collateral fashion from the policy of confiscatory plantation which engrossed much of the government's energy and which was directed principally at Gaelic Irish targets. Towards the end of the reign, religious coercion also slackened in the course of the negotiations concerning the Spanish match. It was in this context that the Catholic church as an institution began to make significant progress. Particularly important in this regard was the revival of a Catholic hierarchy, the only genuine resident Catholic episcopate *in partibus infidelium*. In sharp contrast with England, from 1618 Rome began to reappoint resident bishops once again to the historic sees of the island. While deprived of revenues and thus dependent on voluntary contributions from the laity and the support of their kinfolk and wealthy Catholic families, these bishops claimed the right of jurisdiction over the Catholic clergy in their dioceses. Not surprisingly this could spark some friction with the regular orders on the English model, but in Ireland for a variety of reasons the episcopate managed to arrogate to itself a primary leadership role in ecclesiastical matters.[108] Indeed, in some respects the chief challenge to these Catholic bishops

---

[106] William Lyon to Lord Hunsdon, July 1596 (TNA, SP/63/182/47).
[107] Michael Questier, 'Arminianism, Catholicism and Puritanism in England during the 1630s', *Historical Journal* 49 (2006), 53–78, especially 62–78.
[108] Ó hAnnracháin, 'Alternative establishment', pp. 190–206.

in Ireland could come from the willingness of their own secular priests to denounce them to the state for having exercised a jurisdiction derived from Rome, a crime which the state rated far more seriously than the mere act of saying or hearing Mass. Yet, although bishops suffered considerable harassment and danger in the prosecution of their duties, it was not sufficient to restrict their function. Rather, by making them appear as exemplars of an apostolic mode of life, the disapproval of the state may in fact have had the double disadvantage of increasing the moral authority of the Catholic leadership while not effectively disrupting their activity.

In the later years of James's reign and the first years of his successor, episcopal appointments were made throughout the island until roughly fifteen resident bishops, spread across both Gaelic and Old English Ireland, were present in the island. These prelates presided over a substantial process of reform and reorganization and they benefited also from a marked increase in the numbers of the lower clergy. Many of these were the graduates of the Irish continental colleges and even when bishops were forced to make use of cadres of less educated local clergy they appear to have instituted vicars forane, with responsibility for individual deaneries, which allowed the learning of the continentally educated clergy to be further diffused. This, for instance, was the pattern in Connacht overseen by the Gaelic Franciscan bishop, Boethius MacEgan, who also reported in 1637 on the massive increase in clerical numbers in his diocese over the past thirteen years. Further to the south, the joint diocese of Ardfert and Aghadoe in rural Gaelic Munster possessed by the 1630s in the region of fifty seminary-educated priests, including six doctors of theology and three doctors of canon law.[109] Very importantly, the patterns of Catholic reform which gained increased impetus during the Caroline period were distributed across both Gaelic and Old English Ireland. The first half of the seventeenth century was also a highly significant period in terms of shaping a Catholic literature in the Gaelic language. The most important institution in this regard was the Franciscan order, in particular the college of St Anthony of Louvain which was founded in 1607.[110]

Yet, despite the degree to which the Irish Catholic church was once again taking institutional shape in the course of the reign of Charles I, the difficulties of Catholic landowners and urban elites did not disappear. Instead the Old English community increasingly saw themselves as becoming vulnerable to the same processes of discrimination, marginalization, and plantation which had substantially weakened the position of much of the elite of Gaelic Ireland. During the 1620s, when war broke out with Spain, and again during the 1630s in the context of Charles I's personal rule in England and the ascendancy of Thomas Wentworth in Ireland, the social and political elite of Catholic Ireland believed that they had struck a deal with their monarch which would liberate Catholic landowners from the threat of further confiscatory plantation. In the event, despite paying for these so-called 'Graces', initially in the 1620s, and then again under Wentworth, they were cheated

[109] Brendan Jennings, 'Miscellaneous documents II 1625–40', *Archivium Hibernicum* 14 (1949), no. 9; Archivo Storico 'De Propaganda Fide', SOCG, 140, ff. 69r–77r.

[110] In this regard see, for instance, Raymond Gillespie and Ruairí Ó hUiginn (eds), *Irish Europe 1600–1650: Writing and Learning* (Dublin: Four Courts Press, 2013).

of their expectation.[111] Instead, the final years of the decade raised the spectre of the extension of the policy of plantation throughout the island, even into areas of historically dense Old English settlement.

This was the context in which the Caroline regime suffered an abrupt collapse in Ireland in the winter of 1641–2, ultimately leading to the emergence of a Catholic proto-state, the Confederate Catholics of Ireland, which took advantage of the descent of Britain into the turmoil of civil war to extend its control over much of the island. This train of events was triggered by the rebellion of October 1641 when a botched attempt at a *coup d'état* by some Catholic gentry in the face of the threatening proceedings in the English parliament over the previous year degenerated into a frequently savage sectarian conflict. Protestants were attacked, robbed, and murdered throughout the island and Protestant forces responded with similar ferocity, particularly when reinforced with governmental troops or when given the opportunity to form militias.[112] The Catholic clergy of the island proved critical to the emergence of an organized political body from the inchoate violence of the winter of 1641–2. Their desire to put an end to mere looting and disorder, and to frame an organization which could provide protection against retribution from Britain, was mirrored by the secular leadership of the Catholic community. The island-wide organization and moral authority of the clergy were important factors in allowing ecclesiastical and lay elites to pool their authority. Significantly, the decisive movement towards a national organization grew out of a synod of the entire Irish church convened in Kilkenny in May 1642. While the supreme authority among the Confederate Catholics was the General Assembly, a quasi-parliamentary unicameral body, the membership of the organization were bound together by an oath of association, which was administered by the clergy. Both refusal to take the oath and failure to fulfil its conditions were punishable by *ipso facto* excommunication. While it contained clauses of allegiance to Charles I, and mandated obedience to the legitimate leadership of the association, the oath bound the members to achieve the just rights and prerogatives of all its takers and precluded a Confederate from making a separate peace until these had been established. In the territory under their control, the Confederates transferred the churches and property which had pertained to the established church to their Catholic counterparts.[113]

In the early years of the association the oath was a force for unity among the Confederate Catholics, allowing the nascent body to levy taxes and pay and equip armies to defend and expand its territory. The fact that England was engulfed in civil war was vital in allowing these developments but the progress of that conflict began to impact on the association's internal politics. The parliamentarian party in

---

[111] Aidan Clarke, *The Old English in Ireland, 1625–42* (London: Macgibbon and Kee, 1966), pp. 28–89; Wentworth's regime is analysed in detail in Hugh Kearney, *Strafford in Ireland: A study in absolutism* (2nd edition, Cambridge: Cambridge University Press, 1989).

[112] Canny, *Making Ireland British*; Kenneth Nicholls, 'The other massacre: English killings of Irish, 1641–2' in David Edwards, Pádraig Lenihan and Clodagh Tait (eds), *Age of Atrocity: Violence and Political Conflict in Early Modern Ireland* (Dublin: Four Courts Press, 2007), pp. 176–91.

[113] Ó hAnnracháin, *Catholic Reformation*, pp. 16–38, 68–74.

England was seen as a deadly foe to Irish Catholicism and a victory for the King's English rebels was expected to lead to a savagely punitive expedition of retribution to Ireland. Consequently, with increasing urgency, a party within the Confederates hoped to make a peace with the Royalist party which would allow them to pool their resources with those of the King to oppose parliament. For his part, the King, increasingly hard pressed in England and from the autumn of 1643 involved in open war too with the Scottish covenanters who had precipitated the original crisis, was prepared to barter religious concessions to the Confederates in return for military aid.

The chief stumbling block in these negotiations proved the demands of the Irish Catholic clergy. While the King's representatives were prepared to temper the application of the anti-Catholic statutes, and from 1645 to offer their complete repeal, they were strongly opposed to allowing the churches to remain in Catholic hands or to conceding that bishops appointed from Rome in defiance of the King's laws could exercise jurisdiction in Ireland. The determination of the clerical party among the Confederates to retain the churches was heightened by the arrival of a papal nuncio, GianBattista Rinuccini, in 1645. Ultimately these issues split the Confederate Association. A first military confrontation in 1646 resulted in a triumph for the clergy but military defeats eroded their control of the Association in 1647. A second civil conflict erupted in 1648 which ultimately resulted in the expulsion of the papal nuncio and the conclusion of peace with the royalist party in early 1649, without having attained the chief clerical objectives.[114] The defeat of royalism throughout the archipelago, however, in the period 1649–53 led to the military conquest of Ireland by the Commonwealth regime with horrific demographic consequences. During the 1650s the economic and social bases of Catholic power were profoundly reduced, to the extent that even the Restoration in 1660 of a king conscious of a degree of obligation to former Confederates was not sufficient to restore the fortunes of the Irish Catholic leadership. What was to become the enduring pattern of eighteenth-century Ireland, of an economically as well as politically dominant Protestant elite, perched with a certain insecurity over the main body of a population largely Catholic in religion, was first adumbrated during the 1650s.

The mid-seventeenth century was thus a hinge period in terms of the evolution of Irish Catholicism. Prior to the Commonwealth conquest of 1649–53, Catholics not merely constituted the great majority of the actual population but owned as well as worked the bulk of the land of the kingdom, and a Catholic patriciate largely dominated most of the urban life of the island. The Confederate state of the 1640s represented the high point of an extended process in which Catholic elites had struggled to have their positions of economic and social dominance in the kingdom of Ireland safeguarded within the context of a multiple monarchy in which all the other chief components had embraced varying versions of the Reformed religion. The great confiscations of the 1650s fundamentally altered the confessional complexion of the island's elites. While this led to a considerable Catholic irredentism

---

[114] ibid. pp. 123–67.

in the short term, over a longer period what was confirmed was the marked contraction of elite Catholicism in Ireland, together with the continued survival of the religion among the majority peasantry of the island.

Similarities can be detected in the anti-Protestantism which developed in late sixteenth- and seventeenth-century Ireland and the anti-Catholicism of contemporary England. But whereas in England the actual recusant community was for much of the population only an object of intense distrust at times of extreme crisis and national political uncertainty,[115] with chief loathing centred on a more faceless and international Catholic threat embodied by Spain and the papacy,[116] in Ireland the mirror image seems to have obtained. Despite the ultimate responsibility of the distant and non-resident monarch for the difficulties under which Irish Catholics laboured, it is clear that strong bonds still linked the crown to much of the Irish population. Loyalty to the monarch was expressed with sufficient regularity during the 1640s as to make it clear that it represented a genuine, indeed arguably dominant, strand of Irish Catholic opinion. Thus the deponent Elizabeth Collins noted in 1642 that rebels, quite happy to make ferocious threats to the lives of even Protestant children, were still apparently convinced that they 'had the kings hand & broad seale for what they did',[117] and the Confederate Catholics were insistent on their loyalty to their monarch. In Ireland the object of immediate sectarian hatred was the largely immigrant population which had come to the island in the late Elizabethan and Jacobean periods. Whereas the English recusant population was protected to some extent from the cleavages created by religious change by a shared consciousness of English identity developed over generations, in Ireland the recent provenance (and privileged status) of most of the Protestant community primed a deadly cocktail of ethnic and sectarian hostility.

The workings of this process were already evident in 1614 to George Carew, a former Lord President of Munster, and a respected advisor on Irish affairs. Reflecting on the dangerous changes which had occurred in the Irish population over the preceding decades, he drew attention to the manner in which the 'Old English race', the descendants of the pre-Elizabethan colonists of Ireland, and the 'mere Irish', the Gaelic inhabitants of the island, who had traditionally 'held the other as a hereditary enemy', had now drawn closer together. While more frequent intermarriage and what he saw as the improved civility of the Gaelic Irish formed part of the reason for the improved relations, Carew had no doubt that the real cause was in fact hatred of a third party, the New English and Scottish population which had been introduced into Ireland during the reign of Elizabeth and the early

---

[115] Haigh, *Plain Man's Pathways*, pp. 198–201; Sheils, ' "Getting on" and "getting along" ', p. 80.

[116] Conrad Russell suggests that even the militant anti-Catholic discourse of the parliament in the 1620s did not necessarily translate to hatred of actual English recusants: for the members 'the forces of neighbourhood were even stronger than the forces of religion. They believed that, in principle, no Catholic could be a loyal subject, and yet, at the same time, they knew many of their Catholic neighbours were loyal subjects': Conrad Russell, *Parliaments and English Politics, 1621–29* (London and Oxford: Clarendon Press, 1979), p. 120.

[117] Deposition of Elizabeth Collins, 1 June 1642 <http://1641.tcd.ie/deposition.php?depID=820011r009>, accessed 1 July 2014.

Jacobean period. But although this was the 'first and principal cause of their union' both parties strove to disguise the fact 'under the mask of religion, pretending that nothing but matters of conscience moves them to concur in opposition to the present government'.[118] For their part, it can be suggested that the emphasis on Catholic disloyalty by New English Protestants was also substantially influenced by a realization of the real political and economic benefits which could be obtained by the exclusion of the existing propertied elite of the island from office-holding.

This is not to suggest that Ireland too could not produce examples of 'cross-confessionalism in many areas of life and thought'.[119] Not merely patterns of lending, surety, witnessing, and tenancy linked individuals of different religion but considerable political co-operation became evident in the parliament of 1640 and in the negotiation of the Graces during the 1620s. A shared aristocratic culture also bound together peers of Catholic and Protestant convictions and this laid the basis for quite a successful movement towards the political negotiation of a religious settlement by Royalist and Catholic Confederate forces during the 1640s.[120] Nevertheless, when the Caroline state collapsed in Ireland in 1641 the sectarian violence which developed was significantly more widespread and vicious than even the most exaggerated instances of seventeenth-century English anti-popery. This probably reflected the fact that confessional hostilities and anxieties were less restrained by considerations of neighbourliness and a shared historical experience of the social benefits of a smoothly-working local community.[121]

The vicious sectarian nature of the conflict in Ireland during the winter of 1641–2 ultimately became foundational in terms of wider Protestant patterns of identity in the island. Protestant insecurity and fear of the Catholic majority was heightened by the tradition of commemoration of 1641. The political lessons which were drawn from what became a potent mythology of Irish Protestant suffering were of the need to render Irish Catholics harmless in the future by vigilance, the removal of dangerous leadership cadres, and by depriving Catholics of the economic, political, and military resources to threaten Protestant dominance.[122] On the other hand, the Commonwealth conquest of Ireland, which resulted in appalling mortality of the general population and which in its final stages degenerated into a savage counter-insurrectionary war, was arguably equally foundational in terms of the widespread Irish Catholic sense of grievance and persecution on the grounds of religion.[123]

An interesting by-product of these processes was to be the gradual erosion of ethnic differences between Irish Catholics. During the period under review in this book, parallel if interlinked processes of Catholic reform are visible within both the Old English and Gaelic Irish communities, although these identities in

---

[118] *Calendar of Carew Papers,* pp. 305–6.   [119] Milton, 'A Qualified Intolerance', p. 86.

[120] See Jane Ohlmeyer, *Making Ireland English: The Irish Aristocracy in the Seventeenth Century* (New Haven: Yale University Press, 2012).

[121] Sheils, ' "Getting on" and "getting along" ', pp. 68–73.

[122] Toby Barnard, ' "Parlour entertainment in an evening?" histories of the 1640s' in Micheál Ó Siochrú (ed.), *Kingdom in Crisis* (Dublin: Four Courts Press, 2001), pp. 20–43.

[123] Patrick Corish, *The Catholic Community in the Seventeenth and Eighteenth Centuries* (Dublin: Helicon Press, 1981), p. 49.

the island are probably better conceptualized as distributed along a spectrum rather than as a simple binary opposition. The impact on Old English Ireland of the mores of Catholic reform was probably initially greater than among the Gaelic population. Relative to the population, greater numbers of seminary-educated clergy were active in Old English areas of the island. As elsewhere in contemporary Europe, urban centres which in Ireland were largely Old English tended to be the areas with the highest density of clergy, although this pattern was attenuated to a certain degree by the greater vulnerability of clergy in urban settings to coming to the knowledge of hostile state authorities. The greater economic prosperity of the Old English elite during the Jacobean and Caroline eras, and their markedly lesser exposure to processes of plantation and impoverishment which affected the higher social cadres of Gaelic Ireland, made it easier for Old English clerics to attain a continental education and to function following their return to Ireland.[124] By contrast, the Gaelic Bishop of Raphoe, John O Cullenan, recorded in the 1630s the great difficulties which had been created for him in rural Gaelic Donegal by the Plantation and the economic decline of the local Catholic elite.[125]

Traditional Old English hostility towards Gaelic Irish barbarity was not necessarily expunged by a common embracing of Catholicism. For many Old English of Ireland, their religion linked them primarily to the great cultures of continental Europe and only secondarily to the Gaelic population of the Irish kingdom. It is evident that considerable resentment existed among Gaelic Irish intellectuals of the Old English of Ireland. If the number of continental clergy operating in Gaelic areas was less than that in Old English areas of the country, an increasingly plentiful supply was becoming available by the 1630s. Gaelic Catholic identity, however, emphasized a number of different traits, including the manner in which the wars against the heretical Queen Elizabeth had been principally waged by Gaelic aristocrats. This trope received its canonical form in the work of a second-generation Irish aristocratic exile in Spanish dominions, Philip O'Sullivan Beare, whose *Compendia Historiae Hiberniae* was to become a profoundly influential text in Irish Catholicism. Gaelic scholars also sought in the Irish past a proof of their culture's consistent Catholicism. Massive projects of hagiography were launched in continental centres which sought to refute charges of Gaelic barbarity by enumerating the deeds and lives of Gaelic holy men. This literary project was also able to draw upon powerful currents of contemporary Catholic reform by emphasizing the traditional asceticism and rejection of fleshly pleasure which was characteristic of Gaelic conceptions of holiness.[126]

Yet despite the continued existence of strong mutual antagonisms across the ethnic divide of Irish Catholicism, the most important force in promoting their union

---

[124] Mac Cuarta, *Catholic Revival,* Chapters 5–7.

[125] Archivio Storico 'De Propaganda Fide', SOCG 140, fo. 162r.

[126] Pádraig Ó Riain, 'The Louvain Achievement II: Hagiography' in Bhreathnach, MacMahon, McCafferty, *Irish Franciscans*, pp. 189–200; Mícheál Mac Craith, 'Florence Conry and Hugh McCaughwell', pp. 183–202.

was the totalizing power of the Protestant state. Thus the seventeenth century witnessed a series of initiatives which attempted to articulate a common identity for the Catholic population of Ireland. Politically, this process reached its apogee during the 1640s when the Confederate Catholics explicitly attempted to legislate against ethnic difference and to insist on the shared confessional objectives of their organization. Tensions, however, still remained and they were to be an important factor in the civil conflicts which divided the association in the latter part of the decade when the chief ideologues of what became the anti-clerical party were of Old English extraction.[127] After the dissolution of the association, it was to be a persistent criticism by Gaelic commentators that Old English Catholics had placed their temporal allegiance to their monarch above their fidelity to the Roman church. Yet, despite the bitterness which was engendered by debates around this topic, the political logic of later seventeenth-century Ireland tended to elide the difference between the ethnic varieties of Irish Catholicism. Prior to 1641, the chief victims of governmental discrimination had continued to be from the Gaelic community. After 1649, however, this was no longer the case to anything like the same degree.

Two critically important features of Irish Catholicism, which rendered it atypical in Europe and may have contributed to its unusual, in European terms, vitality late into the twentieth century, were rooted in the period under consideration. The first of these relates to its voluntary character. In the recent debate concerning the difference between American and European religiosity, considerable emphasis has been laid on the manner in which the lack of a state religion promoted a lively vitality among competing American denominations.[128] Uniquely among Western European majority Catholic countries, in Ireland adherence to the church of Rome was not reinforced by state coercion: indeed the opposite applied. What the Irish experience indicated was that very fervent popular Catholicism could be stimulated without active state support although this depended also on the failure of the established church to promote an effective system of repression of Catholicism, except during the 1650s. The second aspect of Irish Catholicism, which arguably links it most closely to a state such as Poland in the East, was the vital connection forged between religion and national identity. That religion rather than language was the chief vehicle for Irish nationalism in the nineteenth and twentieth centuries is something of a truism of modern scholarship. What tends to attract less attention is that the roots of this process in the seventeenth century depended on the success of Catholic reform across the ethnic spectrum of Gaelic and Old English Ireland. Given the importance of the Old English contribution to the shaping of Catholic Reformation in Ireland, it was hardly accidental that an ethno-nationalism centred on religion rather than on language ultimately developed in the island.

---

[127] Tadhg Ó hAnnracháin, 'Conflicting loyalties, conflicted rebels: Political and religious allegiance among the Confederate Catholics of Ireland', *English Historical Review* 119 (2004), 851–72.

[128] In this regard see Peter Berger, Grace Davie, and Effie Fokas, *Religious America, Secular Europe? A Theme and Variation* (Aldershot: Ashgate, 2008).

THE NETHERLANDS

The loss of England from the Catholic fold was undoubtedly experienced as particularly grievous in Rome and the unlikely retention of Ireland, however important in the long term, did relatively little to soften the blow. Not far short of England in terms of its traditional importance was the Netherlands, where another significant peripheral territory of European Catholicism developed. Already in crisis by the 1560s, when widespread evidence of discontent with the existing church was clearly evident, together with significant opposition to Philip II's planned reforms,[129] the evolution of Dutch Catholicism was subsequently critically influenced by the war between the rebellious northern provinces of the Netherlands and Spain. In a manner somewhat reminiscent of England in the 1530s, when the development of the crisis between the regime and Rome impelled Henry VIII to recruit support from an evangelical movement with which he had little native sympathy, the fervent nature of the Dutch Reformed minority's commitment to the anti-Spanish struggle was critical in securing the primacy of their religion among the rebels. In 1572 the States-General declared the Reformed religion to be the public recognized faith of the provinces in revolt and in February 1573 outlawed the public practice of Catholic worship. Stoked by the war against Spain, a violent outpouring of iconoclasm and anti-Catholic sentiment and violence resulted.[130] Over the course of the next eight years the basic legal and economic framework underpinning the dominance of the reformed confession was worked out.[131] In addition to the secularization of church property, between 1580 and 1680 the provincial estates of Holland proscribed the teaching of Catholic doctrine, the reception of priests, the distribution of Catholic literature, attendance at Catholic universities and the ministration of priests at ceremonies of marriage or baptism.[132] The public practice of religion was largely closed off to the Catholic community as the enforcement of law restricted any manifestations of ceremonies deemed offensive to the hegemonic church. While in practice a good deal of private connivance of Catholicism was permitted in the Netherlands in the period under review in the current study, its subordinate status and exclusion from the public sphere was more rigidly enforced. In Amsterdam, for instance, a significant revival and reorganization of Catholicism occurred within the city's cosmopolitan environment in the course of the first half of the seventeenth century. Despite the city's enforcement of anti-Catholic placards, the increase of the number of

---

[129] Benjamin Kaplan, ' "Remnants of the Papal Yoke": Apathy and Opposition in the Dutch Reformation', *Sixteenth Century Journal* 25 (1994), 653–69, at 653–4.

[130] Christine Kooi, '*Sub Jugo Haereticorum*: Minority Catholicism in Early Modern Europe' in Kathleen Comerford and Hilman Pabel (eds), *Early Modern Catholicism. Essays in Honour of John W. O'Malley, S.J.* (Toronto: University of Toronto Press, 2001), pp. 147–62, at 148–51; Judith Pollmann, 'Countering the Reformation in France and the Netherlands: Clerical Leadership and Catholic Violence 1560–85', *Past & Present* 190 (2006), 83–120, at 84–5.

[131] Geoffrey Parker, *The Dutch Revolt* (Ithaca, N.Y.: Cornell University Press, 1977), pp. 116–22, 150–5; Charles H. Parker, 'Paying for the Privilege: The Management of Public Order and Religious Pluralism in two Early Modern Societies', *Journal of World History* 17 (2006), 267–96, at 270–1.

[132] Parker, 'Paying for the Privilege', 288.

Catholics in the city warranted its division into two parishes in 1610 and into five in 1626.[133] In 1640, however, the Catholics of Amsterdam were sharply warned to keep their religious ceremonies unostentatious or face reprisals.[134]

The war against Spain helped to keep hostility towards Catholicism at a high level but the inauguration of the twelve-year truce 1609–21 and the emergence of often savage divisions between Arminians and their opponents within the Reformed church offered something of a breathing space. The renewal of war with Spain and the conclusion of the synod of Dordrecht resulted in increased tensions but, in general, from the second quarter of the seventeenth century the scope of state repression of Catholicism became somewhat milder.[135] Whereas Catholic ceremonies had previously been confined to private houses temporarily converted for worship, gradually fixed mission stations began to develop, which frequently involved the conversion of a large private house into a custom-built space for religious ceremonies but with an unchanged outer appearance which allowed the authorities to overlook its function.[136] Catholic clergy continued to be subject to arrest and imprisonment but, rather than execution, they were liable to be subjected to a system of intimidation followed by ransoms paid by the local Catholic community. These had the dual financial purpose of imposing a financial penalty on the Catholic laity and enriching the coffers of the prosecuting authority. Following payment of sums which could amount to several thousand guilders, priests were generally condemned to exile, with a consequential loss of their sacramental functions to their congregations. As part of an effort to avoid both the humiliation and deprivation which arrest of priests entailed, a system of 'recognition fees' gradually developed which, in a fashion not dissimilar to English recusancy fines, allowed Catholic communities to purchase a degree of immunity from the implementation of anti-Catholic laws by the payment of a negotiated amount. By 1642, the director of the Holland mission reported that he had paid out 50,000 guilders in such fees over a four-year period.[137]

In contrast to Tudor and Stuart Britain and Ireland, however, the Reformed church in the United Provinces did not aspire to conscript the entire population into the ranks of an official national church. Indeed, concerned to establish the genuine nature of the faith of its adherents, the Reformed church placed significant tests before those who wished to join its ranks. Thus, the opposite of Elizabeth's unwillingness to make windows into her subjects' souls, but nevertheless requiring their public obedience by attendance at church, obtained. In the Northern Netherlands, being a Catholic in itself, as opposed to participation in Catholic worship, did not

[133] Christina Kooi, 'Popish Impudence: The Perseverance of the Roman Catholic Faithful in Calvinist Holland, 1572–1620', *Sixteenth Century Journal* 26 (1995), 75–85, at 80.

[134] Robrecht Boudens, 'Présence de la Congrégation dans l'histoire religieuse des Provinces-Unies des Pays-Bas' in Josef Metzler (ed.), *Sacrae Congregationis de Propaganda Fide Memoria Rerum (350 anni a servizio della missioni 1622–1972)* (three vols, Rome, Freiburg, Vienna: Herder, 1971–6), 1, pp. 93–110, at 98.

[135] Kooi, 'Minority Catholicism', p. 156.

[136] Xander Van Eck, 'Paintings for clandestine Catholic churches in the Republic: typically Dutch' in Kaplan et al., *Catholic Communities*, pp. 216–29, at 217.

[137] Parker, 'Paying for the Privilege', pp. 291–2.

place an individual outside the law. By the end of the sixteenth century possibly only twenty per cent of the population were members of the Reformed church.[138]

The emergence of an officially Reformed regime coincided with the final extinction, in 1583, of the Catholic hierarchy in the rebellious provinces. A massive reduction in the numbers of clergy had already occurred. Many went into exile for fear of becoming targets of the soldiery of the rebellion. The real dangers associated with a Catholic identity in the early years of the war were vividly demonstrated at the capture of Leiden in 1572, which resulted not merely in the pillaging of monasteries and the killing of priests but also in attacks on Catholic lay figures.[139] Many more, however, in apparent contrast, for instance, to early Elizabethan England, simply dissociated themselves from their church. This abandonment of the institutions of the church was mirrored at the level of the general population, particularly in Holland and Friesland, where a pattern of lay absence from church membership of any denomination became visible in the later part of the sixteenth century and persisted for decades thereafter.[140] The most important Catholic institution to survive in some semblance from the general disintegration of the latter sixteenth century was the Haarlem Cathedral chapter. Not least because the chapter cooperated with the city government in allowing the confiscation of its assets at the end of the 1570s, it was regarded with considerable leniency and the canons were permitted to remain and function pastorally within the city. Building on this base, the canons under the leadership of a dean developed into a significant pillar of church reorganization in the seventeenth century. [141]

The Clementine papacy marked a vital moment in terms of the reorganization of the Dutch Catholic community. Following his education under Robert Bellarmine in the university of Louvain and ordination in 1572, Sasbout Vosmeer, scion of a regent family in Delft, had gradually emerged as an important figure, operating from the home and under the protection of his parents. In 1583 he was appointed as Vicar General for the diocese of Utrecht and then in 1592 he was created Vicar Apostolic, the first representative of what was to become a key figure of Roman organization *in partibus infidelium*, with jurisdiction over the clergy in Dutch territory.[142] This development occasioned a peak in anti-Catholic activity on the part of the state. In 1594 Rome toyed with the idea of reinstituting a bishop in the Northern provinces but the instability of the situation, which might tend either to a Spanish victory or a complete defeat for Habsburg power, suggested the need for caution.[143] Dutch hostility towards the idea of a Spanish-nominated bishop was understandably considerable and Vosmeer's elevation to the titular archiepiscopal see of Philippi in 1602 precipitated another bout of anti-Catholic

---

[138] Kooi, 'Perseverance of Roman Catholic Faithful in Calvinist Holland', 76.

[139] Kooi, 'Minority Catholicism', p. 148.

[140] Willem Frijhoff, 'Shifting identities in hostile settings: towards a comparison of the Catholic communities in early modern Britain and the Northern Netherlands' in Kaplan et al., *Catholic Communities*, pp. 1–17, at 4.

[141] Charles H. Parker, *Faith on the Margins: Catholics and Catholicism in the Dutch Golden Age* (Cambridge, MA, and London: Harvard University Press, 2008), pp. 37–8.

[142] ibid., pp. 30–1.   [143] Boudens, 'Présence de la Congrégation', p. 94.

activity.[144] Vosmeer's leadership of the *Missio Hollandica* lasted for over two decades until 1614 when he was succeeded by the Vicar Apostolic Philip Rovenius who enjoyed an even longer term of office down to 1651. Thus, for the period under review in the current work, there was an extraordinary consistency of leadership under the direction of just two individuals within Dutch Catholicism, although naturally the actual degree of control which they exerted was by no means absolute. Vosmeer, who had opposed the original decision by the Haarlem Cathedral chapter to cooperate with the city government in the surrender of its property, had a spiky relationship with the canons who asserted the independent authority of their dean in Haarlem. The tensions, however, were largely dissipated by the negotiation of a concordat between Rovenius and the dean which created a practical division of authority and jurisdiction. Significant opposition to the Vicars Apostolic also came from the regular orders. Nevertheless, their privileged position as conduits of Roman authority was not insignificant. As in Ireland during the same time-frame, it can be suggested that the disappearance of the old systems of ecclesiastical patronage facilitated a new ecclesiastical leadership committed to a Tridentine vision of Catholicism in acquiring the control over the lower clergy.[145]

One of the most pressing problems confronting the leaders of Dutch Catholicism was a marked shortage of clerical personnel. At the turn of the century Vosmeer estimated no more than seventy secular priests were active in the area under his jurisdiction. While Vosmeer may in fact have chosen this number for its biblical resonance and thus have under-estimated the actual number of the priests,[146] the still numerous Dutch Catholic population was evidently critically short of ordained personnel and those who were present tended to concentrate in urban areas where they found it easier to mask their identity. In 1592 twelve Papally-funded scholarships were made available to train candidates for the Dutch mission.[147] The founding of a seminary, the Collegium Alticollense, at Cologne in 1602, represented a significant institutional development. Fifteen years later the Collegium Pulcheriae Mariae Virginis was set up in Leuven. Similarly to Ireland, there were certain advantages in the freedom of action in the formation of priests which these colleges conferred on the Vicars Apostolic who led the mission. Nonetheless, the number of priests in the Northern Netherlands in the first half of the seventeenth century was very small in comparison to the size of a Catholic community which was second only to Ireland as the largest to be found in the territory of a non-Catholic Western European state.[148] Even excluding the Generality Lands, at least three hundred thousand Catholics were to be found in the seven northern provinces of the republic at the time of the

---

[144] Joke Spaans, 'Orphans and students: recruiting girls and boys for the Holland Mission' in Kaplan et al., *Catholic Communities*, pp. 183–99, at 193–4.
[145] Parker, *Faith on the Margins*, pp. 38, 42, 66.   [146] Frijhoff, 'Shifting identities', p. 4.
[147] Spaans, 'Recruiting girls and boys for the Holland Mission', pp. 186–7.
[148] A high although contested figure of forty per cent of the population of the Republic's territory as Catholics in the mid-seventeenth century has been advanced: see Kooi, 'Roman Catholic Faithful in Calvinist Holland', pp. 78–9.

Peace of Westphalia,[149] and the number may have been as high as 450,000. Taking the Generality Lands into consideration, it has been estimated that the total Catholic population under Dutch rule may have reached 750,000 in the decade after Westphalia or approximately half the total population.[150] Yet in the mid 1640s, and even including the personnel of the regular orders, only 442 clergy seem to have been available to staff the mission. While this represented a notable increase on the figure of 165 priests in 1614, it still meant that sizeable Catholic communities were frequently deprived of access to sacraments.[151]

This was the context in which *kloppen*, spiritual virgins operating under a simple vow of chastity, became a crucial feature of Dutch Catholic practice. By the middle of the seventeenth century, the number of these women exceeded that of ordained priests by a factor of close to ten to one.[152] The largest concentrations of Catholics were in Holland and Utrecht while far smaller numbers persisted in Zeeland, Gelderland, and Overijssel. In contrast to England, where it has been argued that the distribution of priests failed to mirror the actual size of the Catholic communities in need of ministry, the numbers of Catholics in a given area became a critical criterion for the dispatch of priests by the mission leadership. This was made possible by the fact that, again in contrast to England, the Vicars Apostolic who led the mission fought hard to maintain their control of the allocation of clerical resources and resisted attempts by religious orders, most notably the Society of Jesus, to introduce extra regular clergy. The predominant emphases of the mission were thus on a high quality of seminary-educated clergy, the maintenance of control by the mission hierarchy, and the ability of host communities, not merely to justify the presence of a priest, but also to provide the financial and political resources to support him, and to pay the necessary sums to the authorities to allow him to function in relative security.

In Leiden, for instance, Vosmeer created two stations in 1606 under the direction of Rombout van Medenblik and Govert de Rovere. Four years later van Medenblik was in a position to offer the city authorities sufficient financial incentives to convince them to turn a blind eye to his congregation's activities.[153] By 1629 over two thirds of the resident mission priests were concentrated in the two provinces, Holland and Utrecht, with the largest numbers of Catholics. Areas which lacked the requisite numbers of Catholics to qualify for a resident priest were forced to rely on more occasional provision of sacraments by itinerant clergy, often visiting from more secure centres. The relative shortage of priests and their total dependence on local lay communities for protection and support impacted on the character of lay involvement in Dutch Catholicism. Necessarily the responsibility for a great deal of catechesis devolved onto lay personnel, particularly *kloppen*. Lay patronage

[149] Benjamin Kaplan and Judith Pollmann, 'Conclusion: Catholic minorities in Protestant states, Britain and the Netherlands, c. 1570–1720' in Kaplan et al., *Catholic Communities*, pp. 249–64, at 251–2.

[150] Parker, *Faith on the Margins*, pp. 17–18, 254, n. 54.

[151] Charles H. Parker, 'Cooperative confessionalisation: lay-clerical collaboration in Dutch Catholic communities during the Golden Age' in Kaplan et al., *Catholic Communities*, pp. 18–32, at 20.

[152] Spaans, 'Recruiting girls and boys for the Holland Mission', p. 191.

[153] Kooi, 'Roman Catholic Faithful in Calvinist Holland', 83.

of clergy was also of vital importance and not surprisingly a high proportion of both *kloppen* and male clergy were recruited from the ranks of the social elite.[154]

The intensity of anti-Catholic activity on the part of the state evidently varied according to locality and across time and was susceptible to the personal attitudes and inclinations of governing magistrates. A significant contrast existed, for instance, in the attitude of the magistracy in Dordrecht, where repression of Catholic identity was most consistent and where Protestantization had its greatest successes, and Leiden, where the city refused to promulgate the States-General's 1581 ordinance banning Catholic worship, and a disinclination to enforce anti-Catholic placards became a feature of municipal culture.[155] In practice, therefore, the decentralized nature of governance within the United Provinces made it impossible to impose one consistent policy and the conclusion of the truce in 1612 coincided also with the gradual waning of the generation which had participated in the original revolt. The triumph of orthodox Calvinism at the synod of Dordrecht in 1618–19, followed closely by renewal of war with Spain in 1621, however, created new stresses. In 1631 the withdrawal of safe-conducts from priests was evidently a reprisal against similar actions on the part of Spain in the Southern Netherlands. In the early 1630s, particularly after Gustavus Adolphus's intrusion into German war and the fall of Maastricht in 1632, the prospect of peace, or at least the institution of another long truce, with the aging ruler of the Southern Netherlands, the archduchess Isabella, briefly appeared more hopeful. However, the Swedish King's demise at Lutzen, followed by Isabella's death in 1633, and the reunion of the Habsburg Netherlands with Spain under the governorship of the forceful Cardinal Ferdinand, ensured the continuation of the conflict.

In 1635 France and the United Provinces committed themselves to a mutual alliance against Spain. Dutch Catholics not unnaturally hoped to make use of this alliance to secure better conditions and lobbied the congregation of *Propaganda Fide* to this effect. Pressure from the nuncio in France on Louis XIII resulted in a certain alleviation of the conditions of Dutch Catholics. The leadership of the community in the Netherlands strongly disputed, however, the French contention that Catholics enjoyed freedom of religion. At the most they insisted that mere liberty of conscience was available. With the limits of French intervention clearly visible by April 1635, renewed pressure began to be applied on Dutch Catholicism. In 1636 the States-General once again reinforced anti-Catholic edicts and in 1641 new ordinances saw twelve priests imprisoned in Lingen.[156]

The renewal of war with Spain also resulted in the gradual acquisition of additional territory by Dutch forces in the Netherlands. Rather than the disorganized and in many cases demoralized Catholicism which had confronted the union in the northern provinces, these newly acquired territories had already been the subject of a significant movement of Catholic reform and the population was markedly

---

[154] Parker, 'Cooperative confessionalisation', pp. 21–3.
[155] Kooi, 'Roman Catholic Faithful in Calvinist Holland', 80–2.
[156] Boudens, 'Présence de la Congrégation', pp. 96–8.

hostile to the imposition of the Dutch religious system.[157] From a Dutch perspective, the largely Catholic population of those parts of the Generality Lands which they acquired after 1621 represented a significant challenge, not merely as a potentially disruptive religious community, but also because of the danger that their political sympathies towards Spain might threaten the political and military control of the areas. Not surprisingly, the United Provinces moved to reduce the political power of the Catholic population. The capture of Oldenzaal, for instance, in 1626 led to the deposition of the Catholic magistracy and its replacement with Protestants. The principal church was confiscated and the chapter revenues were devoted to the paying of the salary of a Reformed minister. In 1629, after a textbook investment, Dutch forces successfully conquered the vital fortified position of 's-Hertogenbosch (Bois-le-duc). By 1631 all priests had been ordered to leave the town, all Catholic churches had been closed and public meetings of Catholics were proscribed.[158] In 1632 Maastricht also fell but on the basis of the treaty of capitulation the public exercise of Catholicism continued to be permitted. While wartime conditions made the neutralization of Catholic power in such significant urban areas as Hulst, Bergen op Zoom, Breda, 's-Hertogenbosch and Maastricht a political and military necessity,[159] despite the pressure from Reformed synods and individual ministers for the total prohibition of Catholic worship, the sheer size of the Catholic population made it difficult to put this into practice.

In 's-Hertogenbosch, for instance, although driven underground, Catholic practice continued within the town. Prior to its fall, the Bishop had consecrated a large number of altar stones and within twelve years the city offered eighteen different locations for the celebration of mass and other devotional activities.[160] While these ceremonies were clandestine, and while care was taken to shield them from the authorities, the Catholic population were not at times reluctant to offer violent resistance to attempts to interfere with their activities, which mandated circumspection from the authorities. After the peace of 1648, the States-General had a freer hand to exile Catholic clergy in States Flanders and States Brabant and to close places of worship but even in these changed circumstances the majority of the population obstinately clung to the traditional religion, despite the restrictions which it entailed.[161]

The peace of 1648 finally confirmed the *de jure* status of the United Provinces as an independent state but the provisionality of the border between the Spanish Netherlands and the Dutch in the previous eighty years necessarily impacted on the attitudes of Catholics living under Dutch control. In significant areas, such as Maastricht (1580–1632), Breda (1581–90, 1625–37), Deventer and Zutphen (1587–91), temporary (as it transpired) successes of Spanish arms allowed for the public revival of Catholic worship. And a sense of the common identity of the Low

[157] Charles de Mooi, 'Second-class yet self-confident: Catholics in the Dutch Generality Lands' in Kaplan et al., *Catholic Communities*, pp. 156–67.
[158] Boudens, 'Présence de la Congrégation', p. 96.
[159] de Mooi, 'Catholics in the Dutch Generality Lands', pp. 159–60.
[160] ibid.   [161] ibid., pp. 158–63.

Countries continued to link both Northern and Spanish Netherlands together.[162] The hope of Catholic conquest of the north was probably a factor in the organization of the mission as a kernel of diocesan organization from which larger-scale reconversion could grow when the opportunity arose. For many inhabitants of the Generality Lands, also, the sheer proximity of the Spanish Netherlands offered the possibility of availing of Catholic religious services and participating in devotions with relative geographical ease.

To what extent were certain general characteristics shared by the Catholicism which developed in the Western European fringe of the area considered *in partibus infidelium* in Rome?[163] Certainly neither Britain nor Ireland nor the Netherlands corresponded to the norm exemplified in the Italian and Iberian peninsulae where Catholicism was the state-supported religion of the vast majority of the population. Rather in each area Catholicism occupied a position of legal inferiority within a pluri-confessional state. For Catholics of such societies the casual assumptions of ownership of public space which underpinned the secure centres of the continental mainland were simply impossible. Instead, a sense of marginality was an essential part of their religious inheritance. Necessarily such conditions created different perceptions and identities which could be troubling to visitors from continental centres of Catholicism, such as the papal nuncio to Ireland in the 1640s, GianBattista Rinuccini. While Rinuccini's Italianate inflexibility has been over-estimated in the past, one area where he clearly struggled in Ireland was with the willingness of his Confederate Catholic hosts to make differentiations between the various Protestant identities on the island.

From the beginning of their conflict the Confederates were prepared to draw a distinction between Protestants of their King's sort and Puritans. To some extent this corresponded to an awareness of political realities: it was possible to envisage a coexistence with the King's church on the basis of negotiated conditions which was simply not feasible with the religious zealots who ultimately came to triumph in the English Civil Wars. But for many of the Confederates these distinctions went beyond the merely political. For these, the King's brand of religion was also morally superior to the other competing forms of British Protestantism, not least because of its greater organizational similarity to the Roman church. During the early Stuart era English Catholics too were keenly aware of the different shades of Protestant opinion and clear concerning their preferences. Rinuccini, on the other hand, while he could understand political arguments concerning the utility of making truces or treaties with one faction of heretics, shrank from the religious relativism which he sensed among his Confederate opponents. For the Italian nuncio, heresy was simply heresy and a difference in one small essential from the Catholic church was effectively the same as a whole series.[164]

---

[162] Paul Arblaster, 'The Southern Netherlands Connection: networks of support and patronage' in Kaplan et al., *Catholic Communities*, pp. 123–38, at 124–8.

[163] In this regard see Kooi, 'Minority Catholicism'.

[164] See Rinuccini's relation to Pope Innocent X, 1649 (Aiazzi, *Nunziatura*, p. 432).

Catholics on the margins of Europe, moreover, were especially aware of the international dimensions of their church, not least because of the vital importance of institutions based in the Catholic states of Europe in training the clergy on which the provision of sacraments to the populations of Ireland, Britain, and the Netherlands depended. While significant movements of the laity of the region to Catholic centres also occurred, the importance of international colleges in providing education for clergy, and their consequent exposure to the very different world of Catholic states, can hardly be overstated. The desire of these marginal Catholic communities to emphasize their own people's participation in a wider Catholic family of nations, joined together within the supranational institution of the one true church, was manifested in many ways, not least in the use of history to emphasize the characteristics of their national Catholicisms. This was signified in events such as the controversy which erupted between Welsh and English Catholics concerning the discovery of a tombstone in Rome in the 1570s, which the English party claimed for Caedwalla, King of Wessex, while the Welsh insisted on its commemoration of Cadwaladr the blessed, last king of the Britons. For both parties in this dispute, the desire to claim a historical connection to Rome was part of a greater project to assert the organic connection between Welsh and English identity and the Catholic religion, legitimated by the ancient past.[165] Thomas Stapleton's translation of Bede can also be viewed as the product of a similar preoccupation. Similarly, the first half of the seventeenth century was to prove a particularly fecund era in terms of a Catholic historiography of the Netherlands linking Dutch history to the Roman church.[166]

In the same time-frame an extraordinary multi-dimensional historiographical enterprise, centred largely on the Franciscan college of St Anthony in Louvain, was launched which strove to establish the inextricably Catholic identity of the Gaelic Irish population. Ranging from the massive hagiographical project of John Colgan to the Annals of the Four Masters, this scholarship served a number of vital purposes. In the first place, it asserted Irish ownership over the revered religious figures of the Middle Ages which the use of the Latin term *Scottus* for Gaelic had made vulnerable to Scottish expropriation. Second, such work offered a sharp corrective to traditional English (and Old English) criticisms of Gaelic culture as barbaric. But crucially also this literary activity was designed to equip the Irish to take their place within a Catholic family of nations exhibiting particular national characteristics in a wider pan-national unity centred on Rome.[167]

Yet if a common inheritance of marginality, of creative engagement with the past, and of at least contested entry into, and more commonly exclusion from, public space distinguished the Catholicism of these areas, this should not obscure the very major differences which pock-marked the region as well. Of central importance in this regard was the character and attitudes of the state and of the state-supported church. Fundamental differences distinguished England and Wales, Scotland,

---

[165] Bowen, 'The Battle of Britain, pp. 146–7.   [166] Parker, *Faith on the Margins*, pp. 55–7.

[167] See for instance Mary Ann Lyons, 'St Anthony's College Louvain: Gaelic texts and articulating Irish identity, 1607–40' and Bernadette Cunningham, 'John Colgan as historian' in Gillespie and Ó hUiginn, *Irish Europe*, pp. 21–43, 121–34.

Ireland and the Netherlands and this had profound effects on the nature of the Catholicism which developed. Scotland was the area which enjoyed the most success in obliterating the Catholic past through the remarkably successful educative endeavours of the Kirk. In England, the peculiar Elizabethan settlement, backed eventually by ferocious anti-Catholic legislation, ultimately succeeded in restricting outright recusancy to a tiny minority of the seventeenth-century population, although a much wider penumbra of church papistry and sympathy to Catholic tradition evidently survived than in Scotland. Moreover, English Catholicism was far less politically marginal than its Scottish counterpart and to the end of the period under review its consistent access to the court offered it possibilities of a renegotiation of status.

In the third kingdom of the archipelago, Catholicism survived as the majority confession, not least because the state church lacked both the coercive and evangelical capacity to disrupt it. In one respect, seventeenth-century Ireland down to 1641 resembled Elizabethan England, in that politically Catholicism was the sleeping giant which did not directly challenge the structures of the Protestant state. But, in sharp contrast to sixteenth-century England, this political quiescence was not accompanied by any major success on the part of the state church in winning the religious affiliation of the population. Instead, the period saw an intensifying consolidation of Catholic identity through a very successful programme of pastoral care by a burgeoning shadow church. Consequently only a massive programme of coercion and evangelization offered any possibility of shaking the dominance of the Roman church in the island. In the Netherlands, neither the decentralized system of governance nor the publically-privileged Reformed church demanded religious conformity of the Republic's inhabitants. This was the critical factor in allowing a much larger Catholic minority to survive in the Netherlands than across the North Sea in Britain. The differing coercive powers and policies and educative impulses of the state and state church were thus crucial determinants of the evolution of Catholicism in all of these polities and the size and strength of the Catholic populations which developed had an enormous impact on the nature of the lived experience of the religion.

But as well as a different history of adaptation to political circumstances, the internal evolution of the various Catholic communities differed sharply. In Ireland, for instance, Catholic reform became mapped onto pre-existing and differing ethnic identities to a much greater extent than anywhere else in the region. While a shared religion did in some respects help to draw the Old English and Gaelic Irish of the island together, it certainly did not obliterate ethnic difference and the emphasis on different traits of Catholic identity was used on both sides of the divide to maintain a sense of ethnic difference and superiority. Neither the Netherlands nor Ireland, on the other hand, had any real equivalent to the Court Catholicism of the Caroline era, although certain individual Irish figures such as the earls of Antrim and Clanricard gained entry to its world. The experience of portions of the Dutch Generality Lands of a triumphant Catholic Reformation followed by conquest and subjugation by a Protestant power was also unique in the region, with its nearest equivalent perhaps in the Ireland of the 1640s. On the other hand, although slightly outside the focus of the current study, the Irish experience of conquest during the 1650s, and the appalling demographic losses which the Catholic population endured, had no parallel in either Britain or the Netherlands.

It can also be pointed out that there was no one Catholic church structure which distinguished the area under review. In Ireland, by the second quarter of the seventeenth century, Rome had effectively re-established a resident hierarchy based on the traditional sees of the island. By the 1640s this episcopate emerged as the central leadership of the Irish church but it included among its ranks a significant number of regular clergy. In the Netherlands, the leadership of the *Missio Hollandica* was in the hands of Vicars Apostolic, rather than bishops, drawn from the secular clergy. In England, no one dominant authority structure emerged but rather competing organizations of often mutually hostile regular and secular clergy. In England, the Society of Jesus emerged as a genuinely critical influence on the development of the kingdom's Catholicism, central not merely to its spirituality but also to most of the conflicts which divided it. The Society was the most powerful institution of regular clergy in the Northern Netherlands, supplying in and around half of the personnel supplied by the various orders to the mission. As in England, the Jesuits were also to the fore in offering an alternative vision of a missionary territory in contrast to the diocese-centred order which the secular leadership aspired to create. Against this, in 1629, Jesuits amounted to hardly more than ten per cent of the clerical personnel active on the *Missio Hollandica* and even in mid-century, when their numbers had close to doubled, they still amounted to little more than one eighth of the functioning clergy.[168]

In Ireland, while the Society was certainly not of negligible importance, there is no doubt that the Franciscan order was profoundly more important than the Jesuits and it was the friars, together with the secular clergy, which left the chief stamp on the island's practices and devotions. The very differing influences of Jansenism, significant in both the Netherlands and Ireland, but far less so in England, was arguably related to the relative importance of the Jesuit missions in the various areas. The United Provinces seem also to have differed from both Britain and Ireland in terms of the degree to which the regulation of marriage emerged as a major source of tension. To some extent this reflected the degree to which marriage between Catholics and spouses of other confessions was a much more common occurrence in the Netherlands. While in Ireland, too, significant populations of different confessional background existed in close proximity to each other, the fact that the Protestant population was of relatively recent provenance, and with regard to the Gaelic Catholics both ethnically different and frequently hostile, operated to limit the scope of intermarriage. In England, the paring of the outright recusant community to a hard core possibly resulted in fewer Catholics being willing to enter nuptials across confessional lines. In the Netherlands, on the other hand, intermarriage was common and numerous opportunities presented themselves to the Catholic population to find spouses of different religion who were neither linguistically nor socially foreign to them. Nevertheless, it seems probable

[168] Parker, *Faith on the Margins*, pp. 38–40.

that the reasons why intermarriage became such a source of tension in the Netherlands reflected the preoccupations of the clerical leadership in insisting on the conformity of Dutch Catholicism to Tridentine norms, as well as the sheer dimensions of the phenomenon.

The gender dimensions of the Catholicism which developed on the Roman church's western periphery have been the subject of not insignificant attention. Much of this literature has stressed the manner in which the proscribed position of Catholicism could actually operate to confer a certain freedom of action of action and thought on women. The fact that their religion was restricted from the public sphere, from which women too were increasingly restricted,[169] meant that women in non-Catholic societies paradoxically may have suffered less exclusion in matters of faith and spirituality. By the middle of the seventeenth century between three and four thousand *kloppen*, lay women in a spiritual community committed to an active apostolate of service to the church, were active in the northern provinces of the Netherlands. Far exceeding the number of priests available, these women acted as sextons for Catholic places of worship, not merely housekeeping for their spiritual directors but actually overseeing the upkeep and maintenance of the sacred space and coordinating invitations to services. They provided instruction to the wider community, often from mission centres where priests were less frequently present, collected alms, and ran homes and educational establishments for Catholic girls. The *kloppen* attracted considerable hostility from Protestant authorities because of their perceived importance, not only within the devotional culture of Dutch Catholicism, but even in a mission context, reaching out to seek conversions. To some extent, they also acted as a shield for male Catholics, whether laymen or priests, reducing their need to expose themselves to the danger of state intervention.[170] Across the North Sea, Alexandra Walsham has suggested that the gentry recusant homes of England offered a particular opportunity for the development of communities which represented the very culmination of the attempt to create a devout Catholic laity, while Frances Dolan has pointed out the multiple relationships forged between priests and their female helpers and hosts in late Tudor and Stuart England.[171] Patrick Corish has also emphasized the degree to which Irish Catholicism was influenced by a strong female input, something which he has ascribed to the primacy of the domestic sphere in the spiritual life of the community,[172] which prevented a disjunction between a private, feminine devotion and a more public and masculine practice of religion.[173]

---

[169] Margaret MacCurtain, 'Women, education and learning in Early Modern Ireland' in Margaret MacCurtain and Mary O'Dowd (eds), *Women in Early Modern Ireland* (Edinburgh: Edinburgh University Press, 1991), pp. 160–78, at 175.

[170] Spaans, 'Recruiting girls and boys for the Holland Mission', pp. 188–94.

[171] Dolan, 'Gender and the "Lost" Spaces', 653.

[172] Patrick Corish, 'Women and Religious Practice' in MacCurtain and O'Dowd, *Women in Early Modern Ireland*, pp. 212–20. In this case, the adducing of nineteenth-century evidence to support his thesis is perhaps an indication that the source basis simply does not exist to allow an informed judgement on the subject.

[173] Spaans, 'Recruiting for the Holland Mission', p. 196.

A certain danger in such argumentation is the tendency to downplay the degree to which metropolitan Catholic cultures could also offer a sometimes underestimated degree of space and spiritual autonomy to women. While it is true that in Italy the Inquisition could be highly severe in cases of what it considered to be feigned sanctity, this did not make it impossible for women to be acknowledged as saintly and to acquire considerable charismatic influence. Also in the Netherlands it appears that the first half of the seventeenth century was the era which offered maximum possibilities for female leadership in Dutch Catholicism, thus conforming to a common historical pattern in Christian denominations where moments of extreme vulnerability create particular but often short-lived opportunities for female agency.[174] In Britain and Ireland it could in addition be pointed out that it was evidently more difficult for women to enter religious life than in most other areas of Catholic Europe. The anxiety about the protection of the honour of the brides of Christ meant that most women from the archipelago who wished to become nuns were forced to do so on the continent, something which complicated and raised the expenses of the entire process. Against this, it probably resulted in fewer women from these societies being forced into religious life as a result of familial pressure than in other Catholic communities. The example of the *kloppen* of the Netherlands, and in particular the contrast between their development and the ultimate repression of Mary Ward's Institute, also indicate that wide variations existed between the possibilities open to women religious in marginal Catholic societies.[175] Whereas in Ireland and England the notion of nun which emerged in the Early Modern period was shaped to a considerable degree by Tridentine obsession with secure cloistering,[176] in the Netherlands this obtained to a much lesser degree.

The gendered practice of Catholicism was also affected by the different societal position of the religion on the periphery of Europe. Frances Dolan has pointed out the manner in which gendered privileges, such as the right to bear witness, could be lost by recusant men in England, whereas for women such considerations naturally did not apply.[177] Both in Ireland and in England, the status of men as heads of households ensured that they were more vulnerable to legal penalties than were their wives and daughters. In England, despite the ferocious nature of the statutes, women were executed only for the crime of harbouring priests. Thus while the pressure on men of Catholic inclination towards church papistry could be overwhelming, it seems likely that in many cases their wives were freer to protect what they saw as the spiritual integrity and safety of their families, by not attending the Established church, and that this indeed may have corresponded to another example of an Early Modern division of labour and responsibility.[178] In the Netherlands also, it seems

---

[174] In this regard see Phil Kilroy, 'Women and the Reformation' in MacCurtain and O'Dowd, *Women in Early Modern Ireland*, pp. 179–96, at 188–92.

[175] Spaans, 'Recruiting for the Holland Mission', *passim*.

[176] It is significant that the papal nuncio to Ireland in the 1640s, the rather conventional GianBattista Rinuccini, was highly approving of the discipline and regulation of the nuns whom he encountered which indicates that their mode of organization corresponded to traditional Italian norms: Rinuccini's relation of the kingdom of Ireland, 1 March 1646 (Aiazzi, *Nunziatura in Irlanda*, p. 113).

[177] Dolan, 'Gender and the "Lost" Spaces', 654.   [178] ibid.

that the attraction of office-holding was an incentive for male conformity, a choice probably made easier by the tolerance within Dutch Catholicism for death-bed reconciliation and the fact that such a decision did not mean that the women of the household could not preserve the traditional religion.[179] A lesser vulnerability to the ferocity of the law in England may also have helped to create a space for women to emerge as the comforters and strengtheners of men who felt themselves called to take up a martyr's crown. Michael Mullett has drawn attention to the inversion of roles which could obtain when women came to comfort priests prior to execution.[180] In Ireland, the prominence of women, as well as youths, in riots to protect or rescue clergy from custody probably reflected the perception that they were less liable to prosecution for their actions, although this was not invariably the case.[181]

A major factor influencing the gendering of Catholicism on the periphery was the distinction which the dominant regimes in Ireland, Britain, and the Netherlands drew between private and public exercise of Catholicism. In all three areas, a much greater antagonism was directed at the trespassing of Catholicism into the public (and male) sphere. Even in Ireland, where public exhibitions of Catholicism were so ubiquitous that the state struggled to control them, the very peak of its hostility was directed at the exercise of jurisdiction. Thus similarities can be detected between the conflict of these states with their interior Catholicism and the exercise of male patriarchal power. As Frances Dolan has argued, Catholicism and female identity shared certain characteristics: repressed but subversive, restricted to inferiority but threatening, forced from view but thus liable to appear anywhere, for the public sphere could never be divorced from the domestic and the intimate.[182] The particular type of intolerance evident in these regimes thus had certain gender effects. This tendency was probably least evident in Scotland, for the Scottish Kirk was probably the Protestant institution most concerned with making windows into people's minds as part of a policy of education and control. Ironically, in this regard, Scotland was arguably closer to the dominant culture of European Catholicism in its heartlands where the concern with heresy, precisely in its liminal subversive characteristics, was responsible for much of the energy with which the Italian and Iberian Inquisitions operated.

Rather than one minority Catholicism on the Western fringe of Europe, therefore, what developed was a highly variegated series of communities exposed to varying degrees of harassment and persecution and with very different modes of church organization. Separate from each other and from the other Catholic societies of Europe, their identity was nevertheless sustained by a consciousness of belonging to a religion which crossed international borders. Reacting to this, the

---

[179] Spaans, 'Recruiting for the Holland Mission', p. 195.
[180] Mullett, 'Clergy and laity in a mission territory', pp. 44–6.
[181] Tadhg Ó hAnnracháin, 'Theory in the Absence of Fact: Irish Women and the Catholic Reformation' in Christine Meek (ed.), *Pawns or Players: Studies on Medieval and Early Modern Women* (Dublin: Four Courts Press, 2003), pp. 141–54.
[182] Dolan, 'Gender and the "Lost" Spaces', 659.

intellectuals of the various areas were keen to integrate the history of their own *patria* as a local (and particularly virtuous) variation of a common Catholic inheritance. And the sense of the wider dimension of their religious identity was probably fuelled, in particular, by the systems of clerical training in the Catholic states of Europe which ensured that a very significant portion of the clergy at work in Ireland, Britain, and the Netherlands had lived and been educated abroad before returning to the idiosyncratic conditions of their native societies.

3

East-Central Europe

Because of the degree to which non-Catholic confessions had become strongly-rooted in the region, East-Central Europe represents a particularly interesting territory of Catholic renewal in the period from the end of the sixteenth century down to 1648. This chapter examines four territories in detail, Poland/Lithuania, the *Erblande* of the Habsburgs in Austria, the Czech crownlands, and the kingdom of Hungary. Its primary object is to analyse the manner in which Catholicism made very significant advances throughout this wide swathe of territory, and the different challenges which it faced in areas where confessions derived from the sixteenth-century fracturing of the Latin church had deeply embedded themselves by the beginning of the period under review. The complexity of the religious contours of the area was further complicated in the case of Bohemia by the inheritance of the late medieval Hussite movement, and in the territories of the Polish/Lithuanian commonwealth, in particular, by a strong Orthodox presence and an increasingly significant Jewish community.

POLAND/LITHUANIA

Central to the evolution of the Union of Poland and the Grand Duchy of Lithuania in the post-Reformation period was the pre-existing religious and ethnic heterogeneity of the population contained within its borders. While Poland, including Royal Prussia which had retained an autonomous *Landtag* after its incorporation in 1454, was in the main a Latin Christian kingdom, perhaps three-quarters of the sixteenth-century population of the wide Lithuanian lands was Orthodox. After 1569 this Lithuanian territory contained only two dioceses, Samogitia and Vilna, the latter of which was truly enormous.[1] Although remarkably durable, the union was not without frictions and Lithuanian resentments of Polish dominance, which further militated against the possibility of any programme of religious uniformity that would antagonize the Orthodox community.[2] In 1550, it has been estimated

---

[1] Wioletta Pawlikowska-Butterwick, 'A "Foreign" Elite? The Territorial Origins of the Canons and Prelates of the Cathedral Chapter of Vilna in the Second Half of the Sixteenth Century', *The Slavonic and East European Review*, 92:1 (January, 2014), 44–80, at 44.

[2] Robert Frost, 'Union as process: Confused sovereignty and the Polish-Lithuanian Commonwealth, 1500–1795' in Micheál Ó Siochrú and Andrew Mackillop (eds), *Forging the State: European State Formation and the Anglo-Scottish Union of 1707* (Dundee: Dundee University Press, 2009), pp. 69–92.

that in the region of 150,000 Jews, including a cohort of Khazar origin, were settled in the Confederation, with a notably high concentration in urban areas, especially Poznań and Cracow. By the middle of the seventeenth century the number of Jews had risen to perhaps 350,000. In addition, there were Muslims of largely Tartar origin and a significant Armenian community centred on Lwów. The confederation thus had a tradition of religious pluralism not merely restricted to Christian confessions but which reflected also the evolution of non-Christian community enclaves which disposed of particular juridical rights and privileges. By 1634 roughly eleven million inhabitants lived within the vast territory of the Commonwealth which amounted to about 990,000 square kilometres.[3]

In a fashion similar to other areas of Central Europe, it was through the substantial German population, particularly in the urban areas and in Royal Prussia, that the Reformation first made a sizeable impact on the Confederation. This process was accelerated by the agreement fashioned between the Polish King, Sigismund Augustus II, and the last grand master of the Teutonic knights, Albert of Brandenburg-Ansbach, who had converted to Lutheranism, which transformed the remnant of the Teutonic state into Ducal Prussia under Polish suzerainty.[4] It was to be the areas of highest German inhabitation which witnessed the largest and longest-lasting loss of Catholic parish churches and adherents to Protestantism.[5] In the 1540s Calvinism began to make substantial inroads in Poland and the confessional mosaic was further complicated by the addition of communities of Mennonites, Bohemian Brethren and the development of a significant Unitarian movement. The first Reformed synod was held in 1550 and a Calvinist school was opened in 1551 at Pińczow. The *Sejm* of 1558–9 demonstrated the growing power of the partisans of reform although they failed in their attempts to secure the removal of the Catholic bishops from the Senate.

Although the first edicts against heresy sparked by the Lutheran tumults dated back to 1520, and while attempts were made during the following decade to stem the flow of Polish students to evangelical universities, two principal factors predisposed the Polish monarchs to demonstrate what outside observers considered an extraordinary religious tolerance. The first was the long-established custom of cooperation between the Catholic monarch and local elites of a different religion which was of fundamental importance in administering a territory spanning over three-quarters of a million square kilometres. The second was the recognition of the vital economic role which skilled immigrants, even if of a different religion, could play in the sparsely-populated and under-developed state.[6]

---

[3] Jerzy Kloczowski, 'Some Remarks on the Social and Religious History of Sixteenth-Century Poland' in Samuel Fiszman (ed.), *The Polish Renaissance in its European Context* (Bloomington and Indianapolis: Indiana University Press, 1988), pp. 96–110, at 96.

[4] Laurent Tatarenko, 'Pluriconfessionnalité et politique de tolerance: le cas de la Pologne' in Wolfgang Kaiser (ed.), *L'Europe en conflits: les Affrontements religieux et la genèse de l'Europe modern vers 1500–1650* (Rennes: Presses Universitaires de Rennes, 2008), pp. 239–66, at 240–1.

[5] Stanislaus Litak, 'La paroisse du XVIe au XVIIIe siècle' in Marian Rechowicz et al. (eds), *Millénaire du Catholicisme en Pologne* (Lublin: The Scientific Society of the Catholic University in Lublin, 1969), pp. 109–19, at 110.

[6] Tatarenko, 'Pluriconfessionnalité et politique de tolerance', p. 242.

In the early 1550s, a significant step in the direction of religious tolerance resulted from the case of Stanislaus Orzechowski and the decision that the temporal authorities would no longer execute sentences of excommunication. After the *Sejm* of 1555, the King Sigismund Augustus (1548–72) dispatched an embassy to Rome seeking a national council of the church which could be expected to lead to communion in both species, a vernacular liturgy and to open the way to the end of clerical celibacy. Rome, however, resolutely opposed such propositions.[7] Despite the expressed hopes of the reformers, the King did not abandon Catholicism, both because of the complexion of his personal beliefs[8] and, not least, because of his quest to acquire the vast Sforza inheritance which he claimed through his mother. This amounted to 430,000 ducats, almost six times greater than his annual revenue, and both Austrian and papal assistance were deemed crucial to its acquisition.[9] Consequently, as in France, the widespread but disparate desires for religious reform were not harnessed and focused to support a royal Protestantism. Ultimately, the widespread societal recognition of the need for renewal within the Polish church found its strongest expression in the developments of post-Tridentine Catholicism. A significant factor in this regard was the splintering of the reform movement and in particular the rise of a powerful current of anti-Trinitarianism towards the end of the 1550s, which eventually led to definite division by 1565.[10] Moreover, significant bonds undoubtedly linked Poland to the church of Rome. The King already enjoyed an enviable power over 20,000 ecclesiastical benefices and the Latin bishops occupied critical roles in the Senate and as royal councillors and played a vital part in the administration of the state: indeed the Catholic primate Jakub Uchański twice acted as *interrex* during the 1570s.[11]

The 1560s and early 1570s were a period of particular importance in the political and religious evolution of the confederation. Under the leadership of Stanislaus Hosius, Poland became linked integrally to the movement of Catholic reform. Charged with articulating a Catholic confession of faith by the assembled bishops at the provincial synod of Piotrkow in 1551, Hosius, the newly appointed Bishop of Warmia, produced what ultimately became the much reprinted *Confessio Catholicae Fidei Christiana*. In this text, he presciently emphasized the four notes of the true church, identifying ground where future generations of Catholic controversialists, including his compatriots Stanislaus Sokolowski, Piotr Skarga, and the Polish-based Englishman, Arthur Faunt, proved particularly eager to confront

[7] ibid., pp. 243–4.

[8] Paul Knoll, 'Religious Toleration in Sixteenth Century Poland: Political Realities and Social Constraints' in Howard Louthan, Gary B. Cohen, and Franz A.J. Szabo (eds), *Diversity and Dissent: Negotiating Religious Difference in Central Europe, 1500–1800* (New York and Oxford: Berghahn Books, 2011), pp. 30–52, at 34.

[9] James Miller, 'The Origins of Polish Arianism', *Sixteenth Century Journal* 16 (1985), 229–56, at 230.

[10] Graeme Murdock, 'Un espace-carrefour: l'Europe centrale' in Kaiser, *L'Europe en conflits*, pp. 221–38, at 228.

[11] Theresia Chynczewska-Hennel (ed.), *Acta Nuntiaturae Poloniae XXV Marius Filonardi (1635–43) Volumen 1* (Cracoviae: Academia Scientiarum et Litterarum Polona, 2003), p. 21.

their Protestant opponents.[12] His insistence that God did not make impossible demands of his worshippers and his linking of the doctrines of the reformers to ancient heresies also continued to resonate in Catholic polemic throughout the Early Modern era.[13] Even more important than his adumbration of the future direction of Catholic controversy was his diplomatic and organizational role. Hosius acted as one of the papal legates at the final sessions of the Council of Trent in 1562–3 and following his return to Poland his presence, in conjunction with the efforts of the new and vastly-experienced papal representative, Giovanni Francisco Commendone, helped to secure the acceptance of the council's decrees at the *Sejm* of Parczow in 1564. He was helped in this regard by a certain political reorientation on the part of the King who became the first European monarch to accept the Tridentine decrees and for the rest of the reign Catholicism was to prove a significant advantage in terms of the acquisition of office at the King's hands.

Hosius also played a key role in the introduction of the Society of Jesus into the confederation. Peter Canisius had visited Poland in 1558–9 but, despite a warm welcome from the Catholic hierarchy, the Society's insistence that a new college should be capable of providing for twenty people could not be met. In the event, the Jesuits ultimately agreed to a lesser establishment of ten and a college was founded in Hosius's diocese at Braniewo in 1565. Most of the original Jesuits were German or Dutch and none were Polish. The Bishop of Plock, Andreas Noskowski, invited the Society to set up a second house in Pultusk and two Polish Jesuits established themselves there in 1566. In 1570, animated by collections for a Calvinist academy in Vilna, the Bishop, Valerian Protasewicz Suszkowski, provided the funds to allow twenty-five Jesuits, including ten Poles, to establish themselves in the city. Within a decade, with significant patronage from the Calvinist convert, Jerzy Radziwill, this institution in Vilna had become the university of the Grand-duchy.[14]

The subsequent spread of the Jesuits was dramatic. Initially the Polish branch of the Society was organized as a vice-province of Austria but already by 1576 conditions were deemed sufficient to allow for the establishment of a Polish province. At this point the total Jesuit personnel stood at between 130 and 140. By 1607, the number had increased to 570 religious, of whom 224 were priests. The province divided in 1608 into independent Polish and Lithuanian units. A key element in Jesuit success lay in their provision of a much-prized education in the humanities. Greek was taught in at least ten of the colleges and the Jesuits were consistently willing to import foreign masters to maintain the pedagogic attractions of their schools. While the Society did not typically engage in elementary education, in Vilna a preparatory class was instituted which taught reading from a Ruthene language catechism. Jesuit education proved a formidable attraction to Protestant and

[12] Stanislaus Hosius, *Confessio catholicae fidei Christiana* (Antwerp, 1561), pp. 26–54; Gustave Thils, *Les Notes de l'Église dans l'apologétique catholique depuis la réforme* (Gembloux: J. Duculot, 1937), pp. xix, 9, 87–106.

[13] Hosius, *Confessio*, pp. 30–2, 238–9.

[14] Ambroise Jobert, *De Luther à Mohila: La Pologne dans la crise de la chrétienté, 1517–1648* (Paris: Institut d'Études Slaves, 1974), pp. 241–7.

even more tellingly to Orthodox parents.[15] By 1616 the province of Lithuania boasted 336 members and maintained ten colleges together with another five houses and residences. The Polish province numbered 459 members, with nine colleges and six other houses.[16] The first four Jesuit colleges and seven others in total were founded by Polish bishops but by 1648, when the total number of colleges in the territory of the Commonwealth had swelled to thirty-two, the majority (eighteen) owed their foundation to magnate support.[17]

In addition to their educative roles, from a Roman perspective the Jesuits were evidently perceived as qualitatively superior to the other regular orders of clergy within Polish territories, in particular in the maintenance of much higher standards of discipline.[18] The Society also played a profound role in terms of the provision of Catholic printed material in the Commonwealth. By the end of the sixteenth century Polish Jesuits or Jesuits working in Poland had published 344 works, of which roughly a third were primarily polemical and two thirds were orientated towards the strengthening and deepening of Catholic piety. Several highly significant figures participated in this enterprise. These included Jacob Wujek who produced a Catholic New Testament in 1593 and whose complete bible was posthumously published in 1599, although subsequently revised in the interests of a more faithful reflection of the Latin Vulgate. Wujek, who had apparently flirted with Protestantism in his teens before joining the Society, had previously published a translation of Ledesma's catechism in 1572 as well as counter works against the *Postille* of Nicholas Rey. Polish versions of the Roman catechism, the small catechism of Peter Canisius, and Robert Bellarmine's catechism, also appeared by the beginning of the seventeenth century. In a fashion somewhat similar to the chief architect of the Hungarian Counter-Reformation, Péter Pázmány, the mastery of Wujek's prose was evidently a significant factor in the overall impact of his *oeuvre*.

Shades of Pázmány are also evident in the career of Piotr Skarga, another figure of notable importance. Born in 1536 he joined the Society as a mature adult in 1569 and was a preacher at the court of Sigismund III for over two decades, 1587–1610. One hundred and eighty-six of Skarga's sermons were published in various collections and in their firm grasp of scripture and patristic literature, and their adaptation of Bellarmine's *Controversiae*, they evidently acted as formidable tools in diminishing and restricting the intellectual space available to Polish Protestantism in its various forms. Skarga also produced influential collections of the lives of the Saints, which evidently became a useful source for public devotional readings by the parish clergy and a Polish version of Baronius's great Catholic historical work in 1603.[19] Skarga, in particular, was also noted for his public disputations with Protestant opponents

[15] ibid., pp. 254–9.

[16] Josephus Juvencius, *Historiae Societatis Jesu pars quinta. Tomus Posterior Ab anno Christi MDXVI ad MDCXVI* (Roma, 1710).

[17] Jobert, *La Pologne dans la crise de la chrétienté*, pp. 254–5.

[18] See for example GianBattista Lancellotti to Ludovico Ludovisi 8 June 1623 (Archivio Storico 'De Propaganda Fide', SOCG 337, f. 273rv).

[19] Waldemar Kowalski, 'Change in Continuity: Post-Tridentine Rural and Township Parish Life in the Cracow Diocese', *Sixteenth Century Journal* 35 (2004), 689–715, at 704.

and probably bore a significant share of the responsibility for the confrontational and aggressive reputation which the Society acquired in Poland. His Polish-based English colleague, Arthur Faunt, was another Jesuit who relished the organization of such open set-piece conflicts. Following the uprising (*rokosz*) of 1606–8, which demonstrated the depth of hostility which existed towards the Society and its perceived relationship with a project of royal absolutism and bitter confessional confrontation, and then the condemnation of public disputation by *Propaganda Fide* in 1625, this aspect of the Polish Jesuits' activity seems to have become less salient. Naturally, in Poland as elsewhere, the Society saw missionary visitation as an integral aspect of their *modus operandi* and their impact seems to have been particularly significant in Lithuania in this respect.[20]

Yet, despite the undoubted importance of the Jesuits, and the quality and impact of their personnel, in terms of sheer numbers the various mendicant orders far outweighed them in importance. Although the Dominican order declined in the half century after 1520, it still boasted three hundred friars in 1580. By 1600, their numbers had trebled and they outnumbered the Jesuits by a margin of two to one. By 1648 their numbers stood at about 1750.[21] The trajectory of growth within the Franciscan order in the lands of the Commonwealth was broadly similar. In 1523, in a province which was broadly coterminous with Poland/Lithuania, the order boasted twenty-three convents housing 700 religious. This number had declined to 400 personnel in 1579 but, in a fashion similar to the Dominicans, rapid expansion then ensued. By 1605, having expanded to encompass Royal Prussia, their numbers stood at 1300 in thirty-three houses. In the following forty years absolute membership increased relatively modestly to 1500 but there was a sharp increase in the number of Franciscan houses which mushroomed to eighty in 1648. A strong movement of Observancy also helped transform the Franciscan order in the first half of the seventeenth century. Beginning with a first permanent residence in Zalliczyn in 1622, the Lesser Brothers of the Stricter Observance numbered twenty-six convents adhering to their rule at the onset of the Chmiel-nicki rebellion in 1648.[22] The rapid increase in the number of mendicant clergy was also matched by a growing evidence of lay involvement in the devotional activities of the various orders.

The Rosary confraternities of the Dominican order offer a significant example of such a trend. By 1648 every one of the 114 convents of the order in Poland-Lithuania practised both a Marian Rosary and a Christocentric version centred on the name of Jesus and the devotion proved hugely attractive to the wider population. While the first confraternities in Poland dated back to the fifteenth century, it was the period 1564–1648 which saw a major expansion and consolidation of these institutions. In 1577 the provincial of the order was given permission to erect

---

[20] Jobert, *La Pologne dans la crise de la chrétienté*, pp. 248–54, 261–70.

[21] Piotr Stolarski, *Friars on the Frontier: Catholic Renewal and the Dominican Order in Southeastern Poland, 1594–1648* (Farnham: Ashgate, 2010), pp. 4, 51.

[22] Jobert, *La Pologne dans la crise de la chrétienté*, pp. 298–9; Waldemar Kowalski, 'From the Land of Diverse Sects to National Religion: Converts to Catholicism and Reformed Franciscans in Early Modern Poland', *Church History* 70 (2001), 482–526, at 496–7.

confraternities across Poland. Within Catholic Europe, the battle of Lepanto in 1572 and the wide acceptance of the importance of Marian intercession in the victory was a significant spur in the popularization of the devotion. Given the Commonwealth's proximity and vulnerability to the Ottoman empire and, particularly in the reign of Sigismund III, to Lutheran Sweden, the attractions of Marian protection to Catholic Poles was hardly surprising. Certainly the military border with the Ottoman empire seems to have become something of a hotbed of Marian devotion centred around the Dominican convents in the Ruthenian province of the order. But the confraternities also flourished within the more secure Polish province.

By 1627, 172 towns and villages had established such bodies and the numbers of adherents were often startling. An archconfraternity of the Rosary was established in Cracow in 1585 and by 1627 it boasted over 50,000 members. Similar numbers were attained by the geographically proximate Carmelite confraternity of the scapular at Piasek, which included all social classes in its ranks. The lay role within the Confraternities of the Rosary was considerable, not least in terms of the organization of the social and charitable dimensions of their activity. While the president of the confraternity was a member of the Dominican order there were meant to be fourteen lay elders who had a variety of responsibilities such as collecting charitable donations, visiting sick members, and offering advice concerning sacramental and devotional observance to the ordinary body of the confraternity. Importantly, also, there was a joint responsibility between the laity and the order in terms of the management of financial affairs.[23]

During the 1560s it was becoming increasingly apparent that the monarch Sigismund Augustus was likely to die without a male heir of his body. In 1564 he ceded his personal rights over the Grand Duchy to the Polish crown rather than to his sisters and this prepared the way for the Union of Lublin in 1569, pushed through in the teeth of Lithuanian reluctance at the joint *Sejm* which debated the matter, which created a commonwealth of the two nations (*Rzeczpospolita Obojga Narodów*).[24] A number of highly significant religious changes followed suit. In 1570 the Union of Sandomierz represented an attempt by the Lutheran and Reformed Churches and the Bohemian Brethren to establish a common anti-Unitarian position which would allow for an explicit recognition of their rights. In 1572, the death of Sigismund and the example of religious violence elsewhere in Europe, particularly the St Bartholomew Day's massacre, prompted the confederation of Warsaw of January 1573. Although bitterly opposed by most of the Catholic bishops, the confederation established a concord between nobles of different religion which guaranteed that they could not persecuted in their goods or persons because of differences in religion. This became the constitutional basis of Polish confessional coexistence, since all monarchs were forced to uphold this provision before ascending to the throne.[25]

---

[23] Stolarski, *Friars on the Frontier*, pp.139–45, 154–5, 178.
[24] These details are discussed in Frost, 'Union as process', pp. 70–90.
[25] Murdock, 'Un espace-carrefour', p. 229.

One factor facilitating such limitation of monarchical power was the extinction of the Jagiellonian dynasty with Sigismund August which served to re-emphasize the elective character of the Polish monarchy. Significantly both Henri of Valois and his successor, Stephen Bathory, were the products of different societies attempting to adapt to the coexistence of different confessional groupings within a single polity. In Transylvania Bathory had presided over a system of effective tolerance of four different religious groupings so that the confessional mosaic of Poland/Lithuania was hardly a culture shock. Bathory's demise eventually led to the ascension of a much more overt supporter of projects of re-Catholicization in the person of Sigismund III who was elected and crowned King of Poland in December 1587.[26] But despite his strong personal commitment to Catholicism even in his own family the new King was prepared to acquiesce to differences in religion. His younger sister, Anna Vasa, to whom the King was deeply attached, never converted down to her death in 1625, a decision in which conscience was clearly a significant factor, despite pressure from Rome on a series of nuncios to attempt to bring this about. Sigismund's attempt to maintain his position in Sweden by reassuring his Lutheran subjects there was a further incentive to honour the Polish monarchy's commitment to religious tolerance.

Moreover the historical development of the Polish Lithuanian commonwealth ensured that neither the monarchy nor the church possessed sufficient levels of coercive power to underpin a programme of religious uniformity. The sheer size of the political class disposing of rights, amounting to a least six or seven per cent of the population, dwarfed that extant in any other European polity.[27] Under his rule, while the position of non-Catholics in Poland certainly declined, legal safeguards continued to function to safeguard his Protestant subjects. Not until the middle of the seventeenth century did any Protestant become a victim of religious violence in either Poznań or Lublin and even in Vilna incidents were extremely rare. The desecration of the body of a deceased Protestant, Sophia Mora in 1597, for instance, was punished by the execution of two of the culprits and while the zealous Catholic Bishop, Stanislas Kiszka, escaped personal punishment for the ransacking and burning of a reformed church in Gialowo, he was forced to pay considerable compensation to the victim and surrender his servants to custody. During Sigismund's reign, it is true, there were several executions of non-Catholics. In 1611 both the anti-Trinitarian, Ivan Tyszkowic, and an Italian, Francus de Franco, were put to death for blasphemy and desecration of sacred Catholic objects. In both cases the King's Habsburg consort, Queen Constance, was evidently a factor in ensuring the maximum punishment. However, it was the behaviour rather than the beliefs *per se* of the two individuals, and the fact that they lacked the patronage of strong aristocratic protectors, which rendered them vulnerable in this fashion.[28]

[26] W.F. Reddaway, J.H. Penson, O. Halecki, and R. Dyboski (eds), *The Cambridge History of Poland from the origins to Sobieski (To 1696)* (Cambridge: Cambridge University Press, 1950), pp. 452–3.
[27] Knoll, 'Religious Toleration in Sixteenth Century Poland', pp. 35, 40, 43.
[28] Janusz Tazbir, *A State Without Stakes: Polish Religious Toleration in the Sixteenth and Seventeenth Centuries* (Wzdawniczy: Panstwowy Instytut, 1973), pp. 116–18.

Yet Sigismund's reign, and that of his son and successor Ladislaw IV, did represent a watershed in terms of the erosion of the position of non-Catholics in Poland. In 1572 an estimated 560 Protestant churches existed in the lands of the Commonwealth. By 1648 this number had more than halved to 240.[29] Partly this decline represented the predilections of the first Vasa King and those of his wives and advisors. The King disposed of very wide powers of patronage, appointing to literally thousands of offices. In 1635, the instructions to the nuncio marvelled at the manner in which this had allowed Sigismund gradually and subtly to pressurize his non-Catholic subjects.[30] In 1572 the magnate chamber of the Polish *Sejm* included fifty-two Protestant senators, of whom thirty-six could be considered players of genuine political importance. Together with the Orthodox senators, this amounted to roughly forty per cent of that body's membership.[31] On the accession of Sigismund III twenty-five Protestants still held seats in the Senate but this had dwindled to seventeen by 1606 and to a mere five on his death in 1632. While there was a certain recovery under the less confrontational rule of Ladislaw IV, by 1648 the number of Protestant Senators still stood at only eleven. In 1672, a century after the confessional and constitutional achievements of Polish Protestantism at the confederation of Warsaw, the number had dwindled to five again.[32]

The King's freedom of action in this regard was enhanced by the gradual constriction of Polish Protestantism which had little roots among the peasantry and which was weak in the cities of the realm, except in Royal Prussia. A clear majority of the nobility also inclined increasingly to Catholicism and the appetite of elements of this grouping for more confrontational attitudes towards religious heterodoxy was sharpened by a developing system of Catholic education, particularly in Jesuit colleges. The rejuvenation of the Polish hierarchy by more zealous and aggressive bishops, in which the leadership positions were almost invariably held by graduates of the Roman college, also contributed to a hardening of the atmosphere. In the 1620s, for instance, the bishops of Cracow, Martinus Szyszkowski, and Vladislavia, Paul Wolucki, were warmly commended in Rome for their intransigent stance concerning the decrees of the Council of Trent. By declaring annulled any marriages which had not been celebrated in the presence of a parish priest and witnesses, they placed a formidable pressure on the non-Catholic nobility by calling into question the legitimacy of children of marriages which had not been celebrated in this fashion.[33]

---

[29] Jobert, *La Pologne dans la crise de la chrétienté*, p. 183.

[30] Instructions to Mario Filonardi, 19 July 1635 (Chynczewska-Hennel, *Acta Nuntiaturae Poloniae XXV*, pp. 21–2).

[31] Daniel Tollet, 'Cohabitation, concurrence et conversion dans la confederation Polono-Lithuanienne au tournant des xvie et xviie siècles' in Eszter Andor and István György Tóth(eds), *Frontiers of Faith: Religious Exchange and the Constitution of Religious Identities 1400–1750* (Budapest: Central European University European Science Foundation, 2001), pp. 67–78, at 70.

[32] Jobert, *La Pologne dans la crise de la chrétienté*, pp. 208–9.

[33] Instructions to Giovanni Lancellotti, 14 December 1622 (Thaddaeus Fitych (ed.), *Acta Nuntiaturae Poloniae Tomus XXII Volumen 1 Ioannes Baptista Lancellotti (1622–27)* (Cracoviae: Academia Scientiarum et Litterarum Polona, 2000), pp. 32–4).

Of significance in this regard was the political power wielded by the Catholic hierarchy which was unmatched by any other ecclesiastical establishment in the commonwealth. The Archbishop of Gniezno, for instance, acted as primate, legate, first Prince, and senator of the kingdom, and even as *interrex* in the interval between royal elections.[34] Catholic prelates took precedence in the senate over their lay colleagues and on the royal council traditionally acted as either chancellor or vice-chancellor. Neither the orthodox nor, after 1596, the Uniate bishops of the Commonwealth possessed such political privileges and they were not accorded either to the clergy of even the more mainstream Lutheran and Reformed confessions, let alone to the increasingly pressurized Unitarians.[35] The reinvigoration of Catholic clerical institutions, combined with the supportiveness of increasing numbers of the magnate and noble estates, allowed for a more effective evangelization of the general population. The links between the Catholic church and the mass of the populace were also strengthened from the end of the sixteenth century by the growing importance of ecclesiastical institutions in the provision of charity, an area in which the state performed very little. A multiplication of parish and town hospitals occurred to care for the indigent with the principle gradually developing that each parish had responsibility for its own poor. Even at the beginning of the sixteenth century, a significant number of parish schools had existed but in the period after 1550 more were founded. By the mid-seventeenth century ninety-six per cent of the parishes in the diocese of Cracow boasted a school.[36]

Increasing availability of clergy extended the societal impact of the church, particularly in urban areas which were relatively over-supplied with clergy. By the end of the sixteenth century it is estimated the proportion of laity to secular clergy in Cracow had fallen to 760 : 1 and by the middle of the seventeenth century one in twenty of the town's population was in clerical orders.[37] Inevitably this could also ratchet up the level of sectarian tension. During the reigns of the Vasa kings, mob violence against non-Catholic institutions and personnel sporadically occurred. While churches had been conceded to Protestant confessions by Stephen Bathory in four major cities, the incidents of violence against them during Sigismund's reign meant that Protestant worship became effectively curtailed in both Poznań and Cracow. The Protestant school in Cracow had closed in 1574, its counterparts in Poznań followed suit in 1606 and in Vilna in 1639. Naturally the attractiveness of Catholic-controlled educational institutions for the non-Catholic population was enhanced by the contraction of Protestant alternatives. In 1639 the papal nuncio gleefully reported that for every one of the faithful put at risk by attendance at a heretical institution, fifty heretics were receiving potentially salvific education

---

[34] Wieslaw Müller, 'Structure administrative des dioceses catholiques latins en Pologne du xvie au xviiie siècle' in Rechowicz, *Millénaire du Catholicisme en Pologne*, pp. 105–9, at 106–7.

[35] Antoni Mączak, 'The Structure of Power in the Commonwealth of the Sixteenth and Seventeenth Centuries' in J.K. Fedorowicz, Maria Bogucka, and Henryk Samsonowicz (eds), *A Republic of Nobles: Studies in Polish History to 1864* (Cambridge: Cambridge University Press, 1982), pp. 109–34, at 114–15.

[36] Litak, 'La Paroisse', pp. 117–18.　　　[37] ibid., pp. 112–13.

in Catholic facilities.[38] A burgeoning confessional literature, which associated Protestantism with a threat to social order and which could emphasize the degree to which religious plurality in Poland created potential fifth columns for the Commonwealth's numerous non-Catholic neighbouring powers, also became available.[39] The long series of conflicts in which Poland was involved in the seventeenth century, with Lutheran Sweden, the Transylvania of the Reformed Prince Gabor Bethlen, Orthodox Muscovy, and with the Ottoman Empire and the Tartars, helped to crystallize a sense of an embattled Catholic kingdom which could glory in a sense of itself as a rampart of the Roman church on the borders of the Latin world.[40] To a certain extent, Catholic insistence on the dubious loyalty of non-Catholics could also act as a self-fulfilling prophecy. Disappointed with Sigismund III's rule, it was natural for Polish Protestants to look abroad in search of support and to attempt to barter cooperation in matters of taxation and defence for concessions in point of religion, which naturally accentuated royal distrust.[41]

The traditional line of historiography has tended to emphasize the role of the Jesuits in hardening the lines of confessional confrontation which reached its peak in 1606–8. Even after the *Rokosz* forced the Society towards a somewhat more emollient approach to the tradition of noble egalitarianism, the proliferation of Jesuit alumni in key positions of the state was evidently an important factor in the gradual constriction of Polish Protestantism.[42] But an important factor in the success of Polish Catholicism in the first half of the seventeenth century was evidently the degree of diversity which it encompassed. While monarchical pressure and the Society of Jesus were formidable weapons, of critical importance was the degree to which the Polish nobility came to see projects of Catholicization as consonant with the maintenance of cherished privileges and traditions. Noble opposition to any notion of monarchical absolutism was not, for instance, incompatible with the church of Rome and hostility to the Jesuits was by no means confined to the non-Catholic populations of the confederation.[43]

This became very evident at the great rebellion or *Rokosz* of 1606–8 which confederated some 50,000 nobles across the Polish confessional divide. The rebellion was the culmination of two decades of tension and distrust between the King and the Polish *Szlachta* (nobility) which had already erupted in significant confrontations in 1589, 1592, and 1603.[44] Intermingled with noble wariness of the King's ambitions, and distrust that he was prepared to subordinate Polish interests to policies of war for purely dynastic reasons, were significant tensions with the Catholic church relating to issues of property and a secular concern to ensure that village officials on Church land should be liable for military service, particularly in the

---

[38] Jobert, *La Pologne dans la crise de la chrétienté*, pp. 205–6.

[39] Tazbir, *State without stakes*, pp. 163–4.

[40] Tatarenko, 'Pluriconfessionnalité et politique de tolerance', pp. 258–9.

[41] Tazbir, *State Without Stakes*, pp. 163–7.

[42] Tollet, 'Cohabitation, concurrence et conversion', p. 70.

[43] Stanislaw Obirek, 'Jesuits in Poland and Eastern Europe' in Thomas Worcester (ed.), *The Cambridge Companion to the Jesuits* (Cambridge: Cambridge University Press, 2008), pp. 136–50, at 143.

[44] Reddaway, *Cambridge History of Poland*, pp. 452–61.

context of the level of donation to church foundations which was occurring. But, importantly, prominent figures among the opposition were strongly Catholic in their sympathies. Anti-Jesuit sentiment seems to have functioned as a bridge between anger at the monarch and resentment of the church but in a fashion which ultimately allowed for a strong degree of rapprochement between noble and clerical interests. As Piotr Stolarski has demonstrated, substantial portions of the Catholic elite were happy to voice fierce opposition to the Society of Jesus, not least as part of a process of mustering support for wider anti-Habsburg and anti-clerical grievances, and as a criticism for the perceived political orientation of the Society. But such voices could find alternative modes of expression within the burgeoning Catholic culture of Poland, in particular through patronage of the mendicant orders and their devotional culture, which had strong traditional roots but was far from obsolete or incapable of offering a focus for a genuine religiosity. Indeed, it has been speculated that the importance of the mendicant orders, and in particular their perceived distinction from the Society of Jesus, may have allowed them to act as a bridge for the conversion of Calvinist nobles. Patronage of the mendicants helped to preserve noble autonomy and the notion of free religious choice which had become integral to the political nation, thus acting as a middle road between a distrusted Jesuit Catholicism and increasingly divided and isolated Protestant denominations.[45]

From 1606–7 a prolonged period of negotiation occurred between noble and clerical interests. Important clerical concessions, such as indications of a willingness to accept toleration of religious diversity while maintaining principled opposition to heresy, were adumbrated in 1606. By 1635 the clergy had begun to pay the *subsidium charitativum* and to accept the billeting of soldiers on church lands as a contribution to the Commonwealth's military necessities. They also agreed to restrict appeals to Rome, conceded noble rights to *ius patronatus*, and accepted the need for the consent of the Diet to the creation of new religious establishments. The clergy's willingness to place the extent of tithe demands under discussion resulted, in return, in a noble acceptance of clerical rights in this regard together with a recognition of the validity of powers of episcopal jurisdiction.[46] Thus, while a Catholic tradition centred around the Jesuits and the King and his successive Habsburg wives was undoubtedly a powerful current in Poland during the long reign of Sigismund III, Catholic renewal came to represent a much broader movement. Moreover, in the wake of the *Rokosz*, even Sigismund III seems to have experienced a certain change of orientation in terms of his patronage of religious orders, directing a greater level of support to the mendicants and somewhat lessening his links with the Society of Jesus. This trend was accentuated under his son and successor Ladislaw III who favoured a pluralistic policy of religious patronage in which the Jesuits participated but which, through royal support of the mendicant orders, helped create bonds with those noblemen who distrusted the Society and were glad to see them held at a certain distance, although certainly retaining a degree of influence in court.[47]

---

[45] Stolarski, *Friars on the Frontier,* pp. 182–3.   [46] ibid., pp. 24–7.
[47] ibid., pp. 76–7.

Mendicant spirituality was thus an important constituent factor in the renewal of Polish Catholicism. Recent study of the Dominicans, for instance, who greatly outnumbered the Jesuits within the lands of the Commonwealth, has indicated the importance of this order as a focal point for Catholic female piety which owed little to the leadership of the royal consorts. In contrast with the Jesuits, the Dominicans of course actually provided an outlet for religious women in convents. Women also dominated the confraternities of the rosary which became established as the major Dominican devotional practice. Overall, female patronage of the movement of Catholic renewal was highly significant. The major congregation of post-Tridentine nuns to become established in the territory of the confederation was the reformed Benedictines of Magdalena Mortenska, the abbess of Chelmno, whose rule was confirmed in 1605 and which by the middle of the seventeenth century possessed twenty convents and more than eight hundred members.[48] But female piety found many different outlets in promoting Catholic devotion. Testamentary donations from wealthy women were a key element in the growth of regular establishments. Women sometimes directly founded convents, such as Zofia Magdalena Loknicka-Buckowiecka at Brest, Elżbieta Kamieniecka at Latyczów, and Anna Lubomirska in Cracow, while Mortenska founded a seminary in Poznań in 1616, transferred to Torun in 1618, to train confessors for her convents.[49] Included in the number of important patrons of new foundations were direct female converts from Protestant traditions such as Elżbieta Cieplowska, the founder of the Kamieniec sisters' convent in 1615–16, and Jadwiga Jazlowiecka, who founded a convent at Morachwa and made generous contributions to the Dominican convent at Lwów. And the movement of Protestant women to Catholicism was matched also by the influence of Catholic wives towards the conversion of their husbands and the raising of their children as Catholics, such as the case of the Protestant palatine of Dorpat, Andrzej Leszczyński, whose marriage to the devout Anna Korecka was apparently the key factor in the family's adherence to the church of Rome. Even when a wife did not effect the conversion of a husband of a different confession, she could play a significant role in strengthening the movement of Catholic renewal, as in the case of Katarzyna Ossolińska, the wife of the Calvinist Prokop Ossoliński, whose will in 1624 provided a lavish series of bequests to various religious foundations, including 500 zloty for the Dominican convent in which her own daughter was cloistered. For her part, Elżbieta Kamieniecka persuaded her Reformed husband, Jan Potocki, palatine of Braclaw down to his death in 1611, to contribute an annuity of 200 zloty for her convent at Latyczów.[50]

Yet if the movement of Catholic renewal enjoyed significant successes through a process of blandishment, education and the cultivation of a strong confessional Catholic identity which resulted in the copper-fastening of the church of Rome as

---

[48] Tatarenko, 'Pluriconfessionnalité et politique de tolerance', pp. 248–9.
[49] Karol Gorski, 'L'histoire de la spiritualité polonaise' in Rechowicz, *Millénaire du Catholicisme en Pologne*, pp. 281–354, at 299.
[50] Stolarski, *Friars on the Frontier*, pp. 83–103.

the dominant ecclesiastical denomination in the confederation, there remained limitations to the level of Catholic success. In this regard, the continued value which the Polish nobility and monarchy placed on the attraction and settlement of immigrants, often with highly prized artisan skills, within the vast territory of the confederation ensured a sporadic refreshment of religious heterogeneity within its borders. After the Habsburg expulsions of 1628 large numbers of the Bohemian Brethren settled in Great Poland. A similar influx of mainly Silesian Lutherans also occurred, attracted by a recruiting campaign which offered full religious freedom. New towns such as Rawicz, Szlichtyngowa, Kargowa, and Bojanów resulted and the charters granted to the new settlers were generally extremely generous in the promise of freedom of worship, the right to construct churches and educational establishments, and to establish systems of ecclesiastical governance. Catholic lords such as Adam Przyjemski or Christopher Żegocki proved just as eager as their Protestant counterparts to encourage such immigration and were prepared to offer very wide conditions of religious freedom in order to facilitate the process.[51]

Even more significantly, the Union of Brest of 1596 did not fulfil Catholic aspirations for the integration of the Orthodox population of Ruthenia into the church of Rome. Although the most successful of the attempted unions of the Orthodox and Latin churches, as noted in Chapter 1, the initiative suffered from a series of flaws which greatly limited its ability to attract the Orthodox population. In the decades prior to the Union, a significant movement of lay discontent with the ignorance and spiritual insufficiency of their clergy had become visible within the Ruthenian church. Sharpened both by contact with the ferment of Polish Protestantism and, in the latter years of the century, by the increasing momentum of Catholic organization and activity, this resulted in a search for reform in which lay confraternities at Lwów and the confraternity of the Holy Trinity at Vilna emerged as important actors. They functioned not merely as providers of charity and as a focus for devotional activities but increasingly their members involved themselves also in issues of theology and preaching, areas where the ignorance of the Orthodox clergy made them appear incapable of adequate spiritual ministration. Magnates of Orthodox faith, most notably Konstanty Ostrogski, the principal protector of his confession within the Commonwealth, acted also as patrons of the movement of reform. In 1576 Ostrogski created a school at Ostrih with the intention of forming a learned Orthodox elite through the study of languages, theology, and the liberal arts. While the currents of lay reform in the Orthodox community were not necessarily inimical to any notion of union with Rome, they were not enamoured of the manner in which the bishops of the Ruthenian church, who evidently saw in the Union an avenue towards the reinvigoration of clerical prestige and authority, together with the recuperation of ecclesiastical revenues and properties which in certain cases had been swallowed by lay interests, elected to pursue the project. As noted in Chapter 1, the ungenerous demeanour of the Clementine papacy, and the failure to gain equal status in the senate with the Catholic bishops, also helped diminish the credibility of the proponents of the Union. Consequently, rather than

[51] Tazbir, *State without stakes*, pp. 175–6.

a general embracing of Union an extremely confused and highly embittered situation developed as population and clergy split with mutual recrimination and excommunication. In the actual practice of religion, however, it could be impossible to distinguish the two groupings.

Technically the Orthodox hierarchy was no longer recognized following the Union and in the years after 1596 the Greek Catholic clergy could successfully appeal to the courts to validate their right to benefices and revenues attached to various churches and monasteries. Such decisions, however, were frequently impossible to implement and during the *Rokosz* the rebels extorted from the monarch agreement to a somewhat ambiguous commitment that Ruthenian benefices would henceforth only be conferred on individuals of the true Greek faith. The appointment of Josef Rutski as the Greek Catholic metropolitan in 1613, and his twenty-four-year incumbency in that position, led to a number of initiatives to reinvigorate the Uniate church and to resist certain influences in Rome which considered abandoning the initiative completely. One of the first Ruthenians to attend the Greek College in Rome, Rutski adopted the Greek rite at the behest of Clement VIII and as Metropolitan of Kiev attempted to create an educational network to improve the moral and pastoral capacities of the Uniate clergy. In 1615 he acquired a commitment from Paul V that twenty-two places spread over the colleges of Braniewo, Vilna, Omutz, Prague, Vienna, and Rome would be reserved for Ruthenians from the Metropolitanate of Kiev. He launched a major reform of the monastic order, creating the reformed Basiliens of the congregation of the Holy Trinity, which was intended to provide a standardized seminary education of a high quality. His objective that only members of this congregation would be appointed as bishops was eventually confirmed by Ladislaw IV in 1635. Yet while important in terms of developing a leadership cadre, Rutski's reforms were incapable of regenerating the entire body of the clergy and indeed carried the risk of increasing the distance between the general body of Uniate clergy and their bishops.[52] Roman support for the Union was also somewhat inconstant although officially Rome proclaimed itself indifferent whether the Ruthenian population adhered to the Greek Catholic or to the Latin rite and in 1624 forbade members of the Uniate church to switch to Latin Catholicism.[53]

The most significant problem of the Uniate church, however, was the determined opposition of wide swathes of the Ruthenian population. So extreme was the resentment of the Union in certain areas that even Catholic noblemen in Ruthenian territory could be reluctant to offer much protection to Uniate clergy for fear of the level of religious and peasant unrest which it had the potential to create.[54] In 1623 Josaphat Kuncewicz, the Uniate Archbishop of Polock, was killed by resentful opponents of the Union in Vitebsk, leading to a very strong repression

---

[52] Tararenko, 'Pluriconfessionnalité et politique de tolerance', pp. 249–58.

[53] Instructions from Ludovico Ludivisio to Lancellotti, 14 December 1622 (Fitych, *Acta Nuntiaturae Poloniae Tomus XXII*, p. 38); Tazbir, *State without stakes*, p. 188.

[54] Stolarski, *Friars on the Frontier,* pp. 66–7.

of the urban liberties of the town and punishment of its leadership.[55] Particularly strong reservoirs of resentment towards the Uniate clergy existed among the Cossacks whose military importance to the Commonwealth ensured that even the monarch and his most intransigent advisors were forced to take their attitudes into account. The initial declaration of the Union had led to a Cossack uprising, eventually repressed by Stanislaus Żólkiewski. But the Cossacks subsequently performed invaluable military service against Michael the Brave of Transylvania, in the wars of the false Demetris in Muscovy, in a series of raids on Ottoman territory, and in Prince Ladislaw's 1618 expedition against Moscow, under the leadership of Hetman Peter Sahajdaczny. It was Sahajdaczny who also engineered the revival of an Orthodox hierarchy, not recognized by the monarchy, when the patriarch of Jerusalem ordained a number of bishops and a metropolitan for the Ruthenian dioceses. Cossack forces were in addition vital to the Polish victory at Chocim although even in the wake of this victory Sigismund continued to refuse to recognize the Orthodox hierarchy. However, in 1632, again partly inspired by the desire for Cossack assistance in his war against Muscovy, King Ladislaw IV permitted official recognition of the Orthodox bishops, thus effectively confirming the existence of a schism.[56] The same year saw the opening of an Orthodox college at Kiev.[57] These developments set definite limits on the potential of the Union and in the region beyond the Dnieper it effectively foundered. In Eastern Poland, however, it did establish significant roots which were to ensure its survival as the most successful attempt at Union between Roman Catholicism and the Orthodox church.[58]

Despite the swift monarchical acceptance of the Council of Trent in the 1560s, and the provincial synod in which all the Polish bishops committed themselves to introducing and observing the conciliar decrees in their dioceses,[59] significant problems impeded the actual implementation of Tridentine norms in Poland. In this regard, the general poverty of Polish benefices and the consequent tradition of plurality represented a substantial obstacle.[60] In the latter half of the sixteenth century, as part of the papacy's attempt to secure the implementation of the council, the nuncios to Poland were given general faculties to make dispensations in this matter. However, Clement VIII, who had experience of the system from his time as legate in Poland, removed this power and reserved such dispensations to Rome. Under Paul V Rome once again proved more amenable to granting such dispensations to such an extent that at the beginning of the 1620s Gregory XV, recognizing the difficulty of dealing with the problem, attempted at least to ensure that only two parishes could be conferred on any one individual and then only when revenues were demonstrably inadequate and when the areas were geograph-

---

[55] Mikhail V. Dmitriev, 'Conflict and Concord in Early Modern Poland: Catholics and Orthodox at the Union of Brest' in Louthan et al. (eds), _Diversity and Dissent_, pp. 114–36, at 115–16; Reddaway, _Cambridge History of Poland_, p. 562.

[56] Reddaway, _Cambridge History of Poland_, pp. 508–9.

[57] Tatarenko, 'Pluriconfessionnalité et politique de tolerance', p. 264.

[58] Reddaway, _Cambridge History of Poland_, pp. 562–3.

[59] ibid., p. 409.   [60] Litak, 'La Paroisse', p. 113.

ically proximate.[61] But the practice was still deeply entrenched in the reign of Sigis-mund's successor Ladislaw IV during the 1630s.[62] In addition to plurality, the training of adequate clergy was a consistent problem.[63] Despite the official accept-ance of the Tridentine decrees, very few diocesan seminaries had been established in Poland by the 1620s, a situation which the papal nuncio, Giovanni Lancellotti, was urged to attempt to rectify by mounting pressures on the bishops of the Polish church.[64] Over a decade later, however, identical complaints were made to the new nuncio, Mario Filonardi, that Poland remained severely lacking in the level of sem-inary provision which the size of the dioceses warranted.[65]

Massive discrepancies also existed with regard to the distribution of clergy, particularly between urban and rural areas. While towns such as Cracow were plen-tifully indeed arguably over supplied with clergy, which could lead to unedifying squabbles among the various religious orders when a rival grouping was perceived as trying to muscle in on its turf,[66] the situation in rural parishes was frequently quite the opposite. There was also a sharp distinction between the more ethnically Polish west of the country, with smaller parishes and higher densities of clergy, and the Eastern areas of the Commonwealth where parishes were much larger and Catholic communities were more vulnerable to deprivation of consistent spiritual ministration. In the diocese of Cracow, for instance, parishes corresponded to an average of forty-one square kilometres but in Lublin the average size was over three times greater at one hundred and thirty-four square kilometres. The level of educa-tion and behaviour of the parish clergy, therefore, was not necessarily always in accordance with Tridentine norms. Frequent complaints were made about the drunkenness and moral pettiness of the clergy in the first decades of Sigismund III's reign. Clerical concubinage remained common: in the deanery of Kazimierz thirty-eight per cent of priests still maintained concubines at the beginning of the seventeenth century.[67] At the beginning of the period under review also most churches were poorly endowed with liturgical furnishings and the process of building these up was slow and gradual. The majority of churches were relatively simple wooden constructions. Even in the diocese of Cracow, which boasted the highest level of stone buildings, more than half of the temples were still made of wood in the middle of the eighteenth century.[68]

The functional political role of the Polish episcopate could also operate as an obs-tacle to the processes of pastoral reform on Tridentine lines. As in contemporaneous

---

[61] Instructions from Ludovico Ludivisio to Lancellotti, 14 December 1622 (Fitych, *Acta Nuntia-turae Poloniae Tomus XXII*, p. 42).

[62] See the Instructions to Mario Filonardi, 19 July 1635 (Chynczewska-Hennel, *Acta Nuntiaturae Poloniae XXV*, p. 25).

[63] Kowalski, 'Change in Continuity', 705.

[64] Instructions to Giovanni Lancellotti, 14 December 1622 (Fitych, *Acta Nuntiaturae Poloniae Tomus XXII*, p. 32).

[65] Instructions to Mario Filonardi, 19 July 1635 (Chynczewska-Hennel, *Acta Nuntiaturae Poloniae XXV*, pp. 22–3).

[66] See for instance Giovanni Lancellotti to Maffeo Barberini, 6 October 1623 (Fitych, *Acta Nun-tiaturae Poloniae Tomus XXII*, p. 207).

[67] Litak, 'La Paroisse', pp. 111–12, 115; Kowalski, 'Change in Continuity', 705–6.

[68] Litak, 'La Paroisse', pp. 111–12.

Royal Hungary, the political saliency of the Catholic hierarchy conferred many advantages on the movement of Catholic renewal. But almost inevitably this could reduce the pastoral effectiveness of the hierarchy. Moreover, because appointments to bishoprics frequently reflected a process of reward of individuals for political service to the monarch, the Polish episcopate was naturally inclined to place a high value on its political role. A figure such as Jacob Zadzik, for instance, acted as the King's secretary in 1613 which eventually resulted in his elevation to the hierarchy in 1624 as Bishop of Chelm. He was appointed to the vice-chancellorship in 1627 before becoming chancellor in the following year. He was then appointed to the richer and more prestigious bishopric of Cracow in 1635.[69] Preoccupation with such political responsibilities necessarily impacted on the level of time and concentration which a bishop devoted to his pastoral role.[70] It also helped to diminish the level of residency, one of the key elements of the process of Tridentine reform. The frequent absences of Polish bishops from their dioceses seem to have contributed to the rise to particular importance in Poland of the office of Vicar General, who sometimes effectively came to replace the bishop completely in the day-to-day running of a diocese. Over time, the level of episcopal absence helped to create the office of auditor of the curia who became a significant actor in diocesan affairs.[71] Nor was a figure like Zadzik's movement between episcopal sees unusual. In a fashion once again strongly reminiscent of contemporary Habsburg practice in Hungary, diocese-hopping was a deeply engrained custom of the Polish episcopate. To a considerable extent this reflected the huge disparity in the value of Polish dioceses. A pattern developed, therefore, wherein bishops began their career in a poorer Eastern diocese before moving, sometimes several times, to a richer see.

The primate of Poland during the 1640s, Matthias Lubienski, exhibits this sequence in a very pure form. Born in 1572, he was first elevated to the hierarchy as Bishop of Chelm in 1621. Six years later he was translated to Poznań but within four years had moved to Wloclawek before attaining the archbishopric of Gniezno in 1641 where he remained until his death in 1652.[72] One of Lubienski's predecessors as primate during the 1620s, Ioannes Wezyk (1575–1638), was also appointed to four different dioceses. He began his career in Przemyśl in 1620. In 1623 the Bishop was nominated to Lutsk in the Ukraine but never served there as the more desirable see of Poznań became available in 1624. Three years later the vacancy in the archbishopric of Gniezno enabled him to become the primate of the Polish church.[73] It was thus rare for a Polish bishop to serve in only one diocese. The relatively temporary nature of episcopal incumbencies possibly helped to diminish individual prelates' level of commitment to the particular diocese that they were currently occupying, particularly if they had extensive political commitments. Episcopal visitation, for instance, which a theorist of episcopal government such as GianBattista Rinuccini considered the very core of a bishop's role, was fairly infrequent and when it did occur it was more often the responsibility of deans,

---

[69] Fitych, *Acta Nuntiaturae Poloniae Tomus XXII*, p. 93, n. 11.
[70] Müller, 'Structure administrative des dioceses', pp. 106–7.   [71] ibid., p. 108.
[72] Fitych, *Acta Nuntiaturae Poloniae Tomus XXII*, p. 76, n. 9.   [73] ibid., p. 74, n. 9.

archdeacons and special episcopal delegates.[74] Also, while the level of education of Polish bishops seems to have been high, frequently they did not hold any actual degrees, as the Polish nobility seem to have found the quest for such qualifications somewhat beneath them.[75] Thus, even as late as the reign of Ladislaw IV (1632–48), the perception in Rome was of the Polish realm still having a considerable distance to travel before fulfilling the Tridentine template in matters such as residence, visitation, the supervision of the quality of those ordained to the priesthood, and the lifestyle of the clergy.[76]

Roman dissatisfaction with the regular orders of the Commonwealth was a frequent trope of nuncios' correspondence during the first half of the seventeenth century. The rapid growth of the mendicant orders was a testament to a widely-based current of Catholic renewal which found expression in many different forms and which was not always amenable to easy direction by either the Polish hierarchy, which by 1648 was dominated by products of Jesuit education, or the papacy.[77] From a Roman perspective the older religious orders were far more prone to indiscipline and an abuse of liberty which prevented the inculcation of a new devotional culture. Along with the Jesuits, the Discalced Carmelites represented something of a flagship project for the Polish church in the hope that the introduction in 1605 of an order of friars imbued with a new culture of discipline into Cracow would provide edification for other sectors of the Polish church.[78] But the Carmelites immediately came into competition with long-established orders to the extent that they were unable to source sufficient alms within the city and were forced to maintain horses and carriages to allow them to canvass support over a wider geographical area, which somewhat tarnished the image of simple spirituality which they had originally been intended to represent. In the 1620s the example of the Carmelites suggested that great thought was needed before sponsoring the introduction of the Capuchins to Poland. Although two friars had gone to Poland as early as 1582, there were no permanent establishments of this branch of the Franciscan family. In 1617 Sigismund III appealed to Rome for the introduction of the order[79] but, while it was recognized that the order had much to offer Polish Catholicism, both as an example to other families of regulars and as an instrument

---

[74] Müller, 'Structure administrative des dioceses', p. 108.

[75] See for instance the information process for Michaelis Dzialynski as auxiliary Bishop of Warmia, 26 Nov–2 Dec 1623 (Fitych, *Acta Nuntiaturae Poloniae Tomus XXII*, p. 330; see also the 1631 information process for Henryk Firlej for the diocese of Przemyśl (Adelbertus Bilinski (ed.), *Acta Nuntiaturae Poloniae Tomus XVXIII Volumen 1 Honoratus Visconti* (Rome: Institutum Historicum Polonicum Romae, 1996), p. 349).

[76] Instructions to Mario Filonardi, 19 July 1635 (Chynczewska-Hennel, *Acta Nuntiaturae Poloniae XXV*, pp. 22, 25).

[77] Jobert, *La Pologne dans la crise de la chrétienté*, pp. 256–7.

[78] See Instructions of Cardinal Borghese to Francesco Simonetta, 1606 (Adalbertus Tygielski (ed.), *Acta Nuntiaturae Poloniae Tomus XVIII Volumen 1 Franciscus Simonetta 21 VI 1606–30 IX 1607* (Rome: Institutum Historicum Polonicum Romae, 1990), p. 23; Tatarenko, 'Pluriconfessionalité et politique de tolérance', p. 248.

[79] Gabriele Ingegneri, 'L'opera dei Cappuccini nell'Europa centro-orientale' in Silvano Cavazza (ed.), *Controriforma e monarchia assoluta nelle province Austriache: Gli Asburgo, l'Europa Centrale e Gorizia all'epoca della Guerra dei Trent'Anni* (Gorizia: Istituto di storia sociale e religiosa, 1997), pp. 90–9, at 90.

of conversion, strong fears were expressed that the Capuchins would end up compromising to Polish conditions rather than acting as a beacon of change. Not only the Polish climate in winter, which naturally posed problems to the members of an order for whom braving the elements was of foundational importance, but the sheer distances involved in travelling in the vast Polish territories would naturally militate against the strict observance of the Capuchin rule.[80] Ultimately such doubts were to prevent the introduction of the Capuchins into the territory of the Commonwealth until towards the end of the century during the reign of Jan Sobieski.[81]

Roman criticism of the Polish regular clergy, citing the need for Italian oversight and greatly improved discipline, could be very severe.[82] One factor in precipitating such complaints, in contrast with the Jesuits who were generally exempted from such criticisms, was probably the degree to which the mendicant orders were still linked to older traditions of Polish Catholicism, reflecting their long established position in the region. The numerous bonds which linked the Dominicans, for instance, to noble patrons posed a constant threat to the friars' ability to avoid entanglement in the worldly domain. The assigning of friars as the confessors and chaplains to often highly peripatetic noble families offered significant opportunities for individuals to escape close supervision within the order. That this problem was not insignificant is indicated by the regulation of the 1640 chapter held in Lwów, which ordered excommunication for all chaplains who were not able to demonstrate obedience to their superiors, a willingness to return to their convents regularly, and to account both for their behaviour while in secular society and any alms or donations which they had received. Consumption of alcohol, often in large quantities, was evidently a constant issue concerning mendicant friars, a tendency which presumably was influenced by the ties of sociability which linked them on multiple levels to noble patrons and which was deplored by individuals internal to the order, as well as by Italian nuncios.[83] Significantly, the nuncio to the Confederate Catholics of Ireland during the 1640s, GianBattista Rinuccini, was critical of the Irish regular orders in a fashion quite similar to his colleagues in Poland. In his first major report on Ireland in March 1646, Rinuccini bitterly bewailed the manner in which Irish regulars resisted the imposition of stricter standards of conventual life, and even wearing the habits of their orders, which he ascribed to their experience of too great a sense of liberty prior to the collapse of the Caroline state in 1641.[84]

Both in Poland and in Ireland the adaptation of the mendicant orders to the contours of secular society carried dangers of the erosion of the spiritual mission of the friars, and of their capacity to inculcate respect and promote devotional fervour

---

[80] GianBattista Lancellotti to Ludovico Ludovisi, 8 June 1623 (Archivio Storico 'De Propaganda Fide', SOCG 337, f. 273rv).

[81] Ingegneri, 'L'opera dei Cappuccini', p. 90.

[82] Fitych, *Acta Nuntiaturae Poloniae Tomus XXII*, p. xlvii.

[83] Stolarski, *Friars on the Frontier*, pp. 96–7.

[84] G.A. Aiazzi, *Nunziatura in Irlanda di Monsignor Gio. Baptista Rinuccini Arcivescovo di Fermo negli anni 1645 à 1649* (Firenze, 1844).

in the wider populace. This was recognized by internal critics within the orders in both areas. Yet certain compensatory advantages could also exist. The incorporation of medieval patterns of devotion offered advantages to Catholicism when it chimed with traditional beliefs and expectations.[85] Fear of the contamination of the sacred by the profane was certainly a *leitmotif* of much of the Catholic renewal of the Early Modern period but the mendicant orders, in particular, also represented reservoirs in which the immanence of the sacred in the wider life of the community remained apprehensible. By the multiple nature of their interactions with the laity, and perhaps sometimes because of the laxity with which they preserved the border between the worldly and spiritual, the mendicant orders helped ensure the survival and flourishing of a more variegated Catholicism in the Commonwealth.[86]

The close intersection of the mendicant orders with wide swathes of Polish noble society also assisted in allowing individual friars to adumbrate a vision of elite religious commitment which could harmonize certain traits of Polish noble sensibility with a vision of a renewed Catholicism. A figure such as Adam Birkowski, for instance, the most influential preacher of his era, emphasized noble freedom as the capacity to choose a path of virtue and elaborated the notion of a martial Christian identity which embraced suffering and emphasized constancy, loyalty and service. Identifying Catholicism with a love of a *Patria* in constant danger from incursion by hostile Tartars and Turks, he offered a vision of war as a noble calling which prevented idleness and self-indulgence. For the exceptionally large Polish political nation, highly jealous of its prerogatives and fearful of royal encroachment upon them, the attractiveness of such a vision was probably enhanced by the dignity which it accorded their role within the Commonwealth.[87] Similarly, Szymon Okolski's *Orbus Polonus* (1641–5) has been read as an example of the fashioning of a particular image of Polish noble identity in a manner which emphasized the importance of Catholic morality and reverence for the church, but which also emphasized the excellence of the noble class in their pursuit of virtue, and love of freedom, and of the republic.[88]

Another area of regular life which caused considerable distaste in Rome concerned the laxity of the enclosure of nuns. In particular the manner in which abbesses were prone to leave the cloister in cases relating to their own convents raised the hackles of Roman observers.[89] But, again, such criticisms would appear to reflect more the obsessions of Italian observers rather than any major deficiency within Polish practice. Indeed, the participation of abbesses in a key element of civic and noble culture was probably a distinct advantage in securing the societal position of such institutions.

The period under review in this book was thus one of decisive importance in the evolution of Polish Catholicism and the forging of strong links between Polish

[85] Kowalski, 'Change in Continuity', 713.
[86] In this regard see Obirek, 'Jesuits in Poland', p. 140.
[87] Stolarski, *Friars on the Frontier*, pp. 107–36.   [88] ibid., pp. 193–5.
[89] Instructions to Mario Filonardi, 19 July 1635 (Chynczewska-Hennel, *Acta Nuntiaturae Poloniae XXV*, p. 25).

identity and the church of Rome. A number of factors evidently combined to facilitate the relative triumph of Catholicism over its Protestant competitors. In this regard the fracturing of Protestant unity was clearly an aspect of substantial importance. Not only were both Lutheranism and representatives of the Reformed tradition present in the Commonwealth but a social and ethnic differentiation between the adherents of these two denominations rendered a united Protestant front more difficult. Furthermore, the emergence of Unitarianism, and in particular its easy portrayal as a stalking horse for Islamicization or Judaization, probably contributed to a process wherein conservative Trinitarians came to consider the solid unity of the Roman church attractive. The demonization of Polish Unitarianism was probably also made easier by the strong foreign influences in its organization and direction.[90] Critically, also, the monarchy did not pass into the hands of Protestant sympathizers. Even Stephen Bathory, the post-Jagiellonian king most willing to conciliate his Protestant subjects, who either tacitly or formally yielded authorization for Protestant churches in four major royal cities, used his powers to restore Catholicism in the churches under royal patronage. The re-Catholicization of Livonia also received an important impetus during Bathory's reign, particularly at Dorpat and Riga where he influenced the recovery of several formerly Catholic churches from Lutheran hands.[91] This process was significantly accentuated under Sigismund III. Yet the powers of the monarch were relatively weak. As in Hungary, the King could offer incentives to Catholic nobles in terms of distribution of office and favour, but the unity of the political nation in defending the right to religious expression for their own rank in society meant that Polish Catholicism could not become an ally of a process of royal absolutism. The crown simply lacked the coercive power to make religious dissidence on the part of Polish nobles particularly difficult, let alone impossible. But as it transpired this absence of coercion did not prove an obstacle which could not be hurdled.

A contrast can perhaps be perceived here with Irish Catholicism which was explicitly prohibited but not effectively repressed. The degree of resentment which the state church's inefficient proscription of Catholicism produced in Ireland was arguably a significant obstacle to the acceptance by the Catholic elites in the island of the religion by law established. In Poland, on the other hand, the embracing of Catholicism operated within the context of noble freedom to choose religious affiliation and increasingly the momentum was towards the choice of the Roman church. Thus Polish sociopolitical decentralization and the movement of Catholic renewal operated in tandem with each other rather than in opposition.[92] As elsewhere in East-Central Europe, the attractions of Catholicism for an increasingly dominant noble class were clearly of the utmost importance in securing the confessional triumph of Rome. In this regard, the success of the Roman church in articulating a particular view of its historical evolution and of its Protestant competitors was of real significance. Moreover, Catholicism clearly represented a reassuring power for social order which consolidated noble privileges, especially in the context

[90] Reddaway, *Cambridge History of Poland*, p. 412.   [91] ibid., p. 413.
[92] Stolarski, *Friars on the* Frontier, p. 176.

of the relative failure of the various Protestant confessions to make inroads among the peasantry. In addition, Catholicism offered significant varieties of choice to its Polish noble partisans, with various currents of Ignatian and mendicant spirituality and devotion on offer to allow for a sense of freedom of choice in religious matters within an overall umbrella of unity. Its devotional culture was furthermore clearly attractive at all levels of Polish society, fulfilling a genuine need for spiritual security and agency in an embattled polity. Finally, the revitalization of Catholic institutions, particularly the episcopacy which had never lost the positions of political dominance which it had enjoyed in the medieval period, and the creation of a hugely influential network of educational establishments, firmly consolidated the Roman church's ability to squeeze the space available to its confessional rivals.

AUSTRIA AND BOHEMIA

South and west of the lands of the Polish crown lay the territories of the Austrian Habsburgs, a congeries of different political and administrative units, of which the most significant were the lands of the Bohemian crown—essentially Bohemia itself, the margravate of Moravia, and Silesia—the *Erblande* of the Habsburg dynasty, roughly coterminous with the modern Republic of Austria,[93] and the kingdom of Hungary. This last, in the period under review, was a truncated remnant of its medieval predecessor and divided between Habsburg Royal Hungary, the autonomous principality of Transylvania which acknowledged the suzerainty of the Supreme Porte, and the central plains of the Danube and Tisza, including the ancient capital of Buda, which had been incorporated into the Ottoman empire.[94] In the modern era, this arc of territory is divided between a series of different states, most notably the Czech Republic, Austria, Slovakia, Hungary, Slovenia, and Croatia. In each of these successor states, the most numerous religious confession in the twentieth century was Roman Catholicism, despite the fact that all, with the exception of Austria, fell under Communist rule in the aftermath of World War II.

Significantly this religious geography was sharply different in 1592. Throughout this region, with the exception of certain pockets like the Tirol where Catholicism remained relatively strong,[95] at the end of the sixteenth century Protestantism of various hues had made very considerable strides. In the three central territories of the Austrian Habsburgs, Bohemia, Hungary, and the *Erblande*, Catholicism represented a minority and embattled confession whose long-term prospects of success looked decidedly slim. At the end of the period under review, however, the Roman

---

[93] R.J.W. Evans, *The making of the Habsburg Monarchy 1550–1700* (3rd impression, Oxford: Clarendon Press, 1991), pp. 157–60, 195–6; the duchies of upper and lower Silesia were occupied by Saxony in 1620 and ceded by the Habsburgs in the Peace of Prague.

[94] For an accessible English language description of these three regions see Bryan Cartledge, *The Will to Survive: A History of Hungary* (London: Timewell Press, 2006), pp. 90–101.

[95] Regina Pörtner, *The Counter-Reformation in Central Europe: Styria 1580–1630* (Oxford: Clarendon Press, 2001), pp. 24–5.

church had made a spectacular recovery throughout the region and was on course to emerge as the dominant confession in the major territories of the dynasty.

While a number of shared processes can certainly be distinguished in this transformative process, the following section concentrates on the *Erblande* and the lands of the Bohemian crown because in both cases successful repression of rebellion conferred a free hand on the dynasty to impose highly coercive measures in the quest to achieve political control and Catholic dominance. In Hungary for a variety of reasons, which are investigated in the third section, a similar level of coercion could not be deployed, despite a brief and disastrous flirtation with such confrontational tactics in the latter stages of the early seventeenth-century war against the Ottomans.

A conventional starting point for the study of what can justly be described as an extraordinary recrudescence of Catholicism in Habsburg lands is in the Inner Austrian duchies of Styria, Carinthia, and Carniola for it was here, initially under Archduke Karl II and then under his son, the later Emperor Ferdinand II, that the initial blueprint for a more intransigent confrontation with religious heterodoxy was first developed. By the latter stages of the 1570s, the vast majority of the Inner Austrian nobility had deserted the church of Rome, to the extent that the papal nuncio in Graz estimated in 1580 that there were no more than five Catholic noblemen to be found in the province. The level of influence which the Lutheran nobility enjoyed over the market towns of the area also ensured a dramatic development of urban Protestantism throughout Inner Austria.[96] In the course of the 1570s, the financial difficulties of the Habsburg dynasty had contributed to allowing the Estates of Inner Austria to mount a campaign for recognition of religious freedoms. In 1572, Karl II conceded the Pacification of Graz which offered freedom of conscience to the Estates and to their urban and rural subjects. In 1578 the Estates attempted to secure an assurance of general religious toleration for adherents to the Confession of Augsburg.[97] While the proximity of the Turkish border was a formidable pressure on the Prince to accede to their demands, it also gave the Estates a significant stake in a successful bargain so they eventually moderated their demands in favour of safeguards for the nascent system of Protestant schools and church ministry.[98] Ultimately, they were prepared to accept somewhat equivocal guarantees from Karl II. Their stance in this regard may also have been influenced by Lutheran conceptions of non-resistance to legitimate authority, which seems to have become the dominant political position among the Protestant elites of the area and which helped to influence them towards positions of passive or suffering obedience, even in the context of what was to become in the following decades an all-out assault on religious liberties.

---

[96] ibid., pp. 35–40.

[97] J. Loserth, 'Die Steirische Religionspazifikation und die Fälschung des Vizekanzlers Dr. Wolfgang Schranz', *Jahrbuch der Gesellschaft für die Geschichte des Protestantismus in Österreich* 48 (1927), 1–57, at 12–57.

[98] For a concise analysis of the threat which Turkish power posed to the region see Leopold Toifl and Hildegaard Leitgeb, *Die Türkeneinfälle in der Steiermark und in Kärnten vom 15. Bis zum 17. Jahrhundert* (Vienna: Bundesverlag, 1991), pp. 1–71.

The Prince's personal commitment to Catholicism had already been made clear by his marriage to Maria Wittelsbach, a daughter of Germany's most fervently Catholic dynasty, and by his sponsoring of a Jesuit college and school in Graz in 1572–3, but the concessions won by the Estates were nonetheless important. Protestant grammar schools were established in the main towns of the three duchies of Styria (Graz), Carinthia (Klagenfurt), and Carniola (Laibach) and the organization of schooling and church ministry was put under the authority of a superintendent in Graz. To the frustration of the Jesuits, the education supplied in these institutions was robust enough to resist the competition of the Society's institution in Graz, not least because its Protestant rival in the city was prepared to offer free tuition to able commoners.[99] By the end of the 1570s Protestantism was firmly established in Upper Styria and in the principal towns of Lower Styria, although the rural Slovenian population of the South had been subject to relatively little proselytization in the Lutheran faith. Many of the preachers, it is true, who staffed the Lutheran church were not native to the area. In 1600 roughly two-thirds were still immigrants[100] but the network of schools which had been put into place offered the promise of the creation of a self-sustaining native ministry.

The extent of the concessions extorted from Karl II caused deep alarm in Catholic Germany as well as Rome and led to a meeting in Munich in October 1579 between Duke Wilhelm V of Bavaria, Karl II, and the Habsburg ruler of Tyrol, Ferdinand II, which led to the planning of a concerted programme of re-Catholicization for Inner Austria.[101] It resulted also in the founding of a permanent nunciature at Graz which had been mooted in Rome since 1573.[102] Over the next decade, Karl II strove to implement a programme of curtailment of Protestant liberties and to increase the number of Catholic office-holders and advisors in his administration. Disappointed of significant financial aid from either Bavaria and Rome, and fearful of provoking open revolt, his main achievements tended to halt rather than to reverse the growth of Styrian Protestantism, in particular by a series of restrictive measures against the urban practitioners of the Lutheran faith and by restricting the institutional consolidation of the network of schools and ministers.[103]

The period also saw the further development of Jesuit educational institutions. In 1574 a seminary was created for impoverished students and in 1576 another seminary for the education of priests came into being. The educational range of the Jesuit school in Graz was extended in 1578 and in 1585 it acquired a theological and philosophical faculty and full university status in 1586. It was not until the 1620s however that these institutions managed to make themselves attractive to scions of the higher nobility. One of the objectives of the Jesuit schools was undoubtedly to form a cultivated Catholic elite which would furnish the sovereign with the

---

[99] Pörtner, *The Counter-Reformation in Central Europe*, pp. 46–57.

[100] Evans, *Habsburg Monarchy*, p. 190.

[101] Pörtner, *The Counter-Reformation in Central Europe*, p. 71.

[102] Josef Krasenbrink, *Die Congregatio Germanica und die katholische Reform in Deutschland nach dem Tridentinum* (Münster: Aschendorff, 1972), p. 127.

[103] Pörtner, *The Counter-Reformation in Central Europe*, pp. 51, 71–94.

material to replace Protestant personnel in public offices.[104] Jesuit education was also in part aimed at redressing the need for a better trained and, from a Tridentine perspective, less licentious clergy. In the early 1580s the papal nuncio claimed that out of 220 Styrian priests under the jurisdiction of Salzburg fewer than ten were not living with wives and concubines. However, the favour shown to the Jesuits risked alienating the local clergy, who in particular resented archducal attempts to fund Jesuit institutions by drawing on the resources of existing ecclesiastical foundations.[105] The death of Karl II in 1590 meant that he was succeeded by his twelve-year-old son, Ferdinand. During the regency on his behalf, the Protestant Estates of Styria, Carinthia, and Carniola tried unsuccessfully to obtain Imperial and explicit constitutional recognition for the religious concessions of 1578. In 1595, however, the young Jesuit-educated Ferdinand took power and immediately showed a firm appetite for a harder line which drew ideological support from his Jesuit confessor, and practical and moral assistance from the bishops of Seckau, Martin Brenner, who acted as the Vicar General of the Archbishop of Salzburg, and of Lavant, Georg Stobaeus. Two successive bishops of Lubljiana, Jan Tavčar (1580–97) and Tomas Hren (1577/9–1630), also emerged as formidable supporters of the ruler's programmes of re-Catholicization.[106] The young Ferdinand, like his successors, was a man of genuine religious devotion.[107] His highly pious mother, Maria of Bavaria, was an important formative influence and he spent five years after his father's death in 1590 at the Jesuit university of Ingolstadt.[108]

Over the next two decades, Ferdinand embarked on a campaign of Catholic promotion to governmental, judicial, and court offices, as well as the higher military ranks, often giving posts to Catholic foreigners at the expense of native Protestants. In 1598 he abolished the Protestant ministry centred on Graz by archducal decree, resulting in an exodus of preachers and teachers. In January 1599, hoping to use the crisis of the Turkish war, the Estates refused to vote financial support for Ferdinand unless the decree was reversed but the archduke, asserting his God-given authority as Prince, refused. Eventually, fearful of the advance of the Turkish army and that the archduke would introduce foreign troops, the Estates backed down. In 1600 a decree was issued which gave a stark choice to all burghers in Graz and officials of the Estates of emigration or conversion. Those who opted to leave were forced to pay a tax on their property. The urban Counter-Reformation was supplemented by measures designed to strengthen the power of the ruler over the municipalities, not least by the abolition of annual elections to town offices and their replacement by appointments for life. New charters were issued to towns, based on the recommendations of a series of roving commissions of enquiry and

---

[104] France Martin Dolinar, 'La cultura controriformistica nell'Austria interna: i Gesuiti a Graz e Lubiana' in Cavazza (ed.), *Controriforma e monarchia assoluta*, pp. 99–107, at 103.

[105] Pörtner, *The Counter-Reformation in Central Europe*, pp. 98–107.

[106] Dolinar, 'La cultura controriformistica nell'Austria interna', p. 100.

[107] Silvano Cavazza, 'Religione, cultura e società nelle province austriache. Un bilancio storiografico', in Cavazza (ed.), *Controriforma e monarchia assoluta*, pp. 109–24, at 113.

[108] Robert Bireley, *Religion and Politics in the Age of the Counterreformation: Emperor Ferdinand II, William Lamormaini, S. J. and the Formation of Imperial Policy* (Chapel Hill: University of North Carolina Press, 1981), p. 7.

reform to the urban settlements throughout Inner Austria. In the event of resistance, municipalities and burghers were deprived of rights and troops were billeted to ensure future obedience.[109] The commissions also destroyed Protestant churches and grave yards and burnt heretical literature.[110] In 1601 a general decree of expulsion of Protestant preachers and school masters throughout Ferdinand's lands was issued. Partly because of their grievances against their Hungarian neighbours arising from the Bocskai revolt and peace of 1606, the Estates also failed to make use of the conflict between the Emperor and his brother Matthias to form a common cause with other Protestant Habsburg Estates in order to extort religious guarantees and thus they were excluded from the concessions granted to other parts of Austria, Bohemia, and Hungary. In 1613 Parish priests were ordered to compile lists of their parishioners who had failed to confess and take Easter communion.

Ferdinand's subsequent measures against Protestantism in Inner Austria were taken within the context of his steadily expanding responsibilities. By the end of 1617 he was the designated heir to all the Austrian *Erblande*, as well as the elected King of Bohemia, and he became King of Hungary in the following year, Emperor in 1619, and enjoyed a decade of remarkable success in the first stages of the Thirty Years War.[111] In 1628 this allowed him to complete the jigsaw of political re-Catholicization in Inner Austria by a decree that Protestant nobility had six months to convert or emigrate, initiating a long-drawn-out policy of sale of Protestant lands, which often passed to Catholic members of the various noble families, and which also offered rich possibilities to the higher Catholic clergy of the region who acquired significant pickings. In 1629, 754 people were registered as obliged to go into exile from Inner Austria.[112] Undoubtedly many of those who opted for conversion were anything but convinced of the truths of the Catholic faith. Although in 1634–5 Saxony abandoned its demands on behalf of Protestants in the *Erblande* and the Bohemian lands,[113] crypto-Protestant hopes of a reversal of fortune were sustained for a period by the steady tide of defeats sustained by the Habsburgs after 1636. However, the terms of the Peace of Westphalia in 1648, which more or less offered *carte blanche* to the dynasty in terms of the imposition of confessional conformity everywhere in their hereditary lands, other than Silesia, ended this possibility.[114] Indeed, not even the relatively generous terms of emigration for the Protestant subjects of the dynasty which had been agreed at Westphalia were subsequently honoured by Ferdinand III.[115]

---

[109] Pörtner, *The Counter-Reformation in Central Europe*, pp. 144–80.

[110] Peter Vodipivec, 'Reformation and Counter-Reformation in Inner Austria' in Tóth (ed.), *Frontiers of Faith*, pp. 203–12, at 209.

[111] Johann Rainer, 'L'assolutismo politico e confessionale in Austria nei secoli XVI e XVII' in Cavazza (ed.), *Controriforma e monarchia assoluta*, pp. 11–28, at 22–3.

[112] Friedrich Edelmayer, 'La Nobilità Austriaca nella prima metà del Seicento' in Cavazza (ed.), *Controriforma e monarchia assoluta*, pp. 61–70, at 66.

[113] Bireley, *Religion and Politics*, pp. 209–10.

[114] Miroslav Hroch and Ivo Barteček, 'Die Böhmische frage im Dreissigjährigen Krieg', *Historische Zeitschrift Beihefte* New Series 26 (1998), 447–60, at 457–8.

[115] Pörtner, *The Counter-Reformation in Central Europe*, pp. 108–43, 225–8.

The coercive and restrictive measures which Ferdinand II introduced were also accompanied by a classical Tridentine attempt to improve the quality, and eventually numbers, of the Catholic clergy, particularly those with pastoral responsibilities. Significant obstacles existed in this respect. Clerical concubinage remained deeply engrained with a flagrant example set by the Archbishop of Salzburg, the chief prelate in the region down to his imprisonment in 1612, Wolf Dietrich Von Raittenau, who was the father of fifteen children with his partner Salome Alt. In 1592 it was recognized in Rome that the problem of concubinage was so widespread that a universal deprivation of clergy with partners would result in the effective denudation of the parish ministry. Consequently it was temporarily decided to turn a blind eye to the practice if the doctrinal orthodoxy of priests was not suspected. Gradually, however, pressure was applied. Between 1607 and 1614 Bishop Brenner of Seckau proceeded against thirty-six concubinary priests. In 1617–19 his successor Jakob Eberlein reported at least ten cases from the 160 clergy examined, which evidently represented a significant diminution if not elimination of the practice, which continued to persist into the second half of the seventeenth century. These changes were partially effected by a willingness to import clergy from the empire. During Eberlein's incumbency in Sechau the majority of the parish priests were not locally recruited. By this stage there was evidence of a definite if modest improvement in the educational standard of the clergy and increasing pressure was being levied on practices such as clerical drunkenness, gambling, and other aspects of conviviality with the laity considered scandalous by Tridentine standards. The parish clergy were increasingly tasked with the inculcation of Tridentine norms and beliefs by the provision of catechesis, the keeping of parish registers, and the regulation of sexual activity and its transgressive consequences in terms of abortion and infanticide. These processes were aided by governmental support for the recovery of alienated church property, although the power of the Protestant nobility down to 1628 was an important brake on this development.[116]

Additional Jesuit schools were opened in Laibach (1597), Klagenfurt (1604), Leoben and Gorizia (1615), and Judenburg (1621), in each case with attached residences, and they had a steady impact both on the urban areas which they served and on the surrounding rural parishes.[117] The Jesuits introduced the forty-hours prayer to Graz in 1594 and by the second decade of the seventeenth century this had become entrenched as a popular devotion. The Society, which conducted collective exorcisms in Graz in the period 1599–1600, offered themselves as an important source of thaumaturgic power to a society highly fearful of demonic presence.[118] By 1600 also the banning of local Protestant publication gave a free hand to the Jesuit press in Graz.[119] This press largely concentrated on Latin and German texts, restricting Slovenian to instruction and preaching,[120] although

[116] ibid., pp. 182–93, 232, 244.
[117] Dolinar, 'La cultura controriformistica nell'Austra interna', p. 102.
[118] Cavazza, 'Religione, cultura e società', p. 118.
[119] Pörtner, *The Counter-Reformation in Central Europe*, pp. 196–203, 217–23.
[120] Vodipivec, 'Reformation and Counter-Reformation', p. 210.

the three catechisms of Peter Canisius, which were a vital element of the Jesuit instruction of the general populace, were translated into Slovenian in 1613–15.[121] Thereafter, however, for the rest of the period under review no further Slovenian texts were issued.

The rapid expansion of the Capuchins also added another important aspect to the matrix of Counter-Reformation activity. By 1608 Styria was elevated to the status of an independent province of the order.[122] Initially, the presence of an Italian administrative and mercantile cadre provided the first *point d'appui* for the settlement of Italian Capuchins in Gorizia in 1596. Other convents were also established in places such as Graz (1600), Cilli (1611), Pettau (1615), Radkersburg (1617), and Marburg (1620) which had significant Italian communities.[123] Italian evidently functioned as something of a *lingua franca* in the region and offered some possibilities of communication to non-Italian linguistic groups.[124] Yet while Italians spearheaded the order's penetration of the area, as elsewhere in Central Europe, the attractions of the simple and austere mode of life of the Capuchins rapidly led to an influx of local novices.[125] Consequently, the most important ministry of the Capuchins was soon to the German- and Slovenian-speaking populations, where, as in many other areas of Catholic Europe, their activities as preachers became particularly noted. Capuchin preaching to the Slovenian population, in particular, was evidently a significant factor in the almost totally successful re-Catholicization of that linguistic group.[126] While the Capuchins were arguably the single most successful order in terms of new foundations in Inner Austria, other branches of the Franciscan family enjoyed more modest success, with the creation of six new convents in the period 1632–69. The impact of the regular orders on the devotional life of the population was heightened by the mushrooming of confraternities. By 1669, twenty such bodies existed in Graz organized by the various mendicant orders, the parish clergy and, pre-eminently, the Society of Jesus.[127]

Yet while steady, indeed spectacular, advances in terms of re-Catholicization were recorded in Inner Austria under Ferdinand II and his successor through a potent combination of piecemeal coercive measures and an intensive attempt to foster a Catholic revival in the general population by campaigns of clerical reform, missionary outreach, improved pastoral surveillance and spiritual provision, and catechism, these processes suffered from significant limitations. The fact that the Austrian territories were not the seat of a major bishopric made a smooth line of ecclesiastical control more difficult. Various different enclaves existed which were immune to episcopal visitation, such as the diocese of Seckau itself, which was subject to the jurisdiction of the head of the chapter. Even new foundations, such as

[121] Dolinar, 'La cultura controriformistica nell'Austria interna', p. 105.
[122] Ingegneri, 'L'opera dei Cappuccini', p. 90.
[123] Pörtner, *The Counter-Reformation in Central Europe*, pp. 233–9.
[124] Cavazza, 'Religione, cultura e società', p. 111.
[125] Ingegneri, 'L'opera dei Cappuccini', p. 91.
[126] Vodipivec, 'Reformation and Counter-Reformation', p. 210.
[127] Pörtner, *The Counter-Reformation in Central Europe*, pp. 233–9.

the Society of Jesus, which had acquired jurisdiction over several different parishes, proved reluctant to surrender such rights to episcopal visitation. It is clear that very uneven success was enjoyed in terms of the creation of parish registers and the rate and efficacy of catechism varied considerably. The attempt to provide a sound economic basis for a new and more educated pastoral clergy through the imposition of ecclesiastical fees risked alienating an over-burdened peasantry which rose in revolt several times during the first half of the seventeenth century, most notably in 1635, which resulted in widespread devastation of ecclesiastical lands and a consequent diminution of clerical income. In Upper Styria, in particular, clerical poverty, the large size of the parishes, and the difficult geography combined to severely limit the capacity to inculcate new norms and devotions among the general population. The proximity of the Hungarian border also acted as a lifeline to Lutheranism in Upper Styria and Upper Carinthia as even peasants proved capable of travelling to attend services in a jurisdiction where Habsburg coercive measures were not capable of implementation.[128] In certain mountain valleys in Upper Carinthia, Protestantism managed to hang on until the tolerant era of Joseph II allowed it to emerge into the light again in 1781.[129]

Ferdinand II was certainly the decisive figure in what became an expanding movement of counter-reform and his experiences in Styria, and the conjoint approaches of coercion and evangelization which he brought to bear there, were destined to serve as a model in others of his expanding dominions. Moreover, the process of re-Catholicization was mutually reinforcing within the Habsburg lands. Not only did co-religionists in other Habsburg territories offer Protestants moral and sometimes political support, but the piecemeal nature of the dynasty's holdings in Central Europe meant that Protestants under pressure in individual areas could often locate spiritual services in other contiguous territories, perhaps most notably and consistently in Royal Hungary. The expanding nature of Ferdinand II's re-Catholicization projects, therefore, was significant in the process of cutting off these redoubts and sources of comfort. Yet, as in Styria itself, the movement of re-Catholicization by no means began *ab initio* with Ferdinand II. In the 1590s his first onslaught on Inner Austrian Protestantism occurred in the context of a determined campaign waged by the Emperor Rudolf II to effect Catholic reform in the ducal municipalities of Upper Austria following the suppression of a major peasant revolt in 1597.[130] In Lower Austria the Emperor struck against Protestant schools, forcing their transfer from Vienna to smaller towns in the region. There was a gradual reduction in the numbers of Protestants at court and a policy of promotion of Catholics was beginning to prompt conversion, as in the case of Karl von Liechtenstein.[131]

The events of the next decade, however, revealed both the fragility of the dynasty's internal cohesion and its financial and military power to sustain processes of

---

[128] ibid. pp. 186, 227–8, 230, 232, 244–6.
[129] Vodipivec, 'Reformation and Counter-Reformation', p. 210.
[130] Pörtner, *The Counter-Reformation in Central Europe*, p. 169.
[131] Edelmayer, 'La Nobiltà Austriaca', p. 64.

re-Catholicization. As a contest for power developed between Rudolf and his brother Matthias, Estates in Hungary, the *Erblande*, and Moravia were able to extort wide-ranging religious concessions, while in Silesia and Bohemia the Estates received the Letter of Majesty, which offered liberty of conscience to all subjects and granted further rights to the nobles, knights, and free towns.[132] Although the widespread nature of the crisis in the Habsburg lands was the key to the success of the dynasty's Protestant subjects in extracting religious concessions, the various Estates nevertheless failed to establish a sufficiently durable union to establish a system of collective security for freedom of worship. And although Protestant pressure forced Matthias to admit large numbers of Lutherans into the Lower Austrian Estate of Lords between 1600 and 1609, he largely halted this process after securing his position against Rudolf. From 1613 only one Protestant family was promoted. Furthermore, service to the state, with the substantial rewards which it entailed, was increasingly restricted to the Catholic nobility so that by 1620 almost two thirds of the Catholic nobles in Lower Austria enjoyed office as opposed to little more than ten per cent of their more numerous Protestant counterparts. Significantly, none of the Lower Austrian nobles who joined the rebellion belonged to this cohort of office-holders.[133] The Aulic Council had also become a Catholic bastion prior to 1620.[134] The reunification of the dynasty under the leadership of Ferdinand II, and the military and financial support which he received from his Habsburg cousin in Madrid, and his Wittelsbach cousin in Munich, gave the new Emperor the opportunity to exploit the weaknesses of the positions of the various Estates as guarantors of Protestant liberty.

Ferdinand's victory at the White Mountain in 1619 was of crucial importance not merely for Bohemia, which is discussed below, but also for the *Erblande*. Over a third of the nobility of Upper and Lower Austria were directly implicated in the revolt.[135] The consequences were cataclysmic. Because of its stronger support for the uprising, Upper Austria was perceived as guilty of rebellion and vulnerable to the same system of punishment as Bohemia itself. Although the archduchy was pawned to Bavaria until 1628, by 1624 a policy of expulsion of Protestant preachers and teachers had begun. An attack on the municipalities followed in 1625–6, in tandem with a savage repression of a peasant uprising which had been partially inspired by resistance to the imposition of parish priests and the undermining of what were conceived to be rights of self-administration of parishes.[136] In 1627 the nobility were confronted with the choice of emigration or conversion.[137] Because

[132] Evans, *Habsburg Monarchy*, pp. 52–3.

[133] Karin J. MacHardy, 'The Rise of Absolutism and Noble Rebellion in Early Modern Habsburg Austria, 1570–1620', *Comparative Studies in Society and History* 34 (1992), 407–38, at 418–22, 432.

[134] Karin J. MacHardy, 'Cultural Capital, Noble Identities and Family Strategies in Early Modern Habsburg Austria, 1579–1620', *Past & Present* 163 (1999), 36–75, at 70.

[135] MacHardy, 'The Rise of Absolutism and Noble Rebellion', 408.

[136] Hermann Rebel, 'The Rural Subject Population of Upper Austria' (PhD dissertation, University of California, Berkeley, 1976), pp. 322–5.

[137] Concerning the violent conflicts in Upper Austria see Hans Sturmberger, *Adam Graff Herberstorff: Herrschaft und Freiheit im konfessionellen Zeitalter* (Vienna: Verlag für Geschichte und Politik,1976), Chapters 3 and 4.

most of the estates of Lower Austria had remained loyal, there was no formal retraction of their religious rights but the greatly increased power of the dynasty allowed for a much stronger system of pressure. Preachers were expelled and the number of noblemen who could claim the right of liberty of conscience was highly circumscribed. By the end of Ferdinand's reign, practically all administrative posts in Lower Austria were in the hands of Catholics.[138]

As in Inner Austria, such coercive and repressive measures were then complemented by a positive and aggressive campaign of Catholic renewal and the Peace of Westphalia of 1648 copper-fastened the dynasty's ability to maintain this two-pronged approach. Inevitably the Society of Jesus and the Capuchins acted as shock-troops in the campaigns of evangelization. But Austria as a whole was also distinguished by a strong revival of the regular orders which had implanted themselves in the area prior to the Reformation. The Austrian provinces contained over twenty Benedictine houses to which were attached a number of celebrated schools, which fed many pupils to the order's university in Salzburg, and fifteen major Cistercian foundations. More numerous than either were the regular canons of the rule of St Augustine. After a precipitous decline in the sixteenth century, the monastic orders enjoyed a sharp renaissance in the period under review. Although a large part of the membership, including much of the leadership, was recruited from abroad, the monasteries themselves were rooted in the localities. Extremely wealthy, they came to serve as local foci of Catholic revival and of Baroque expressions of devotion. Monks frequently took over *cura animarum* in parishes within their sphere of influence and abbots were important and, in the case of Lower Austria, exclusive members of the clerical estate. The culture of pilgrimage became intimately tied up with monastic foundations, such as that of St Lambrecht, and monasteries acted as the centres of saints' cults. St Coloman, for instance, whose cult enjoyed wide local popularity was centrally associated with the abbey of Melk where he was buried. The monasteries with their deep historical embedding in the local landscapes of the Austrian provinces were also an important constituent in the gathering attempt to forge a notion of 'Catholic Austria', the idea of an intrinsically Catholic identity for the region, validated by tradition, history and the lives of Austrian saints, beside which Lutheranism was made to appear both transitory and deeply foreign.[139] The capstone of this process was arguably the *Pietas Austriaca* of the ruling dynasty itself, a notion of the special and extraordinary piety of the Habsburgs, which reached its climax in the seventeenth century, finding among its special expressions a devotion to the doctrine of the Immaculate Conception of the Virgin Mary in an era when the Barberini papacy fairly openly indicated its unwillingness to countenance official recognition of this doctrine.[140]

[138] Evans, *Habsburg Monarchy*, pp. 71, 76; Pörtner, *The Counter-Reformation in Central Europe*, pp. 138, 142.

[139] Evans, *Habsburg Monarchy*, pp. 181–91.

[140] Anna Coreth, *Pietas Austriaca. Österreichische Frömmigkeit in Barock* (Vienna: Verlag für Geschichte und Politik, 1982); Andrew H. Weaver, 'Music in the Service of Counter-Reformation Politics: The Immaculate Conception at the Habsburg Court of Ferdinand III (1637–57)', *Music and Letters* 87 (2006), 361–78, at 363–5.

The Habsburgs' in large part successful confrontation with Protestantism in the *Erblande* was the result of the coincidence of a number of different factors. The single-minded nature of Ferdinand II's commitment to the process of re-Catholicization was undoubtedly of key importance.[141] Alongside his personal religious convictions, the Emperor generated a political vision in which heresy became more or less synonymous with dubious loyalty. The narrowness of this vision undoubtedly had terrifying implications for the Protestant nobility of Austria, most notably perhaps in Styria itself, where the political quiescence of the Estates during the crisis of the *Bruderzwist* and the Bohemian insurrection failed to save them. But a corollary to this narrow intolerance, namely that conversion to Catholicism could yield extraordinary political dividends, was also of crucial importance.

In this regard, a useful contrast with late Tudor and Stuart rule in Ireland can be drawn. From the accession of Elizabeth I the English state in Ireland showed remarkably little inclination to incentivize the Old English elites of the island, let alone its Gaelic lords, to embrace the state church. Most tellingly, that great bastion of governmental support in Elizabethan Ireland, Black Tom of Ormond, so fundamental in the suppression of the Desmond rebellion of the 1580s, and in protecting the Queen's authority when it was most fragile in the late 1590s, was never given the lord deputyship. Over the course of a long century, English policy effectively operated to liquidate the existing elites rather than to convert them.[142] But the Habsburgs proved highly accommodating of converts, not merely in Austria but more generally throughout their domains. This pattern was set prior to Ferdinand II's accession to power outside Styria, as evidenced by the vertiginous career of the convert Karl Liechtenstein (and his two convert brothers, Maximilian and Gundakar)[143] who managed to court favour under both Rudolf and Matthias before becoming a key element in Ferdinand's repressive government of Bohemia.[144] Hans Ulrich Eggenburg offers another prime example of a convert who became Ferdinand II's first minister and was rewarded with a princely title as well as significant largesse from the conquest of Bohemia. In Styria itself families such as the Stubenbergs, Herbersteins, Sauraus, Trautmannsdorfs, and Windischgrätzes, which had flirted with Protestantism and lost some members to confessionally-necessitated exile, prospered splendidly through commitment to the church of Rome.[145] Critical in this regard was the political and cultural capital which nobles acquired through the holding of office for which Catholicism was increasingly indispensable.[146] Exclusion from the court was also erosive of noble status since it acted as a key locus for the forging of marriage networks.[147]

---

[141] In this regard see Robert Bireley, 'Ferdinand II: Founder of the Habsburg Monarchy' in R.J.W. Evans and T.V. Thomas (eds), *Crown, Church and Estates: Central European Politics in the Sixteenth and Seventeenth Centuries* (London and New York: Palgrave Macmillan, 1991), pp. 232–40.

[142] Tadhg Ó hAnnracháin, 'Plantation, 1580–1641' in Alvin Jackson (ed.), *The Oxford Handbook of Modern Irish History* (Oxford: Oxford University Press, 2014), pp. 291–315, at 308–9.

[143] Thomas Winkelbauer, *Fürst und Fürstendiener: Gundaker von Liechtenstein, ein österreichischer Aristokrat des konfessionellen Zeitalters* (Vienna: Oldenbourg Verlag, 1999), pp. 90–158.

[144] Evans, *Habsburg Monarchy*, p. 171.   [145] ibid., pp. 171–5.

[146] MacHardy, 'Rise of Absolutism and Noble Rebellion', 429–30.

[147] MacHardy, 'Cultural Capital, Noble Identities and Family Strategies', 71.

Many factors obviously influenced such conversion processes in addition to the possibility of court favour. The severity of peasant rebellion in Austria during the period, with major outbreaks in the 1590s, the 1620s, and the 1630s, probably made the church of Rome seem a reassuring bulwark of social order, particularly when Protestantism could be viewed as enabling questioning of the established order.[148] The disunity of Protestantism in the region generally was a major advantage to the cause of the Counter-Reformation. An inability between the Protestant parties of the various Habsburg domains to maintain coherent pressure on the dynasty ultimately allowed for their religious freedoms to be diluted in a piecemeal fashion. The political quiescence of Austrian Lutheranism, which had theological as well as political roots, was probably also of importance. In addition, Catholicism itself obviously had purely religious attractions. Polemically, Rome took increasing advantage of Protestant disunity to dismiss the credentials of any other confession to claim the identity of the church against which the gates of Hell would not prevail. And a sharpening Catholic historicism both bolstered the Roman church's sense of an identity reaching back to the apostles and increasingly dismissed the various forms of Protestantism as religions of innovation and recent development.[149] Programmes of clerical reform, and attractive practices of devotion, also acted as a draw but, possibly because pragmatic and material reasons played a significant role in encouraging conversion, a certain Baroque zeal became particularly evident in the religious devotion of some convert families. It is notable that convert houses, such as the Sauraus and Stubenbergs, for instance, were to the fore in the establishment of Capuchin convents in Styria.[150] A florid embracing of Catholicism in this fashion thus served to foreground the religious and devotional aspects of conversion rather than the murkier issues of ambition and self-promotion.

One of the reasons why conversion could offer such splendid rewards was the manner, as elsewhere in the dynasty's holdings, in which the great aristocratic families emerged as the key players in the control and administration of Habsburg Austria. Rather than seeking to clip the wings of over-mighty aristocrats, the dynasty encouraged their prominence and Habsburg rule depended on a close coincidence of interest between ruler and magnates. Nor was this surprising, for the social conditions of the area offered no other conceivable source of support for the Prince.[151] The relationship offered significant advantages to both parties. For the Habsburgs the manner in which a religion which emphasized values of devotion, respect for legitimate (namely Catholic) authority, and reverence for a church which validated the dynasty's rule, came to underpin the identity of the Austrian aristocracy offered a solid guarantee of loyalty and reliability. The magnates, for their part, not only enjoyed vast estates but came to dominate provincial administration. Loyalty to the dynasty was also rewarded with the conferring of honours and titles, both local

---

[148] In this regard see Joseph F. Patrouch, 'Who pays for building the Rectory? Religious conflicts in the Upper Austrian parish of Dietach, 1540–82', *Sixteenth Century Journal* 26 (1995), 297–310.
[149] In this regard, see in particular the section on Péter Pázmány below.
[150] Pörtner, *The Counter-Reformation in Central Europe*, p. 235.
[151] MacHardy, 'Rise of Absolutism and Noble Rebellion', 438.

and imperial. Furthermore, political reliability allowed for prominent aristocrats to benefit from the processes of consolidation of Habsburg power by acquiring lands and positions outside the *Erblande*.[152]

THE CZECH CROWN LANDS

The most important of the Habsburg possessions was arguably the kingdom of Bohemia, the crown of which passed into the dynasty's hands in 1526. The crown lands of Bohemia had a population in the sixteenth century of over three million, greater than contemporary England, and they were also rich both in terms of agricultural fertility and in mineral resources. Prague was one of Europe's major cities and the crown of Bohemia was a critical player in the electoral college of the Holy Roman Empire, effectively the key to the retention of the Imperial title by a Catholic candidate.[153] The re-Catholicization of Bohemia shows many similarities to the contemporary process in Austria, conducted under the same monarchs and utilizing broadly similar tactics, in which both stern coercion and evangelization played their parts. Yet while many parallels clearly exist between what occurred in the crown lands of St Wenceslas and Austria, the complex historical identity of the Czech lands, and their different ethnic and linguistic composition, combine to ensure that Bohemia represents a particularly striking case of Catholic Reformation.

This is not to suggest that the *Erblande* themselves were historically or linguistically homogenous. Significant communities of Slovenians and Italians, for instance, complicated the ethnic patterns of Austria. Nor were the Czech lands devoid of significant German communities, particularly in urban centres and in frontier regions which proved notably receptive to the Lutheran Reformation.[154] Multilingualism was to be a feature of the literary production of seventeenth- and eighteenth-century Bohemia.[155] The Teutonic identity of the Habsburgs themselves can perhaps be over-estimated. Rudolf II made Prague his effective capital rather than Vienna, Ferdinand III spoke Czech, and his successor Leopold was not intolerant of the language.[156] Yet even when such factors are taken into account, there were formidable reservoirs, not merely of confessional, but also of national and historical identity, which represented potential obstacles to the imposition of a Habsburg religious reformation in Bohemia.

In the fifteenth century, Bohemia was home to contemporary Europe's most successful heterodox religious evolution in the shape of the Hussite movement which successfully resisted annihilation against five crusading attempts sent against

[152] Evans, *Habsburg Monarchy*, pp. 169–70.
[153] Howard Louthan, *Converting Bohemia: Force and Persuasion in the Catholic Reformation* (Cambridge: Cambridge University Press, 2009), p. 13.
[154] Winfried Eberhard, 'Die deutsche Reformation in Böhmen 1520–1620' in Hans Rothe (ed.), *Deutsche in den böhmischen Ländern* (Cologne: Böhlau, 1992), pp. 103–23.
[155] Martin Svatoš, 'Zur Mehrsprachigkeit der Literatur in den böhmischen Ländern des 17. und 18. Jahrhunderts', *Wiener slavistisches Jahrbuch* 46 (2000), 33–42.
[156] Evans, *Habsburg Monarchy*, p. 214.

it by Pope and Emperor. The legacy of the fifteenth century was complicated by the onset of the Reformation. By the end of the sixteenth century, more than ninety per cent of the population of the Czech lands had abandoned the church of Rome. The strongest confession in the crown lands of the kingdom was the Utraquist church, the majority inheritor of the Hussite tradition, which offered the Eucharist in both species but which retained cognate features with Catholicism, such as veneration of images and relics and belief in the intercession of saints, which the Protestant confessions which emerged after Luther's breach with Rome dismissed as superstition. A more radical Hussite outcrop was the Bohemian Brethren. Anabaptism had emerged as a minority community in Moravia, many of the nobility were Lutheran and strains of the Reformed tradition were also present in the kingdom.[157] Since 1575, while Catholicism and the Utraquist church were legally recognized, tacit recognition had been given also to adherents of the Augsburg Confession and to the Bohemian Brethren and in 1609 the Letter of Majesty extorted from Rudolf II granted both these groupings full legal status.[158]

Bohemia's Counter-Reformation was largely a product of the seventeenth century although, as in Austria, some stirrings were visible in the previous century. The Society of Jesus was introduced to Prague in 1555 and the archiepiscopal see, vacant since 1431, was revived six years later. The first incumbent, Antonín Brus (1561–80), had attended the Council of Trent, and like his two successors, Marin Mohelnicky (1580–90) and Zbynek Berka z Dube (1590–1606), was a proponent of Catholic renewal.[159] The Premonstratensian monastery at Bruch in Moravia became something of a cultural centre for a revivified Catholicism while, at Strahov, Johann Lohelius instituted a movement of reform which gained him wide recognition. Critically also a number of important aristocrats emerged as key actors in the Catholic party, most notably Jaroslav Martinic and the convert Vilém Slavata.[160] Nevertheless, before 1620 at best a quarter of the kingdom's aristocrats were Catholics and the proportion was significantly lower among the lesser nobility.[161] Undoubtedly, therefore, it was the victory at the White Mountain in 1620 which opened the way to a thorough campaign of re-Catholicization.[162] Not only was the Emperor given a new freedom of action by military success but he was imbued with the conviction that the crime of rebellion had released him from the obligation to stand by past precedents and agreements.[163]

[157] Louthan, *Converting Bohemia*, pp. 5–6.

[158] Zdeněk David, 'Lutherans, Utraquists and the Bohemian Confession of 1575', *Church History*, 68 (1999), 294–336, at 298, 336.

[159] James R. Palmitessa, 'The Prague Uprising of 1611: Property, Politics and Catholic Renewal in the Early Years of Habsburg Rule', *Central European History* 31 (1998), 299–328, at 302, 315.

[160] Petr Maťa, 'Constructing and Crossing Confessional Boundaries: The High Nobility and the Reformation of Bohemia' in Louthan et al. (eds), *Diversity and Dissent*, pp. 10–29, at 25; Evans, *Habsburg Monarchy*, pp. 47–8.

[161] James Van Horn Melton, 'The nobility in the Bohemian and Austrian lands, 1620–1780' in H.M. Scott (ed.), *The European Nobilities* (two vols, New York: Longman, 1995) 2, pp. 105–11.

[162] Jaroslav Pánek, 'The Religious Question and the Political System in Bohemia before and after the Battle of the White Mountain' in Evans and Thomas, *Crown, church and estates*, pp. 129–48.

[163] Hans-Wolfgang Bergerhausen, 'Die "Verneuerte Landesordnung" in Böhmen 1627: ein Grunddokument des habsburgischen Absolutismus', *Historische Zeitschrift* 271 (2001), 327–52, at 330–1.

The campaign of Catholic renewal occurred in a series of phases. In the immediate wake of the victory a series of confiscations was launched, producing a significant amount of largesse for redistribution by the dynasty, in which the Catholic minority of the indigenous Czech nobility were notable participants.[164] This was accompanied by an orchestrated execution of twenty-seven rebels in Prague constructed as symbolic cleansing of the kingdom of the crime of rebellion. In sharp contrast with previous experiences of Habsburg leniency, the victims included prominent members of the Czech nobility. Immediately after the executions, all Calvinist and Brethren teachers and preachers were proscribed, causing severe damage to the educational infrastructure of the kingdom. In 1622 the Anabaptist community in Moravia was forced into exile and the following year all non-Catholic clergy were officially proscribed in the Czech lands. A year later a series of laws were introduced aimed at forcing Protestants to conform to Catholic norms, including fasting on Fridays and cessation of work on saints' days. Training for the professions was limited to Catholics and restrictions were imposed on Protestant participation in a variety of economic activities. Ordinances were supplemented by the use of military force. The billeting of soldiers on non-Catholic households offered a crude but effective inducement to consider conversion to the church of Rome. In a fashion similar to the tactics first utilized in Styria, commissions were created to review the conditions of the parishes.[165] In 1627 a new constitution was decreed which abolished the elective character of the monarchy, vested the right to grant patents of nobility in the crown alone, reconstituted the Catholic clergy as the first Estate of the kingdom, abrogated the Letter of Majesty, proscribed all Christian confessions other than Catholicism, and granted German equal status with the Czech language. Non-Catholics were given six months in which to convert before being forced to leave the kingdom. In the event between twenty and twenty-five per cent of the nobility went into exile, a proportion almost matched by the emigration of burghers from urban settlements. For such emigrants, the possibility of a Protestant victory in the Thirty Years War represented the chief hope for a restoration of their status but, in the event, despite significant incursions into the Czech lands by Protestant forces in the course of the conflict, the Peace of Westphalia copper-fastened Habsburg control over the kingdom. Over the course of the decade after White Mountain a series of edicts was issued by Karl Von Liechtenstein attempting to restrict the printing and circulation of non-Catholic material. A commission was created to oversee all printing houses and to inspect the wares of booksellers and a programme of censorship was instituted, although its effectiveness was clearly hampered by the difficult conditions of 1630s and 1640s Bohemia and rivalry for control between the Archbishop of Prague and the Society of Jesus.[166]

[164] Victor L. Tapié, *The Rise and Fall of the Habsburg Monarchy* (London: Pall Mall Press, 1971), pp. 93–9.

[165] Louthan, *Converting Bohemia*, pp. 22–34, 179–81, 190.

[166] Evans, *Habsburg Monarchy*, pp. 198–9; Louthan, *Converting Bohemia*, pp. 7, 214–15; Berger-hausen, 'Die "Verneuerte Landesordnung" in Böhmen 1627', 331–52.

As in Austria, the coercive elements of the Habsburg programme were supplemented by attempts to create structures which would allow for the inculcation of a new devotion to Catholicism. Central in this regard was the educational role of the Society of Jesus and in the decades following the reassertion of Habsburg control nineteen new Jesuit colleges were founded in the lands of the Bohemian crown, which were to be critically important in the task of forming a new Catholic elite.[167] Moreover, in the wake of the White Mountain the Jesuits emerged as key players in the publishing trade through their effective control of the academic press. The Society also actively engaged in missionary evangelization, although they were by no means the only Catholic body involved in this activity. A significant factor in increasing their efficiency in this respect was the increasingly local provenance of the membership in Bohemia. By 1623 the Czech section of the Society was sufficiently numerous to justify the formation of an independent province. Even at the highest intellectual echelon natives came increasingly to the fore: by the middle of the seventeenth century the majority of the professors in the Jesuit University at Prague traced their origins to the Crown lands rather than any exterior location.[168] Both in their patronage of Christmas nativity scenes, which they first introduced in the 1560s and which became extremely popular as foci of Catholic devotion, and in their wider exploitation of religious theatre, the Society played a vital role in inflecting the urban culture of the Czech lands with a new sense of Catholic devotion. Much of their drama was explicitly polemical but it also sponsored practices of piety, not least because the Marian confraternities organized by the Society were frequently involved in the production of religious plays. But while the towns were a central aspect of the programme of religious renewal, extensive attempts were also made revive Catholicism in the countryside and among the peasant population. Although originally a largely urban phenomenon, confraternities spread rapidly into the countryside as well in the period after 1620.

The process of outreach to the localities was certainly impeded by the extreme conditions of war which afflicted Bohemia down to the Peace of Westphalia. Nevertheless, it is evident that a great deal of energy was expended in a multifaceted attempt to bring the mass of the Bohemian population into closer contact with the church. The diocese of Prague was divided into vicariates, more than twenty by the early 1640s, to facilitate a more intense process of surveillance and education. The success of Catholic endeavour in this regard was probably facilitated by the numerous practices which had continued within the Utraquist church and which could serve as bridges to ease transition into patterns of Catholic devotion. The Hussite mass, for instance, was structurally highly similar to its Catholic equivalent and the liturgical calendar of the two confessions was largely identical. Visitors to Bohemia of a more advanced Protestant stamp, such as Fynes Moryson, could be surprised at the extent to which beliefs which they labelled as Popish

---

[167] Olivier Chaline, *La Reconquête Catholique de L'Europe Centrale XVIe–XVIIe siècle* (Paris: Les Editions du Cerf, 1998), pp. 47–8, 76.
[168] Olivier Châline, 'Frontières Religieuses: La Bohême après la Montagne Blanche' in Tóth, *Frontiers of Faith*, pp. 55–65, at 58.

superstition survived among the Utraquist population. The cult of St Wenceslas, for example, which had retained real currency within the Utraquist community offered significant possibilities to Catholic missionaries. In sharp contrast to the Winter King, Ferdinand II identified strongly with the martyr and promoted his cult and Wenceslas rapidly became a prominent figure in the burgeoning Catholic hagiography of Bohemia.[169]

Catechism was naturally a fundamental aspect of the processes of re-Catholicization. In 1572 a Czech version of Peter Canisius's *Small Catechism* was published in Prague, the first of more than twenty editions down to the mid-eighteenth century. In the 1620s František Rozdrażewski produced a handbook aimed primarily at combatting Utraquist championing of communion under two species, *Roudnice nad Labem* (*The Dispute of the Chalice*) and a wide array of catechetical material continued to pour off the presses to underpin the activity of missionaries of various orders. Yet while catechetical material was primarily aimed at providing the basis of orthodox belief, missionary activity also operated to woo the rural population of the Czech lands. It provided rituals and practices of comfort and support, such as widespread use of Holy Water and of *Agnus Dei*, and accommodated and integrated aspects of folk practice, such as painted Easter eggs, celebratory bonfires, and the burning of effigies on Laetare Sunday, into the rhythm of Catholic devotion. Bohemian Catholicism also actively cultivated a wide array of sensory material to underpin the process of mission. As in Hungary, music had been an important part of non-Catholic culture and Catholic missionaries recognized the necessity to confront traditions of Protestant hymns by the propagation of Catholic alternatives. In the hands of a figure such as the Moravian priest, Jan Rozenplut, this provision of Catholic hymns became part of a wider project of combatting the accretions of centuries of error through which the Czech population had been led away from salvation.[170]

To an even greater extent than in Austria, Catholic reformers were faced with a challenge in constructing an image of *Bohemia Sancta*. For two centuries the kingdom had been renowned as a centre of religious heterodoxy. Yet, despite the magnitude of the challenge, it was a task into which Czech advocates of Catholic renewal poured themselves with gusto. Central to this process were projects of antiquarianism which uncovered the pre-Hussite Catholic heritage of Bohemia, and in doing so providing the historical underpinning for the notion of a naturally Catholic Czech identity. By highlighting the sufferings of Catholic martyrs, not least in the Hussite period, they offered an alternative vision of Czech history which foregrounded the constancy of its martyrs rather than its susceptibility to heresy. An important tool in this regard was the practice of pilgrimage which came to the fore as one of the defining features of the Catholic devotionalism which emerged in Bohemia after White Mountain. Pilgrimage became a staple expression of Catholic identity for all social classes. The road between Prague and Stará Boleslav,

---

[169] Louthan, *Converting Bohemia*, pp. 163–6, 184–8, 201–3, 216–17, 250; Châline, 'Frontières Religieuses', p. 61.
[170] Louthan, *Converting Bohemia*, pp. 192–4, 205–8, 234–6.

the site of Wenceslas's martyrdom, became an expression of the commitment of the social elite, including the imperial family, to the person and legacy of the saint. But, equally, large swathes of the general population found in pilgrimage an opportunity to express their need for, and faith in, divine intervention to assist them in their earthly trials. Particularly significant pilgrimage practices developed around the sacred past of the Czech lands, commemorating the Catholic evangelists who brought the Roman faith to the region, the holy figures who flourished in the pre-Hussite era, and the Catholic martyrs to Hussite and Protestant violence.

Of critical importance in this regard too was the cult of saints. As Howard Louthan has pointed out, the heretical past of Bohemia brought a new urgency to the task of creating reservoirs of Czech sanctity which could be used as foundational capital in the creation of Catholic identities. In this regard, he has highlighted the role of the translation of the remains of St Norbert from Magdeburg to Prague at a cost of almost 11,000 thalers in 1626 as a ritual injection of sanctity into a kingdom tainted by heresy, a pattern replicated by figures such as Archbishop Harrach and the Capuchins in their importation of the bodies of martyrs and relics.[171] The cult of saints was thus an important tool in constructing a new Czech Catholicism. Similarly to Austria, saints' cults operated at both a transnational and local level. In this regard the universal saints of the church helped link Bohemian Catholicism to the wider family of the Roman church. Not surprisingly given the nature of the Habsburgs' championing of the Immaculate Conception and their attribution of victory at the White Mountain to the Virgin Mary's support, Marian devotion became an intrinsic element of Catholic renewal but a proliferation of cults of native saints played a role in copper-fastening the notion of an indigenous Catholic identity. In particular, the devotion to the child of Prague came to play an important role.

The development of this cult brought together a number of important features of the renewal of Bohemian Catholicism. In the first place, it demonstrated the manner in which the translation of an originally Spanish devotion to the new context of reviving Catholicism could take on an extraordinary vigour and life of its own within an environment where the promotion of Catholic devotion had become imbued with such cultural and political significance. Of critical importance in terms of the devotion to the Infant of Prague, too, was the role of female patrons. The original statue of the child of Prague was brought to Bohemia by Isabella Manrique de Lara y Mendoza. Her daughter Polyxena Pernstein then bequeathed the artefact to the Discalced Carmelites, who as an order were to make great use of the prestige of the miraculous statue to build their own reputation in Bohemia. A major figure in consolidating the reputation of the statue was Alžběta Kolovratová who attributed her recovery from illness to the Infant Jesus. She and her husband became generous donors to the convent. Other aristocratic women too, most notably Anna Polyxena Slavatová and Benigna Kateřina Lobkovic, made major financial contributions. The cult of the child of Prague thus offered a space both to aristocratic patrons, particularly women, to invest in a devotion which rapidly came to appear intrinsically Bohemian, and to the Discalced Carmelites to boost their prestige and establish their reputation within the city of Prague.

A similar trajectory can be seen in the cult of the Loreto shrine which resulted in the construction of forty-five Loreto chapels on Czech lands between 1584 and 1729. Significantly the majority of these were founded by members of the Czech nobility. Once again women and a religious order, namely the Capuchins, played a prominent role, most notably Markéta Lobkovic who provided the property for the first Capuchin cloister in Prague and then Benigna Kateřina Lobkovic. The Capuchins heavily promoted the Loreto devotion which offered them an outstanding opportunity to forge links with a Czech nobility for whom a florid Catholicism was becoming increasingly necessary as a marker of the new identity of a ruling caste.[172] While the Capuchins represented a new and dynamic post-Reformation element in the renewal of Czech Catholicism, older religious structures also revived. Close to moribund in the 1570s, the Observant Franciscans began a slow but successful revival from the turn of the century. This involved a marked effort to ensure that Franciscan ideals of strict poverty were not only realized but made manifest and that the conduct of the friars would lead to general edification rather than scandal of the populace.[173]

The importance of these alternative and non-Jesuit reservoirs of Catholic practice and identity has run the risk of being under-estimated. To a considerable extent the *modus operandi* of the Society of Jesus is one which is particularly comprehensible to a modern sensibility. With its streamlined structures of authority, its long Early Modern Generalships which allow for a clear apprehension of the preoccupations of its leadership, and the abundant and self-promoting source material which the Jesuits produced, the Society offers itself as a relatively accessible matrix of Early Modern sensibility. Particularly in East-Central Europe the Jesuits as a grouping can be easily assimilated within the contours of a general theory of Catholic confessionalization. By contrast, the various mendicant orders, rooted in a pre-Reformation past, and a spirituality constantly informed by their medieval heritage, with far more complex outlines of constantly shifting authority, can appear less easily comprehensible. Yet, as in Poland, in both Austria and Bohemia re-Catholicization was a more super-abundant process than mere dynastic and Jesuit-driven programmes of control. As Regina Pörtner has noted, for instance, Jesuit resistance to allowing aristocratic ostentation in their churches disturbed the continuation of patterns of late medieval piety which found an alternative expression with the mendicant orders.[174]

In this regard the tension which accumulated around the resistance of traditional Catholic institutions of pedagogy to Jesuit intrusion into their domain in Cracow, Vienna, and Prague is of particular interest. Throughout East-Central

---

[172] ibid., pp. 61–5, 133–4, 160–1, 248–62.

[173] Martin Elbel, 'The Making of a Perfect Friar' in Jaroslav Miller and László Kontler (eds), *Friars, Nobles and Burghers—Sermons, Images and Prints: Studies of Culture and Society in Early-Modern Europe in memoriam István György Tóth* (Budapest: Central European University Press, 2010), pp. 149–78, at 170–2.

[174] Pörtner, *The Counter-Reformation in Central Europe*, p. 11.

Europe the role of the educational establishments of the Society of Jesus was undoubtedly of key importance both in terms of forming a cultivated lay elite confessionally committed to Rome and in the training of better-educated clergy imbued with Tridentine conceptions of their responsibilities. However, this should not obscure the degree to which older educational institutions resented Jesuit prominence and interference into what they perceived as their rightful territory and the manner in which they engaged in often successful resistance. In Cracow, Prague, and Vienna,[175] particularly high-profile conflicts occurred. Such frictions were frequently deplored by Catholic observers but the power of such institutions, and in particular their capacity to appeal to notions of traditional rights, was not necessarily an obstacle to processes of Catholic reform. Internal competition possibly served as a spur to excellence for both the Jesuits and their opponents. Moreover, the existence within Early Modern Catholicism of alternatives to the Jesuits, and in particular to the close connection which was perceived to exist between the Jesuits and both the Habsburg dynasty and Sigismund III in Poland, was probably a source of strength rather than weakness.

It is clear that, as in contemporaneous Austria, it was the nobility which became the central linchpin of the new Catholic society erected in the aftermath of the Habsburg triumph at the White Mountain. The movement of nobility back towards the church of Rome took on increasing momentum during the 1590s. It became evident in the increasing use of certain Christian names, such as František and Ignác, and in the conscious self-identification of confessional allegiance to Rome in testamentary documents. It may have been facilitated by the fact that many members of the nobility in sixteenth-century Bohemia and Moravia seem to have been reluctant to make clear confessional choices[176] and that the drift towards Protestantism was of relatively recent origin with many conversions not occurring until after 1550.[177] As in Austria conversion brought great rewards and having family members tainted by heresy and implication in rebellion was not necessarily a bar to spectacular advancement. For example, although Heřman Černín's eldest brother was executed for his close involvement with the Winter King, he himself became chief judge and high steward of Bohemia. The revolution which occurred after the White Mountain opened opportunities for new families to establish themselves within the crown lands, as the Habsburgs rewarded military service with Czech estates and opened the door to Austrian magnates such as the Eggenbergs

---

[175] Stolarski, *Friars on the Frontiers*, pp. 28–41; Louthan, *Converting Bohemia*, pp. 88–96; Bireley, *Religion and Politics*, p. 10.

[176] Josef Válka, 'Die "Politiques": Konfessionelle Orientierung und politische Landesinteressen in Böhmen und Mähren (bis 1630)' in Joackim Bahlke, Hans-Jürgen Bömelburg, and Norbert Kersken (eds), *Ständefreiheit und Staatsgestaltung in Ostmitteleuropa: Übernationale Gemeinsamkeiten in der politischen Kultur vom 16–18. Jahrhundert* (Leipzig: De Gruyter, 1996), pp. 229–41.

[177] Maťa, 'Constructing and Crossing Confessional Boundaries', pp. 23–5; Petr Maťa, 'Vorkonfessionelles, überkonfessionelles, transkonfessionelles Christentum: Prolegomena zu einer Untersuchung der Konfessionalität des böhmischen und mährischen Hochadels zwischen Hussitismus und Zwangskatholisierung' in Joachim Bahlcke, Karen Lambrecht and Hans-Christian Maner (eds), *Konfessionelle Pluralität als Herausforderung: Koexistenz und Konflikt in Spätmittelalter und Frühen Neuzeit. Winfried Eberhard zum 65. Geburtstag* (Leipzig: Leipziger Universitätsverlag, 2006), pp. 307–31.

and the Trautmannsdorfs and, in Moravia in particular, to Hungarians to establish themselves. Nevertheless, the key to Habsburg administration of Bohemia remained a restricted circle of Czech magnates.[178]

The contrast here with Ireland is again instructive. Broadly speaking, the thrust of late Tudor and Stuart policy was to entrust political power and land to ethnically English families. In the decades following the Williamite wars in Ireland up to seventy-five per cent of members who actively participated in the House of Lords of the Irish parliament traced their origin to settlers who had entered the kingdom since the onset of the Irish Reformation in the 1530s. A mere five active parliamentary families can be easily classified as indigenously Gaelic, despite the fact that Irish was still the vernacular of the bulk of the population.[179] While other factors certainly affected the Irish case, it can be surmised that a sense of ethnic and historical difference from the general population may have played a part in the lack of promotion of effective evangelical activity on the part of the Irish Protestant nobility. By contrast, a particular feature of the Bohemian nobility who embraced Catholicism with such fervour after 1620 was their patronization of processes of indigenization of the religion among the general population. In Bohemia this was exemplified by the Lobkovic and Martinic families who proved ardent supporters of the movement of Catholic renewal in their considerable territories. In Moravia, similarly, the role of the Dietrichstein and Lichtenstein families proved key. Their influence in this regard was enhanced by the growing power of the magnate families who by the last quarter of the seventeenth century controlled almost two thirds of the landed wealth of the kingdom, almost double the proportion in their possession in 1615. Land, titles, and office were obvious blandishments for the attachment of the nobility to Catholicism, as was the opportunity to acquire a foothold in other Habsburg domains through loyal service, but the religion also offered somewhat more subtle attractions. The cosmopolitanism of Catholicism lay not merely in the possibility of integration into the wider world of the Habsburg territories including the court[180] but also into a far broader system of Catholic culture centred in particular on the metropolitan centres of France, Spain, and Italy. In addition, for a nobility naturally wary of social unrest the ceremonial forms of Catholicism provided a set of rituals which centred the elite in a hegemonic system of power and control.[181] In this regard it is apparent that the movement of Catholic renewal was based on a system of social discipline of the Bohemian peasantry which apparently remained largely constant during the process of religious change.[182]

---

[178] Evans, *Habsburg Monarchy*, pp. 201–14.

[179] Toby Barnard, *A New Anatomy of Ireland: The Irish Protestants, 1649–1770* (New Haven and London: Yale University Press, 2003), pp. 23–4.

[180] Petr Maťa, 'Der Adel aus den böhmischen Landern am Kaiserhof 1620–1720: Versuch eine falsche Frage richtig zu lösen' in Václav Bůžek and Pavel Král (eds), *Šlechta v habsburské monarchii a císařský dvur, České Budějovice Opera historica*, 10 (2003), 191–203.

[181] Louthan, *Converting Bohemia*, pp. 48, 50, 58–9, 81–2.

[182] Sheilagh Ogilvie, ' "So that every subject knows how to behave": Social Disciplining in Early Modern Bohemia', *Comparative Studies in Society and History* 48 (2006), 38–78, at 49.

Significant limitations naturally existed on the Habsburg programme of re-Catholicization. Yet in terms of creation of identity, the processes instituted after the White Mountain certainly enjoyed very considerable successes. By 1651 the regime was confident that Bohemia was no longer home to any publically significant heretical population, even if figures such as Cardinal Harrach and the Capuchin, Valerio Magni, entertained doubts about the nature of the conversions which had been obtained.[183] Indigenous Protestantism eventually largely withered away and when toleration was finally extended in the late eighteenth century only a tiny minority of the population took advantage of the relaxation of the law to claim a Protestant identity. Naturally, as in Lutheran Scandinavia, or Anglican England, where Catholicism dwindled in a similar fashion, this did not necessarily mean the successful inculcation of a complete religious revolution. Huge challenges existed for the Catholic church, as for other state churches throughout Europe, in reaching out to the dark corners of the land, to equip the general population with the basic understanding of faith which was believed necessary to salvation. It has been pertinently argued that the most measureable achievement of the Bohemian Counter-Reformation represented the triumph of Catholic orthopraxy and that it is far more difficult to appreciate the degree to which the inculcation of a genuine sense of religious understanding of Catholicism actually occurred.[184] Yet, on the other hand, it is clear that a self-consciously Catholic native elite was formed which both internalized the self-understanding of what the post-Tridentine church saw as the essence of religion and attempted to bring it to a wider audience. In addition, bringing the population into contact with the sacraments of the Roman church, and establishing the Catholic clergy as their authentic intermediaries with the sacred and thus cutting them off from the heretical wolves in sheep's clothing who would lead them to their inevitable damnation, was for Catholic reformers the *sine qua non* of possible salvation for the Bohemian population. While often conscious of the limitations of what they could achieve, they had a united perspective on the vital importance of these aspects of religion and it was this which underpinned the missionary fervour which they displayed.

The successes of the Bohemian Counter-Reformation are also particularly interesting because of the manner in which the Habsburgs managed to prevent the process from being subverted by ethnic or national resentments. Given the harshness of the manner in which the dynasty deployed an extensive coercive apparatus to underpin the religious authority of the Roman church, this is especially significant. In this regard, the fact that Bohemian re-Catholicization was allowed to take on Czech habiliments, in the construction of a sense of reconnection with a glorious Catholic past, in the evangelical use of the vernacular, and in the central role played by native magnates in overseeing the administration of the kingdom, was surely of importance. Thus despite the brutality of much of what occurred, a sufficient space was created which allowed for collaboration and the sharing of significant rewards between the dynasty and native elements of Czech society.

---

[183] Châline, 'Frontières Religieuses', p. 62.
[184] Louthan, *Converting Bohemia*, pp. 8, 320–1.

HUNGARY

As a vital element of the Habsburg domains, Hungary offers an intriguing parallel, not only with Austria and Bohemia, but also with Poland because of the degree to which the dynasty lacked the free hand in the period under review to deploy coercion to assist in the programme of re-Catholicization. Moreover, the fact that the Habsburgs considered themselves as the rightful heirs over the entire territory of the medieval kingdom of St Stephen, most of which was actually under the authority of the Ottoman empire or its semi-autonomous client state, the principality of Transylvania, also offers the possibility of evaluating the degree to which the dynasty was able to promote Catholic renewal in areas where it lacked, not merely a coercive apparatus, but also the softer power of monarchical favour and the promise of office and title.

First constituted as a Christian kingdom in the eleventh century, and then reconstituted after the Mongol invasions, by the fifteenth century the crown of St Stephen was a major power in Central Europe. The shattering defeat of Móhács in August 1526, however, led to a prolonged occupation of much of the kingdom by the Ottoman Turks, including the traditional capital Buda, the establishment of a largely autonomous principality in Transylvania, and the acquisition of the crown of St Stephen and a limited north-western portion of the old kingdom by the Habsburg dynasty. The reality of this tripartheid division coexisted uneasily with the historical memory of the greater and unified kingdom of the early sixteenth century. From the perspective of the Habsburgs and their *Magyar* supporters, the Turkish *Hódoltság* was a temporary occupation of lands which still by right pertained to the throne of St Stephen. The military might of the Ottomans, however, meant that no significant inroads were to be made into this occupation during the period under review.

Not only was Royal Hungary a truncated expression of a larger aspiration but in Transylvania it faced a genuine competitor for the allegiances of the *Magyar* population. The succession of *Magyar* princes who emerged in Transylvania represented an alternative political and cultural focus for the population of Habsburg Royal Hungary. Habsburg aspirations to acquire the Transylvanian lands of the old kingdom and the Transylvanian interest in adding portions or all of Royal Hungary to their own principality was an inevitable recipe for conflict which boiled over in a particularly devastating fashion during the long war between the Habsburgs and the Turks at the beginning of the seventeenth century. Frustrations with the failure to make military advances against Ottoman power and resentment of the intemperate attempts of Hungarian Catholics (with dynastic support) to undermine the dominant position of Protestantism in the kingdom, through the trial of the Lutheran magnate, István Illésházy, the attempted gagging of the *országgyűlés* (Diet) from discussing religious grievances, and a use of military power to further the repossession of churches in north-eastern Hungary, provoked a massive rebellion under the leadership of István Bocskai. The rebellion resulted in the ruin of the Habsburg coercive strategy and in the Peace of Vienna of 1606, concluded in the same year as the Treaty of Zsitvatörök, Bocskai was recognized as Prince of

Transylvania and freedom of religion was granted to the main non-Catholic denominations of the orders of the kingdom.[185] The Peace of Vienna effectively precluded the use of Bohemian-style repressive tactics for the rest of the period under review, not least because the frequent assembly of the Hungarian Diet gave a consistent forum for Protestant opinion.[186]

While it is difficult to put precise figures on the confessional complexion of the Hungarian population, it is clear that the overwhelming majority had abandoned allegiance to the church of Rome by the end of the sixteenth century.[187] The lack of coercive power available to the Habsburg regime in Hungary was lamented by native Hungarian Catholics. Miklós Dallos, the Bishop of Vács, reported sorrowfully to the newly founded congregation of *Propaganda Fide* in 1622 that in Hungary, where the workings of the Inquisition were not permitted, there was no possibility of using law or punishment to uphold the Catholic faith and acquire conversions. In the same year the single most influential figure in the movement of Catholic renewal in Hungary, Péter Pázmány, rather bitterly echoed the same message: even Catholic bishops lacked the power to coerce their own serfs into the Catholic faith. It was only 'suavi tractu', by gentle means, that the movement of conversion could be advanced.[188]

A concern not to provoke the Protestant population was also heightened by the legitimate fear that interference with religious liberties might lead to a general defection to the Princes of Transylvania who during this period were not merely Protestant in religion but presided over a system of confessional tolerance in their own domain.[189] Three times in the period under review this emerged as a real possibility. The Bocskai rebellion was followed by a series of conflicts between Gábor Bethlen and the Habsburgs. In 1620 Bethlen successfully invaded Royal Hungary and occupied the capital, Bratislava (Pozsony). A Hungarian Diet offered him the crown of Hungary which had been surrendered into his possession and he ultimately accepted the offer repeated to him at another Diet convened in Besztercebánya in August 1620.[190] The renaissance of Habsburg power following the victory at the White Mountain subsequently forced Bethlen to renounce the crown in the Peace of Nikolsburg of December/January 1621/1622.[191] However, the Prince of

---

[185] Evan, *Habsburg Monarchy*, pp. 51–2.

[186] In the immediate background to the rebellion of the 1640s were strong feelings of resentment at the monarch's failure to convene a Diet within the mandatory three-year period: see István Hajnal (ed.), *Esterházy Miklós Nádor Iratai I. Kormányzattörténeti Iratok: Az 1642 Évi Meghiúsult Országgyűlés Időszaka (1640 December–1643 Március)* (Budapest: Esterházy Pál Herceg Kiadása, 1930), pp. xiv–xv.

[187] István György Tóth, 'Old and New Faith in Hungary, Turkish Hungary, and Transylvania' in R. Po-chia Hsia (ed.), *A Companion to the Reformation World* (Oxford: Blackwell Publishing, 2004), pp. 205–22, at 206.

[188] István György Tóth, 'A Propaganda megalapítása és magyarország,' *Történelmi Szemle* 42: 1–2 (2000), 19–68, at 42–5.

[189] Teréz Oborni, *Erdély Fejedelmi* (Budapest: Pannonica Kiadó, 2002), p. 105; Vilmos Fraknói, *A Magyar Királyválasztások Története* (Máriabesnyő-Gödöllő: Attraktor Kft., 2005), p. 190.

[190] Fraknói, *A Magyar Királyválasztások Története*, pp. 204–6.

[191] Ervin Liptai (ed.) *Magyarország Hadtörténete* (two vols, Budapest: Zrínyi Katonai Kiadó, 1984), 1, p. 259; Oborni, *Erdély Fejedelmi*, pp. 116–17.

Transylvania did substantially increase his Hungarian territory at Habsburg expense, gaining lifetime control of seven counties from Royal Hungary, the so-called *partium*. During the 1640s another popular Protestant Prince of Transylvania, György I Rákóczi, similarly threatened to make use of the dynasty's reverses in the Thirty Years War to overthrow Habsburg rule in Hungary completely, although eventually he too, like Bethlen, was forced to make do with the territorial acquisition of the *partium* rather than the actual crown.[192]

The alienation of the affections of their Hungarian subjects to the Princes of Transylvania was not the only danger of a coercive confessional policy. Religious conflict also risked opening the door to the Ottoman threat. As Zsigmond Forgách, the *nádor* or palatine of the kingdom, noted in 1618 prior to the Bethlen invasion of Hungary, history demonstrated that confessional strife was a key factor in Turkish expansion, evidencing the fall of Esztergom to Turkish arms during the long Habsburg–Turkish war in this context.[193] Prior to the Rákóczi invasion, another *nádor*, the extraordinarily influential Hungarian convert, Miklós Eszterházy, strongly echoed this same message in a memorandum to Ferdinand III. In Hungary, Eszterházy insisted, accommodations simply had to be made with the non-Catholic subjects of the realm.[194] Given the constant Ottoman attempts to make gains from Hungarian dissensions, the regime could not afford to use the coercive measures which had been applied in other Habsburg territories. As the *nádor* noted:

> this kingdom of Hungary and its inhabitants are placed in the very vicinity and jaws of the Turks and to their great misfortune have experienced in various motions and changes Turkish savagery, which in our turbulent waters in the manner of some fisherman tries to extend its nets, and ever deeper, and has always wished to be and been the happy third between two disputing parties. Which enormities, [of toleration] even if they are far too harmful to the propagation of the catholic religion, neither however do I esteem them capable of being removed by those means which Your Majesty has used in others of his realms and provinces both because of the concessions made and also because of the vicinity of our perfidious Turkish enemies, lest in some way seeking to bend the tree, we are broken, with great detriment both to religion and to the region.[195]

---

[192] Lászlo Makkai, András Mócsy, and Zoltán Szász (eds), *Erdély Története* (three vols, Budapest: Akadémiai Kiadó, 1986), 2, pp. 674, 707.

[193] Georgius Fejér (ed.), *Jurium ac Libertatum Religionis et Ecclesiae Catholicae in Regno Hungariae Partibus adnexis Codicillus Diplomaticus* (Buda: Typis Regiae Scientiarum Universitatis Hungaricae, 1847), p. 142.

[194] Hajnal (ed.), *Esterházy Miklós Nádor Iratai*, pp. 251–3.

[195] 'regnum hoc Hungariae ac incolas eius in ipsa vicinitate et faucibus Turcarum positos, in quolibet motu seu mutatione, malo suo ingenti expertos fuisse ferociam Turcicam, quae in nostris turbidis aquis instar piscatoris alicuius, sua retia laxare contendens, imo laxans, tertius semper inter duos litigantes gaudens esse voluit et fuit. Quae etsi enormia sint catholicaeque religionis propagationi nimium nociva, nequaquam tamen ea illis mediis, quibus Sua Mattas in alienis suis regnis et provinciis usa est, tolli posse existimo, tum propter concessiones factas, cum etiam propter vicinitatem perfidorum hostium nostrorum Turcarum, ne forte alioquin arborem inflectere satagentes, rumpamur, cum summo detrimento tam religionis, quam etiam regionis.': 1642 memorial of Miklós Eszterházy in Hajnal, *Esterházy Miklós Nádor Iratai*, p. 253.

Thus *realpolitik* demanded the recognition of the right of the Hungarian estates to the free exercise of their religion, the tolerance of heretical ministers on their lands by Catholic lords, and an acceptance of the limitations on their ability to enforce religious conformity even on the serf population.[196] Eszterházy's submission to Ferdinand III rehearsed the various settlements that provided the framework for the concession of religious diversity, principally the articles of 1606 and 1608, which had been renewed in 1622, on the coronation of Ferdinand II and following the Peace of Nikolsburg, and reaffirmed again in 1628. Such concessions were not, however, to the population at large but rather they represented an agreement between the monarch and the orders of the kingdom entitled to representation at the Diet.[197]

Yet despite the lack of coercive power available to the dynasty, the period under review in this study was one of significant Catholic renewal in Hungary. To a considerable extent, the triumph of Hungarian Catholicism was accomplished in the eighteenth century following the reversal of the Turkish conquest and the assimilation of Transylvania but equally the mould of the Catholic kingdom which was to emerge was set to a significant degree in the first half of the seventeenth century. As elsewhere in Habsburg territories, a key factor in this regard was the relationship between dynastic and aristocratic power.[198] From the end of the sixteenth to the mid-point of the seventeenth century a veritable revolution in the confessional alignment of the upper echelons of the Hungarian nobility occurred. The importance of this development was enhanced by the increasing political, social, and economic salience of magnates within the Hungarian kingdom during the sixteenth and seventeenth centuries, together with an evolving sense of magnate identity which stressed its superiority towards the rest of the noble population.[199] The confessional shift was already becoming visible at the beginning of the seventeenth century. In 1601, the Hungarian Diet was attended by twenty-three secular Protestant magnates as opposed to seventeen Catholics, the majority of whom owed their presence to the conferral upon them of hereditary titles by the dynasty.[200] By 1618 the Catholic party held a clear majority in the Upper House of the Diet which materially assisted the *nádor*, Forgách, himself a convert, in preventing the *országgyűlés* from agreeing to the overtures from the Bohemian, Moravian, and Austrian Estates' attempts to recreate the political coalition which had forced the dynasty to concede wide-ranging religious concessions in 1608. By 1649, the magnate order, which had undergone significant expansion, was overwhelmingly Catholic even in its secular dimension with eighty-eight Catholics, who vastly outnumbered their thirty-three mutually divided Lutheran and Reformed counterparts.[201]

---

[196] ibid., pp. 252–62.   [197] ibid., pp. 247–55.
[198] Tadhg Ó hAnnracháin, 'The Maintenance of Habsburg Rule in Early Modern Hungary' in McKillop, *Forging the State*, pp. 87–100.
[199] Péter Schimert, 'Péter Pázmány and the reconstitution of the Catholic Aristocracy in Habsburg Hungary, 1600–1650' (unpublished PhD dissertation, University of North Carolina, Chapel Hill, 1989), pp. 25–151.
[200] ibid., p. 51.   [201] ibid., p. 108.

The Catholicization of the magnate order was the result of two conjoint processes. A very significant part was played by the dynasty's creation of new magnates. Up to the end of the sixteenth century the grounds which allowed an individual to take a place among the magnates at the *országgyűlés* lacked clarity. The major officers of the realm naturally occupied such positions and letters of invitation were then dispatched to men of clear economic and political importance, although not necessarily figures in possession of hereditary titles of nobility. During the next century, however, the importance of hereditary titles, such as *báró* or *comes*, assumed escalating importance as the most important criterion of membership of the magnate group at the Hungarian Diet. Such titles were eagerly sought because they had become indispensable in guaranteeing the protection of elevated status for subsequent generations of the family, particularly because of the relatively large proportion of the population which could claim *nemes* or noble status.[202] The dynasty's control over the conferring of such titles was thus an important arrow in its quiver of influence. While Protestants were not entirely excluded from grants of titles, a clear pattern of favouritism of Catholics by the dynasty became increasingly apparent, particularly after 1608.[203] But conversion of magnates was also a key development during this period. Between 1613 and 1637 twenty-one magnates became reconciled with the church of Rome, including the hugely influential Croatian, György Zrinyi, and Adám Batthyány, the only surviving son of one of the most important aristocratic families in western Hungary, whose vast holdings became subject to the close religious interest of the man who had master-minded his conversion, Péter Pázmány. A study of these series of converts has suggested a number of common characteristics: conversion tended to occur at a relatively young age, almost invariably before an individual's thirtieth birthday. Such converts moreover tended not to have been particularly prominent as political champions of Hungarian Protestantism, or as patrons of major preachers or Protestant scholars.[204]

It is naturally extremely difficult to establish the precise factors which governed individual conversions because the records of this process either never existed or failed to survive. While Adám Batthyány was the most strikingly evident example of a startling and personal spiritual alteration, it seems clear that none of these conversions was forced, although many of them probably owed something to a keen sense of political expediency. It rapidly became evident to the Hungarian nobility that monarchical favour and support, appointment to military and political office, and the eagerly sought gift of hereditary titles, which alone could guarantee the transmission of privilege to future generations, were far more likely to be gained by Catholics. By 1643, for instance, practically all the military commands in Upper Hungary were in the hands of Catholics, despite the fact that most of the local

[202] ibid., pp. 26–9.
[203] ibid., pp. 120–1; suitable Catholic candidates were identified to the Habsburg authorities by trusted Hungarian advisors, such as favoured bishops: see for instance the memorial from the Archbishop of Esztergom to Archduke Matthias, 23 March 1601 (Magyar Országos Levéltár, Magyar Kancelláriai Levéltár, Litterae Archiepiscoporum 1589–1710, A30 (no folio or letter number)).
[204] Schimert, 'Reconstitution of the Catholic Aristocracy', p. 104.

nobility were not adherents of the church of Rome.[205] Yet such inducements were tacit and implied rather than crude and outspoken. The monarch and his Catholic supporters constantly insisted that royal favour was conferred according to grounds of merit rather than religion, and instances of Protestant promotion could always be adduced to support this claim. The covert blandishments towards Catholicism did not emanate merely from the foreign Habsburg court but were supplemented and brokered by native Hungarian figures. In this regard, the role of the *nádor* or palatine was crucial,[206] particularly during the tenure of Miklós Eszterházy. Like Pázmány, the other most important figure in seventeenth-century Hungarian Catholicism, Eszterházy was himself a convert, largely because of his education in a Jesuit school. Even before he attained the position of *nádor* which he held from 1625 until his death twenty years later, Eszterházy operated as a powerful influence in attracting others to Catholicism. One of his most notable coups was his marriage to Orsolya Dersfy, the daughter and sole heiress of a militant and vastly influential Lutheran family. Her conversion utterly transformed the relative position of the Catholic and Lutheran confessions in the county of Saros. Eszterházy's second marriage was to another Protestant who conformed to her husband's religion. The conversion of the Revay family, who ultimately supplied several reliable magnate figures in the Catholic camp, also owed most to Esterházy's influence. Eszterházy ultimately became the wealthiest aristocrat in Hungary but he repaid the dynasty with vital service in terms of keeping Hungary under Habsburg rule, although he evidently felt that his service was valued more cheaply than it should have been.[207]

That the Habsburgs' most important secular supporter in Hungary was also a proud and frustrated Hungarian patriot might at first sight seem somewhat surprising but that such sentiments could fuse with a militant Catholicism certainly helps explain the gravitational pull which the Roman church was to exercise over many of the Hungarian nobility. For Eszterházy, and indeed for Pázmány, also an ardent defender of the rights of the Hungarian nobility from whom he sprung, Catholicism was not a religion of German imposition but the native creed of the great Hungarian nation which still struggled to maintain its historic responsibility as *propugnaculum christianitatis*. And while the Princes of Transylvania offered a model of accommodation to the reality of Turkish power, it was the Habsburg dynasty which could supply the only real hope for the reversal of the Ottoman conquest, as indeed was to happen in the late seventeenth century.[208] Such a prospect could help counteract a widespread resentment of *nemetek*, or Germans. Indeed, in this regard, even a figure such as Eszterházy himself was evidently not without

---

[205] Lippay to Ferdinand III, 6 March 1643 (Magyar Országos Levéltár, Magyar Kancelláriai Levéltár, Litterae Archiepiscoporum 1589–1710, A30, 161).

[206] In this regard see the 1619 address of the *nádor*, Sigismund Forgách, to the Hungarian Diet (Fejér (ed.), *Jurium ac Libertatum Religionis et Ecclesiae Catholicae*, p. 145) which emphasized the central importance of the palatinate in allowing a native Hungarian to preside over the hearing of grievances in the kingdom.

[207] Eszterházy to Ferdinand II, 20 September 1636 (Magyar Országos Levéltár, Magyar Kancelláriai Levéltár, Litterae Palatinorum, 1614–1765, A21, 165).

[208] Ó hAnnracháin, 'The Maintenance of Habsburg Rule', pp. 92–100.

certain anti-German prejudices. Johannes Hodik, a Lutheran preacher, has left a record of a rather uncomfortable lunch to which he was invited by Eszterházy, at which he was forced to defend his Hungarian identity against the palatine's gibes about his Teutonic character.[209]

Prejudice aside, however, that lunch time conversation also revealed two more important elements of Eszterházy's anti-Protestant antagonism: the first of these was his view of the Reformation as innovation and his distaste for its willingness to dispense with 1200 years of tradition.[210] Hodik's own account indicates that Eszterházy and his priestly advisors at the colloquy were able to force him to insist that even St Augustine would have to be abandoned on certain points, in order to maintain the authority of *sola scriptura*, an attitude which Eszterházy castigated as presumptuous and arrogant. Linked to this was the even more vital element of authority. To the palatine Lutheranism was a prescription for personal interpretation of the word of God which inevitably rendered even those of the lowest social status insolent and lacking in due deference to their betters.[211] One can surmise that in this regard Eszterházy's social and religious prejudices combined in a particularly potent way and it was probably an attitude which he shared with other magnate converts of the era. Certainly the natural harmony between social and religious hierarchy within the Roman church was a theme constantly emphasized by contemporary Catholic apologists. Given the highly unsettled conditions in seventeenth-century Hungary, the Catholic church also offered itself as a potential refuge to widows attempting to safeguard their children's inheritance. The leaders of the Hungarian church evidently saw the protection of vulnerable women and their children as an important aspect of their role and an awareness of their influence acted as a stimulus to women to seek their assistance.[212]

The historical evolution of the Turkish conflict also evidently underpinned the world view of a figure such as Eszterházy and presumably others of his peers. In October 1642, he prepared a memorandum on the religious situation in Hungary. Although his purpose was to convince the Emperor of the need to make some religious concessions to Protestants, Eszterházy nevertheless bluntly ascribed the Turkish scourge to God's punishment of the Hungarian people for their desertion of the Catholic faith. In this he was certainly not alone. The seventeenth century witnessed in Hungary an orchestrated propagation of this idea which represented a conscious attempt to wrest a vitally important piece of intellectual ground from the Protestant cause. Sixteenth-century Hungarian Protestant confessions had made much play of, and much hay from, the devastation of the Turkish conquest. In brief, the Turks had been portrayed as God's punishment for Catholic idolatry

---

[209] 'Ex diario Johannis Hodik Delineatio Mensalis Colloquii' in László Szelestei (ed.), *Naplók és útleírások a 16–18 századból* (Budapest: Universitas Könyvkiadó, 1998), p. 152; for a discussion of Esterházy's political attitudes as palatine see Katalin Péter, *Esterházy Miklós* (Budapest: Gondolat, 1985), pp. 73–82.

[210] In this regard see Evans, *Habsburg Monarchy*, pp. 111–12.

[211] 'Ex diario Johannis Hodik', p. 152.

[212] See for example Pázmány to Ferdinand II, 10 November 1624 (Magyar Országos Levéltár, Magyar Kancelláriai Levéltár, Litterae Archiepiscoporum 1589–1710, A30, 16); Lósy to Ferdinand III, 18 February 1639 (ibid., 107); same to same, 5 September 1642 (ibid., 125).

and Protestant preachers had strongly pushed the message that a renewal of religion would give relief from the heavy hand of God's enemies. The popular theology of the Hungarian Reformation portrayed Christ as the suffering redeemer and suffering was given an educational purpose: if people would repent and reform, suffering would cease.

By the beginning of the seventeenth century, the historical situation provided ample ammunition for a Catholic counter-attack. Rather than Catholicism as the source of the Turkish punishment, the disasters of the sixteenth century were pinned on the reformers themselves. Lutheran ideas had first penetrated Hungary, like harbingers of disaster, according to the Catholic account, in the decade prior to 1526. The Hungarians' unwillingness to excise the evil lost them God's favour at Móhács and in the decades that followed more of the people had abandoned God. The result: the Turkish occupation grew worse and worse, more land was lost. The message: renewal of the Catholic faith would turn the tide and restore God's favour. By the early seventeenth century, Catholic polemicists had good historical wood from which to fashion these particular arrows: the most disastrous era in Hungarian history coincided almost exactly with the abandonment of Rome by the mass of the people. Moreover, in the course of the seventeenth century, there could be no doubt that the champions of Hungarian Protestantism, the Princes of Transylvania, depended on Turkish support, and it was evident that the Protestants of Eastern Hungary and Transylvania were less militant towards the Ottoman threat than those living west of the Danube. Indeed, this factor may have been one of the reasons why it was the west Hungarian nobility in particular, where anti-Turkish sentiment could be given freer rein, which was attracted in the greatest numbers back towards Catholicism.[213]

As in much else in the movement of Catholic renewal the colossal figure of Péter Pázmány, Jesuit controversialist and later primate of Hungary, played an important role in framing this Catholic narrative of the Turkish disaster. This was the theme of the *Felelet*, his first major vernacular work, produced in answer to what he saw as the calumniation of Hungarian Catholicism by the preacher István Magyari. In this text, Pázmány offered an alternative providential explanation for the disaster of the Turkish conquest in sixteenth-century Hungary. In his published work, according to what had become a traditional trope, Magyari had ascribed the Turkish invasion to divine chastisement of the Hungarian nation for the sins of its people, heavily foregrounding the idolatrous nature of Catholic worship. Drawing heavily on the Old Testament, Magyari had argued that the Chosen People had been heavily punished for idolatry on several occasions and suggested that only the pure religion of Hungary's Lutherans had preserved a remnant of the old kingdom from the Turks. Pázmány's text offered an alternative reading which linked the fall of the Hungarian kingdom to the advent of Lutheranism so that a realm which had stood for hundreds of years while the Catholic faith had been preserved was swiftly overthrown when heresy began to sap it from within. Not only did the text offer a different historical interpretation but

---

[213] Schimert, 'Reconstitution of the Catholic Aristocracy', *passim*.

Pázmány engaged closely also with Magyari's biblical examples. While accepting that idolatry was a feature of God's anger with the Chosen People (and naturally denying any idolatrous component in Catholic worship), his discussion concentrated on the punishment of the Jews for the crime of *innovation* in religion, in effect for heresy.[214] Rather than a denial of the providential paradigm, therefore, Pázmány offered a potent appropriation and reinterpretation of historical events. The implication of Pázmány's argument was that by preserving the critical element of the Hungarian past, its Catholic identity, the nation could once again find a future as God would assist in the turning back of the Turkish conquest.

As in many other elements of his varied career, Pázmány in this respect was by no means unique nor necessarily an originator. Nevertheless, his footprint within the Hungarian Counter-Reformation was truly gigantic. Born in 1570 to Calvinist parents, his education at the Jesuit college of Kolozsvár was evidently a key factor in his conversion to Catholicism. Having entered the Society of Jesus himself, he was sent first to Poland and then to Rome where he came into contact with Robert Bellarmine, among others. His first mission experience was in 1600 and in 1602 he was appointed as theological advisor to one of the key figures of the early movement of Hungarian Catholic renewal, the Bishop of Nyitra and later primate, Ferenc Forgách. Prior to 1600 there had been relatively little evidence of vitality within Hungarian Catholicism. The then primate, Miklós Oláh, had introduced the Jesuits to Hungary in 1560 but the Society made relatively little impact, although later foundations in Transylvania did bear some important fruit. Oláh was followed by two important figures, Cardinal Drašković and the administrator of the see of Esztergom, Miklós Telegdi, who set up a Catholic printing press, but their wider societal impact was relatively minimal. Forgách, himself a convert, was an advocate of uncompromising attitudes towards Protestant pretensions which Pázmány came gradually to see as counter-productive. In 1608 he produced a famous memorandum for Matthias which offered a series of reasons why religious rights could be conceded to Hungarian Protestants.[215]

In his later career as an important political advisor to Emperor Ferdinand II, he acted as a counter-balance to the more intransigent views of William Lamormaini, believing that the confrontational policy in other lands of the dynasty had a detrimental effect on the situation in Hungary by increasing Protestant insecurity as well as actual immigration of non-Catholics forced out of other Habsburg territories for confessional reasons.[216] For Pázmány, the key to Catholic revival was educational development, missionary outreach and institutional reform to create

---

[214] Péter Pázmány, *Felelet Magyari István Sárvári Prédikátornak as Ország Romlása Okairul Írt Könyvére*, ed. Emil Hargittay (Budapest: Universitas, 2000), esp. pp. 235–48.

[215] Ferenc Hanuy (ed.), *Pázmány Péter összegyujtött levelei* (two vols, Budapest, 1910–12), 1, pp. 26–9.

[216] Bireley, *Religion and Politics*, pp. 29–30; this position was echoed also quite crudely by Eszterházy: see his memorial of 7 April 1633 where he compared the arrival of heretics from other Habsburg domains as the expulsion of their faeces into Hungary (Magyar Országos Levéltár, Magyar Kancelláriai Levéltár, Litterae Palatinorum, 1614–1765, A21, 144).

the structures necessary to win over hearts and minds and his elevation to the primatial see of Esztergom in 1616 gave him the opportunity to further this vision. Despite the low number of actual adherents, the movement of Catholic revival benefited from the fact that bishops in particular retained an institutional importance within Hungary, including the symbolic rights of the Archbishop of Esztergom to cast the first vote in the Diet and to crown the king. And although the Peace of Vienna restricted the ability to use coercion there were legal avenues to assert Catholic rights under its provisions, to make claims for properties which had passed into Protestant hands in the course of the Bocskai revolt, to open Catholic schools in Protestant-dominated towns such as Bratislava, and to seek punishment for preachers on the grounds of calumniation of Catholic institutions if not for actual religious practice.[217] On the other hand, bodies such as chapters could be highly resistant to the attempts to restructure church resources to promote the goals of Catholic renewal, particularly when this involved favouring the Society of Jesus over traditional ecclesiastical institutions.[218]

Pázmány himself placed the utmost significance on education and towards the end of his career he was to estimate that two-thirds of his revenues were devoted to this end. He assigned a very high priority to the *Collegium Germanicum-Hungaricum* in Rome which he did not believe was performing adequately, striving to ensure that the twelve Hungarian places in the college were constantly filled and that sufficient funds were available to cover the necessary expenses. He promoted also the education of Hungarian- and Croatian-speaking priests at the University of Graz. In 1624 he was responsible for the opening in Vienna of an institution with the primary objective of training clergy for service in the Hungarian crown lands, the *Pázmáneum*. By 1638 over sixty students were in training at this college and more than sixty had already graduated. The Archbishop, who became a cardinal in 1629, was also a supporter of the seminaries which were opened in Győr and Bratislava. Arguably his most significant achievement in the educational field, however, was the creation first of a national seminary at Nagyszombat in 1631 and then the university at the same town in 1635. The university was centred in the metropolitan see of Esztergom and under the supervision of the Archbishop but the teaching was supplied by the Society of Jesus. It rapidly developed into a key institution of Catholic renewal, although Pope Urban VIII, in sharp contrast to the Emperor, withheld recognition of the university.[219]

---

[217] Pázmány to Ferdinand II, 14 October 1634 (Magyar Országos Léveltár, Magyar Kancelláriai Levéltar, Litterae Archiepiscoporum 1589–1710, A30, 75); Lósy to Ferdinand III, 1 March 1642 (ibid., 115); same to same, 31 March 1642 (ibid., 120;) Eszterházy to Ferdinand II, 19 February 1626 (ibid., Litterae Palatinorum, 1614–1765, A21, 51).

[218] See for instance the bitter letter of complaint from the Chapter of Győr to the Council of War, 1 July 1637 (Magyar Országos Levéltár, Magyar Kancelláriai Levéltár, Litterae Capitolorum, Capitulum Jauriense 1632–1741, A31, 2); Lippay to Ferdinand III, 16 December 1642 (ibid., Litterae Archiepiscoporum 1589–1710, A30, 132).

[219] The Archbishop's grant of establishment and Ferdinand II's recognition of the university are reproduced as documents 41 and 42 in László Szögi, (ed.), *Régi Magyar Egyetemek Emlékezete: Memoria Universitatum et Scholarum Maiorum Regni Hungariae 1367–1777* (Budapest: Eötvös Loránd Tudományegyetem, 1995), pp. 198–208.

Aware of the importance of secular education as well, Pázmány successfully helped to face down local urban opposition to the creation of Catholic schools in the towns of Pozsony, Sopron, Homonna, and Szatmár.[220] Pázmány's emphasis on education reflected his awareness of the importance of local linguistic skills in promoting Catholic renewal. He increasingly became frustrated with the Roman congregation of *Propaganda Fide*'s tendency to dispatch Italian missionaries to Hungarian territory believing that, although certain individuals among them could be of utility, larger numbers were actually counterproductive because of their linguistic inadequacies.[221] Pázmány's infrastructural developments merged with the growing support for Catholicism in the higher social echelons of Hungarian society, particularly when magnates opened their territories to the ministration of priests.

Yet, while critical as an ecclesiastical organizer and in terms of his political counsel, Pázmány had an equally important career as a writer and controversialist. He was a theologian of real substance who published extensively in Latin and who demonstrated a subtle and nuanced understanding of Thomist thought. Much of his ecclesiology and his controversial writings were influenced by Robert Bellarmine, although the English theologian, Thomas Stapleton, was also of key importance in this respect. Spanish influences were also very evident. Pázmány's discussions of the Incarnation owed much to Francisco Suarez, while Valencia's understanding of faith and Vasquez's positions concerning the theology of grace were highly formative.[222] Although his Latin writings were intellectually significant, it was his relationship with the Hungarian vernacular which set him apart from most of his contemporaries. As primate he eventually chose to short-circuit the foot-dragging of the Holy Office to equip Hungarian Catholicism with a vernacular translation of the Bible, which he saw as a vital tool in combatting Protestantism, by personally authorizing its publication.[223] His own production was staggering in terms both of quantity and of range. Among his most significant texts were his collected sermons, which subsequently became a significant source of reference for the Hungarian priesthood.[224] His translation of Thomas à Kempis's *Imitation of Christ* was also destined for extended recognition long after his decease.[225]

---

[220] Miklós Őry and Ferenc Szabó, 'Pázmány Péter (1570–1637)' in Miklós Őry, Ferenc Szabó, and Péter Vass (eds), *Pázmány Péter Válogatás Műveiből* (Budapest: Szent István Társulat Az Apostoli Szentszék Könyvkiadója, 1983), pp. 48–53; István Bitskey, 'Pázmány Péter és a Római Collegium Germanicum Hungaricum' in I. Bitskey and A. Tamás (eds), *A Debreceni Kossuth Lajos Tudományegyetem Magyar Irodalomtörténeti Intézetének Közleményei*, XXIII (Debrecen: Debrecen University Press, 1985), pp. 29–40; see also idem., 'The Collegium Germanicum Hungaricum in Rome and the Beginning of the Counter Reformation in Hungary' in Evans, *Crown, Church and Estates*, pp. 110–22.

[221] See Bonaventura da Genova to the Cardinals of *Propaganda Fide*, 2 June 1635 (István György Tóth (ed.), *Litterae Missionariorum de Hungaria et Transilvania (1572–1717)* (two vols, Roma and Budapest: Biblioteca Academiae Hungariae, 2002), 1, pp. 584–6.)

[222] A detailed discussion of Pázmány's theology can be found in Ferenc Szabó, *A Teológus Pázmány: A grazi 'theologica scholastica' Pázmány művében* (Roma: Metem, 1990), see esp. pp. 254–66.

[223] Antal Molnár, 'A horvát és magyar katolikus Biblia-fordítás és a romai inkvizíció', *Magyar Könyvszemle* 118 (2002), 24–37.

[224] Antal Molnár, *Katolikus missziók a hódolt Magyarországon I (1572–1647)* (Budapest: Balassi Kiadó, 2002), p. 431.

[225] Őry and Szabó, 'Pázmány Péter', p. 48.

Pázmány's controversial writing in Hungarian became particularly important as an intellectual foundation for the process of Catholic renewal. In the course of the sixteenth century Catholic literary production in Hungarian had been extraordinarily restricted. Almost single-handedly Pázmány began to redress this imbalance.[226] One of his early masterpieces, *Őt Szép level*, the *Five Beautiful Letters*, mounted an ingenious attack on the staple Protestant accusation of Catholic idolatry, as an increasingly frustrated Calvinist was made to appeal in vain to the famous preacher, Péter Alvinczi, for assistance in mounting arguments against an unshakeable Catholic case. The high point of Pázmány's literary endeavours in this regard was *Isteni Igazságra Vezérlő Kalauz* (*Guide to the Divine Truth*), which was first published in 1613 and subsequently revised several times down to its final redaction in the year of his death in 1637. The essential goal of this text was to demolish the credibility of all non-Catholic faiths. While his major targets were the traditions which had emerged from the Reformation, as the product of a highly confessionally-mixed society he was to the fore in contemporary Europe in accepting the need to prove the rational basis of Christian belief in a manner which could engage with non-Christians. This emphasis on rationality was a key theme of the text. Without the clear proof of the Godly origin of Christ's teaching then a refusal to believe in his message would not, he argued, render an individual culpable, but such open proof existed that it was impossible for a person of any intelligence to entertain doubts. Faith and intelligence thus harmoniously supported each other in a highly comforting manner.[227] The apprehension of God, too, depended on the exercise of rational faculties. For Pázmány, the goodness of the Creator God demanded that a way should be available to his creatures to distinguish the true religion, outside of which there was no salvation.[228] And because it was impossible in a true religion for believers to be uncertain about essential doctrine, only Catholicism could provide the necessary security of belief. The church of Rome was thus the reassuring refuge from doubt, which fulfilled the promise made to the primitive church that it would be supported to the world's end.

Critically, he argued that it was the tradition of this church which both defined the canon of Scripture on which faith was based and provided the key to authoritative interpretation of that canon. On the other hand, the Reformed and Evangelical confessions were hopelessly riven by doubts about everything.[229] Moreover, how could it be consonant with God's grace that so many saints could have been abandoned to the darkness that Protestants called papistry and how was it possible that there could be no record of opposition to what the reformers called the church of Antichrist for a thousand years before Luther? Only a tyrant God, such as the God he identified with Calvin, could allow such a development. From a Hungarian perspective, he argued that it was abundantly clear that Protestantism of any shape could not be the true faith for it had come to flourish in the kingdom in

---

[226] István Bitskey, *Hitvitak tüzében* (Budapest: Gondolat, 1978), p. 175.

[227] Péter Pázmány, *Hodoegus. Igazságra vezérlő Kalauz* (Nagyszombat, 1637), pp. 42–5; Tadhg Ó hAnnracháin, 'The Miraculous Mathematics of the World: Proving the existence of God in Cardinal Péter Pázmány's *Kalauz*', *Studies in Church History* 46 (2010), 248–59.

[228] *Kalauz*, p. 77. [229] ibid., pp. 91–2, 287–9, 335, 399, 402.

tandem with the Turkish assault and who could believe that God wished to establish the purity of the gospel in such a fashion? He identified a clear providential link between God's abandonment of Hungary and Lutheranism: it was Luther's preaching which ensured no aid came to the kingdom at the disastrous battle of Móhács. And God's ire was clearly visible in the extinction of so many great Hungarian houses which had abandoned Catholicism. In typical fashion Pázmány looked back also to the medieval past as the source of a more authentic Hungarian identity before the clouding of the Reformation. Traces still remained: Hungarians could not even tell the days of the year without reference to the feasts of the Virgin and the Saints and to Lent.[230] Thus, as in the manner previously discussed with regard to Bohemia and Austria, the idea of an alternative national and Catholic identity which could be resurrected and lead to a new future bubbled through his writings and indeed through his political activity as, for instance, in his attempts to ensure equality of a Catholic right to office in the municipal government of Pozsony, on the grounds that the ancient privileges of the city, which its patricians were attempting to defend against the pressure of the regime, had all been originally granted to Catholics prior to the Reformation.[231]

The comprehensive nature of Pázmány's attacks on the Reformed and Evangelical traditions, in his masterwork in particular, naturally demanded responses, one of the most important of which was commissioned in Wittenberg and undertaken by the distinguished theologian, Friedrich Balduinus. Ten years later his rejoinder appeared in print but Pázmány rapidly wrested back the controversial initiative by having his own riposte published within a year. This was a telling demonstration of the indigenization of the movement of Catholic renewal in Hungary and its increasing institutional solidity.[232] One of the most interesting features of Pázmány's career was the personal success which he enjoyed in the process of conversion. Rather than being an ivory-tower intellectual, he engaged in quotidian contact with individuals of different faiths and evidently had a clear apprehension of the usefulness of various arguments in advancing the process of conversion, rather than mere point-scoring. As a convert himself, like so many other major figures of the Hungarian Catholic Reformation such as Forgách and Eszterházy, and markedly unlike figures such as Bellarmine and Stapleton, he evidently had a personal insight into the thought processes and doubts of his adversaries which he exploited to the full.

The gigantic footprint of Pázmány renders him a particularly visible figure but of crucial importance was the degree to which his was not an isolated voice. One of the major successes of the Habsburg policy of Catholic renewal was the manner in which it was forwarded by native figures who occupied key political and

---

[230] ibid., pp. 138–9, 161–2, 184, 218, 309–10, 371, 467.

[231] See the (more precisely undated) 1626 'Humillima Supplicatio' of Pázmány to Ferdinand II (Magyar Országos Levéltár, Magyar Kancelláriai Levéltár, Litterae Archiepiscoporum 1589–1710, A30, 26).

[232] Friedrich Balduinus, *Phosphorus Veri Catholicismi: Devia Papatus, & viam regiam ad Ecclesiam vere Catholicam & Apostolicam fideliter monstrans, facemque praelucens legentibus Hodegum Petri Pazmanni olim Jesuitae, nunc Cardinalis Ecclesiae Romano-Papisticae* (Wittenberg, 1626); László Barta, 'Adatok a Kalauzra Adott Wittenbergi Válasz Készítéséhez' in Emil Hargittay, *Pázmány Péter és kora* (Piliscsaba: PPKE BTK, 2001), pp. 268–73.

ecclesiastical roles, some of whom did not necessarily even possess good German linguistic skills.[233] In this regard, the Hungarian Catholic episcopacy offers a particularly interesting contrast with the hierarchy of the Established church in Ireland where the office of bishop was largely monopolized by New English or English appointees in the course of the seventeenth century. While William Bedell in Kilmore proved an honourable exception to the rule, these bishops and their lower clergy demonstrated a low level of evangelical zeal, in particular towards the Gaelic population of the island, placing a much greater emphasis on ministration to the immigrant English community and thereby largely abandoning the field to their Catholic counterparts.[234] By contrast figures such as Forgách, Pázmány, and their successors Imre Lósy and György Lippay were fiercely committed to the revival of Catholicism among their native community. This was strongly evidenced by the concern which they and their other episcopal colleagues demonstrated concerning the necessity of the advance of Catholic renewal being given due prominence in the exercise of their monarch's rights of *iuspatronatus* to ecclesiastical positions such as bishoprics, praepositories, abbeys *in commendam*, and church properties and rights in general.[235]

The importance of the relationship between the Hungarian episcopate and their monarch was enhanced by the mobility between sees which the bishops demonstrated. In a fashion similar to contemporary Poland, Hungarian bishops changed dioceses with great rapidity. As in Poland this reflected the incredible differential in the value of particular sees. A Hungarian bishop frequently started his episcopal career by being appointed in a merely titular capacity to a church in Turkish territory, such as Bosnia, Szerém, or Tinnin. The next step on the ladder was then often to a see under Turkish influence but capable of supplying some limited revenue. Such appointments included the dioceses of Pécs, Várad, and Csanád. A further upgrade would lead to the conferring of a see with at least portions in Habsburg territory, most notably Vác, Veszprém, and Nyitra. At the apex of the scale were the dioceses of Győr, Eger and the archbishopric of Esztergom.[236] A death of a bishop in a valuable diocese thus generally caused a ripple of movement throughout the

[233] See for example Lippay's comments on the suitable candidates for the Hungarian Chancellorship: Lippay to Ferdinand III, 15 August 1644 (Magyar Országos Levéltár, Magyar Kancelláriai Levéltár, Litterae Archiepiscoporum 1589–1710, A30, 173).

[234] Tadhg Ó hAnnracháin, 'The consolidation of Irish Catholicism within a hostile Imperial framework: A comparative study of Early Modern Hungary and Ireland' in Hilary Carey (ed.), *Empires of Religion* (Basingstoke: Palgrave Macmillan, 2008), pp. 25–42.

[235] See for example Pázmány to Ferdinand II, 29 April 1623 (Magyar Országos Levéltár, Magyar Kancelláriai Levéltár, Litterae Archiepiscoporum 1589–1710, A30, 15); same to same, 12 March 1625 (ibid., 23); same to same, 13 August 1628 (ibid., 49); Pázmány and István Sennyey, Bishop of Győr, to same, 14 October 1630 (ibid., 56); Pázmány to Ferdinand II, 19 June 1635 (ibid., 79); Imre Lósy to Ferdinand II, 14 September 1637 (ibid., 97); same to Ferdinand III, 27 July 1639 (ibid., 98); same to same, 14 September 1639 (ibid., 98); György Lippay to Ferdinand III, 28 October 1642 (ibid., 124); same to same, 20 September 1643 (ibid., 141); same to same, 13 July 1643 (ibid., 148); same to same, 11 June 1643 (ibid., 158); same to same, 16 June 1644 (ibid., 179); same to same, 24 July 1644 (ibid., 175); same to same, 11 September 1644 (ibid., 171).

[236] Antal Molnár, 'A kalocsai érsekség a XVII századi püspöki processzusok tanúvallomásainak tükrében' in Zsuzsanna J. Újvári (ed.), *Ezredforduló—századforduló—hetvenedik évforduló. Ünnepi tanulmányok Zimányi Vera tiszteletére* (Piliscsaba: PPKE, 2001), 140–63, at 140–2.

hierarchy. In 1630, for instance, István Sennyey, who had previously moved from his initial see of Bosnia, first to Vács and then to Vesprém, was appointed to the rich bishopric of Győr. This resulted immediately in attempts by himself and Pázmány to have the vacant see of Veszprém occupied by the bishop-elect of Vács which would allow the Bishop of Pécs, György Drastkovith, to replace him in Vács and offer the opportunity to Benedict Vinković to be elevated to the hierarchy in Pécs, as eventually occurred in 1633.[237] A factor facilitating such mobility was the tendency for Hungarian bishops to take up their functions on royal nomination alone, often omitting to obtain papal confirmation, a practice which developed into a considerable source of tension between the Habsburgs and the papacy of Urban VIII.[238] As kings of Hungary, the Habsburgs claimed:

> superior prerogatives to all the kings of Christendom, even as an apostolic king. And he has among others the faculty of conferring bishoprics and the other kings have only the faculty of presentation...the crown of Hungary puts bishops in possession *in spiritualibus et temporalibus* without pontifical bulls and causes them to exercise administration and to draw revenues.[239]

Nor was this claim confined to the dioceses situated in the portion of the medieval kingdom of Hungary which was actually under Habsburg control but rather it was extended, often in a most exaggerated fashion, to all the territories which were believed to have once pertained to the crown of St Stephen.

Among the reasons why Rome was reluctant to entertain such claims was the patent inability of the Habsburg-appointed bishops to minister to the Catholic populations outside Royal Hungary. The Archbishop of Kalocsa, for example, whose titular see was entirely in Turkish hands, was forced to confess to the papal nuncio in 1622 that he was ignorant even of the religion which was professed by the inhabitants of his archdiocese.[240] Partly under the spur of pressure from *Propaganda Fide*, and concerned also to protect their jurisdictional rights, the titular bishops of Royal Hungary did from the 1620s begin to make attempts to foster contact with their sees, and to try to extract some revenues.[241] Ultimately, however, it was only after the late-seventeenth-century reconquest of the Hungarian crown lands that genuine pastoral episcopal functions could be exercised by Habsburg-nominated bishops. Nevertheless, the role which the dynasty played in protecting the perceived rights and jurisdictional integrity of the Hungarian church was an indication of the manner in which Habsburg rule provided the space for the development of a genuinely indigenous sense of Hungarian Catholic identity. As

---

[237] Pázmány and Sennyey to Ferdinand II, 14 October 1630 (Magyar Országos Levéltár, Magyar Kancelláriai Levéltár, Litterae Archiepiscoporum 1589–1710, A30, 56).

[238] Péter Tusor, 'Az 1639. Évi Nagyszombati Püspökkari Konferencia', *Századok* 134 (2000), 431–59.

[239] 'prerogative superiori à tutti i Rè della Cristianità, tamquam Rex Apostolicus. E fra l'altri ha facoltà di conferire i vescovati e l'altri Rè solo han facoltà di presentare...la corona d'Ongheria mette i vescovi in possesso in spiritualibus et temporalibus senza Bolle Pontificie, e li fà esercitare l'amminstratione e tirar l'entrate': 'Risposta alle ragioni addotte da Ministri della Sacra Congregatione contra il Vescovo di Bosna', memorandum dated to 1648 concerning the King of Hungary's rights over the bishopric of Bosnia (Magyar Országos Levéltár, Litterae Roma Exaratae, A29, 31).

[240] Molnár, *Katolikus missziók*, p. 211.   [241] Molnár, 'Kalocsai érsekség', 155–6.

the patron of Hungarian Catholicism, supporting for example the canonization of Margaret of Hungary and the maintenance of St Stephen's position within the new Roman breviary,[242] rather than as an imposer of a German model, the dynasty's strategy helped prevent Hungarian resentments becoming ruinous to the process of re-Catholicization. Crucially, and similarly to Bohemia, neither ethnic identity nor convert status was a bar to high office and influence. Indeed, rather than mere Habsburg place-men, the leaders of the Hungarian church could display a certain conditionality in their loyalty to the dynasty. Pázmány himself certainly seems to have appreciated the importance of the Transylvanian principality as a counterbalance to *nemet* dominance in Royal Hungary.[243] And in the 1660s Lippay became involved in actual conspiracy against the dynasty in the aftermath of the humiliating Peace of Vasvár.[244]

Nowhere were the limitations of the process of Catholic revival more evident than in those areas of the ancient kingdom which lay outside Habsburg control. In real terms the recrudescent church of Royal Hungary did remarkably little to foster either the maintenance of Catholicism or missionary outreach to populations under Turkish control or in Transylvania.[245] Even in Habsburg Hungary itself, the position of the church of Rome was significantly weaker than in the dynasty's other possessions at the conclusion of the period under review, a factor clearly linked to the inability of the regime to exert effective coercion against the non-Catholic clergy and lay elites of the kingdom. Hungarian Catholicism was weaker too than its Polish equivalent, with which it shared many structural similarities, most notably the framework of religious coexistence, a supportive but relatively weak monarchical institution which was largely confined to the exercise of soft power, its juxtaposition with a multiplicity of different confessional perspectives, and the omnipresent external threats, not least from the Ottoman empire. Yet coming from a much weaker base than in Poland, Hungarian Catholicism had made hugely important strides in the period under review. In this regard three factors would appear to have been of preeminent importance: first, the reconstruction of Catholic institutions, most notably in the educational field which had begun to produce native clergy capable of forwarding the movement of Catholic renewal; second, the increasing salience of Catholicism among the higher nobility and the manner in which this opened the way to a fruitful collaboration between local interests and the dynasty in terms of administering the country and advancing a movement of evangelization; and third, the successful elaboration of the idea of a Catholic identity native to the crown lands of St Stephen which was capacious

---

[242] Pázmány to Ferdinand II, 14 October 1630 (Magyar Országos Levéltár, Magyar Kancelláriai Levéltár, Litterae Archiepiscoporum 1589–1710, A30, 57); Lósy to Ferdinand III, 11 May 1641 (ibid., 113); Father Antonio O.P. to Ferdinand III, 9 August 1642 (ibid., Litterae Roma Exaratae, A29, 10).

[243] Őry and Szabó, 'Pázmány Péter', p. 54.

[244] Evans, *Habsburg Monarchy*, p. 260.

[245] The contrast here with Ireland is striking: see Tadhg Ó hAnnracháin, 'The Bishop's Role in Two Non-Catholic States: the Cases of Ireland and Turkish Hungary Considered', *Church History and Religious Culture* 95 (2015).

enough to accommodate not merely a significant *Magyar* constituency but also Slovak and Croat elements.

The great advances in Catholic renewal throughout East-Central Europe were largely the product of developments in the late sixteenth century and in the century that followed. In assessing its successes it would certainly be unwise to under-estimate the essential intolerance of the confession. Even in Hungary, where figures such as Pázmány or Eszterházy recognized the futility of coercive tactics, there was no recognition of any validity for different confessional perspectives. As Pázmány bitterly informed the citizens of Pozsony, who attempted to enlist his support for a preacher threatened with expulsion in 1634, had he possessed the power he would have ensured that not a single preacher could stay in his diocese.[246] Not only was genuine brutality exercised in the course of the re-Catholicization of Bohemia and Austria, in particular, but it can be surmised that the often vicious repression of peasant disturbance by Catholic authorities during this period was actually a factor in ensuring the increasing attractiveness of the church of Rome to the social elites of the region. Even in areas such as Poland and Hungary, where the state's hands were tied with regard to coercive measures, it is clear that a significant amount of conscious discrimination helped promote Catholic renewal among elite groupings. Thus a panoply of measures ranging from outright violence to exclusion from office and favour underpinned the increasing institutional strength of the church of Rome in East-Central Europe.

The salience of these factors makes clear the essential importance of the various monarchs. That neither the Vasa kings of Poland nor the Habsburgs were tempted to break from Rome during this period was a huge source of strength for Catholicism, for even in a monarchy as weak as Poland the crown could act as a source of patronage and soft power which in the long run could accomplish a great deal. Even more importantly, the Catholicism of the monarchs denied such essential sources of influence and legitimacy to non-Catholic confessional groupings. The manner in which Catholicism largely failed to gain ground in contemporaneous Transylvania, despite the avowed tolerance of the principality under its Reformed rulers, is another indication of the importance of the monarchical institution as a promoter of particular confessional perspectives.

Why the monarchs of the region adhered with such vigour to Catholicism during the period under review was obviously due to many reasons. Some of these were undoubtedly structural. The power which the Polish monarch enjoyed over the conferring of ecclesiastical positions clearly reduced the necessity to seek a breach with Rome, particularly when the papacy on the whole proved eager to support and conciliate the monarch. For the Habsburgs, Catholicism undoubtedly came to function as a supra-national identity which allowed for the creation of strong bonds between the dynasty and the various elites of their multi-ethnic territories. Given the essential weakness of the dynasty's power, this coincidence of

---

[246] Pázmány to Ferdinand II, 14 October 1634 (Magyar Országos Levéltár, Magyar Kancelláriai Levéltár, Litterae Archiepiscoporum 1589–1710, A30, 75).

interest was of vital importance in allowing for the political consolidation of control. To some extent also, figures such as Ferdinand II and Ferdinand III and Sigismund III were simply typical of their era as pious princes. Maximilian of Bavaria was certainly similarly motivated in religious terms. For his part, Louis XIII of France was arguably the most zealous king of France in the Early Modern period. And while the Habsburgs of Spain in the seventeenth century may not have surpassed Philip II in their piety they did not represent a significant falling-off in standards of religious zeal. In this respect, the refinement of Catholic education was clearly a factor of some importance, together with the growing importance of monarchical confessors and their pressure towards the development of personal conscience. A homology can also be distinguished between Catholic emphasis on legitimate authority and hierarchy in the ecclesiastical sphere and its comfortable endorsement of monarchical power.

Of equal importance with monarchical support was the increasing attractiveness throughout the region of Catholicism to elites, particularly magnates, who became a critical social force behind the movement of Catholic renewal.[247] Many of the factors which influenced monarchs to support Catholicism clearly operated at the level of aristocracy as well. The provision of effective Catholic education and the degree to which it was so highly prized in outfitting aristocrats for a life at court and in office certainly had an effect on the higher echelons of society. The cosmopolitanism of Catholic culture was evidently another draw. And the reassuring social bulwark which the Catholic church represented, its strong support for societal hierarchies, was naturally attractive to a highly privileged class who presided over large populations which suffered greatly in times of major upheaval and warfare. The very effectiveness of Catholic devotionalism in reaching out to the peasant population and providing orderly rituals which helped promote societal cohesion naturally provided preeminent benefits to the highest social classes.

The sheer plethora of competing non-Catholic confessions also contributed to the emergence of the church of Rome as the strongest religious grouping in the region. Catholic advantages over the disunities of its rivals were accentuated by the elaboration of controversial viewpoints which emphasized the weak points of the Reformed and Lutheran confessions, particularly their lack of agreement on matters considered central, and which could portray Unitarianism as part of a slippery slope towards Judaism or Islam. At a time of massive political and economic change, accentuated by the onset of harsher climatic conditions, the Catholic emphasis on the rationality of the Roman church's beliefs evidently provided a great deal of reassurance, although it is eminently arguable that the confessional viewpoints so well equipped to confront seventeenth-century Protestantism ultimately proved something of an intellectual strait-jacket at the onset of the Enlightenment.

In addition to reassuring uniformity, Early Modern Catholicism also supplied significant variety. In this regard the various religious orders offered a menu of spirituality and a complex web of cultural affiliations which allowed for a variegated appeal. While capable of confronting Protestantism on equal intellectual ground as

---

[247] Winkelbauer, *Fürst und Fürstendiener*, pp. 90–158.

a result of the development of effective educational institutions, and of institutional reforms which allowed the Catholic clergy to mirror the development of the ministers of the various confessions which sprang from the Reformation, the Catholic church also proved hospitable to a wider accommodation with older forms of spirituality and it allowed for acculturation to the type of religion which the impoverished peasantry evidently found meaningful and comforting. Thus while some Catholic devotions, such as pilgrimage, could act as a bridge and promote social cohesion in all orders of society, in other respects Catholicism could function in a surprisingly varied fashion. In particular, it can be suggested that the emphasis on the hostility of Early Modern Catholicism to superstitious practices can be overstated. A considerable element of tolerance for traditional practices still persisted, provided they were not seen as offering a gateway to heresy. On a whole variety of levels, it is clear also that throughout the regions Catholicism proved attractive to many women. In a period of real military disturbance and upheaval the church evidently acted as an important source of support to women, particularly widows. But Catholic devotionalism also offered real opportunities for women to participate in meaningful spiritual activities and gave an outlet to many for acts of piety and charity which provided a sense of reassurance, control, and sanctity.

4

Opposition to Islam

This chapter offers a case study of papal diplomatic involvement in conflict against the Ottoman empire, a consistent impulse of pontifical policy which deeply influenced the relationship between the south-eastern periphery of European Catholicism and Rome. As the chapter demonstrates, the Early Modern papacy was at the heart of a formidable diplomatic web yet its capacity to exert pressure on the Catholic powers of Europe was limited by many constraints. Particularly in the period immediately after Trent the diplomatic servants of the papacy tended to be recruited from pastoral bishops who had been present at the council and as a result it was hoped that they would act as leaders for religious reform in the countries to which they were sent. While this was not an unimportant aspect of overall papal policy, experience at Trent or as pastoral bishops was not necessarily the best training for diplomatic service. Much more importantly, the perceived best interests of individual states was, almost invariably, the strongest factor in determining the foreign policy pursued. At times this could cut directly across papal ambitions, as for instance when Charles IX and the Medici Queen Mother not only failed to support papal plans for a Holy League in 1571 but worked hard to detach Venice from the project.[1] When states did commit themselves to wars in the Catholic interest they considered themselves entitled to both material and moral support from the papacy and were not slow about expressing their displeasure if it was not forthcoming. Thus even as junior a government as the Confederate Catholics of Ireland in the 1640s, which owed a significant element of its political legitimacy to papal recognition, expressed its disappointment about the lack of monetary support from the papacy in quite sharp terms to their representatives in Rome.[2] When material papal support was forthcoming for 'Catholic' wars, it was frequently seen as no more than their due by local forces in arms for religion. This lack of reciprocity was particularly evident in the case of Venice which ignored papal attempts to recruit the state for an anti-Turkish war for decades between 1573 and 1645 but *La Serenissima* immediately considered itself entitled to assistance from Rome on the outbreak of the war of Candia.[3]

---

[1] Lynn Martin, 'Papal Policy and European Conflict, 1559–1572', *Sixteenth Century Journal* 11: 2 (1980), 35–48.

[2] J.T. Gilbert (ed.), *The history of the Irish confederation and war in Ireland, 1641–1649 containing a narrative of affairs of Ireland... with correspondence and documents of the confederation... with contemporary personal statements, memoirs, etc.* (seven vols, Dublin: 1882–91), 4, pp. 35–6.

[3] Tadhg Ó hAnnracháin, 'Vatican diplomacy and the mission of Rinuccini to Ireland', *Archivium Hibernicum* 47 (1993), 78–88.

Dynastic ambition was as constant a factor as martial notions of noble honour in defining the contours of state interaction and of papal diplomacy. Susceptibility to the lure of titles and territories and the enhancement of status was an integral aspect of the culture of the princely houses of Early Modern Europe which could often cut across material interests and trigger conflicts. Philip III's refusal to abandon his claim to the crowns of Bohemia and Hungary during the first decades of the seventeenth century, for instance, not only disrupted the interests of the Central European branch of the dynasty but ultimately redounded materially to Spanish and papal disinterest. The attempts of his father, Philip II, to acquire the throne of France for the Infanta of Spain during the 1590s similarly operated to weaken the case of Spanish allies among the papally-backed *ligue*. In the same decade Archduke Maximilian's unwillingness to abandon his pretensions to the crown of Poland in the early years of the Clementine pontificate obstructed papal attempts to bring Poland into a coalition of Christian states to preserve the Habsburg foothold in Hungary.[4] The noble houses which occupied the papal throne during this period were themselves creatures of this system and not immune to such behaviour but a consistent thrust of papal policy was the attempt to harness and channel dynastic ambition towards the perceived interest of the church in a cognate fashion to its attempts to inflect the noble martial culture of Europe towards war on behalf of religion.

A number of key although sometimes conflicting themes can be identified in terms of the papacy's perception of its mission within the Catholic world which are explored in the following three chapters. First the fracturing of the Latin Christian world at the Reformation had ensured that the border between Christendom and the Islamic world in Europe was effectively divided between the territories of the Catholic and Orthodox churches. It was an integral part of papal policy as spiritual leader of the *Republica Christiana* to assist and participate in the Christian struggle against Islam, with particular reference to the Ottoman empire. Second, throughout the period of this book the papacy aspired to patronize the struggle against the Protestant Reformation. Strongly intermixed with both these themes was a concern to fulfil a function as the reconciler of the warring Catholic powers of Europe, both in the context of a Christian pastor and with an eye to more efficient implementation of the anti-Protestant and anti-Islamic struggles. Fourth, having identified itself with a particular conception of the Tridentine legacy, the papacy actively sought to foster the acceptance of the decrees of Trent and the implementation of that legacy throughout the Catholic world. Fifth, with increasing emphasis the papacy evinced a desire to actively involve itself in and promulgate policies of missionary evangelization.[5]

---

[4] Magdalena S. Sanchez, 'A House Divided: Spain, Austria and the Bohemian and Hungarian Successions', *Sixteenth Century Journal* 25: 4 (1994), 887–903; Paula Sutter Fichtner, 'Dynastic Marriage in Sixteenth-Century Habsburg Diplomacy and Statecraft: An Interdisciplinary Approach', *The American Historical Review* 81: 2 (1976), 243–65.

[5] Although not the explicit focus of the following chapters it can also be noted that, throughout this period, successive popes demonstrated a keen concern to preserve the independence and if possible to increase the territorial power of the papal state in Italy. In addition, it might be said that all holders of the papal office showed a consistent desire to advance the social and financial interests of their families.

This chapter offers a case study of the first of these themes which was particularly resonant on the Eastern periphery of Catholic Europe, namely the struggle against Muslim and, in particular, Ottoman power. The extended borders between the Catholic and Islamic world, the vulnerability of Italy itself to Islamic raiding, and the awareness that the Supreme Porte as the successor to the Byzantine empire considered the peninsula as rightly pertaining to his dominions, all contributed to the anxiety of what was essentially an Italian institution *vis-à-vis* the Ottoman empire.[6] Moreover, the presence of a significant *Morisco* community in Spain and the weakness of Catholic mechanisms of conversion of Muslims, in contrast to the relative success which these were perceived to enjoy by the end of the sixteenth century in confronting Protestantism, combined to make the threat of Islam appear more insidious and destabilizing. The chapter concentrates on the first decade of the Clementine pontificate, which represented the highpoint of the papacy's involvement in the anti-Islamic struggle during the period of this book. This was principally because after the conclusion of hostilities between Venice and the Ottoman empire in 1573–4, a serious conflict between these two powers did not break out again until 1645 in the war of Candia. The lessening of the Ottoman investment in naval warfare also reduced the interest of Spain in committing major resources against the Supreme Porte. Similarly, after the Treaty of Zsitvatörök which brought an end to the long war in 1606, a major struggle between the Austrian Habsburgs and the Turks did not occur for another five decades.

Without conflict between the Ottoman empire and a major Christian power, there was no opportunity for the papacy to apply leverage in support of an anti-Islamic crusade, although this certainly never implied a lack of interest in Rome in this subject. Rather the Sultan in Istanbul continued to be perceived as 'the most potent and formidable enemy of Christianity' and throughout the period under review Rome attempted to patronize anti-Ottoman campaigns.[7] The first Polish-Ottoman war of 1620–1, for instance, and in particular the heavy defeat inflicted on the Turks at Chotin in September/October 1621, did raise hopes in Rome that a new campaign against Turkish power was possible. At the beginning of his pontificate in 1621 Gregory XV still hoped to unite the Austrian Habsburgs and Poland for a war against the Turks and was bitterly disappointed when this opportunity was lost as a result of events in Central Europe and the Polish sense of grievance that their assistance in preserving Bohemia and Hungary for the Habsburg dynasty had not been sufficiently appreciated.[8] In the 1630s this was still seen as a major opportunity lost and the military successes enjoyed by Ladislav IV of Poland in the Smolensk war 1632–4 lifted Pope Urban VIII's hopes that he might be the figure

---

[6] Kenneth Setton, *Venice, Austria and the Turks in the Seventeenth Century* (Philadelphia: The American Philosophical Society, 1991), pp. 8–9.

[7] 'La Christianità non ha nemico più potente e formidabile del Turco': Instructions for Alessandro del Sangro, 5 April 1621 (Klaus Jaitner (ed.), *Die Hauptinstrucktionen Gregors XV für di Nuntien und Gesandten an den Europäischen Fürstenhöfen 1621–1623* (two vols, Tübingen: Max Niemeyer Verlag, 1997), 2, pp. 575–601, at 582.

[8] Instructions for Giovanni Battista Lancellotti, 14 December 1622 (Thaddaeus Fitych (ed.), *Acta Nuntiaturae Poloniae Tomus XXII Volumen 1 Ioannes Baptista Lancellotti (1622–27)* (Cracoviae: Academia Scientiarum et Litterarum Polona, 2000), pp. 44–7).

to bring about the destruction of Ottoman power in the Balkans, for which enterprise the Pope was prepared to offer any diplomatic aid in his power.[9] In 1639 Urban VII's renewed attempt to bring an end to what seemed, from a papal perspective, a ruinous internal Catholic conflict between the houses of Bourbon and Habsburg, by dispatching three extraordinary nuncios to the Emperor, France and Spain, was prompted by rising fears of an Ottoman assault on Europe.[10]

Nevertheless, from the last decade of the sixteenth century down to the Peace of Westphalia, it was the papacy of Clement VIII which allowed for the greatest manifestation of anti-Ottoman papal activity. The incorporation of Ferrara into the papal state, the textured non-resolution of the *De auxillis* controversy and, above all, the reconciliation of Henri IV have been seen as the chief successes of the Clementine papacy.[11] Yet the attempt to create a Christian coalition against the Turks was one of the *leitmotifs* of his reign, and his endeavours in this respect reveal much about the scope, aspirations, and limitations of papal diplomacy.

Papal knowledge of the Balkans increased in the decades after Trent as part of wider processes of engagement and renewal. Under Gregory XIII the notion of a Roman centre for missionary activity had been promoted by Jean de Vendeville and Antonio Possevino[12] and a number of Apostolic visitations had been made into the Balkans and into the Turkish-subjugated part of Hungary. In 1580 Pietro Cedulini, the Bishop of Nona, visited throughout the south Balkans and Constantinople and made use of a Franciscan, Girolamo Arsengo, and a Dominican, Giovita da Brescia, to push the scope of investigation as far as the Crimean peninsula. Meanwhile, the Bishop of Stagno, Bonifacio Drakolica, who had been employed as a visitor to the Bosnian Franciscan province under Pius V in 1571, was dispatched to a wide arc of territory through Dalmatia, Slavonia, Croatia, Bosnia, Serbia, and Hungary. Cedulini's recommendations in terms of reconstructing a local hierarchy, missions of regular clergy, financial aid for the reconstruction of churches, and a Jesuit mission to Istanbul to counteract the effect of Protestant influence in the entourage of the English ambassador, were influential in terms of shaping future papal missionary policy, but also helped to furnish Rome with a more acute sense of the political and confessional contours of the area.[13] Drakolica's apostolic visitation to the north was assisted by acquiring permissions from the *Bey* of the *Sanjak* and the *Qadi* at Sarajevo to conduct visitation and instruction of the Christian population without molestation from Turkish officials. He was

---

[9] See the Instructions for Mario Filonardi, 19 July 1635 (Theresia Chynczewska-Hennel (ed.), *Acta Nuntiaturae Poloniae Tomus XXV Marius Filonardi (1635–43) Volumen 1* (Cracoviae: Academia Scientiarum et Litterarum Polona), pp. 16, 35–8).

[10] See the common Instructions to Gaspar Mattei, Cesare Fachinetti, and Ranuccio Scotti, 1639 (Pierre Blet (ed.), *Correspondance du Nonce en France Ranuccio Scotti (1639–41)* (Paris and Rome: E. de Boccard, 1965), pp. 58–90, at 58–60, 85–90).

[11] In this regard see Maria Teresa Fattori, *Clemente VIII e il Sacro Collegio, 1592–1605: Meccanismi istituzionali e accentramento di governo* (Stuttgart: Hiersemann, 2004).

[12] John Patrick Connelly, 'Antonio Possevino's Plan for World Evangelization', *The Catholic Historical Review* 74: 2 (1988), 179–98.

[13] Antal Molnár, *Katolikus missziók a hódolt Magyarországon I 1572–1647* (Budapest: Balassi Kiadó, 2002), pp. 124–5; István György Tóth (ed.), *Litterae Missionariorum de Hungaria et Transilvania (1572–1717)* (two vols, Roma and Budapest: Biblioteca Academiae Hungariae, 2002), 1, p. 83.

impressed by the tenacity with which local Catholics had adhered to their faith—in Sarajevo he encountered an estimated 5000 Catholics—but he and his party were also depressed by the effect which a lack of educated priests and contact with Orthodox and Protestant communities had had on their grasp of Catholic doctrine and practice. He reported also of the financial pressure which was leading to Islamicization.[14]

In 1580, observing the disorder which had begun in Ottoman territories in the wake of Suleiman's long reign, Germanico Malaspina raised the idea of a Christian Balkan insurrection in tandem with an assault on the Ottomans by Christian powers.[15] In the decade that followed Roman interest in Eastern Europe was further sharpened by Antonio Possevino's peregrinations. Possevino was deeply struck by the possibilities for the augmentation of the Catholic religion in Transylvania, Wallachia, and in the areas around Timisoara and Belgrade. He was impressed by the fidelity of Catholics in these areas who were prepared to undertake long journeys to avail themselves of the sacraments of the church, often exposing themselves to significant dangers of attack while doing so. As an Italian, his enthusiasm was particularly animated by the Romanian-speaking populations which he encountered. Seeing them as the abandoned remnants of old Italian colonies, still speaking a corrupted form of 'our' language, he believed that they were ripe for Catholic evangelization. It was true that they were 'Greeks' (Orthodox) but in an 'idiotic' manner, knowing nothing of their religion, and therefore he did not anticipate the same difficulties in winning them over as occurred with more educated Orthodox populations. How many souls would be lost in Italy, he speculated, if there were only six or seven priests?

But nowhere he journeyed was Possevino struck with the impossibility of conversion. On the contrary, in a cognate fashion to how other members of his Society saw the Americas and Asia as a fruitful source of souls to replace those damned in Europe by the Reformation, he detected the possibility of conversion not only among the Germans and Hungarians of Hungary and Transylvania but even among those he termed Tartars, Goths, and Scythians, remarking on the openness and hospitality which had been shown to him by all. Possevino's dream was that intense evangelical work in this area could open up a corridor for Catholic evangelization into Asia.[16] From the same date also Possevino had noted the childish promise of Sigismund Bathory on whom Clement VIII was to hang so many hopes in the Balkan wars against the Turks during the 1590s.[17]

Even before ascending to the papal throne, Clement had professed a keen interest in the Turkish threat but in the first months of his pontificate the level of disunity within the Christian world had rendered any thoughts of an anti-Turkish

[14] Bartolomeo Sfondrato S.J. to Oliver Manareo, 15 December 1580 (Tóth, *Litterae Missionariorum*, 1, pp. 113–14); Molnár, *Katolikus missziók*, pp. 125–36.

[15] Augustin Theiner (ed.), *Vetera Monumenta Slavorum Meridionalium* (two vols, Rome and Zagreb, 1863–75), 2, pp. 75–7.

[16] See for instance Antonio Possevino to Pope Gregory XIII, 12 April 1583 (Andreas Veress (ed.), *Epistolae et Acta Jesuitarum Transylvaniae Temporibus Principum Báthory (1571–1613)* (Budapest: Atheneum, 1911), pp. 279–83).

[17] Same to Cardinal Antonio Galli Ptolemeo, 6 March, 1583 (ibid., pp. 260–1).

coalition nugatory. Immediately upon the escalation of hostilities in 1592 on the Turkish–Habsburg border, however,[18] he urged the Emperor to convene the Imperial Diet to prepare an effective resistance and exhorted the princes of Italy to contribute assistance. Following the fall of Bihac in June 1592, where a reported 5000 Christians were killed and 800 children carried off into captivity, he redoubled these efforts in the hope that the war might become, not merely an effective defence of Christian territory, but an anti-Islamic offensive.[19] The destruction of the regional Turkish army at Sisak, a key Imperial defensive position for the valley of the Sava, by a greatly out-numbered Christian force, ignited an open war between the Emperor Rudolf II and the Ottoman sultanate in July 1593 and it fired the Pope's enthusiasm.[20] Sisak seemed to offer itself as a providential sign that perhaps the time had come to drive back the Turkish threat. In that context it behoved all Christians to seek to seize the presented opportunity, in the belief that God would increase the graces on offer to those who recognized and accorded with his will.[21]

Clement's diplomatic policy reflected the Pope's personal convictions. The congregation for Hungary, whose membership he constantly tampered with in the course of the first years of his pontificate, and which met relatively infrequently, was largely restricted to the deliberation of the concrete manner in which papal policy was to be implemented, rather than being given a voice to explore the overall value of what became a massive drain on papal resources in the course of his pontificate.[22] From the beginning of the war the Pope attempted to encourage the King of Spain to come to the defence of the patrimonial lands of the house of Austria. On the other hand, and more hopefully in view of Spanish involvement in the war against Henri of Navarre in France, he explored the possibility of creating an Eastern Christian alliance. Although the tensions between the Turks and the Poles which he had witnessed first-hand in his time as legate had diminished,[23] the Pope was hopeful that he could draw Poland into an anti-Turkish coalition and prevail upon the Catholic Prince of Transylvania, Sigismund Bathory, to revolt

---

[18] For an accessible English language summary of the Habsburg–Turkish war 1593–1606 see István György Tóth, 'The Century of Ottoman Wars (1526–1606)' and 'Between the Sultan and the Emperor (1604–1711)' in idem (ed.), *A Concise History of Hungary: The History of Hungary from the Early Middle Ages to the Present* (Budapest: Corvina, 2005), pp. 181–212.

[19] Instructions to Camillo Borgese, 6 October, 1593 (Klaus Jaitner (ed.), *Die Hauptinstruktionen Clemens' VIII. für die Nuntien und Legaten an den europäischen Fürstenhöfen, 1592–1605* (two vols, Tübingen: Max Niemayer Verlag, 1984), 1, pp. 156–7); Setton, *Venice, Austria and the Turks*, p. 6.

[20] Jan Paul Niederkorn, *Die europäischen Mächte und der 'Lange Turkenkrieg' Kaiser Rudolfs. II (1593–1606)* (Vienna: Verlag der österreichischen Akademie der Wissenschaften, 1993), pp. 70–102, 499, offers a comprehensive treatment of papal diplomatic commitment to the war and Rome's financial support which he estimates as amounting to roughly 2.85 million florins.

[21] Instructions to Camillo Borgese, 6 October 1593 (*Die Hauptinstruktionen Clemens' VIII.*, pp. 157, 158, fn 4, 161): the fact that the war had ignited almost by accident as a result of the actions of the Pasha of Bosnia when neither Turks nor Habsburgs were seeking conflict was seen as another possible example of divine intervention.

[22] Fattori, *Clemente VIII e il Sacro Collegio*, pp. 88, 116–18.

[23] Instructions to Camillo Borgese, 6 October 1593 (*Die Hauptinstruktionen Clemens' VIII.*, 1, pp. 157–8); C.M. Kortepeter, 'Ġāzī Girāy II, Khan of the Crimea, and Ottoman Policy in Eastern Europe and the Caucasus, 1588–94', *The Slavonic and East European Review* 44: 102 (1966), 139–66, at 150–2.

against the Supreme Porte. While continually frustrated in the first of these objectives, Clementine diplomacy enjoyed its most spectacular successes in Transylvania. In August 1594 the Prince broke the power of the pro-Turkish party within the principality and veered to the Christian alliance, culminating in an agreement with the Emperor in early 1595 which acknowledged Rudolf as his heir if he died childless and which guaranteed Sigismund the Silesian territories of Oppeln and Ratibor were he to lose Transylvania in the course of hostilities. The Prince was also promised a Habsburg bride, Maria Christina, daughter of Archduke Charles.[24]

The instructions furnished to Fabio and Valerio Orsino and to Paolo Sanvitale, who were sent as extraordinary nuncios to the Italian princes of Urbino, Ferrara, Mantova, Savoy, Parma, and Florence, and to the republics of Lucca and Genoa in January 1594 to encourage them to furnish forces for an anti-Turkish campaign, offer an interesting series of insights into the attitude of the Clementine papacy towards the war. Not surprisingly, in view of the policy of peace with the Ottomans which it had followed since the 1570s, the papacy had little expectation that Venice would be proactive in committing forces but hoped that it might, in time, participate if it saw successes for the Christian forces.[25] The view of the Turkish threat hovered between a genuine fear of its future expansion and the hope that it might be utterly overcome.[26] Throughout this period, a providential understanding of Turkish power was a key element of papal engagement with anti-Islamic activity.

The instructions to Clement's diplomatic representatives in Italy demonstrate this motif clearly. Ottoman strength was perceived as having grown as a result of the intestinal dissension of the Christian world. The first ingress into Europe derived from the quarrels between the Greek emperors of Trabizbond and Constantinople which had opened the door to the destruction of Byzantium and the gradual subjugation of the Balkans.[27] The great naval victory of Lepanto some two decades previously was seen as a lost opportunity, as the Christians failed to prosecute their advantage and then, while the Turks were preoccupied with warfare against the Persians 1578–90, Christian solidarity was dissolved in renewed civil conflicts.[28] The cessation of hostilities on the Ottomans' eastern flank, and their strengthened position in Transcaucasia and Tabriz, now meant that Europe was once again in danger. Yet the battle of Sisak and a number of other smaller victories against superior Ottoman forces offered themselves as a 'great sign of compassion

[24] Tóth, 'Century of Ottoman Wars', p. 203.

[25] In 1599, with peace having been secured between France and Spain and nourishing hopes that both powers would join forces against the Turks, he was optimistic that Venice too would finally enter the war: see Niederkorn, *Die europäischen Mächte und der 'Lange Turkenkrieg'*, pp. 322–3.

[26] See Instructions to Paolo Sanvitale, 24 January 1594 (*Die Hauptinstruktionen Clemens' VIII.*, 1, pp. 216–25) and to Sanvitale and Fabio and Valerio Orsino, 30 January 1594 (ibid., pp. 232–45): see also the Instructions for Alfonso Visconti, 15 January 1595 (Veress, *Relationes Nuntiorum Apostolicorum*, p. 59) which spoke of the 'speranza di ricuperare non solo tutto quello, che s'è perduto in centinaia d'anni sino a Constantinopoli, ma forse anco di distruggere tutto l'impero ottoman'.

[27] Instructions to Sanvitale and Fabio and Valerio Orsino, 30 January 1594 (*Die Hauptinstruktionen Clemens' VIII.*, 1, p. 233).

[28] Instructions to Paolo Sanvitale, 24 January 1594 (ibid., p. 219).

and the placation of the divine wrath'[29] which had allowed such damage to Christendom. As an intimation that God wished his people to know that they should now play their part and that he was prepared to assist them, it was possible to understand the battle as a source of a great hope and the promise of fiercer Turkish aggression in revenge. Thus, the necessity of preparing for a great struggle had made itself apparent.[30] It was taken as another favourable portent that the Imperial forces were already committed in defence of Hungary, which had been one of the great objectives that Pope Pius V had been unable to achieve and which had now been accomplished without any diplomatic activity on the part of the papacy.

The providential framework within which the conflict was understood was of genuine importance. Islamic–Christian enmity was a fundamental constitutive factor of Early Modern Catholic identity, symbolized by the excommunication of all who conveyed war supplies to Muslims in the annually published bull, *In Coena Domini*. The unexpected nature of the war, followed by even more unexpected Christian victory at Sisak, seemed to indicate the workings of divine power. In a longer perspective, the historical successes of the Ottomans were seen as God's punishment of the Christian world. The Turks had been granted the role of God's 'castigo dei popoli' and previous attempts to create an effective union had not succeeded because divine providence evidently wished to move the hearts of the Christian people to a more ardent supplication for relief.[31] Such an understanding of the Turkish conflict continued throughout the period under review.[32] Cognate to this providential understanding of defeat was the assumption that, just as the Chosen People had known victory under Joshua when obedient to their God, but suffered defeat when sullied by Achan's sin, if Christians could unite in lives uncontaminated by heresy and sinfulness then they too would always enjoy victory against the Muslim enemies of God.[33]

In this conflict both the papacy and the powers of Italy were seen as having a special role. Throughout the diplomatic documentation of the Clementine era, the notion of the *Republica Christiana* is constantly reiterated and the term was evidently still freighted with significant resonance and relevance. Interestingly, it is difficult to distinguish any sense that the Protestant powers of Europe could be comprehended under this term but it evidently did not exclude Orthodox Christians, with whom the possibility of future union was not discounted. This notion of the *Republica Christiana* was also understood in the context of a corporeal metaphor that 'Christendom, or at least that which existed in Europe under Christian

---

[29] 'segno grande della misericordia et placatione dell'ira divina' (ibid., p. 219).

[30] Instructions to Sanvitale and Fabio and Valerio Orsino, 30 January 1594 (ibid., p. 235).

[31] 'col timore di tal flagello voleva la divina providenza tirare il cuore d'huomini christiani a chiederle con più viva fede et con più ardente devotione misericordia di tante perdite et desolationi' (ibid., p. 233).

[32] See for example the Third Instruction for Giuseppe Acquaviva, 16 October 1621 (*Die Hauptinstrucktionen Gregors XV*, 2, pp. 798–9):'Iddio permise che quasi per gastigo della Grecia infedele e per vegogna e percossa dell'arme latine, che dall'Oriente furon del tutto cacciate'.

[33] In this regard see the 1611 text of Szántó (Arator) István S.J., *Confutatio Alcorani*, Mihály Balász (ed.) (Szeged: Scriptum KFT, 1990), pp. 50–1.

princes, was one sole body composed of many kingdoms and provinces' and whose oppressed members had need of the aid of the others in order to preserve the health 'each one of them and of all together'.[34] The popes, 'to whom God had entrusted the care of the entire Christian flock'[35] as spiritual leaders, were perceived as having moral responsibility to animate the various constituent elements of this *Republica Christiana* in a common policy of defence.

The reasons to participate in this enterprise were twofold: on the one hand it was seen as a clear aspect of spiritual duty. All those who owed their redemption, endowment with miraculous sacramental and temporal goods, and a perpetual celestial inheritance to the 'most precious blood'[36] of Christ, were obliged to become ardent propagators and warriors on behalf of the Christian religion. Not to do so would result in condemnation before the awesome tribunal of the lord on the day of their judgement. On the other hand, particularly for the princes of Italy, it made compelling sense to carry the war outside the peninsula rather than to wait for its arrival. With a keen sense of the history of antiquity, it was noted that from Otranto the sails of a Turkish fleet in Albania could be espied and that Turkish territory was close enough to allow fresh figs to be brought from there to Rome, the ancient sign for the Romans of the need to take heed of the proximity of a foe.

In addition to their Roman ancestors, the parallel between contemporary Italy and ancient Greece suggested itself: like the Persian threat which forced the different states of Greece to combine in resistance, so the politically fragmented Italian people needed to confederate to protect their cultural and religious inheritance from an Oriental foe. Another lesson from the past concerned the folly of defensive warfare. The entire unhappy history of the wars against the Turks indicated the ineffectiveness of this approach which had led to the progressive weakening of the Christian world.[37] It was noted that the Venetians were fortifying Udine but the individual defence of territories, while not unimportant, could not address the roots of the problem. Only common action, preferably by taking the war to Hungary or Thrace, offered genuine hope.[38]

One of the great advantages which the Clementine papacy hoped to achieve from a determined Christian offensive against the Supreme Porte was the uprising of Christian populations within Turkish dominions and the rebellion of the vassal states on the Ottoman empire's northern border.[39] Following on from the missionary contacts of the previous decades, papal interest in this possibility had become increasingly aroused, particularly after the Venetian peace with the

[34] Instructions to Paolo Sanvitale, 24 January 1594 (*Die Hauptinstruktionen Clemens' VIII.*, 1, p. 218).

[35] 'a' qual ha racomandata la cura di tutto 'l gregge christiana': Instructions for Lotario Conti, 3 October 1594 (ibid., p. 270).

[36] 'pretiosissimo sangue': Instructions to Paolo Sanvitale, 24 January 1594 (ibid., p. 217).

[37] Instructions for Giovanni Francesco Aldobrandini, 10 November 1594 (ibid., pp. 278–303, at 294.)

[38] Instructions to Sanvitale and Fabio and Valerio Orsino, 30 January 1594 (ibid., p. 234).

[39] Grounds for optimism did exist in this regard: see István György Tóth, 'Between Islam and Catholicism: Bosnian Franciscan Missionaries in Turkish Hungary, 1584–1716', *The Catholic Historical Review* 89 (2003), 409–33, at 411.

Ottomans in 1573 which seemed to sacrifice the advantages gained at Lepanto. In the 1580s a Bosnian, Friar Angelo, had offered to organize the betrayal of military positions in Dalmatia. Following his accession, Clement activated a diplomatic web of envoys in South-Eastern and Eastern Europe. His most notable success in this regard was certainly in Transylvania. The Catholic sensibilities of the Prince, Sigismund Bathory, were worked on by his Jesuit confessor, Alfonso Carillo, and by various papal envoys. Eventually the Prince became inclined to join the anti-Turkish coalition.[40] But Clement's envoy to Eastern Europe, Alexander Komulovic, the rector of the Illyrian College in Rome, was not merely sent to Transylvania, but was instructed also to make contact with the Zaporozhian Cossacks across the Dnieper to encourage them to attack the Ottoman empire and to offer them financial support in doing so. He was also to investigate whether through the medium of the Cossacks the Precopensian Tartars, the Mengrellians, a people on the Black Sea between the rivers Rion, Zchenis-Zkali, and Ingur, and the Circassians could be induced to launch attacks on the eastern flank of the Ottoman dominions. In addition, Komulovic was one of the envoys who was to explore the possibility of creating a rising in Wallachia and Moldova, both of which were under Ottoman suzerainty.[41] Since his wide peregrinations through the Balkans as apostolic visitor 1584–87, Komulovic had been impressed by the possibilities of creating a general uprising among the Turkish-subjugated Christian populations. In 1594 he was hopeful that a Habsburg victory over the main Turkish forces in the field could lead to a triple thrust comprising the Imperial forces, the conjoint armies of Transylvania, Wallachia, and Moldova, and a fleet dispatched from the western Mediterranean, that could aspire to take Istanbul itself.[42]

The plan of a joint attack on the Ottomans under the leadership of the Transylvanian Prince was greeted with interest in Wallachia and Moldova. Papal enthusiasm was also sharpened by rumours that the Christian commander of the vital fortress of Klis, situated in the mountains interior to the port of Split in Dalmatia, which Christian forces had been trying to suborn since the 1580s, was prepared to betray it to the Christian alliance. Consequently, another envoy, Giovanni Francesco Allegretti, was dispatched to investigate the possibilities of gaining and holding the stronghold and to hammer out the terms.[43] In addition, contacts were explored

---

[40] Carillo's correspondence is collected in Endre Veress (ed.), *Epistolae et Acta P. Alfonsi Carrillii S. J., 1591–1618: Monumenta Hungariae Historica Diplomataria 32* (Budapest: Magyar Tudományos Akadémia, 1906).

[41] Instructions for Alexander Komulovic, 10 November 1593 (*Die Hauptinstruktionen Clemens' VIII.*, 1, pp. 186–204); Endre Veress (ed.), *Relationses Nuntiorum apostolicorum in Transsilvaniam Missorum a Clemente VIII, 1592–1600: Monumenta Vaticana Historiam Regni Hungariae Illustrantia* (2nd edition, Budapest: Metem, 2001), p. xxiv; Setton, *Venice, Austria and the Turks*, p. 9.

[42] Komulovic to Cinzio Aldobrandini, 16 February 1594 (Veress, *Relationses Nuntiorum apostolicorum*, pp. 42–5).

[43] Instructions for Giovanni Francesco Allegretti, 11–13 April 1594 (*Die Hauptinstruktionen Clemens' VIII.*, pp. 256–61). These negotiations eventually bore fruit when the city was taken in a daring surprise attack in 1596 but strong Venetian hostility to the enterprise helped ensure that the garrison was inadequately reinforced and the town was rapidly retaken: see James Krokar, 'New Means to an Old End: Early Modern Maps in the Service of an anti-Ottoman Crusade', *Imago Mundi* 60: 1 (2008), 23–38.

with the warlike Serbian communities along the lower Danube and most fruitfully in southern Albania for participation in the campaign.[44]

The high hopes of early 1594 were soon swiftly dashed. The overtures to the Tartars proved completely unsuccessful with a large Precopensian force entering Hungary in 1594 in a mission of pillage and destruction in support of the Turks, although their subsequent heavy defeat was one of the few Christian successes of that year. The Turks recorded significant advances, in particular the capture of the key fortress of Győr in Hungary on 2 October 1594. Yet, despite what he saw as the disastrous leadership of the Emperor, Clement's government's interpretation of the importance of maintaining war against the Turks was heightened by the sense that the entire Christian world now stood on the brink of disaster. In effect, it was feared in Rome that the fall of Győr opened the way for potential annihilation of the entire Eastern wing of the house of Austria, with the exception of the Tirol and Lorraine. Győr, one of the strongest fortresses in Europe, situated and protected by the confluence of the rivers Danube and Raab, had been the linchpin of Habsburg defences. It was assumed that its fall could precipitate the collapse of the remaining portion of Hungary, since the remaining fortresses at Kassa (Košiče), Kanizsa, and Szatmár were too small, and too difficult to relieve in the event of a siege, to hold out much prospect of a successful defence against the main Turkish forces.

Once again the road to Vienna was seen to have been opened to Turkish arms and, given the state of its defences, the appalling performance of the Imperial armies in the Hungarian campaign, and the strength of alienated Protestant opinion within the city itself, the Curia was not hopeful that the city could withstand a determined Turkish attack. It was true that in the past the city had twice successfully withstood Turkish arms but the leadership previously provided by the Palgrave of Neuburg in 1529 and then by Charles V was now unlikely to be provided by Rudolf. Moreover, the successful deliverance of Vienna in the past was seen to have owed much to the pious prayers of the inhabitants and the faith of its defenders, uncontaminated by heresy. Neither urban population nor Imperial army could now offer such proof of Catholic fidelity and thus were less likely to attract divine favour. Indeed, one of the chief reasons why the destruction of the Habsburg dominions was so feared in Rome was the conviction that the Turks as the 'castigo de' populi'[45] generally discharged their divinely-sanctioned mission against people who had abandoned union with the Catholic church.[46]

This conception which was to become a common trope of Hungarian Catholic controversy, for instance, was founded on a historical analysis that no truly Catholic state had ever fallen to the Turks. However, given the propensity to heresy among

[44] Instructions for Giovanni Francesco Aldobrandini, 10 November 1594 (*Die Hauptinstruktionen Clemens' VIII.*, 1, p. 300).

[45] Instructions for Lotario Conti, 3 October 1594 (ibid., p. 273).

[46] As an attempted counterweight Clement published a jubilee in December 1594 to excite all Catholics to pray for the situation in Hungary, Germany, and France: see Arnold d'Ossat to Villeroy, 6 December 1594 (*Lettres de l'Illustrissime et Révérendissime Cardinal d'Ossat, éveque de Bayeux au roy Henry le Grand et à Monsieur Villeroy* (Paris, 1627), p. 23).

the Hungarian, Austrian and German peoples, it seemed legitimate to fear that they too might be about to follow the dire example of the Orthodox populations of the Balkans. Such considerations would not necessarily affect Italy itself, of course, but this was cold comfort compared to the awful prospect of further Turkish advances into the heart of Christendom. It was also gloomily assumed that if the Ottomans chose to strike north there were equally poor prospects of successful defensive war. Bohemia was considered to lack any major fortress capable of breaking the waves of a Turkish assault, nor, except for the weak fortress of Ujvár, was there any obstacle to the ravaging of Moravia.[47]

In this context Clement believed it imperative that Spain throw its weight into the struggle to preserve the Central European branch of the Habsburg dynasty and in November 1594 Giovanni Francesco Aldobrandini was dispatched to Philip II in an effort to persuade him to contribute significant forces. In Rome's estimation, only the provision of a major army of 30,000 to 40,000 men, preferably not of German troops in view of their poor record against the Turks, offered a concrete hope of preserving Vienna. It was also considered of prime urgency that the Spanish fleet be sent to Sicily by May of the following year.[48] In urging Philip II to follow the example of his father in preserving Austria, the Clementine government was aware that certain influences at court were not necessarily averse to Turkish advances in Croatia. In a wider geopolitical context, the threat on their eastern flank might be expected to induce Venice to behave in a more cautious manner with regard to the support of Navarre in France, and might even incline certain Lombard cities under Venetian domination to look for a more potent Spanish protector.[49]

Rome was conscious too of a coldness of relationships between the Emperor and Madrid. But that this should serve as a pretext to deny aid was considered unconscionable. Moreover how could the pontiff prevail upon other princes, particularly in Italy, to furnish aid to the Emperor if his own kinsfolk were not prepared to do so? Rome also expected reluctance from Spain on the grounds of lack of finance. Here again the Clementine line was harsh. The throne of Spain was granted extensive use of ecclesiastical revenues amounting to well over one million ducats annually which had been granted for the sole end of mounting resistance to the enemies of Christendom.[50] If Philip chose to harden his heart to the necessity of his blood, and the supplications of the Vicar of Christ, and ignore the many evident divine

---

[47] Instructions for Lotario Conti, 3 October 1594 (*Die Hauptinstruktionen Clemens' VIII.*, 1, p. 271).

[48] First Instruction for Giovanni Francesco Aldobrandini, 10 November 1594 (ibid., pp. 278–303).

[49] Instructions to Camillo Borgese, 6 October 1593 (ibid., p. 159).

[50] The 'Cruzada' was worth about 750,000 ducats annually to the monarch of Spain at the end of the sixteenth century. Revenues from the 'Subsidio' amounted to 420,000 ducats and the 'Excusado' provided another 250,000 ducats. Together these three taxes, which could only legally be levied with papal approval, approximated to one quarter of the King's annual income: Sean T. Perrone, 'The Procurator General of the Castilian Assembly of the Clergy, 1592–1741', *Catholic Historical Review* 91 (2005), 26–59; Patrick O'Banion, 'Only the king can do it: Adaptability and Flexibility in Crusade Ideology in Sixteenth-Century Spain', *Church History* 81: 3 (2012), 552–74.

favours which had been showered upon him,[51] then the Apostolic See would be forced to consider revoking the concessions and to publicize the reasons why it had been moved to take this step.[52] The appeal was also to Spanish self-interest. The dilatory dispatch of the Armada to Sicily in 1594 had allowed the Turkish fleet to ravage Spanish possessions, sacking and burning Reggio in Calabria, while Messina itself lay helpless against them. Thus, providing naval assistance was in Spain's own interest. If the commander of the Turkish fleet, Sinan (Scipione) Cicala, a native of Italy, made use of his knowledge of the area to seize a port in the coming year then this would be of manifest detriment to the kingdom of Naples. Moreover, if the Emperor, deserted by his kin, was forced to make a humiliating peace with the Sultan then it was unimaginable that the Supreme Porte would consent unless the Adriatic littoral, which had provided a base for Uskok piracy, and which had been one of the principal reasons for the war, was ceded to Turkish control.[53] This, however, would open the way for Ottoman armies into Italy itself and the Spanish possessions at Milan. The range, urgency, and indeed menace of the arguments which the papacy was prepared to make to the most important Catholic monarch is an indication of the significance which was placed on the struggle against Ottoman power in the Balkans.

Clement was keenly aware, however, that Spanish involvement in the war largely depended on the contemporary situation in France. And it was during 1594 that the papacy came to the momentous conclusion that it would be necessary to accept Henri of Navarre's reconciliation with the Catholic church, although only in September 1595 was this process finally brought to a conclusion.[54] Many factors, both spiritual and temporal, evidently influenced this decision. In terms of the former, the Holy See was clearly determined to assert its own primacy and the envoy to Spain was instructed that a decision 'on the absolution of Navarre should be absolutely reserved' to the Pope who 'with the assistance of the Holy Spirit, and being well-intentioned, without any interest, it could be believed that he should take the decision most useful to the glory and service of God'.[55] Clement was undoubtedly aware that any decision to absolve Navarre would be met with bitter hostility in Madrid but increasingly he saw little other choice. A king was

[51] 'un Prencipe, che Dio ha circondato di tante sue gratie...non esaudisca la voce del Vicario suo che le chiede aiuto non per sè, ma per li parenti di lei: First Instruction for Giovanni Francesco Aldobrandini, 10 November 1594 (*Die Hauptinstruktionen Clemens' VIII.*, 1, p. 284).

[52] Under papal prompting Spain did offer some 300,000 ducats to support the war but at least half of this sum does not seem to have been paid; the prospect floated by Spain of raising 8000 foot for the Hungarian war was also not fulfilled: see d'Ossat to Villeroy, 20 May 1595 (*Lettres de Cardinal d'Ossat*, p. 110).

[53] See Emra Safa Gürkan, 'The Centre and the Frontier: Ottoman Cooperation with the North African Corsairs in the Sixteenth Century', *Turkish Historical Review* 1 (2010), 125–63, at 155; D'Ossat to Villeroy, November 1596 (*Lettres de Cardinal d'Ossat*, p. 336).

[54] Michel de Waele, 'Autorité, Legitimité, Fidelité: le Languedoc Ligueur et la reconnaissance d'Henri IV', *Revue d'histoire moderne et contemporaine* 53: 2 (2006), 5–34, at 7; Fattori, *Clemente VIII e il Sacro Collegio*, pp. 57–8.

[55] 'l'assolutione di Navarra, sia assolutamente riservato a N.S.'; 'con...l'assistenza dello spirito Santo et con la buona intentione, lontana da ogni interesse, si può credere che debba pigliare quella risolutione che più converrà a gloria et servitio di Dio': Second Instruction to Giovanni Francesco Aldobrandini, November 1594 (*Die Hauptinstruktionen Clemens' VIII.*, 1, pp. 304–20 at 315, 306).

necessary in France, who evidently had to be Catholic in religion and French by nationality, as the xenophobic reaction to the candidatures of Archduke Earnest and the Infanta had revealed. Six years of war had revealed the impossibility of imposing a Spanish-favoured king on France. The efforts of both the papacy and Spain had been sufficient to maintain a civil war in France but now far more resources would be needed as the anti-Navarre party in France had lost momentum. Neither the dukes of Lorraine, Guise, nor Mayenne offered real hope of mounting successful resistance to the Bourbon pretender and the exhausted house of Savoy had more chance of drawing the war into Italy than of unseating Navarre. The *Ligue* offered no hope: without a leader, money, or troops, it was a mere ghost of its former self. At a popular level, too, it was clear that the French wished an end to war. While the cause of religion had kept them in arms before, now that the King had abjured, hatred of Spain was a more potent motivation than loathing of heresy in a leader whose conversion the French people were prepared to accept.[56] Any future war, therefore, would effectively become an international contest between France and Spain rather than a French civil war. That Spain could win such a war was doubtful.

Genuine religious concern for France, impressed upon him by his spiritual advisors, also inclined the pontiff towards this decision. If Navarre could not be driven from the realm by force, and if the French accommodated themselves to his rule despite the papal censures, then millions of souls would be damned. Was it not better to accept one man than condemn so many to perdition? And was there not an active danger of pushing France into open schism by denying an absolution which the French people thought merited?[57] The menace of a patriarchate in France, to which the French were considered naturally inclined, represented a significant threat. Venetian advice that a schism was a clear and active possibility, that Clement VII had lost England for Catholicism by seeking to ingratiate himself with Charles V, and that an obvious threat existed that Clement VIII could lose France by refusing to stand up to Charles's son, was not without substance.[58] The idea that as king Navarre could return to heresy and use his powers to drag the realm in his wake was considered less likely than a situation where the King could use the excuse that he had been wrongfully denied absolution to justify a return to Protestantism. If, on the other hand, the Holy See showed mercy and benignity then any future lapse on the part of the King would be perceived as an ungrateful rebuff to God rather than a justified rejection of the Holy See's hard-heartedness. And while the Pope had previously

[56] The Parisian acceptance of Navarre as king in March 1594 was followed by twenty-seven other towns in the following four months: de Waele, 'Autorité, Legitimité, Fidelité', 22.
[57] Clement was aware that many in France who considered themselves fervently Catholic were prepared to accept the King. The Catholic consuls of Lyon had written to the Pope in February 1594 insisting that the King had formally promised that no other religion than Catholicism would be tolerated in Lyons and it was on this basis that they had accepted him: see de Waele, 'Autorité, Legitimité, Fidelité', p. 27.
[58] *La Legazione di Roma di Paolo Paruto 1592–95: Monumenti storici publicati dalla R. Deputazione Veneta di storia di patria*, G. De Leda (ed.) (three vols, Venice, 1886–87), I, p. 309.

rejected Navarre's attempts through the Duke of Nevers,[59] the situation in France had changed significantly. Navarre had effectively gained the kingdom despite the censure and had demonstrated over a year of perseverance in the Catholic faith.

While many purely French factors inclined Clement to make the decision to accept Navarre's reconciliation, it is evident that the Turkish war was also a highly significant issue. From the beginning of the conflict until its conclusion in 1606, the level of European interest in the war was manifested in the number of pamphlets and other publications which events such as the sack of Bihac or the victory at Sisak stimulated throughout the continent.[60] Already in 1593 the Pope's preference had been for the Spanish to scale back their involvement in France, either by offering the *Ligue* merely enough support to maintain its position, or through the medium of a military truce, in order to free up resources for the Turkish war, on the basis that the dangers which the Protestant party in France represented were neither as imminent nor as common to all of Christendom as the threat from the Ottomans.[61] The reverses in Hungary in 1594 formed the proximate background to the decision to break with previous policy in France. While Roman fears of the possible destruction of the eastern branch of the house of Austria, as well as the hopes that a successful campaign might lead to the fall of Istanbul and the expulsion of the Ottomans from Europe, were both exaggerated, there can be no doubting the urgency with which Clement VIII viewed the situation in eastern Europe in 1594. One of the major advantages which the Pope evidently hoped to reap from the absolution was that peace with France would allow Spain to turn its forces to the Turkish war.[62] That in the long term it might even lead to the application of French resources to that conflict was another tantalizing possibility.[63] Thus the Turkish war played a significant role in what was arguably the most important papal decision of the Early Modern period. As it transpired, few of the advantages of which Clement had dreamed in terms of mobilizing French and Spanish resources to support the Balkan war against the Turks ultimately came to pass although Spain's contribution to the war increased significantly after peace was finally concluded in 1598.[64]

---

[59] Clement refused to accept Nevers as the ambassador of a king and although two audiences were granted the Pope was unmoved by the arguments put forward: indeed the ecclesiastics in his company who had participated in the King's reconciliation were required to present themselves to the Holy Office: de Waele, 'Autorité, Legitimité, Fidelité', 21–3.

[60] Setton, *Venice, Austria, and the Turks*, p. 7.

[61] First Instruction for Camillo Borghese, 6 October 1593 (*Die Hauptinstruktionen Clemens' VIII.*, 1, p. 160); 'Considerationi et occorrenze intorno all'instruttione data all'Auditor della Camera', 6 October 1593 (ibid., 2, pp. 795–7).

[62] 'non lasciando di mettere in consideration a Sua Maestà che per questo mezzo porá dare assetto alle cose de' suoi stati et applicate l'animo con maggior forza et ardore alla Guerra contro il Turco': Second Instruction to Giovanni Francesco Aldobrandini, November 1594 (ibid.,1, p. 319).

[63] In 1596 the curia believed that peace in France would lead to the destruction of the Ottoman empire: see Instructions for Cardinal Alessandro de' Medici, 10 May 1596 (*Die Hauptinstruktionen Clemens' VIII.*, 1, p. 466).

[64] Niederkorn, *Die europäischen Mächte und der 'Lange Turkenkrieg'*, p. 253.

If the most influential effects of Clement VIII's preoccupation with the anti-Ottoman war were in some respects actually in France, the details of his papacy's actual involvement in the struggle, and in particular his diplomatic efforts to create an alliance to prosecute the war, offer a keen insight into the limitations which afflicted Rome in its dealings with Catholic states. The Eastern coalition on which Clement had pinned very considerable hopes suffered from significant fractures and mutual suspicion between the participants. With regard to the rebellion of the Ottoman empire's client states, the papal legate Alexander Komulovic began to nourish suspicions that the Prince of Transylvania, Sigismund Bathory, rather than allying with the rulers of Moldova and Wallachia, intended merely to occupy both territories and put the incumbent rulers to death.[65] The conduct of the Emperor also gave considerable cause for worry. Despite the alliance between Transylvania and Rudolf II, fears existed that the Emperor might be tempted to look for a peace with Turks, in which case the papal diplomats were instructed to ensure that Bathory was not left exposed to the wrath of the Supreme Porte. The possibility that Bathory might be the one to look for peace could not be ignored either. It was partly to prevent this that a figure of the importance of Alfonso Visconti, the Bishop of Cervia, was sent to Transylvania in 1595 to act as nuncio to Bathory and his court. Visconti accompanied the Prince on his campaigns during that year as the Transylvanian ruler enjoyed remarkable success and interposed his influence to counteract two Ottoman delegations which tried to abstract Transylvania from its alliance with the Habsburgs. He also operated to sooth tensions between the Prince and the Emperor as a result of the dilatory arrival of his promised Habsburg bride, the archduchess Maria Christina of Austria. The victories which Bathory enjoyed in 1595, especially at Tirgiviste against a large Turkish force under the command of the seasoned general, Sinan pasha, before which the Prince served at the papal nuncio's mass and then kneeled to receive Visconti's blessing in the sight of the whole army, seemed to confirm to the Prince the providential advantages of following the advice and direction of the Vicar of Christ.[66]

Several possible sources of tension smouldered between the Emperor and Transylvania, which the papal nuncios were constantly forced to confront. As holder of the crown of Hungary, Rudolf maintained a claim to both Moldova and Wallachia (as well as to Transylvania itself as a former territory of the crown of St Stephen). While it had been impossible for him or his predecessors to vindicate any of these claims against the Turks, this did not mean that the Imperial court looked with equanimity at the prospect of the fusion of all three under the rule of Sigismund Bathory. Bathory's potential attractiveness to Rudolf's Hungarian subjects was another node of friction. In 1595 plans were floated that the forces of Royal Hungary should join with Bathory for a direct assault on Belgrade, ignoring Esztergom and Buda, on the grounds that this would allow them to join their forces to rebellious Serb, Bosnian, and Bulgarian contingents. Furthermore, the fall of Belgrade would

[65] Alexander Komulovic to Cesare Speciano, nuncio in Prague, 28 February 1594 (Veress, *Relationes Nuntiorum Apostolicorum*, p. 48).
[66] Alfonso Visconti to Cinzio Aldobrandini, 18 October 1595, (ibid., p. 121); same to Peter Aldobrandini, 25 May 1595 (ibid., p. 78); same to Germanico Malaspina, 1 May 1595 (ibid., p. 77).

leave the Turkish garrisons in Hungary isolated and almost impossible to supply and could potentially ignite a general Christian rebellion in the Balkans. Yet the Emperor's advisors were deeply reluctant to countenance this plan, despite its tactical advantages, because of the danger that his Hungarian subjects would desert him to follow Bathory in the event of such a spectacular victory, particularly if the threat of Turkish invasion was removed.[67]

Tensions also existed between Poland and Transylvania, as well as between Poland and the Habsburgs. The various members of the Bathory family considerably muddied the waters in Eastern Europe. Sigismund Bathory's uncle had been a celebrated King of Poland as well as Prince of Transylvania before sponsoring Sigismund's own elevation to the latter position. This however embittered the three sons of Andrew Bathory, Sigismund's cousins, namely Balthasar, an experienced soldier, Cardinal Andrew Bathory, and Stephen, who also aspired to the principality. In 1592 the offices of Clement's first nuncio to Transylvania, Attila Amalteo, who hoped in this manner to create a united Catholic party in the Transylvanian Diet, brought about a short-lived reconciliation between the cousins.[68] In 1594, however, in the context of the crisis provoked by Sigismund's desire to join the Christian coalition, the Prince managed to gain the upper hand over his older relatives. On the grounds of having conspired against him, he caused a number of men to be imprisoned and then strangled, including Balthasar Bathory.[69] Cardinal Andrew and Stephen Bathory were then declared traitors and their possessions confiscated by the Prince. The Cardinal had been a contender for the throne of Poland during the 1580s and still nourished ambitions to advance his status, either by making use of Sigismund Vasa's preoccupations with his second kingdom of Sweden to gain the throne of Poland, or to become Prince of Transylvania himself. He disposed of considerable influence in Poland where Sigismund's behaviour since his accession had aroused substantial resentments.

In 1595 Sigismund's Bathory's acquisition of Moldova and Wallachia created new tensions. Prior to the Turkish occupation Poland had asserted suzerainty over both Moldova and Wallachia and claimed that the insignia of both were displayed among the other dependencies of the crown in the royal standard of Poland. Poland maintained also that the right of both subject states to government by native Christian rulers was guaranteed by the terms of the Polish–Ottoman agreements, which also mandated that the *voivodes* of both maintain amity and correspondence with the Commonwealth.[70] The acceptance of Bathory's overlordship by the *voivodes* both of Moldova and of Wallachia was greeted with natural reservations in Poland. Opportunities to destabilize the new dispensation were not lacking. Despite the manner in which *voivode* Aaron of Moldova had transferred his allegiance, the Prince of Transylvania doubted his reliability and replaced him with Stephan Răzvan in 1595. On the invitation of certain Moldovan nobles who resented this

---

[67] Instructions for Alfonso Visconti, 15 January 1595 (ibid., p. 55).
[68] Relation of the business treated in Transylvania by Monsignor Amalteo, October 1592 (ibid., pp. 382–93).
[69] ibid., p. xxv.
[70] ibid., p. 405; Germanico Malaspina to Alfonso Visconti, November 1595 (ibid., p. 150.)

behaviour, and under pretext of defending Moldova from a Tartar incursion, Polish troops under the command of the chancellor, Jan Zamoyski, therefore moved into Moldova. Răzvan was forced to flee to Sigismund and most of the troops from Moldova, on which Bathory had been counting for the campaign against the Turks, consequently failed to arrive. This was extraordinarily embarrassing for Visconti who, on the basis of information from the nuncio in Poland, had assured Bathory that he need not worry about Polish interference.[71] Visconti's efforts, however, were successfully directed at preventing the Prince of Transylvania from attacking the Poles rather than the Turks, which resulted in the capture by Sigismund of Tîrgoviște, Giurgiu, and Bucharest. This evident and prompt demonstration of God's pleasure at his Christian restraint was noted by Rome as having made the Prince less likely to place his private interests over those of his religion and strengthened Visconti's hand in calming the Prince's ire. Consequently, at the end of a successful season's campaigning in 1595 Sigismund opted to visit the Emperor in Prague rather than attempting to take vengeance on the Poles and Jeremiah, the *Voivode* whom they had installed, although he did allow his own nominee for that post, Răzvan, to take troops for that purpose.[72] Again Visconti's influence was important in convincing the Prince to offer to have the Pope as the mediator between himself and Poland concerning the ultimate disposition of Moldova.[73] As it transpired, it seemed better to Rome that Poland would acquire Moldova while Wallachia would go to Transylvania. This, it was hoped, would bring Poland into the Turkish war.

In order for this objective to be achieved, however, the tensions between the Emperor and the key elements of the anti-Habsburg faction in Poland, principally the chancellor, Jan Zamoyski, needed also to be resolved. Poland had several principal demands of the Habsburgs as a condition for their entry into the conflict. One of these concerned the Archduke Maximilian's claim to the Polish throne which, the papacy agreed, was a complicating factor in Polish politics, particularly in the complex context of Sigismund III's attempts to manage a second crown in Sweden. The prospect that Maximilian would in fact gain the military command of the Habsburg forces against the Turks was similarly unappetizing. Second, partly from a concern to obviate the possibility that an eventual Habsburg/Ottoman peace would leave them exposed to carry on a war unaided against the Supreme Porte, Poland desired the prospective alliance to be forged with the Diet of the Empire and the estates of Bohemia, Hungary, and Austria, rather than merely with Rudolf personally.[74] Third, they wished also that other Christian princes be solicited

---

[71] Alfonso Visconti to Cesare Speciano, 12 September 1595 (ibid., p. 110).

[72] ibid., p. 407; it was the opinion of Germanico Malaspina, the papal nuncio to Poland, that the majority of the *Sejm* would prefer peace with the Turks but that the King was more interested in joining the Christian coalition: see Malaspina to Cinzio Alsobrandini, 29 December 1595 (ibid., pp. 408–9).

[73] Visconti to the Emperor, 13 November 1595 (ibid., p. 140); Cinzio Aldobrandini to Visconti, 9 March 1596 (ibid., p. 188).

[74] At the end of 1595, *pourparlers* indicated that the Supreme Porte was considering peace on the basis of ceding Győr back to the Emperor and Timisoara to Transylvania, something which the papacy, flushed with recent victory, opposed completely: see Cinzio Aldobrandini to Visconti, 20 January 1596 (ibid., p. 171).

to join the League. Finally, the Poles insisted that they could not commit to a Turkish war without significant monetary subventions. During the papacy of Gregory XIII King Stephen Bathory had offered to maintain an anti-Turkish war with an army of 60,000 horse, plus the requisite supporting infantry and artillery, in return for 400,000 scudi per annum. In the 1590s the Poles demanded similar sums.[75] The Imperial court in Prague, on the other hand, placed little or no reliance on the prospect of Poland joining the union. While showing evidence of respect for the King, Sigismund Vasa,[76] they were deeply distrustful both of the Polish constitution, which limited his power, and of the chancellor, Zamoyski, and his party.[77] For their part the Poles complained that the Imperial envoys who appeared at their Diet lacked the necessary instructions and clear directions to facilitate a definitive resolution of the matter of the alliance.[78]

The responsibilities for composing these various difficulties fell principally on the papal diplomatic network and in particular the three nuncios, Alfonso Visconti, the Bishop of Cervia, in Transylvania, Cesare Speciano, the Bishop of Cremona, in Prague, and Germanico Malaspina, the Bishop of San Severo, in Poland, who naturally were forced to operate with acute political sensitivity and in the face of grave difficulties of communication. When these factors are taken into account, the degree of success which was achieved was not insignificant. Visconti, in particular, forced to deal with a young and impressionable Catholic Prince, evidently played a major role in preventing the disintegration of the Christian alliance and in maintaining a highly successful year's campaigning against the Turks in 1595 which, in conjunction with the uprising of Michael the Brave, substantially weakened Ottoman control in the provinces adjacent to the Black Sea.

All three nuncios, however, faced a wide array of problems. Each of the rulers to which they were accredited, Rudolf, Sigismund Vasa, and Sigismund Bathory, were necessarily aware of strong non-Catholic influences within their courts, and in the representative institutions of their various domains, which were frequently distrustful of Rome's objectives and which restricted their freedom of action in responding to papal pressure. The papal court considered the Austrian Habsburgs' non-Catholic advisors to be especially pernicious and wished in particular to see the influence of David Ungnad over Archduke Matthias, and of Christoph Von Teuffenbach over Archduke Maximilian, reduced. Rome also deeply distrusted the politics of Ferdinand Hofmann, the president of the Hofkammer.[79] In Transylvania, Visconti had to reckon with numerous non-Catholic advisors around the Prince, perhaps most significantly István Bocskai, a figure who excited a reluctant

---

[75] Setton, *Venice, Austria, and the Turks*, p. 13.

[76] Sigismund informed the nuncio in Cracow that he feared deposition if he entered the war against the Turks without the accord of the *Sejm*: see Veress, *Relationes Nuntiorum Apostolicorum*, p. 169, fn 3.

[77] Cesare Speciano to Alfonso Visconti, 13 May 1595 (ibid., p. 74).

[78] Instructions to Benedetto Mandino, 7 January 1596 (*Die Hauptinstruktionen Clemens' VIII.*, 2, p. 403); Rome sympathized with the Poles in this regard, complaining frequently of the dilatoriness of the Imperial court: see for instance Cinzio Aldobrandini to Visconti, 27 April 1596 (Veress, *Relationes Nuntiorum Apostolicorum*, p. 202).

[79] Instructions for Benedetto Mandina, 7 January 1596 (*Die Hauptinstruktionen Clemens' VIII.*, 2, p. 418).

admiration among the papal diplomats.[80] Neither Rudolf, Sigismund Vasa, nor Sigismund Bathory were easy figures for their respective nuncios to deal with. All were prone to fits of melancholy, although in Bathory's case this was interposed with periods of intense activity. Both Sigismund Vasa and Rudolf, in particular, were regarded as inefficient and tardy in the management of business, even if the piety of the Polish King was highly esteemed.[81] From August 1595 the coming to light of Sigismund Bathory's impotence and his inability to consummate his marriage with Maria Christina intensified the Prince's emotional fragility.

Moreover, the diplomatic chain was only as strong as its various links. Communications between Prague, Cracow, and the necessarily peripatetic Visconti were anything but reliable and there were frequent complaints of letters not having arrived. While the string of Jesuit colleges in much of Central and Eastern Europe provided a network experienced in communicating with Rome of which the nuncios could avail, Visconti, in particular, was vulnerable to thwarted communication or deliberate tampering. Indeed, revealingly, his first communication openly informing Rome about certain worries which he entertained about the Prince of Transylvania was penned from Vienna because of the availability of a secure line of communication there which suggests that he was not convinced that even ciphered material was safe.[82] Even when letters securely arrived their information was only as reliable as their sources. By the end of 1595 the reports emanating from Poland and Prague, particularly about what had happened in Moldova and the prospects of Poland joining the Turkish war, were so contrary that the Cardinal-nephew, Cinzio Aldobrandini, confessed that it was as difficult to decipher what had actually happened as to determine what action to take next.[83] Visconti, for his part, was convinced that his colleague Malaspina had been badly blind-sided in the Polish court and the sense of panic in some of the latter's letters, especially at the end of November 1595, when he secretly broke a confidence which had been entrusted to him, suggests that this was correct.[84]

It was probably for this reason that in January 1596 Clement dispatched Benedetto Mandina, the Bishop of Caserta, as a special nuncio to Poland. Mandino's brief was to make a major endeavour to bring Poland into the war and to convince the Poles of the impossibility of binding the empire as a whole into any league, since the Diet had never been willing even to commit itself to a defence of a Hungarian kingdom which was the personal patrimony of the Emperor, on the grounds that it lay outside Imperial frontiers. Rather than seeing the Emperor's unwillingness to involve the representative estates of the territories over which he presided as a reason for suspicion, Mandina was to impress upon the Polish Diet that they should trust to Imperial goodwill and Clement's oversight and his known affection

[80] Visconti to Speciano, 5 December 1595 (Veress, *Relationes Nuntiorum Apostolicorum*, p. 155); Speciano to Visconti, 29 December 1595 (ibid., p. 164).

[81] Instructions for Claudio Rangone, 20 February 1599 (*Die Hauptinstruktionen Clemens' VIII.*, 2, pp. 603–4).

[82] See Visconti to Cinzio Aldobrandini, 12 March 1596 (Veress, *Relationes Nuntiorum Apostolicorum*, pp. 190–2).

[83] Cinzio Aldobrandini to Visconti, 6 January 1596 (ibid., p. 165).

[84] Malaspina to Visconti, end of November 1595 (ibid., pp. 152–3).

for Poland to join a simple alliance with Transylvania and the Emperor in which each party would agree to enter no negotiations about peace without the consent of the others. The Poles should also accept the Imperial offer of 200,000 florins per annum and the promise of what additional monies the Pope could supply, placing reliance on his proven generosity in the course of the war.[85] On the other hand, the papal court accepted that Maximilian's pretensions to the Polish throne were a destabilizing irritant and in the course of his journey to Poland Mandino was to bring Rudolf and Maximilian to promise an open renunciation of this claim as soon as Poland made a resolution to enter the war.[86] In April the papacy dispatched an even more senior figure, Cardinal Enrico Caetani, the brother of the nuncio to Spain, as envoy to the Imperial court and most importantly as Legate to Poland.

The Emperor subsequently ceded to papal pressure on a series of points and indeed professed willingness to offer the Poles the substance of their other demands, although with a lower level of subsidy and no guarantee of commitment from the Empire as a whole to the alliance.[87] Frustratingly for Rome, however, the communication of Imperial proposals remained bedevilled by various organizational difficulties arising from what was seen as simple negligence.[88] Caetani complained, for instance, that the Imperial agents sent to Poland to negotiate the terms of Polish participation in the war only possessed the power to propose terms but lacked the authority to conclude anything. The details of Habsburg renunciation to claims on Poland continued to cause difficulties. The Emperor's proposal for a three-year alliance was also regarded unfavourably with the Poles preferring the idea of a binding league until the conclusion of peace. Polish preference was for a joint offensive against Turkish power in which their contingent would be heavily subsidized while the Imperial delegates favoured the idea of separate forces. By August Caetani accepted that there was no prospect of Polish forces coming to reinforce the Christian alliance in the course of 1596.[89]

In addition to intense diplomatic activity and the application of moral pressure on various Christian rulers, the papacy also made a significant military and financial contribution to the war. At the beginning of 1597 Clement claimed to have already expended 1,500,000 thalers on the war against the Turks in Hungary despite the major pressures on the papal purse, including the need to fund papal forces in France, and the effects of famine in Italy. The Pope naturally expended substantial sums of money on the numerous diplomatic missions and *nunciaturae* which he maintained but he also supplied direct subventions to the participants. In 1593 he engaged himself to supplying 30,000 florins a month to the Imperial forces. When Transylvania joined the war it too became a recipient of papal

---

[85] In the course of 1594–5 papal expenditure on the war had amounted to *circa* 800,000 florins: Setton *Venice, Austria and the Turks*, p. 11.

[86] Instructions to Benedetto Mandino, 7 January 1596 (*Die Hauptinstruktionen Clemens' VIII.*, 2, pp. 403–18).

[87] Instructions for Cardinal Enrico Caetani, Legate in Poland, 13 April 1596 (ibid., p. 437).

[88] Cinzio Aldobrandini to Visconti, 15 March 1596 (Veress, *Relationes Nuntiorum Apostolicorum*, p. 193).

[89] Caetani to Visconti, 27 August 1596, (ibid., p. 242); same to same, 30 August 1596 (ibid., pp. 244–5).

largesse.[90] Moreover, Clement also committed three papal armies to the war. The first of these in 1595 consisted of 260 horse and 7648 foot under the command of his nephew, Giovanni Francesco Aldobrandini, whom Clement appointed as general despite significant doubts among the cardinals concerning his fitness for the office.[91] Joining with the Imperial forces under Count Mansfield in August they assisted in the capture of the primatial seat and castle of Esztergom, and then Aldobrandini distinguished himself in the taking of the famous fortress of Visegrad, which opened up the possibility of the recapture of the ancient Hungarian capital of Buda.[92] In addition to the papal forces, a number of other Italian states contributed small numbers of soldiers to the war, largely as a result of papal encouragement. The Tuscan contingent, which numbered about a hundred, made a notable contribution to the successful attack on Girgiu at the end of October 1595, first when its captain, Silvio Piccolomini, provided the advice which rendered the previously impotent artillery barrage against the fortress's walls effective, and then by leading the attack on the subsequent breach.[93]

At the end of 1594, Clement and his advisors had been fearing the spring would bring about the fall of Vienna. In the event by the end of 1595 the Christian coalition had recorded a string of successes, both on the border between Royal and Turkish Hungary and through Bathory's Transylvanian army in Wallachia. The significant successes of 1595 raised optimism in Rome that the coming campaign might finally bring about the liberation of the Balkans. Bathory's successes as a 'bravo, pio e ben fortunato'[94] prince against superior Turkish forces in particular fired the imagination that a Christian liberator had been sent by God. The decision was taken that the Transylvanian Prince would be honoured by the gift of a papally consecrated 'stocco', symbolic of his new status as a Christian hero and the recipient of special graces both from God and from his vicar on earth.[95] When Bathory opted to go to Prague during the winter to negotiate personally with the Emperor this aroused certain apprehensions in Rome where reservations about Rudolf were freely entertained. In the event, the manner in which the Emperor offered to support the Prince in the coming campaign with 3000 cavalry, a similar number of foot, and a monthly subsidy of 20,000 thalers for seven months, greatly pleased the Roman Curia which resolved to complement the Imperial subsidies with a major donation of 40,000

---

[90] Instructions for Giovanni Battista Doria, 5 July 1594 (*Die Hauptinstruktionen Clemens' VIII.*, 1, p. 262). In 1596, for instance, the Pope provided 60,000 florins to enable Bathory to prepare his army for the summer campaign: see Amalteo to Visconti, 30 April 1596 (Veress, *Relationes Nuntiorum Apostolicorum*, p. 202).

[91] Fattori, *Clemente VIII e il Sacro Collegio*, pp. 116–27, provides a detailed analysis of the various congregational tensions and discussions concerning the dispatch of pontifical troops under Giovanni Francesco Aldobrandini.

[92] Setton, *Venice, Austria and the Turks*, pp. 10–11; Veress, *Relationes Nuntiorum Apostolicorum*, p. xxxii.

[93] Visconti to Cinzio Aldobrandini, 31 October 1595 (Veress, *Relationes Nuntiorum Apostolicorum*, pp. 129–30).

[94] The expression was used by Cardinal Enrico Caetani, see his letter to Visconti, 5 July 1596 (ibid., p. 224).

[95] Instructions to Ludovico Anguisciola, 23 January 1596 (ibid., p. 172).

scudi.[96] The capture of Klis which commanded the sole pass into Bosnia, and news that Bathory had moved to attack the fortess of Temisoara, combined with news from informants in Constantinople that the Turks were experiencing difficulties in gathering an army of vengeance, raised expectations further.[97] While Caetani in Poland was unable to bring that kingdom into the coalition, he was given guarantees, which he communicated to Transylvania, that Polish forces would protect Moldova and Transylvania in 1596 from any flanking attack by the Crimean Tartars, thus allowing Bathory to concentrate his army on the Turkish threat to the south.[98]

Yet storm clouds swiftly gathered. In Prague Bathory's actions had already greatly alarmed Visconti whose view of the Prince was considerably more jaundiced than the Roman perception. The Prince, weary of the intrigues of his Bathory cousins and their Polish backers against him, in fact was already contemplating renouncing the principality of Transylvania to the Emperor in return for more secure territories within Habsburg domains.[99] Visconti, aware of the depth of anti-Habsburg feeling in the principality, was aghast at this notion and together with the nuncio in Prague worked feverishly on both the Prince and the Imperial court to prevent any agreement. In the event Rudolf's doubts on the matter, and his offer of significant aid, convinced Bathory to maintain the principality and continue the war and, as had been planned from the end of 1595, he concentrated his forces on the fortress of Timisoara.[100] By July 1596, however, Rome was grieved to hear that Bathory had been forced to raise the siege of Timisoara, not least because of the lack of the promised Imperial supplies which, in contrast to the papal subsidies, were not punctually disbursed.[101] The retaking of the supposedly impregnable stronghold of Klis by the Turks, coming in the wake of the open hostility demonstrated by Venice to the initial Christian capture of that fortress, took the wind out of the sails of insurrection in Bosnia and Hercegovina.[102] In an effort to stiffen the war effort, Clement authorized an extra payment of 30,000 florins to Bathory

[96] Cinzio Aldobrandini to Visconti, 3 February 1596 (ibid., p. 177); Visconti to Peter Aldobrandini, 21 February 1596 (ibid., p. 181); Cinzio Aldobrandini to Visconti, 11 April 1596 (ibid., p. 198); in the summer of 1596 the mission of Sigismund's confessor, Alfonso Carrillo, to Spain also yielded a promise of 80,000 ducats in aid for Transylvania from Spain: see Carillo to Peter Aldobrandini, 10 August 1596 (Veress, *Epistolae Carrilli*, pp. 188–9).

[97] Cinzio Aldobrandini to Visconti, 20 April 1596 (Veress, *Relationes Nuntiorum Apostolicorum*, p. 200); same to same, 5 May 1596 (ibid., p. 207); G.E. Rothenberg, 'Christan Insurrections in Turkish Dalmatia, 1580–1596', *The Slavonic and East European Review* 40: 94 (1961), 136–47, at 144–7; Elisabeth Springer, 'Kaiser Rudolf II, Papst Clemens VIII und die bosnischen Christen: Taten und Untaten des Cavaliere Francesco Antonio Bertucci in kaiserlichen Diensten in den Jahren 1594 bis 1602', *Mitteilungen des Österreichischen Staatsarchiv* 33 (1980), 77–105.

[98] Cinzio Aldobrandini to Visconti, 2 March 1596 (Veress, *Relationes Nuntiorum Apostolicorum*, p. 186); Caetani to Visconti, 2 August 1596 (ibid., p. 235).

[99] Visconti to Peter Aldobrandini, 28 February 1596 (ibid., p. 183); same to Cinzio Aldobrandini, 12 March 1596 (ibid., p. 191); he was also open to the idea of becoming a cardinal: cf. Veress, *Relationes Nuntiorum Apostolicorum*, p. 173, fn 3.

[100] Carrillo to Cinzio Aldobrandini, 23 December 1595 (Veress, *Epistolae Carrilli*, p. 171).

[101] Responses of Prince and Council of Transylvania to Visconti's propositions, July 1596 (Veress, *Relationes Nuntiorum Apostolicorum*, p. 230); Cinzio Aldobrandini to Visconti, 10 August 1596 (ibid., p. 238).

[102] Cinzio Aldobrandini to Visconti, 22 June 1596 (ibid., p. 222).

from a sum of 200,000 scudi which he had deposited in Vienna to underpin Caetani's mission to Poland.[103] The Turks then recorded a major success in taking the fortress of Eger, which had been previously and famously held against the invincible armies of Suleiman the Magnificent. Finally, in arguably the most significant battle of the war, the joint forces of Archduke Maximilian and Bathory were defeated at Mezőkeresztes by the Turkish army under the command of the Sultan on 23 October 1596, largely because the Imperial forces scattered to plunder the Turkish camp in the belief that the battle was won. When news of this reached Rome the Cardinal-nephew did not dare inform the Pope, who was recovering from a severe illness, for fear that it would bring about a relapse.[104]

This roll-call of failure was a crushing blow to papal hopes in 1596. Yet, while bitterly disappointed at the turn of events, and despite a rising tide of opinion within the congregation of Hungary against the application of pontifical resources on behalf of the Emperor, the Pope's appetite for supporting the war did not disappear.[105] After the fall of Eger, 30,000 florins were immediately disbursed to Transylvania to bolster its defences although the coming of winter precluded any immediate Turkish assault.[106] Mario Farnese was dispatched to the Imperial court as papal envoy to impress on Rudolf the importance of an active response to these setbacks and to urge him to cease making use of non-Catholics in important offices. He was to convince Maximilian to renounce definitively his pretensions to the crown of Poland, not least because of Caetani's belief that the Christian defeat at Mezőkeresztes would make the Poles more inclined to support the war.[107] Papal desire for a long truce between France and Spain which would free Spanish resources to come to the assistance of the beleaguered Austrian branch of the family, as well as to facilitate an enterprise against England, became even more vehement, and an inevitably unsuccessful appeal to support the Hungarian war was also launched directly to the French King.[108]

By early 1597 the inability of the Turks to make use of their victories helped to soothe papal worries about a collapse of the Imperial position in Hungary, prompting the belief that a peace between Spain and France might well be enough to cause the Sultan to sue for peace.[109] The events of 1596, however, had greatly reinforced

[103] Amalteo to Visconti, 31 May 1596 (ibid. p. 217); Cinzio Aldobrandini to Visconti, 27 July 1596 (ibid., pp. 233–3).

[104] Cinzio Aldobrandini to Visconti, 16 November 1596 (ibid., p. 262).

[105] Fattori, *Clemente VIII e il Sacro Collegio*, p. 126, fn 117. Clement's willingness to spend the resources of the Holy See, in particular when the King of Spain showed no inclination to match the Pope's level of commitment, became the subject of significant criticism in Italy generally: see ibid., pp. 122–3.

[106] Cinzio Aldobrandini to Visconti, 2 November 1596 (Veress, *Relationes Nuntiorum Apostolicorum*, p. 260).

[107] Instructions for Mario Farnese, December 1596 (*Die Hauptinstruktionen Clemens' VIII.*, 2, pp. 478–81).

[108] Arnold d'Ossat to Villeroy, 16 January 1597 (*Lettres de Cardinal d'Ossat*, pp. 360–2); same to same, 18 February 1597 (ibid., pp. 379–84). Clement can hardly have believed this appeal for aid for the House of Austria would be successful while France was at war with Spain and it may have represented merely a gambit to allow the ventilation of French opinions in the context of the Pope's hopes to broker peace between the two powers.

[109] Arnold d'Ossat to Villeroy, 1 February 1597 (*Lettres de Cardinal d'Ossat*, pp. 374–6).

Bathory's inclination to abandon the Transylvanian principality and he journeyed to Prague for this purpose in February 1597. Visconti believed that he was motivated by a personal desire to lay down the burden of rule, extreme distaste for his marriage, and the belief that Transylvania could only be preserved from Turkish vengeance by the Emperor directly assuming responsibility for its protection. Once again Visconti and Prague united to oppose the idea. The Prince insisted that if the transfer was not made his only recourse was to make peace with the Sultan, which placed the Imperial counsellors and the papal representatives in considerable difficulties, not aided by Rudolf's disinclination to take the matter in hand personally.[110] Rather to his own surprise, Visconti eventually managed to convince both parties of the dangers involved and, on the promise of 6000 Imperial troops for the coming campaigning season in 1597, Bathory consented to continue in the principality. In addition, he was promised and received 24,000 thalers from papal funds. By 20 June 1597, however, he was complaining of the non-arrival of the promised assistance from the Habsburgs, of which only 1500 cavalry had made an appearance. Towards the end of that month 500 infantry also joined his forces and the lack of a major Turkish offensive on the Wallachian front allowed the Transylvanian army to return to the siege of Timisoara in October.[111]

By 1597 Clement was increasingly assuming personal control over the papal contribution to the war without reference to the congregation of Hungary and he opted to increase his level of involvement.[112] In that year his principal investment in the anti-Turkish struggle was in direct assistance to the Imperial campaign by raising and sending at papal expense a force of 7157 mercenary troops, again under the command of Giovanni Francesco Aldobrandini, to the Hungarian war where they participated in the attack on Buda. Even after the outbreak of the crisis in Ferrara, Clement opted not to withdraw them, although his involvement in that adventure necessarily impeded his capacity to subvent the Turkish war. Joining with Imperial forces, the allied Christian army occupied Pápa but failed in its major objective of recovering Györ.[113]

At the end of 1597 Visconti's long run of luck in restraining the Prince of Transylvania finally came to an end. In December he reported to Rome that if an agreement was not made between the Emperor and Bathory then the latter would make peace with the Turks, who almost since his entry into the Christian coalition had been dispatching envoys to persuade him to that decision.[114] By February 1598 the news that a deal between the Emperor and the Prince was being negotiated had become public knowledge even in Italy although, astonishingly, Rudolf's envoys to

[110] Visconti to Cinzio Aldobrandini, 17 February 1597 (Veress, *Relationes Nuntiorum Apostolicorum*, p. 275); same to same, 22 February 1597 (ibid., pp. 276–9); same to same, 24 February 1597 (ibid., pp. 280–1).
[111] Visconti to Cinzio Aldobrandini, 20 June 1597 (ibid., pp. 290–1); same to same, 30 June 1597 (ibid., pp. 293–4); same to Speciano, 12 October 1597 (ibid., pp. 295–6).
[112] Fattori, *Clemente VIII e il Sacro Collegio*, p. 122.
[113] Setton, *Venice, Austria and the Turks*, p. 14.
[114] Visconti to Cinzio Aldobrandini, 11 December 1597 (Veress, *Relationes Nuntiorum Apostolicorum*, pp. 299–300); same to Speciano, 11 December 1597 (ibid., pp. 296–7).

the Transylvanian Diet assembled to legitimize the transfer were late in arriving.[115] Yet, although Bathory had been negotiating for the transfer since the winter of 1595–6, he was not content and over the next two years he was central to a series of bewildering shifts. Having resigned office he apparently rapidly repented of the decision, disavowed the bargain and resumed the principality, recuperating the garrisons which had been taken over by the Emperor.

While this understandably created tensions with the Emperor, the need to keep Transylvania in the war, and the fact that the initial impetus for the original agreement had come from Bathory, inclined the Imperial court to swallow the insult, provided that the Prince did not make peace with the Turks. Bathory, however, disillusioned with the progress of the war, seems to have believed that such a peace was in his best interests and the Sultan made constant efforts to attract him in that direction. Bathory's conscience and the oath he had sworn never to make such a peace with the Turks may have been one of the chief deterrents.[116] Certainly, it is otherwise difficult to rationalize his following move when he again laid down the principality at the Transylvanian Diet in March 1599 but this time to his long-time foe and cousin, Cardinal Andrew Bathory. The Cardinal was a known advocate of peace with the Sultan and Sigismund may in this way have hoped to obtain peace without violence to his conscience. The Cardinal summoned the Transylvanian diet in July 1599 where it was clear that a peace would be popular with the generality of the population exhausted by the constant demands of the war and very fearful of Turkish invasion.[117] The Cardinal then became engaged in a three-pronged diplomatic project, attempting to smooth the feathers of the Imperial court, opening discussions with Poland, where he had been domiciled for many years, about incorporation of Transylvania into the kingdom, and direct negotiations with the Supreme Porte.[118] Istanbul was prepared to offer very generous peace terms to the Cardinal and did not close the door to the idea of the incorporation of Transylvania into the Polish kingdom, which was particularly attractive to the new Prince who continued to dream that he might himself become king of such a union if Sigismund Vasa was forced to lay down the Polish throne in an attempt to maintain his status as king in Sweden.

This complex weave of events in 1599 created a diplomatic minefield for the Apostolic See. In yet another indication of the emphasis which Clement placed on the Turkish war, Rome determined to accept the risks of a proactive policy and dispatched Germanico Malaspina, a veteran diplomat with experience as papal representative both to the Habsburgs and to Poland, as nuncio to the Cardinal. Malaspina's principal qualification for the role was his long personal experience of dealing with Andrew Bathory while both had been domiciled in Poland.[119] Both Malaspina and his superiors were aware that the Emperor might easily take offence

---

[115] Visconti to Pezzen Bertalan, 20 March 1598 (ibid., pp. 312–13); Cinzio Aldobrandini to Visconti, 28 February 1598 (ibid, pp. 310–11).
[116] Malaspina to Cinzio Aldobrandini, 19 August 1599 (ibid., p. 334).
[117] ibid.
[118] Malaspina to Cinzio Aldobrandini, 7 September 1599 (ibid., pp. 339–43).
[119] Instructions for Germanico Malspina, 11 June 1599 (ibid., pp. 316–20).

at the extension of papal recognition to what, in Imperial eyes, was a usurping prince. This indeed was precisely the tenor of the first Habsburg reactions expressed both to the nuncio in Prague, Spinelli, by several Imperial envoys, and to Malaspina personally by Archduke Matthias, who had been dispatched to Vienna to interview him on his way north.

Both papal ministers attempted to soothe wounded Habsburg feelings. In an unusual step, a copy of the instructions which Malaspina was carrying had already been forwarded to Prague to be viewed by the Emperor. The Imperial council, however, took a good deal of umbrage at these. In view of what they saw as Cardinal Bathory's usurpation of a principality to which the Emperor had so many claims, both by virtue of its original status as part of the kingdom of Hungry, and in view of the recent agreements concerning Sigismund Bathory's renunciation, they wished to see a far more severe tone in the instructions. They also had reservations about Malaspina himself, suspecting that his personal acquaintance with the Cardinal might prejudice him against Imperial interests.[120] The two nuncios responded that the papal briefs which were being sent to Andrew Bathory were addressed to him as cardinal rather than prince.[121] In effect, Malaspina would proceed to Transylvania only with Imperial permission and would transmit the Emperor's conditions for accepting the Cardinal under his protection. The thrust of the papal argument was that, without diplomatic intervention, Cardinal Bathory would either make peace with the Sultan or pursue his Polish aspiration, which Malaspina was confident could be blocked by the papal relationship with the Polish King. A major stumbling block for the Emperor's advisors, however, was the person of the Cardinal himself whom they viewed as entirely hostile to Imperial interests. His close relationship with Zamoyski, the Polish Chancellor, also rendered them intensely suspicious. Rumours of a plot by the Poles to join the forces of Transylvania and Moldova to depose the *voivode* of Walachia, Michael the Brave, in order to incorporate all three provinces into Poland increased their antipathy.[122] The Emperor eventually decided that it was in his interests to allow a papal attempt at mediation. Malaspina, therefore, made a hurried journey to Transylvania, arriving in Gyulafehérvár on 20 August 1599.

As a manoeuvre this was hardly without risk for it placed an enormous onus on the papal nuncio to broker an agreement between two highly distrustful parties who were not in direct negotiation and each of which was desirous of guarantees. That the papacy was prepared to allow Malaspina to place the dignity and credibility of the Holy See in the centre of this imbroglio was another indication of Roman perception of Transylvania as a vital aspect of the anti-Turkish war. The Emperor had finally yielded to the papal arguments that it would be futile for the nuncio simply to demand Cardinal Bathory's abdication from a seat which he had

---

[120] Spinelli to the Emperor, 26 June 1599 (ibid., pp. 431–2); same to Cinzio Aldobrandini, 28 June 1599 (ibid., pp. 433–4); same to same, 5 July 1599 (ibid., pp. 434–6).

[121] Malaspina to Spinelli, 21 July 1599 (ibid., p. 324).

[122] Spinelli to the Emperor, 26 June 1599 (ibid., pp. 431–2); same to Cinzio Aldobrandini, 28 June 1599 (ibid., pp. 433–4); same to same, 5 July 1599 (ibid., pp. 434–6); Instructions for Claudio Rangone, 20 February 1599 (*Die Hauptinstruktionen Clemens' VIII.*, 2, p. 604).

connived so long to attain, not least because of the option which he held of making peace with the Sultan. Nonetheless, in view of his extreme distrust of the Cardinal, Rudolf insisted on the hard security of fortified places, namely Varad, Huszt,[123] and a number of the smaller garrisons, to be given into his hands.

For their part both the Cardinal and the Transylvanian nobles whom he involved in the discussions clearly underestimated the level of affront which the Emperor had been asked to stomach. They believed that the Cardinal should be offered the same terms from Rudolf as had previously been extended to Sigismund, down to marriage with Sigismund's estranged wife, the Archduchess Maria Christina. From their perspective, they had undergone significant risks for five years on the frontier of the Turkish war on behalf of the entire Christian world for which they deserved appreciation and gratitude. Passing lightly over the manner in which the Transylvanian Diet had endorsed the transfer of power to Rudolf, they were inclined to ascribe all blame for previous breaches of faith to Sigismund Bathory. Having solicited terms from the Turks, they now feared that to reject them would bring down on Transylvania the full vengeful weight of the Ottoman army assembling near Belgrade. Consequently, their inclination was to accept peace with the Turks until they had finalized terms with the Emperor and then once again to join the Christian alliance when adequate defensive preparations had been made. But this was a non-negotiable point for Malaspina. Although desirous of re-establishing agreement between the Emperor and Transylvania, such a development could not be accommodated within the contours of Roman diplomacy. If the Cardinal accepted a Turkish standard, the traditional mechanism of ratifying subordinate relations between the Supreme Porte and its vassal states, then Malaspina would abandon negotiations and leave immediately. However, he was prepared to pledge that the Emperor would not make any offensive movements against the Cardinal or the principality while negotiations were on-going.

In making this latter commitment, Malaspina was offering a sizeable hostage to fortune. Once what he had done was communicated to Rome, his superiors became nervous that the reputation of the Holy See as an honest broker between Catholic powers had been left exposed to the whims of Rudolf's court.[124] Faced with Malaspina's intransigence on the subject of peace with the Ottomans, Bathory and his advisors backed down and committed not to accept the Turkish standard until the conclusion of negotiations with the Emperor. Yet despite his firm stance on this matter, Malaspina's basic sympathies lay with the Transylvanian position. A sizeable party of the Transylvanian nobility clearly preferred an alliance with Christians rather than with the Turks.[125] Essentially Malaspina believed that the best hope for the Emperor of maintaining Transylvanian involvement in the war was to build upon this by according Cardinal Bathory very similar terms to those which had been used to bring Sigismund into an alliance. These would include a Habsburg

---

[123] Huszt was a particularly sensitive point because it was part of the personal patrimony of Cardinal Bathory of which he believed he had been wrongfully deprived by Sigismund.

[124] Cinzio Aldobrandini to Malaspina, 2 October 1599 (Veress, *Relationes Nuntiorum Apostolicorum*, p. 353).

[125] Carillo to Peter Aldobrandini, 9 September 1599 (Veress, *Epistolae Carrilli*, pp. 339–40).

marriage, probably with Sigismund's own estranged wife, the dissolution of whose union with the former Prince the papal nuncios consistently saw as a relatively minor affair. The Imperial insistence on the yielding of additional fortresses was in his opinion a mistake.[126] Essentially the nuncio did not believe, and the events of the following decade were to prove him correct, that the Emperor possessed the power to hold Transylvania without the active cooperation of its nobility while simultaneously at war with the Turks. Therefore, Rudolf's best option was to trust in the principality's willingness to re-instigate the alliance.

Malaspina's attempts at mediation, however, were rapidly undercut by alternative Imperial provisions. While his mission did contribute to the eventual abandonment of the threatening movement towards the frontiers of Transylvania of George Basta, the Imperial commander in Kassa, in October 1599 Michael the Brave, the *voivode* of Wallachia, who also felt threatened by Cardinal Bathory's Polish and Moldovan connections, erupted with an army into the principality, claiming to be acting under Imperial orders. Cardinal Bathory hurriedly assembled his own forces and went to confront the *voivode*, accompanied by Malaspina who hoped to convince Michael that the Emperor had entrusted negotiations to his direction. Michael, however, to whom the nuncio's interventions were unwelcome, subverted Malaspina's attempts and an inconclusive battle ensued. Despite having had the better of the encounter, the Cardinal's nerve then broke and he fled his camp during the night with a small retinue which proved insufficient to guard him from a subsequent attack in which he lost his life. Desperately trying to control events, Malaspina then exerted himself to ensure that any oaths sworn to Michael by the leaders of the Saxon community and the nobility should be merely as the Emperor's representative. His efforts in that respect, however, were short-circuited by Michael's determination to have him leave the principality.

Malaspina undoubtedly felt betrayed by the Imperial court. He had first heard of Michael the Brave's *pourparlers* with the Emperor in July 1599. Nevertheless in pursuing his mission, and in particular in the guarantee which he had offered to Bathory that the Emperor would neither directly with his own forces nor through any intermediary attempt to unseat the Cardinal while negotiations under Malaspina's auspices were on-going, he believed that he had been acting according to an agreement with Archduke Matthias.[127] Malaspina especially blamed the Emperor's non-Catholic advisors, most notably David Ungnod who had long been a papal *bête noire*, for intriguing with Michael the Brave and thus ensuring the ruin of his own negotiations with Cardinal Bathory. The violation of Malaspina's guarantee necessarily cast a sinister light on papal activities. Not only were there imputations that Malaspina had conspired with the Imperial court to trick the Cardinal but even in Prague a good deal of hostility continued to exist concerning the manner in which he had attempted to present the Transylvanian position in

---

[126] See his long memorials to Cinzio Aldobrandini of 7 September and to the nuncio in Prague, Spinelli, of 13 September 1599 (Veress, *Relationes Nuntiorum Apostolicorum*, pp. 339–43 and pp. 345–50).
[127] Malaspina to Cinzio Aldobrandini, 2 December 1599 (ibid., pp. 368–70).

the negotiations.[128] While Rome was inclined to forgive Malaspina his mistakes, the embarrassment for the Pope increased in early 1600 as the Emperor's desire for the Cardinal's posthumous excommunication clashed with an argument from the nuncio in Cracow that his killers should be declared anathema in order to mollify Polish anger at his death.[129]

Malaspina's return signalled an end to the special relationship with Transylvania which Clement had cultivated almost since the beginning of his pontificate. From this point on, lacking any real leverage in the principality, papal diplomatic attempts with regard to the Turkish war were concentrated on attempts to persuade Spain, France and Venice to commit large-scale resources to assist the eastern branch of the House of Austria and in keeping the peace between the Emperor and Poland, which at times threatened an open rupture, particularly over the issue of Wallachia and Moldova.[130] But direct papal aid to the Imperial cause did not cease. In 1601, a year in which the Pope still hoped that the final destruction of Ottoman power could be accomplished through the means of a united Christian force combining the power of both France and Spain,[131] the Pope committed the largest papal force of the war, totalling 9000 men, under the command of Giovanni Francesco Aldobrandini, who died in the course of the campaign, which assisted in the siege of Kanisza.[132] In this expedition, as in the previous campaigns of 1595 and 1597, the papal troops suffered very heavy casualties. They complained of local hostility towards them and certainly all three expeditions suffered from difficulties of supply.

Throughout the war, the local Christian forces generally preferred subventions of money to foreign troops. The Prince of Transylvania, for instance, in the 1590s proved noticeably unwilling to receive German cavalry into his forces, arguing that they did more damage to his own people than the enemy. His chief desire was for money and Hungarian cavalry and the right to recruit Hungarian troops from the Habsburg portion of Hungary.[133] This third expedition marked the last attempt by the Clementine papacy to send major forces into the actual theatre. From this point on, papal assistance chiefly took monetary and diplomatic form. In 1602 100,000 scudi was provided to assist in the siege of Buda and a further 50,000, despite the strongly negative attitude of the *Congregatione d'Ungheria*, was contributed in 1603. In 1604 the news of the death of the Sultan Mehmed III and the

---

[128] Spinelli to Cinzio Aldobrandini, 6 December 1599 (ibid., pp. 446–7).

[129] Arnold D'Ossat to Nicholas Villeroy, 13 January 1600 (*Lettres Cardinal d'Ossat*, pp. 710–12).

[130] Instructions for Giovanni Stefano Fereri, 20 January 1604 (*Die Hauptinstruktionen Clemens' VIII.*, 2, pp. 722–3); instructions for Tommaso Lapi, December 1604 (ibid., p. 771); Spanish contributions to the war eventually totalled about 3.75 million florins and the level of support was greater following the conclusion of peace with France in 1598 and with England in 1604: in this regard see Niederkorn, *Die europäischen Mächte und der 'Lange Turkenkrieg'*, p. 253.

[131] Instructions for Innocenzo del Bufalo, July 1601 (Bernard Barbiche (ed.), *Correspondance du nonce en France Innocenzo del Bufalo évéque de camerino (1601–1604)* (Rome, Presses de l'Université Grégorienne/Editions E. de Boccard, Paris, 1964), pp. 160–1).

[132] The Roman accounts for the first and third of these armies indicate that the cost to the papal exchequer of these two forces amounted to 1,101,938 florins: Veress, *Relationes Nuntiorum Apostolicorum*, pp. xxxii–xxxiii.

[133] Cinzio Aldobrandini to Visconti, 4 November 1595 (ibid., p. 136); Tomasso Contarini to the Doge of Venice, 13 February 1596 (ibid., pp. 412–13); Visconti to Cinzio Aldobrandini, 3 November 1595 (ibid., p. 135).

opening of hostilities on the Ottoman empire's eastern borders again fired the Pope's optimism concerning the possibility of actual victory in the long struggle if France, Spain, and Venice could be induced to participate enthusiastically in the conflict and another 50,000 scudi was authorized. Clement's death in March 1605 did not completely put an end to papal involvement. Rather to the surprise of the Imperial envoys in Rome, Paul V and the *Congregatione d'Ungheria* authorized further substantial subsidies in that year.[134] Under Lala Mehmed Pasha, however, who was assisted in 1605–6 by the new Prince of Transylvania, István Bocskai, Ottoman forces stormed Esztergom and retook Veszprém and Palota. In 1606 peace was finally concluded. Rather than either the major Christian defeat or victory which the papacy had dreaded or dreamed of for a decade, the long Habsburg–Turkish war had resolved itself into an exhausted stalemate.

As is well–known, at Nantes in 1598, and at Westphalia fifty years later, the basic religious complexion of the most important territories of the contested European mainland, France and the Empire, was established. Both were processes which had been the subject of intense papal diplomacy, although the first was perceived in Rome with less extreme bitterness than the second. The peace of 1606 is rarely considered in the same light as these indubitably important settlements but it too was profoundly important in terms of the religious boundaries of Europe. The end of the papally-supported Habsburg war against the Turks signalled the long-term postponement of the crusading dream of the expulsion of the Ottomans from European soil. The Austrian triumphs of the later seventeenth century meant that the borders of Catholic Europe did alter south to some significant degree outside the period under review in this study but the failure of Catholic arms in the Balkans which Zsitvatörök represented had long-term effects on the position of Catholicism in the peninsula. It was the decades after this peace which saw the intensifying Islamicization of what had been the most significant Balkan Catholic population, in Albania, and the migration of significant southern Slav Catholic populations. Ultimately these latter were reintegrated into the Catholic kingdom of a reconstituted Hungary but south of the territories of the crown of St Stephen was to remain under Turkish domination into the twentieth century.

The case study of papal patronization of the Habsburg war against the Ottoman empire in the 1590s and early seventeenth century provides a revealing insight into the motivations which underpinned policy, as well as permitting an assessment of the resources which Rome could mobilize, and the limitations on the influence which it could exert. The extent of Clement VIII's commitment to the long war in Hungary certainly highlights the importance which was placed upon the anti-Islamic struggle in Rome. At a conservative estimate, papal expenditure on the war exceeded two million thalers but it may even have amounted to almost twice that sum, at a time when the disposable income of the Holy See amounted to considerably less than one million scudi per annum.[135] Such an expenditure relative to

---

[134] Niederkorn, *Die europäischen Mächte und der 'Lange Turkenkrieg'*, pp. 80–3.

[135] Peter Partner, 'Papal Financial Policy in the Renaissance and the Counter-Reformation', *Past & Present* 88 (1980), 17–62, at 27; Mario Caravale and Alberto Caracciolo, *Lo Stato pontificio da Mar-*

income was for instance on a scale similar to that committed by Elizabeth I of England in the nine-year struggle to subdue Ireland in the period 1594–1603. Fear of Ottoman expansion was a critical aspect of this massive papal involvement but it is noteworthy that Venice, a comparable Italian state with even more reason to feel anxiety about Turkish power, resolutely kept aloof from the struggle. A sense of papal mission and responsibility to the entire Catholic world was undoubtedly a vital aspect of papal involvement.[136] Increasing papal contact with the Christian population of the Balkans in the previous decades also played a part in shaping papal policy. Rome arguably over-estimated the rebellious inclination of the Christian population of the Balkans, although it was correct in its assumption that these communities had little fidelity to their Turkish overlords. That these populations could be Catholicized as well as liberated was another factor in Roman aspirations. In 1595, as the prospect that union with the Orthodox metropolitanate of Kiev might provide the template for union with the liberated Orthodox peoples of the Balkans appeared on the horizon, these aspirations seemed more than ever possible.[137] The manner in which Michael the Brave, the *voivode* of Wallachia, dangled the prospect of his accepting papal authority also helped to keep this end in view.

Another ever present and vitally important aspect of papal involvement concerned the providential framework within which the war with the Turks was viewed. Intense oscillations between hope and trepidation were characteristic of the Early Modern Catholic understanding of the Turkish empire. That God would ultimately grant the Christian people victory over their enemies was considered inevitable, but prophecies existed too that this might not occur until practically all Christian realms had been exposed to Ottoman depredations as a consequence of their monstrous sins. Hope that they might be among the blessed generation that would see such a victory, therefore, coexisted with the fear that they might be among the cursed ones who were to suffer tribulation.[138] This providential conception of the Turks tended to accentuate illusions of control even over essentially external factors. Throughout the war, papal ministers interpreted its events in a providential fashion and the hope that perseverance in a cause clearly pleasing to God would excite further outpourings of divine grace was ever present.

Clement's own personal role in this regard was highly significant. Undoubtedly many cardinals questioned the wisdom of such massive investment on the part of the papacy on behalf of the Austrian Habsburgs, particularly in light of the limited Spanish commitment to the Turkish war. Yet the manner in which Clement's government operated, with the consultative and assistant role of the cardinals discharged not by the consistory as a whole but by smaller congregations to which the Pope

---

tino V a Pio IX (Torino, UTET, 1978), pp. 387–9; Niederkorn, *Die europäischen Mächte und der 'Lange Turkenkrieg'*, p. 499 estimates the papal contribution at 2.85 million gulden.

[136] Niederkorn, *Die europäischen Mächte und der 'Lange Turkenkrieg'* contrasts this with all other powers involved in the conflict: see in particular pp. 70–102.

[137] See Cinzio Aldobrandini to Germanico Malaspina, 24 July 1595 (Veress, *Relationes Nuntiorum Apostolicorum*, p. 405).

[138] In this regard see *Confutatio Alcorani*, esp. pp. 143–5.

himself appointed,[139] meant that it was far more difficult to restrain the Pope's entrepreneurial optimism about the war. That papal ministers would incessantly preach peace and reconciliation between Catholic powers while exulting in the most bloody details of victory over the Turks was also in no wise surprising. It was not merely that the Turks were considered *ipso facto* as treacherous and untrustworthy people, with whom no legitimate relationships could be had,[140] but the accommodation of Early Modern Catholicism to martial codes of noble honour was so complete that the legitimacy of warfare as a Christian activity could not be challenged but only inflected towards the idea of violence in the interest of religion.

An analysis of papal involvement in the long war also demonstrates the extraordinary reach of Roman diplomacy which included missions to Moscow, the Zaporozhian Cossacks beyond the Dnieper in Central Ukraine, Balkan communities and Persia, as well as constant diplomatic activity in the Catholic capitals of Europe. The adherence of Transylvania to the Imperial alliance was to a significant extent the fruit of papal diplomacy and arguably the most concrete achievement of Clement's involvement in the Turkish war. While his desire for personal aggrandizement was a necessary factor, the Prince's Catholic sensibilities and susceptibility to the moral persuasion of Rome were critical influences in distinguishing his activities from the anti-Habsburg policies of his later successors, Gábor Bethen and György Rákóczi. Without papal oversight and pressure it seems probable that the alliance would have fallen apart far sooner. Certainly the policies implemented by the Habsburgs in the area after the removal of the papal diplomatic mission to Transylvania proved disastrous and provoked a general revolt, which not only placed the principality in the anti-Habsburg camp for most of the following century but significantly threatened Habsburg control over Royal Hungary as well.

An important factor in facilitating the deployment of papal influence was the employment by Rome of capable and trusted diplomatic personnel, in particular Visconti in Transylvania and Speciano in Prague, who provided a high level of communication, both with each other and with Rome. Consequently, and especially in the context of the huge geographical distances involved, Roman policy was remarkably coordinated throughout the 1590s and the role of the papacy as mediator and moral broker between the various Christian dynasts was a significant element of the war.[141] Yet the limitations on papal policy were severe. In particular, Clement and his ministers had to work with two highly difficult personalities in the shape of Rudolf and Sigismund and within a highly complex Polish political context where very significant anti-Habsburg tensions existed. The inconstancy of the Prince of Transylvania and the constant dilatoriness of the Emperor, especially

---

[139] Fattori, *Clemente VIII e il Sacro Collegio*, pp. 88, 116–18.

[140] This is evident in the almost routine references to Turkish barbarity and infidelity in papal correspondence. Consider also the extraordinary bitterness of George Zbaraski's reproaches in 1623 to Bethlen Gabor about his alliance with Turkish power: 'Rem vix aliquando auditam, per se abominabilem et nescio quo ingenio orbi Cristiano excusandam' (Biblioteca Apostolica Vaticana, Barb Lat. 6583, ff. 119v–120r).

[141] Veress, *Relationes Nuntiorum Apostolicorum*, p. 57.

concerning the late provision of promised resources to Transylvania, materially impacted on the alliance. Judicious application of papal finance, most notably to Transylvania where papal subsidies were of relatively greater budgetary importance, to some extent added another arrow to the pontifical quiver, but the resources of the Holy See were too exiguous to allow it to assume the chief burden of subsidizing the Transylvanian forces.

The limitations on Clement's diplomacy were even more evident in Poland. Despite constant diplomatic pressure and the existence of a cordial personal relationship founded on his experience as legate in Poland between the Pope and King Sigismund Vasa, Poland did not adhere to the Christian coalition. Indeed, Zamoyski's interference in Moldova and his installation of Jeremiah as *voivode* as well as Polish negotiations with Cardinal Andrew Bathory in 1599 proved substantially damaging to papal attempts to maintain the unity of the anti-Ottoman alliance. The degree of resentment which was manifested in Poland to Malaspina's opposition to Polish involvement in Transylvania in 1599, and the far less reasonable criticism of his conduct in Prague by Imperial minsters, also reflected the constant tendency of Catholic states to interpret papal policy within the light of their own interests.

The Malaspina nunciature to Transylvania in 1599, in particular, demonstrates the real limitations under which papal diplomacy operated. From the moment of his entry into Transylvania his communications with Rome were effectively severed, despite his diligent letter writing. Moreover, the distances involved in the communications between Prague and Transylvania, effectively around two weeks for letters to be sent from Gyulafehérvár to Prague, and double that for even an immediate response, were also an enormous obstacle. Much more pertinently, Malaspina's mission was fatally undermined by the attempt of both parties, but in particular the Emperor whom he trusted more, to manipulate his embassy. While he believed himself an honest broker, the Imperial court were not prepared to entrust matters to his discretion and their involvement with Michael the Brave destroyed his chances of success.

It is eminently arguable that Malaspina's analysis of the situation was more effective and realistic than the Emperor's counsellors in Prague, which can be interpreted as a compliment to the efficiency of papal gathering of information. Whatever about the general population's desire for peace and the degree of anti-Catholic sentiment in the principality, the doubts of major figures within the nobility that the Sultan would ever forgive their support for Sigismund in his war against the Supreme Porte, allied to their distaste as Christians in siding with the traditional enemy of their faith, and the experience of five years' reasonable, or at least not disastrous, cooperation with Imperial forces, meant that the grounds for a new accommodation with Prague on similar terms to those enacted with Sigismund were available. That the Emperor had drawn significant benefits from this arrangement is incontestable, as the events of the following century, and in particular the Bocskai revolt and Gábor Bethlen's harassment of the Habsburg eastern flank during the Thirty Years War, were to demonstrate. Not only had the resources of Transylvania been joined with those of the Habsburgs since 1594, rather than arrayed against them, but Sigismund's campaigns had also denied the Turks the use of Wallachia and Moldova, the breadbasket of Istanbul, for their war against the Emperor. Nothing demonstrated the strategic value of Transylvania to the Imperial cause more than Turkish eagerness to offer generous terms to its princes in order to detach them from the Christian coalition. Nevertheless, for all the acuity of his perception, the complete failure of the Malaspina mission can also be seen as an example of how Roman enthusiasm for the anti-Turkish war carried the Clementine papacy beyond the limits of diplomatic prudence and ended in corroding to some degree the Holy See's reputation as an honest diplomatic broker.

Ultimately, analysis of the papal involvement in the long Habsburg–Turkish war is revelatory chiefly of the intensity of interest in Rome concerning anti-Islamic military activity and the genuine limitations which restricted the ability of the papacy to create durable bonds between rival Catholic powers. Relative to its overall income, the Clementine papacy poured vast sums of money into the attempt to create and maintain a durable military coalition but ultimately for little reward. It engaged also in constant and intense diplomatic activity. Despite the overall failure, however, the championing by the Holy See of the anti-Turkish war, its manifest commitment of men and money, and its repeated diplomatic endeavours throughout Europe to create support for the Christian coalition, represented an important aspect of the papacy's claim to moral authority within a supra-national confession united in common cultural convictions. According to the French prelate and later Cardinal, Arnold d'Ossat, Clement claimed to have no political agenda between Catholic states and that he was:

> the most disinterested Pope ever. That there could have been others as and more holy than he, but not more disinterested, wherever he sends, whatever he does, he does not aim at any particular interest and refers all to the glory and common good of Christendom.[142]

Such an assertion of moral leadership inevitably lacked traction when deployed against the grain of international state or dynastic interests but it was not necessarily entirely in vain. In particular, the public endeavours of Rome in advancing what could be widely accepted as the common good of Christendom boosted the credibility of the pontifical institution and thus formed an important background influence over papal attempts to assert a leadership role in the wider field of Catholic renewal.

---

[142] 'le moins interessé Pape qui fut jamais. Qu'il y en pouvoit avoir eu d'aussi saincts & plus que luy: mais de moins interressez, non…qu'où qu'il envoye quoy qu'il fasse, il ne tend à aucun interest particulier, & referre le tout à la gloire, & au bien commun de la chrestienté.': D'Ossat to the King, 4 January 1595 (*Lettres de Cardinal d'Ossat*, p. 62).

5

Catholicism and Missionary Activity
in the Northern Balkans

The principal focus of this chapter is on the northern sections of the Balkan peninsula and Hungary, an area which traditionally has received relatively little attention in English-language historiography of the movement of Early Modern
Catholic renewal. As such it complements the previous chapter's analysis of the
papal patronage of war in the same region. One of its objectives is to investigate the
distribution and nature of the Catholic communities within the area. Second, this
region offers itself as an interesting case study which demonstrates both the perceived importance and limitations of Catholic mission activity during this period.
This was an area where missionaries from Rome were forced to confront a bewildering range of linguistic and confessional groups, where their actions were circumscribed by the reality of Turkish power and by the jurisdictional claims of the
Habsburg holders of the crown of Hungary, and by the existence of Catholic institutions, most notably the province of the Bosnian Franciscans, which had adapted
to the peculiar conditions of the area since the Ottoman conquest.

Mission was certainly one of the defining characteristics of Early Modern Catholic renewal and the intensity and breadth of its mission impulse was arguably one
of the most important features in distinguishing Catholicism from the Protestant
denominations which emerged in Europe in the course of the sixteenth century. In
this regard, Catholic missionary strategies were certainly affected and inflected by
the Protestant threat in Europe. Significant effort was devoted to the support of
missionaries charged with the conversion of Protestants in multiple different environments. In areas such as Bohemia and Austria missionaries operated in tandem
with policies of state coercion. In Bourbon France they could rely on the benevo-
lence of state authorities although there actual repression of Protestant worship was
more difficult to attain. Missionaries sought conversions also in the much more
difficult territory of hostile Protestant powers.

Yet while the reaction to Protestantism certainly constituted one of its defining
constituents, the Early Modern Catholic missionary impulse derived from forces
significantly more copious than the confrontation with the Reformed churches
alone. Indeed the greater salience of this characteristic within Early Modern Catholicism than in the Reformed churches is a testament to its wider ancestry. The
'dark corners' of Protestant Europe certainly resembled the internal 'Indies' of the
Catholic portion of the continent and here the different confessions came closest

in their missionary preoccupations.[1] Yet these commonly used metaphors communicate very different associations: the 'dark corners' testify to a sense of a closed and bounded space while the phenomenon of internal Indies suggests a much wider and less confined frontier. More crucially, the dominant metaphor within Catholic parlance itself testifies to the far greater influence which contact with non-European societies and religions exerted over the understanding and practice of Catholic missionary endeavour. In addition, the intellectual frameworks which underpinned evangelical work among the ill-educated Europeans of the Early Modern era differed in subtle ways.

In the Protestant north, as in England for instance, the struggle against ignorance and superstition formed part of a seamless spectrum with the rooting out of popery and the remnants of Catholicism. While Catholic missionary work often aimed at armouring the flock against Protestantism, this was soon a diminishing characteristic in much of the Catholic heartland of the continent which, over the course of several centuries, was to transform the countryside from neglected periphery of the urban centres of Catholicism into the bastion of Catholic piety. Theatricality and emotional intensity of religious belief seems also to have been a more significant long-term result of Catholic missionary activity in southern Italy, for instance, than doctrinal understanding.[2]

With regard to the mission activity of the Early Modern period, the regular clergy of Catholicism were especially significant. New orders, such as the Jesuits, as well as the various revitalized families of friars, found in mission a vocational outlet for the active apostolic spirit which was to be the hallmark of the renewed Catholicism, and to which they were ideally suited. Mission activity, whether internal or external to Europe, thus contributed to a remodelled understanding of the *raison d'être* and role of the regular orders and helped preserve this central structural differentiator between the old church and its new counterparts deriving from the Reformation. Mission not only provided a field of action but also a powerful recruitment tool for the most dynamic orders of the Early Modern period. The ideal of mission activity, up to and including glamorous martyrdom, was carefully promoted by the Society of Jesus, for instance, although in the actual dispatch of missionaries and the practice of missionary work, more sober criteria of selection were then utilized.[3] Catholic theological principles also favoured a heightened emphasis on mission activity in comparison with the churches which stemmed from the Reformation. It is true that the necessity to preach the gospel to all peoples was accepted generally by Protestant denominations. However, in practice a number of factors could operate to weaken enthusiasm for the possibilities of mission success, even within, let alone outside, Protestant national boundaries. These included the emphasis on the central role of faith in salvation, and the concomitant requirement

---

[1] J.E.C. Hill, 'Puritans and the "Dark Corners of the Land"', *Transactions of the Royal Historical Society* Fifth Series 13 (1963), 77–102.

[2] David Gentilcore, 'Methods and Approaches in the Social History of the Counter-Reformation in Italy', *Social History* 17 (1992), 73–98, at 81.

[3] Jennifer Selwyn, *A Paradise Inhabited by Devils: The Jesuits' Civilizing Mission in Early Modern Naples* (Aldershot: Ashgate, 2004), pp. 95–137.

of often sophisticated comprehension of Christian doctrine, together with an under-standing of the inability of the human will to offer any meaningful cooperation to Divine power in the salvific process, and an acceptance that perhaps only a fraction of humanity would be saved.[4] This was notably evident in England and the Nether-lands, the two largely Reformed powers whose maritime expansion brought them into greatest contact with non-European populations. Even in the United Prov-inces, as noted in Chapter 3, the hegemonic church, for instance, placed significant obstacles in the face of full participation by the entire population in its communion services.[5] In Ireland, it has been noted that attempts to translate the Gospel require-ment to preach to all nations into an active evangelization of the Gaelic and Old English inhabitants of the island may have been undermined by the suspicion that the Irish population were numbered almost entirely among the reprobate. Certainly, by the 1630s, Bishop William Bedell was to complain of the widespread assumption that parishes without a significant English colonial element could simply be treated as *sine cura* by the parochial incumbents. It was for this reason that he prioritized clergy who could speak Gaelic over more qualified Anglophone preachers on the Pauline model to 'rather speak five words with my understanding, that by my voice I should teach others also, than ten thousand words in an unknown tongue', but his was to be a voice in the wilderness.[6]

For their part, many Catholic theologians certainly doubted that the mass of humanity was destined for salvation. The heavenly community might in fact be dominated by those fortunate enough to die after baptism and before the corrup-tive effects of concupiscence could take hold.[7] Yet such an understanding could be an important underpinning of mission activity. Whereas an orthodox Reformed position derived from Calvin maintained that unbaptized elect infants were saved and that baptism did not automatically confer salvation,[8] the Tridentine decree *De peccato originali* of the fifth session confirmed the Catholic doctrine of complete remission of Original Sin in infants through baptism.[9] Thus a missionary might hope to save a certain number of souls simply by administering this sacrament to young children, who might then die in a state of grace. The grim implications of Augustinian theology that those who were not baptized were destined for damnation

[4] Patrick Collinson, *The Birthpangs of Protestant England: Religious and Cultural Change in the Six-teenth and Seventeenth Centuries* (London: Macmillan, 1988), p. 76 has noted 'successful practice of the Protestant religion required literate skills'. This made mission activity even more daunting.

[5] Benjamin Kaplan and Judith Pollmann, 'Conclusion: Catholic Communities in Protestant States, Britain and the Netherlands, c. 1570–1720' in Benjamin Kaplan, Bob Moore, Henk Van Nierop, and Judith Pollmann (eds), *Catholic Communities in Protestant States, Britain and the Nether-lands, c. 1570–1720* (Manchester: Manchester University Press, 2009), pp. 249–64.

[6] I Cor 14: 19; E. Shuckburgh, *Two biographies of William Bedell, Bishop of Kilmore: with a selection of his letters and an unpublished treatise* (Cambridge: Cambridge University Press, 1902), pp. 40–2; Alan Ford, *The Protestant Reformation in Ireland, 1590–1641* (2nd edition, Dublin: Four Courts Press), pp. 172–176, 225.

[7] Jean Delumeau, *Le péché et la peur: La culpabilisation en Occident (Xiiie–XVIiie siècles)* (Paris: Librarie Arthème Fayard, 1983), pp. 296–302.

[8] Christie Sample Wilson, *Beyond Belief: Surviving the Revocation of the Edict of Nantes in France* (Bethlehem, Penn.: Lehigh University Press, 2011), Chapter 2.

[9] H. J. Schroeder, *Canons and Decrees of the Council of Trent* (Rockford, Ill.: Tan Books, 1978), 92.

was an additional spur in this regard. In addition to baptism, the sacrament of confession was particularly important within the Catholic economy of salvation. This understanding was to become a key aspect of Jesuit spiritual activity and a principal cause of Jansenist hostility to the Society[10] but in mission terms it opened up significant avenues of optimism concerning the possibility of salvation for large numbers of people through evangelical zeal.

As this chapter demonstrates, the provision of the sacrament of penance was seen by missionaries as a key element of their mission in saving souls. The Augustinian inheritance was important, too, in the notion of criminal ignorance leading to damnation which further intensified the importance of mission activity in reaching out to provide instruction.[11] The importance of a basic level of imparted knowledge in constructing a gateway to the sacraments of the Eucharist and Penance has recently been emphasized for the peculiar mission conditions of Ireland but it was hardly unique to that island.[12] Moreover, the Catholic theology of good works exerted a particular fascination for missionaries themselves, for this offered itself as a means of personal salvation. Particularly in the first half of the seventeenth century, mission activity, whether in or outside Europe, thus became crystallized as the most perfect manifestation of vocation, favouring in a double movement both the salvation of the individual missionary and the souls of those redeemed from heresy or ignorance.[13]

From the later part of the sixteenth century, the papal attempt to assert leadership in the movement of Catholic reform resulted in an increasing Roman interest in the subject of mission and a growing desire to play a more important role in the coordination and direction of missionary activity. While interest in evangelical performance was sharpened by the progressive increase of contact with non-European populations in the era of exploration, the loss of much of the heartland of Latin Christendom to the Reformed churches also operated to sharpen the urgency of the missionary impulse within the Catholic world. As is well known, Catholic missionary activity operated on many different levels. The lure of the extra-European was certainly intense. In the Neapolitan province of the Society of Jesus, for instance, the numbers desirous of undertaking mission work in exotic circumstances significantly exceeded the number of those deemed suitable for such a career by the administration of the province.[14]

[10] Richard Parish, *Catholic Particularity in Seventeenth Century French Writing* (Oxford: Oxford University Press, 2011), p. 153.

[11] Delumeau, *Le péché et la peur*, pp. 289–91.

[12] Salvador Ryan, ' "New wine in old bottles": implementing Trent in early modern Ireland' in Thomas Herron and Michael Potterton (eds), *Ireland in the Renaissance, c.1540–1660* (Dublin: Four Courts Press, 2007), pp. 122–37, at 128–9.

[13] Bernard Dompnier, 'La France du premier XVIIe siècle et la frontiers de la Mission', *Melanges de l'École Française de Rome: Italie et Méditerranée* 109 (1997), 621–52; it also promised significant rewards for those who favoured the missionary enterprise: see for instance Bartolomeo Kašić to Savary de Brèves, 17 November 1613 (Mihály Balázs, Ádám Fricsy, Lukács László, and István Monok (eds), *Erdélyi és Hódóltsági Jezsuita Missziók* (two vols, Szeged: Scriptum KFT, 1990), 1, pp. 165–6).

[14] Selwyn, *Paradise Inhabited by Devils*, pp. 95–137; in Austria, too, many Jesuits had a passionate desire to embark on missions outside Europe: see Regina Pörtner, *The Counter-Reformation in Central Europe: Styria 1580–1630* (Oxford: Clarendon Press, 2001), pp. 203–7.

In this regard, the desire to retain their best personnel for service within their own provinces undoubtedly influenced leadership cadres within regular orders. It has been noted that even the Society of Jesus, whose extra-European missions were of profound importance, had a tendency to reserve its most promising members for activity in Europe.[15] The same phenomenon was visible in the Ottoman Balkans where, despite much prodding from both the general of the Society and the papacy, neither the Austrian nor the Roman provinces were enthusiastic about turning the attentions of their best operatives to Turkish territory, despite the great dearth of priests to minister to the Catholic populations of the area.[16] Such a tendency was heightened by the phenomenon of internal mission which influenced religious authorities, not merely in the manner in which it impacted on their area of personal responsibility, but also in the way that it could mobilize feelings of patriotism. The Irish province of the Observant Franciscans, for instance, were reluctant to commit resources to a Scottish mission in the Hebrides and Highlands, preferring to concentrate on Ireland itself, despite the enthusiasm demonstrated in Rome for the project and the fact that the local population was basically Gaelic speaking.[17] The internal Indies of Europe, the dark corners of apparently barely Christianized populations which lurked within all Catholic lands, preoccupied ecclesiastical organizers all over the continent and demanded intense missionary activities, such as areas of the Dauphiné in France where Capuchin missionaries considered themselves to be dealing with a virtually pagan population.[18]

In addition to the widespread problems of superstition and ignorance, Catholic Europe contained non-Catholic populations which acted as a major spur to internal mission activity and which could attenuate the enthusiasm of local ecclesiastical leaderships in providing key personnel for areas outside their borders. In Royal Hungary, the existence of a majority Protestant population and the tenuous state of clerical resources was certainly one of the reasons why the Hungarian ecclesiastical establishment paid little or no attention to the Catholic communities under Turkish rule, particularly since many of these were relatively recent South Slav immigrants. Even in Italy itself, in maritime centres such as Livorno, Genoa, and Venice, or a tourist zone such as Florence, heretical merchants and visitors posed a constant threat to the purity of faith which seemed to require mission activity. Even more frightening was the tract of Italian territory under Swiss

[15] Simon Ditchfield, 'Of Missions and Models: The Jesuit Enterprise (1540–1773) Reassessed in Recent Literature', *Catholic Historical Review* 93 (2007), 325–43, at 342.
[16] Antal Molnár, *Katolikus missziók a hódolt Magyarországon I 1572–1647* (Budapest: Balassi Kiadó, 2002), pp. 256–8.
[17] Tadhg Ó hAnnracháin, 'Introduction: Religious acculturation and affiliation in Early Modern Gaelic Scotland, Gaelic Ireland, Wales and Cornwall' in Tadhg Ó hAnnracháin and Robert Armstrong (eds), *Celtic Christianities in the early modern world* (Basingstoke: Palgrave, 2014), pp. 1–16, at 3–4.
[18] Dominique Deslandres, *Croire et faire croire: Les missions française au xviie siècle* (Paris: Fayard, 2003), p. 58; Bernard Jacqueline, 'Missions en France' in Josef Metzler (ed.), *Sacrae Congregationis de Propaganda Fide Memoria Rerum (350 anni a servizio delle missioni 1622–1972)* (three vols, Rome, Freiburg, Vienna: Herder, 1971–6), 1, pp. 111–48, at 111–15; Bernadette Majorana, 'Une pastorale spectaculaire: Missions et missionnaires jésuites en Italie XVIe-XVIIIe siècle', *Annales, Histoire, Sciences Sociales* 57 (2002), 297–320.

control, from Balerna to Lucerne with the valleys of Mendrisia and Lavizzara, from which it was feared that the contagion of heresy might creep into the Italian heartland. And Italy, moreover, contained sizeable communities adhering to Greek rites, particularly in Mezzogiorno and Corsica, who presented a constant missionary challenge.[19]

Within the Catholic states of Western Europe in the period under review in this book the missionary challenge of religious heterodoxy was at its greatest in France, particularly after the Edict of Nantes brought peace to the kingdom while guaranteeing the right of religious practice to more than one million French Huguenots.[20] In the 1590s César de Bus founded a native missionary congregation, the priests of the 'Doctrine Chrétienne', which was then followed by a female equivalent, the 'Filles de la Doctrine Chrétienne'. Between 1594–8 François de Sales, who was to represent a critically important example for French missionary activity, engaged in evangelical activity in the Chablais. In 1607 a papal-authorized Barnabite mission was mounted to Béarn while the following year Michel Le Nobletz commenced his missions in Brittany.[21] Under Henri IV, French Jesuits mounted missions in Chablais and Vivarais, and in 1618 made major evangelical efforts in the Paris region. Louis XIII founded ten missions attached to the Jesuit college at Agan in 1621 and in the 1630s the subsequently canonized Jesuit, François Regis, proved a turbo-charged purveyor of missions among the Reformed population of Vivarais and of Vivay. In addition to conversion, mission activity also served to shore up confessional boundaries, thus inoculating the Catholic faithful from what was seen as the danger of heretical contamination.[22]

The most dynamic figures within French Catholicism of the seventeenth century all contributed to French missionary culture. In 1613 the Oratoire of Pierre Bérulle accepted the charge of preaching missions and Vincent de Paul was to emerge as an indefatigable correspondent with the Roman congregation of *Propaganda Fide* founded in 1622.[23] Of central importance in France was the role of the Capuchins who through Richelieu's *eminence grise*, Père Joseph, came also to exercise significant influence on the formulation of royal policy towards Huguenot conversion. As the Capuchin superior in the Protestant stronghold of Saumur in 1611, Père Joseph initiated intense mission activity and in 1617 he inaugurated the mission of Poitou at Lusignan, followed two years later by the mission of Touraine. Capuchin activity rapidly extended to Rheims, Paris, Normandy, Brittany, Aquitaine, Toulouse, La Rochelle, Cevennes, Bourgogne, the Dauphiné, and

---

[19] Pietro Chiocchetta, 'La S. Congregazione e gli Itali-Greci in Italia' in Metzler, *Congregationis de Propaganda Fide Memoria Rerum*, 1, pp. 3–23; Instructions for Giovanni della Torre, nuncio to the Swiss, 10 November 1595 (Klaus Jaitner (ed.), *Die Hauptinstruktionen Clemens' VIII. für die Nuntien und Legaten an den Europäischen Fürstenhöfen, 1592–1605* (two vols, Tübingen: Max Niemayer Verlag, 1984), 1, pp. 365–89, at 374–5).

[20] Joseph Bergin, *Church, Society and Religious Change in France 1580–1730* (New Haven: Yale University Press, 2009), p. xiii.

[21] Deslandres, *Croire et faire croire*, pp. 118–40.

[22] Keith P. Luria, *Sacred Boundaries, Religious Co-existence and Conflict in Early-Modern France* (Washington D.C.: Catholic University of America Press, 2005), pp. 47–102.

[23] Jacqueline, 'Missions en France', pp. 111–20.

Lorraine.[24] The fervour of the regular clergy also was echoed by French bishops. Between 1623 and 1648 the congregation of *Propaganda Fide* received nineteen requests for missionary faculties from French dioceses.[25]

Yet while the internal missions of the Catholic church and missionary endeavours outside Europe have rightfully attracted a great deal of attention, by the end of the sixteenth century much of Europe itself lay *in partibus infidelium*. As a result of the Reformation, huge swathes of Northern Europe had been reconfigured as Protestant states. This presented a series of variegated challenges to Catholic missionary zeal. The Protestant societies which emerged in the wake of the Reformation were not uniform in their internal organization or their level of harassment of Catholic clergy. As noted in Chapter 2, while all subjects of the throne of England were technically required to belong to its church and the harbouring of clergy became a capital offence, in the Netherlands the Reformed church actually placed significant obstacles in the way of potential members and there Catholic clergy underwent less significant dangers.[26] Even within the domains of the Tudor and Stuart monarchs, massive differences existed between England and Ireland. At the end of the sixteenth century the former represented probably the most dangerous mission territory in the world while in Ireland the presence of a massive Catholic population not only offered protection for clergy returning to the island from continental seminaries, and a haven for English Catholic exiles, but even allowed Rome to create a resident Episcopal hierarchy during the 1620s.

South-eastern Europe also represented territory *in partibus infidelium*. The current chapter offers a case study of Catholic missionary activity in the Turkish Balkans and Hungary, much of which was taken by the Turks after the fall of Belgrade in 1520. Turkish Europe represents a particularly striking field of study of Catholic mission activity because there impulses of post-Tridentine Catholic reform encountered an entirely individual situation. The Ottoman presence ensured that the Balkans, despite its European population, also demonstrated characteristics of non-European societies. Within this area an immense variety of different religious perspectives, each with its particular challenges for Catholic missionaries, coexisted. In addition to the Muslim faith of the Turks themselves there were a plethora of Christian denominations—Orthodox, Unitarian, Reformed, Lutheran, even Paulician—as well of course as Jews, including exiles from Spain. But critically there were also important Catholic communities and ecclesiastical structures which had adapted to Turkish rule over the course of several centuries.

In the north of the zone, the tripartheid division of Early Modern Hungary between the Habsburg kingdom, the principality of Transylvania and the Turkish occupied region created highly complex political, ethnic, and religious contours. As István György Tóth has noted, in Hungarian territory the phenomena of internal

---

[24] For details of the Capuchins' claims of success in their conversion activity see Archivio Storico 'De Propaganda Fide', Acta 4, ff. 129, 212, 321, Acta 6, ff. 154, 166, 283; see also Jacqueline, 'Missions en France', pp. 124–32.

[25] Jacqueline, 'Missions en France', pp. 118–20.

[26] Kaplan and Pollmann, 'Catholic Communities in Protestant States', pp. 249–64.

and external mission occurred in sharply contiguous spaces so that Italian missionaries could consider themselves operating in either Germany or Turkey when actually they were in the same geographical zone.[27] The linguistic diversity of the area was also striking. In 1669 the missionary Joannes Vanoviczi noted that ten languages were necessary in the kingdom: Hungarian, German, Slovak, Croat, Polish, Ruthene, Serb, Romanian, Turkish, and Latin. While five of these languages were Slavonic, which meant that missionaries with a proficiency in one could rapidly acquire communication skills in one of the others, Hungarian, German, Romanian, and Turkish were completely distinct.[28]

For the papacy the Balkans were a missionary field of particular interest given the nature of the Turkish threat yet, although it attempted to acquire a freedom of action in Ottoman lands, echoes of the jurisdictional problems created by the *Padronado* also surfaced in terms of Balkan missionary organization.[29] In this area, too, the problems of rivalry between different regular orders and ethnic antagonisms which complicated the task of mission organization all over the world come clearly into focus. Ultimately the failure of Rome to safeguard significant Catholic communities in Bosnia and Albania from creeping Islamicization in the course of the seventeenth century, despite the lack of systematic persecution by Turkish power, also offers an insight into the limitations of Catholic missionary activity in the post-Tridentine era, and another example of the manner in which Catholic confessionalization proved so unsuccessful in its encounters with Islam.

The gradual Turkish conquest of the Balkans wrought havoc on the medieval system of Catholic church organization in the Balkans which had been centred in particular on the three archbishoprics of Raguza (Dubrovnik), Bar as the metropolitan seat of the Albanian and Serbian churches, and the southern Hungarian archbishopric of Kolocsa, which from 1247 exercised ecclesiastical jurisdiction over the bishopric of Bosnia.[30] In the first half of the sixteenth century the bishoprics of Scardona, Tinini, Duvnói, and Makarskai fell entirely under Turkish control. Similarly the Ottoman conquest of much of Hungary in the decades following the victory at Mohács in 1526 resulted in the territories of the archbishopric of Kalocsa and the bishoprics of Pécs, Csanad, Vác, Várad, Veszprém, and Zágreb falling either wholly or partially under Turkish rule. In addition, the cathedral seat of the archbishopric of Esztergom and its immediate environs was in Turkish hands for most of the period of this book.

Venice and the Habsburg Emperor, by virtue of his assumption of the title of King of Hungary, both continued to claim the right of nomination to dioceses

[27] István György Tóth, *Politique et religion dans la Hongrie du XVIIe siècle: Lettres des missionnaires de la Propaganda Fide* (Paris: Honoré Champion, 2004), p. 14.
[28] Relazione di Joannes Vanoviczi, 1669 (István György Tóth, *Relationes Missionariorum de Hungaria et Transilvania (1627–1707)* (Rome and Budapest: Biblioteca Academiae Hungariae, 1994), p. 151); István György Tóth (ed.), *Litterae Missionariorum de Hungaria et Transilvania (1572–1717)* (two vols, Roma and Budapest: Biblioteca Academiae Hungariae, 2002), 1, *passim*.
[29] Ignacio Ting Pong Lee, 'La actividad de la Sagrada Congregación frente al Regio Padronado' in Metzler, *Congregationis de Propaganda Fide Memoria Rerum*, 1, pp. 353–438.
[30] Molnár, *Katolikus missziók*, pp. 39–40.

which had pertained to the jurisdiction of the *Serenissima* or to the crown lands of St Stephen prior to the Turkish invasion. The status of both as among the chief enemies of the Supreme Porte ensured that prelates appointed by either power were not welcome in Turkish territory, thus removing any possibility of providing these dioceses with resident bishops. Indeed in Dalmatia fears of Turkish raids ensured that even in those sees where a portion remained under Venetian rule the activities of the Italian bishops tended to centre on safer urban areas, where, in addition, their general linguistic deficiencies in Croatian were less of an obstacle. It was in this context that Catholic ecclesiastical institutions internal to the Ottoman empire, most importantly the Bosnian province of the Franciscan order, came to play a significantly increased role in terms of providing pastoral care throughout the European portion of the empire.

Even prior to the collapse of the Bosnian kingdom in 1463, the Bishop of Bosnia had not resided within the territory and the *Vicaria Bosniae* of the Franciscan order had developed into the chief institution of the area's Catholicism. This was recognized by Sultan Mehmet II whose *firman* of 1463 offered protection to the order and its personnel, property, and churches.[31] While this did not prevent a steady contraction of the order's establishments, fourteen convents still remained by the end of the sixteenth century and, despite suffering constant extortion and attempts by Orthodox bishops to assert jurisdictional rights, the order's membership flourished in the period under review. In 1587 the province counted seventy-five friars but by 1600 this had practically doubled to 149 and in 1623 its size had more than doubled again to 355 members. According to seventeenth-century visitation reports, the number of Catholics in Bosnia was between 100,000 and 300,000, and the steady migration north of Bosnian Catholics into parts of Turkish Hungary helped reinvigorate Catholicism in those areas. It also opened up new fields of resources to support the Bosnian convents under pressure from Turkish extortion and creeping Islamicization.

The mission church model of the Bosnian Franciscans in fact proved highly suitable to Ottoman rule and the province's leadership was notably resistant to the reinvigoration of Episcopal power which was to become a keynote of the post-Tridentine church. They strove to keep the right of filling parishes within the order while restricting the role of bishops, even those appointed from within the ranks of the friars of their own province, to largely sacramental functions. As the last surviving institution of the medieval Bosnian kingdom, the Franciscan province saw part of their role as preserving its legacy. Similar to the contemporary developments among Gaelic Irish Franciscans, this resulted in a reinvigoration of literary endeavour from the end of the sixteenth century.[32]

The relationship between the province and the strengthening mercantile elite of Bosnia during the seventeenth century was particularly strong. The financial support of Bosnian merchants was critical in the upkeep of the order's convents and it was

---

[31] David Do Paço, '"La demeure de la paix"? Conflits, religions et sociétés en Europe ottoman, 1453–1683' in Wolfagng Kaiser (ed.), *L'Europe en conflits: Les affrontements religieux et la genèse de l'Europe moderne vers 1500–1650* (Rennes: Presses Universitaires de Rennes, 2008), pp. 267–86, at 274.

[32] Molnár, *Katolikus missziók*, p. 86.

from this social group that the Franciscans drew much of their membership. In the course of the seventeenth century commercial rivalry between merchants from Bosnia and Ragusa (Dubrovnik) began to intensify and this was to have important effects on Catholic missionary activity, particularly as papal interest in the Balkans became more acute, since Rome's natural tendency was to make use of Ragusan networks to facilitate missionary penetration. The closer relationship between the Bosnian friars and Turkish authorities, where many even of the order's leadership had Muslim relatives, then became an important factor in the Franciscans' protection of the position of ecclesiastical prominence which they had gained all over the northern Balkans following on from the Turkish conquest.[33]

The city of Ragusa proved another key element in the ecclesiastical system of the Balkans since it represented a Catholic city state, tributary to the Supreme Porte, whose merchants enjoyed significant commercial privileges and rights of travel, as well as the tacit right of free practice of their religion and the construction of churches, within Turkish dominions. According to local legend, St Francis had guaranteed that the city could maintain its independence as long as Catholicism remained the only permitted religion within its territory and the open practice of other faiths was forbidden by city law. The urban religious life of Ragusa corresponded to that of contemporary Italian city states. In addition to the three principal dignitaries of archbishop, papally-nominated and invariably Italian, archdeacon, and archpresbyter, 120–30 secular clergy and a somewhat greater number of regular clergy, including a Jesuit residence after 1609, ministered to the 16,000 Catholic population of the archdiocese, which was latticed also with numerous lay associations and confraternities. Ragusan caravans travelled throughout the Balkan peninsula. Various Ragusan colonies were also set up, most importantly in Belgrade and in Sofia, where the Ragusan chapel became the most important Catholic institution in the Eastern Balkans. The Catholic merchants from the city provided a vital conduit of information to Rome concerning the Turkish empire and Ragusa was the natural entry port for clergy from Italy entering the Balkans. The mercantile network was also of crucial importance in terms of ecclesiastical visitation and ultimately of missionary work. Travel with Ragusan merchants offered otherwise impossible opportunities of mobility for Catholic missionaries since the caravans provided protection and the various colonies offered hospitality, a vital web of local contacts and, not infrequently, direct financial assistance.[34]

Both Ragusa and the Bosnian Franciscans offered important support to the numerically small Bulgarian Catholic community which, while it perhaps represented only one per cent of the total population, played a more important role in the articulation of Bulgarian identity than its mere numbers might suggest.[35] The three major components of Bulgarian Catholicism comprised a compact band of

---

[33] István György Tóth, 'Between Islam and Catholicism: Bosnian Franciscan Missionaries in Turkish Hungary, 1584–1716', *The Catholic Historical Review* 89 (2003), 409–33, at 411–13.

[34] Molnár, *Katolikus missziók*, pp. 66–7.

[35] Georgi Nešev, 'La propaganda catholique dans les terres bulgares au XVIIe siècle et le développement historique du Sud-Est européen', *Bulgarian Historical Review* 3 (1975), 43–52; Ekaterina Večeva, 'L'église catholique et le peuple bulgare (XVIIe–XVIIIe siècle)', *Bulgarian Historical Review* 11 (1983), 65–84.

territory originally settled by Saxon miners centred around the town of Čiprovici and the villages of Kopilovci, Železna, and Klisura; the Ragusan colonies and the converts which they attracted; and the followers of the Paulician heresy who converted wholescale to Catholicism under the influence of Bosnian Franciscan missionaries between 1595 and 1650, thereby continuing to maintain an identity distinct from the surrounding Orthodox majority. The Bosnian Franciscans were also critical in terms of providing pastoral care to the community at Čiprovici where they built both a school and a convent which became the seat of the Catholic bishopric of Sofia from 1601 to 1688.[36]

The third major Catholic reservoir in the Balkans was in the northern part of Albania. While Albania was ultimately to become perhaps the most heavily Islamicized area in the region, and while the nobility adopted the religion of the conqueror relatively early, most of the popular conversion to Islam occurred in the course of the seventeenth and eighteenth centuries and this phenomenon was more marked in the Catholic north than in the Orthodox south.[37] The decline of Albanian Catholicism, and of the Albanian Catholic communities which had been colonizing the Kosovan Serb lands since the fifteenth century, thus represents one of the most important failures of the post-Tridentine mission impulse within the Balkans. In Albania, the ancient metropolitan seat of Antivari or Bar remained an important ecclesiastical dignity even after its fall to Turkish power in 1571 and its archbishops attempted to exercise oversight over the Catholic communities of Serbia and Bulgaria as well as Albania. The general lack of Catholic priests which characterized the Balkans in the period under review was less pronounced in north Albania. In fact, like Bosnia, Albania was to be an exporter of priests in search of better material conditions to other Balkan Catholic communities during the sixteenth and seventeen centuries. So pronounced was the exodus indeed that it contributed to the weakening position of Catholicism in Albania itself. Of more importance in this respect, however, were the failures of Roman missionary policy.[38] Missionaries dispatched with a direct mandate from Rome, who often despaired at the beliefs and practices of the local Catholic communities which they encountered, recognized the urgent need for local educational institutions.[39] But Rome failed to found an independent college with responsibility for Albania and much of Roman missionary work became entrusted to Italian regular clergy who signally failed to alter the process of Islamicization.[40]

---

[36] Molnár, *Katolikus missziók*, pp. 97–101.

[37] The process has sometimes been interpreted as part of a process of preserving Albanian ethnic identity: see Lino Sciarra, 'L'Islam in Albania', *Oriente Moderno* new series 15 (1996), 1–77, at 1–7; the manner in which subordinate peoples can adopt the religion of high-status outsiders in order to demonstrate independence from dominant neighbours is discussed in Robert Hefner, 'Multiple Modernities: Christianity, Islam and Hinduism in a Globalizing Age', *Annual Review of Anthropology* 27 (1998), 83–104, at 95.

[38] Molnar, *Katolikus missziók*, pp. 87–96.

[39] See for example Bartolomeo Kašić to Claudio Acquaviva, 15 June 1615 (Balázs et al., *Jezsuita Missziók*, 1, pp. 122–3).

[40] In Serbia, for instance, the Archbishop of Antivari and papal visitor Pietro Massarecchi numbered the mostly Albanian Catholic community at 20,000 but also noted now a lack of priests was leading to Islamicization. Ten years later his reports suggest a significant decrease: see Molnár, *Katolikus missziók*, p. 97.

The Turkish conquest of Hungary resulted in the dismemberment of the ancient throne lands of St Stephen. The southern and middle parts fell under direct Turkish rule, while Transylvania became an Ottoman satellite state which officially recognized four Christian confessions, Reformed, Lutheran, Unitarian, and Catholic, but whose princes for most of the period under review were Reformed in their sympathies. Only in the truncated Royal Hungary did the outline of the medieval ecclesiastical inheritance survive, although even there Catholicism rapidly became a minority faith. Catholicism, however, was not entirely swept away from Turkish Hungary, although this part of the ancient kingdom naturally became subject to very similar conditions to the rest of the Turkish Balkans and significant southern Slavonic immigration resulted in the importation of the Balkan ecclesiastical system, spearheaded by Bosnian Franciscans, into Ottoman Hungary.

A number of islands of Catholicism continued to persist within Turkish Hungary at the onset of the seventeenth century. East, north, and north-west of the town of Pécs was a group of about sixty villages with a significant Catholic population.[41] Within the town of Pécs itself, Jesuit missionaries in the early seventeenth century estimated the Catholic community at about 500 people.[42] South of Lake Balaton in North Somog lay another sizeable Catholic community which was reinforced by South Slav Catholic immigration. By the 1640s Jesuit missionaries reported some fifty settlements with a strong Catholic presence in the area. Further east between the river Tisza and the Danube, three surviving Franciscan convents at Gyöngyös, Jászberény, and Szeged provided the pastoral network to maintain a Catholic presence in the surrounding villages. In the 1670s, seventy-three Catholic communities were noted by the bishop in the Turkish-occupied bishopric of Vács and it seems probable that these had survived in the area since the sixteenth-century conquest. South of Pécs, in Slavonia, the Catholic community amounted to about a third of the population by the end of Turkish rule, largely the result of substantial Slavonic immigration since the sixteenth-century destruction of the medieval kingdom. This represented the largest Catholic population in the Hungarian crown lands. The Turkish settlement of soldiers in their Hungarian lands and the arrival of Slavonic farmers to replace the fled *Magyar* population, while in the main Serbians, also resulted in a Croatian and Bosnian Catholic minority moving in to settle along the Danube. In the seventeenth century more Catholic Slavs settled along the Drava river with some moving north also towards Kanizsa. In addition, south of the Maros river around Lippa and Timisoara significant Catholic communities were to be found. In the mid-seventeenth century it was estimated by Matej Benlić that 170,000 Catholics were living in Turkish Hungary. While this is hardly a reliable figure, it seems probable that, after Bosnia, Turkish Hungary represented the second largest Catholic community in the European section of the Ottoman empire.[43]

[41] Molnár, *Katolikus missziók*, pp. 101–2.
[42] Bartolomeo Kašić to Claudio Acquaviva, 15 June 1615 (Balázs et al., *Jezsuita Missziók*, 1, p. 123).
[43] Molnár, *Katolikus missziók*, pp. 101–6.

As noted in Chapter 4, the period prior to Clement's ascension to the pontifical throne in 1592 had witnessed a gradual increase of contact between Rome and the Christian population of the Balkans. This had formed the backdrop to enthusiastic papal involvement in the Habsburg struggle with the Ottomans between 1593 and 1606, which had been animated by an optimism that major military success by the Habsburgs and their allies would lead to an uprising by the Christian population of the Balkans and the final elimination of Ottoman power in Europe. The committed participation of the papacy in the anti-Turkish war naturally impeded the formation of a coherent missionary policy in the Balkans. The Treaty of Zsitvatörök finally put paid to these hopeful imaginings and in the absence of another major war it was through the medium of mission and not military liberation that the heartland of Catholicism was to communicate with the Christians of Turkish Europe. In this regard Roman institutions, and in particular the *Congregatio de Propaganda Fide*, founded in 1622, were of critical importance. As previously outlined in Chapter 1, this held certain continuities with the first congregation of the same name, founded by Clement VIII in 1598, but other institutions, in particular the religious orders who represented the shock troops of Catholic missionary activity throughout the world, both before and after the founding of the congregation, were also of crucial significance.

Down to 1612, Rome's chief missionary involvement in the northern part of the Turkish zone was the provision of missionary authorization to Bosnian Franciscans and to the Ragusan Benedictine congregation of Meleda which resulted in the expansion of both orders in other areas of the Balkans. By the second half of the sixteenth century, bishops from the Bosnian Franciscan province were given the right to visit in Belgrade and the order also exercised missionary faculties in Hercegovina and had begun pastoral work in southern Hungary. The Ragusan Benedictines ultimately developed several centres of missionary activity, particularly around Pozsega, and their faculties were renewed by both Clement VIII and Paul V. Friction between the two orders was considerable however. The Ragusans complained to Rome of the licentious life of the Bosnian friars, and of the general ignorance which characterized the Catholic communities, while the Bosnians bitterly resented what they saw as Ragusan interference in their sphere of influence.[44] The apparent ending of the Benedictine mission in 1612, however, resulted in a new round of inter-order strife as a papally-authorized Jesuit mission was launched in a two-pronged direction, from Graz in the Habsburg dominions, and from Ragusa. The reports of these Jesuit missionaries provide a particular insight into the conditions under which Catholicism was practised under Turkish rule.

Turkish terrain certainly presented particular challenges for the renewed Catholic church. The Ottoman empire did not, of course, aspire to the massive and forced Islamicization of the Christian populations which the conquest of the Balkans brought under its rule. Cooperation with local Christian elites had significantly assisted the movement of conquest and their continued collaboration was necessary

---

[44] ibid., pp. 140–50.

for the administration of the new territories. Consequently the Sultan was prepared to offer articles of protection to the non-Muslim religious communities which had come under his control.[45] On religious grounds the Turkish authorities did not necessarily discriminate between the various Christian denominations within their empire, and local *beys* were generally prepared to weigh conflicts between conflicting Christian groups in light of their own pecuniary interests. Nevertheless, in practice, due to its supranational character and the geographical proximity of Catholic powers, Catholicism was less well suited to adaptation to Ottoman structures and in the course of the sixteenth century generally represented the least favoured denomination by the Turks. The ecclesiastical leadership of the Greek, Serbian, and Armenian churches resided within the territory of the Ottoman empire and their church organization largely did not reach into enemy territory. Similarly, the large Protestant communities of subjugated Hungary and dependent Transylvania were potential allies against the Sultan's Catholic enemies. On purely religious grounds, too, Catholics tended to be the least respected Christian denomination. As evident monotheists, Ottoman officials demonstrated most sympathy for the Unitarian communities of the lands which came under their control but it was a persistent Muslim belief that believers in the Trinity were polytheists.[46] While numbered among the Trinitarians, the Lutheran and Reformed denominations at least were vehemently opposed to the use of images in worship. Indeed this had become one of the most visible points of differentiation between Protestants and Catholics, which was entirely comprehensible to Muslim sensibilities.[47]

Yet religious factors were effectively of secondary importance. Whatever their internal differences no Christians were followers of the prophet and the Turks were rarely disposed to allow minor gradations in the level of falsity in religion influence policy. The principal Turkish desire was for internal stability within Christian denominations, and it was also in the authorities' interest to maintain disunion between Christian groups, which could sometimes operate to protect the existence of smaller Catholic minorities. The influence of diplomats in Istanbul could also act to favour particular denominations with the ambassadors of France and Venice playing the most important role from a Catholic perspective.

In the years prior to 1612 Jesuit activity in Royal Hungary in a mission at Alsólindvár, on the lands of the Lutheran convert Kristóf Bánffy, had opened the way for increased contact with the Turkish-occupied zone. The exorcisms performed by one of the Jesuit fathers, Gergely Vásárhelyi, came to the attention of the Turkish authorities who requested that he come to Kanizsa to assist two Turks who were tormented by demons. Given the number of Slavs in the Turkish settlement of Hungary, there is every chance that the two in question were of Christian origin. The Jesuit general Claudio Acquaviva was eager to make use of this entrée

---

[45] Do Paço, "'La demeure de la paix"?, p. 273.

[46] In 1613, for instance, the Jesuit Bartolomeo Kašić made use of a metaphor of the sun, the sun's light and the sun's heat to demonstrate that the Trinity represented one God, not three, to a deeply surprised Turkish scholar: see his letter to Claudio Acquaviva, 15 June 1615 (Balázs et al., *Jezsuita Missziók*, 1, pp. 126–7).

[47] Tóth, *Politique et religion dans la Hongrie*, pp. 37–8.

and urged the Viennese provincial to facilitate it.[48] Thereafter Vásárhelyi asked permission to mount a mission to Turkish-controlled Pécs which, coinciding with renewed requests to the Pope for spiritual assistance from within the Turkish territories, ultimately resulted in his employment, together with Zachariás Jékel, on a papally-authorized Jesuit expedition. Both Acquaviva and Cardinal Scipione Borghese involved themselves personally in this enterprise and asked the aid of the Hungarian primate, Ferenc Forgách, in promoting it.

A second aspect of the mission involved another two Jesuits, Bartolomeo Kašić and István Szini, who were dispatched from Ragusa to Belgrade in the company of a secular priest, Don Simone Matkovic. Both pairs thus contained one Jesuit proficient in Hungarian and the other a native speaker of a Slavonic tongue. Kašić acted as the overall superior of the mission and was one the significant figures in Croatian intellectual life of the seventeenth century, composing and translating significant philological, hagiographical, catechetical, and devotional texts, although his supreme work of translation of the scriptures into his native language was not to see publication until after the second Vatican council. The instructions given to the departing Jesuits epitomize the sense of mission which Acquaviva had attempted to make central to his generalship of the Society. The objective was to be service to others and the glory of God with no ulterior motivation. The principal goal of the mission was to make contact with the region's Catholics in order to assist them and to confirm them in their faith. The missionaries were emphatically warned to avoid any trouble, and indeed contact, with the Turks and, in particular, to avoid any attempt at converting Muslims which could bring down persecution on the missionaries' heads. They could offer spiritual consolation to Christian slaves but only with the permission of their masters and were to involve themselves in no attempts at escape or flight. Although Kašić was equipped with a copy of Bellarmine's *Controversiae*, it was not intended that the Jesuits should seek to involve themselves in any public debates with Protestants, not least because the outcome of such disputations in the eyes of the general population was always doubtful. They were to seek no monetary recompense of any kind for their work and to embrace poverty, showing themselves content with the most mediocre hospitality which might be offered them. It was inevitable that they would encounter many incompetent Catholic clergy but were to use no public reproofs nor to give any impression that their role was one of inspection or correction. Instead, only through good example were they to seek to edify and improve such clerics. They were to be wary not to cause any conflict through indiscreet fervour and to take adequate time for eating and sleeping. The ideal of mission was thus patience, perseverance, gentleness, moderation, altruism, and restraint.[49]

The interest of the Borghese papacy in the mission was considerable. Not only was Kašić equipped with letters from the Pope to prominent figures in Ragusa, as well as indulgences to promulgate, but the mission's expenses were supported by papal funds and Acquaviva evidently communicated the information he received

---

[48] Claudio Acquaviva to Giovanni Argenti, 8 January 1611 (Balázs et al., *Jezsuita Missziók*, 1, p. 32).
[49] Instructions for Bartolomeo Kašić, 1 September 1612 (ibid., pp. 55–6).

concerning its progress directly to Pope Paul V.[50] Such overt support, however, was something of a two-edged sword because the rumour that they were acting as apostolic visitors actually put the mission in Belgrade in considerable danger.[51]

Partially this was occasioned by their association with Matkovic who was a local figure with significant enemies. Originally educated by the Bosnian Franciscans, he left their cloisters at the age of twenty-two and thereafter a strong hostility existed between him and the order. Matkovic's strong championship of the new Gregorian calendar also created antagonism. For many Catholics in Eastern Europe, largely divorced from the intellectual and spiritual ferment which erupted in later sixteenth-century Catholicism in the wake of Trent, the essence of their religion consisted of a fierce attachment to traditional practice. During the 1580s in Transylvania, for instance, passionate opposition ignited to the synodal attempt of primate Miklós Olah to abolish a variety of traditional Hungarian and Transylvanian feast days which were not observed within the universal church. To many traditional Catholics attachment to such traditions was precisely what distinguished them from the heretics who surrounded them.[52] The Gregorian calendar represented a similar challenge, particularly given the number of Orthodox Christians who regarded it with open hostility, in the Balkans. The Jesuits in their turn soon encountered difficulties in persuading local populations that adhering to the new calendar did not characterize them as another new denomination which had spring up since the Reformation.[53]

Prior to the sending of the Jesuit mission, Matkovic's conflict with the Serbian Orthodox Archbishop over the calendar had also intersected with Catholic resentments at taxation by the Orthodox clergy, whose favoured position within Turkish dominions needed to be safeguarded annually with significant financial contributions to the Supreme Porte. In search of redress for this, Matkovic went to Istanbul, probably in 1608, and secured a wide-ranging immunity for Catholics from Orthodox and Protestant jurisdiction, although it needed to be authorized by the Pasha of Buda and, as was customary with such documents, its points were not necessarily observed to the letter by other Turkish authorities. In 1609–10, however, this authorization helped to protect the massive assembly of pilgrims at Olovo, which was a major site of pilgrimage for the entire Balkan peninsula.[54] In 1610 Matkovic, with Turkish assistance, secured half the Unitarian church in Pécs for Catholic worship and in 1612 he joined the Jesuit mission in Ragusa. Acquaviva was delighted at the prospect that his missionaries could benefit from his knowledge, and journey under Matkovic's protection, and indeed instructed them not to leave Ragusa except in his company.[55] Kašić, however, soon had to disabuse

[50] See Acquaviva to Kašić, 2 March 1613 (ibid., pp. 79–80); same to same, 16 March 1613 (ibid., p. 81).

[51] Acquaviva to Gergely Vásárhelyi, 8 June 1613 (ibid., p. 109); same to Theodor Busaeus, 8 June 1613 (ibid., p. 111).

[52] See the memorial by Stephen Arator, 15 March 1583 (Andreas Veress (ed.), *Epistolae et Acta Jesuitarum Transylvaniae Temporibus Principum Báthory (1571–1613)* (Budapest: Athenaeum, 1911), pp. 266–71).

[53] Bartolomeo Kašić's relation of the mission, 31 January 1613 (Balázs et al., *Jezsuita Missziók*, 1, p. 75).

[54] Molnár, *Katolikus missziók*, pp. 166–8.

[55] Acquaviva to Szini, 10 November 1612 (Balázs et al. *Jezsuita Missziók*, 1, p. 60); same to Kašić, 29 December 1612 (ibid., p. 61).

Matkovic of the notion that he was the superior of the mission rather than merely its guide and protector. In Belgrade also their association with Matkovic earned them the hostility of the Bosnian Franciscans.

However, it seems probable that the Jesuits would have encountered opposition from the Bosnian friars in any event. Throughout the period under review the Bosnian Franciscans exhibited a marked hostility towards all other Catholic groups or institutions which attempted to interfere in what they considered their own sphere of influence. This included papal visitors such as Pietro Massarecchi, the Archbishop of Antivari, in the 1630s, Matkovic and other secular priests who associated with him, and the bishops of the historic sees of Turkish-dominated Hungary, as well as Jesuit missionaries. By the end of the sixteenth century the Franciscan province of Bosnia was locked in a highly exploitative relationship with Ottoman power. While enjoying legally recognized status, the order's convents were the subject of constant extortion. It was in this context that the order was eager to acquire pastoral care of Catholics outside Bosnia, especially in the comparatively richer lands which had once been in the Hungarian kingdom, now heavily populated by southern Slavs. The resources from these areas which they received in return for their ministry were vital in terms of up-keeping the cherished fabric of the order's institutions. In 1632, the apostolic visitor Pietro Massarecchi, a hostile witness it is true, penned a highly critical account of Bosnian activities. He was incensed at the manner in which a friar, charged with the pastoral care of the incredibly poverty-stricken Catholics of Karassevó, had raised money and goods to the value of 300 scudi for the area, by virtue of an extended tour which had even taken him to Vienna, but had then decamped to convey the money to his convent in Bosnia. Massarecchi compared the order's friars to bees who swarmed from their convents in order to bring back honey for the hive.[56]

The Jesuit mission represented a considerable threat to the Franciscan position. On a series of levels the Jesuits threatened to undermine the local prestige of the friars. Their lack of solicitation of recompense for their spiritual services was naturally welcome to the laity but cast into relief the Bosnian expectation of higher levels of support in return for ministry. The papal authority and indulgences at the Jesuits' disposal were also unwelcome as they further diminished the relative standing of the friars, especially because the publication of indulgences was one of the most cherished missionary privileges of the Franciscans. Not surprisingly, therefore, the Bosnian chaplain in Belgrade, Tommasso Jukovic, attempted to prevent the promulgation of the Jesuits' indulgences and also strove to prevent the newcomers from preaching to any substantial number of people. Christmas became a flash point when he forbade the Jesuits to say public mass, even going so far as to take away Matkovic's chalice from the altar.[57] Bosnian preaching in addition became directed at the Jesuits, accusing them of ambition and avarice and disobedience to the Franciscan Bishop of Bosnia, and alleging that all who went to

---

[56] Pietro Massarecchi to the cardinals of the congregation, 4 March 1632 (Archivio Storico 'De Propaganda Fide', Visite, Vol. 10, fos 13r–14v).

[57] Kašić to Lorenzo Paoli, 9 January 1613 (Balázs et al., *Jezsuita Missziók*, 1, p. 66).

hear them preach would incur excommunication. It was apparently also asserted from the friar's pulpit that the sacraments offered by his rivals were inefficacious and that confessions made to the Jesuits were null and void.[58]

The education and demeanour of the Jesuits apparently contrasted sharply with the vast majority of the local Franciscans. The Bosnian province was not totally divorced from developments in contemporary western Catholicism, sending some of its most promising novices for education in Italy, but it was far less infused with the current of reformed spirituality which characterized the Jesuits. It is true that many of the witnesses who supplied evidence about the Bosnian Franciscans to Rome were deeply hostile but it seems clear that many of the friars conducted themselves in a manner very far removed from contemporary ideals of regular behaviour. While a reluctance to wear habits corresponded to a reasonable desire not to attract unwelcome attention from hostile observers of a different religious persuasion, many Franciscans were accused of attiring themselves like Turkish soldiers in scarlet robes. Accusations of concubinage, drunkenness, gluttony, and violent behaviour were frequent.[59] Matters were made worse by the order's expansion during the seventeenth century. Social factors evidently favoured this growth since membership of the order conferred significant prestige. Not surprisingly, however, the bulging numbers seem to have resulted in a decline in discipline. Moreover the tendency towards conflict with other Catholic groups seems to have been accentuated by the Bosnian practice of keeping the cream of the order within Bosnia and dispatching the more difficult friars outside the traditional borders, particularly to the north. The Bosnian leadership may also have favoured friars with good Turkish contacts for this enterprise. Increasingly in the seventeenth century this factor became a significant criterion for advance within the order as influence with the authorities was critical for the protection of the Franciscans in general. Not surprisingly, however, it also created a tendency for members of the order to look to use their leverage with the Turks against rivals.[60]

The Society of Jesus, on the other hand, by the early seventeenth century had cultivated an ideal of behaviour and had streamlined structures of selection in order to produce a cadre of highly-motivated and disciplined priests for missionary activity. The Jesuits sent to the Balkans seem to have been remarkably diligent. István Szini, for instance, hardly had time to fulfil his duties of regular communication by letter due to the demands of work. In June 1613 he managed to snatch time to send a letter to the mission leader Kašić explaining that he had already given six sermons in Belgrade that week and that he was preparing at least one and possibly two more in the next day.[61] Kašić's successor as superior, Marino de Bonis, reported frequently having to preach up to six times in one day while on a mission in Slavonia and of standing entire days and nights to hear confession.[62]

[58] Marino de Bonis's relation of the mission in 1617 (ibid., 2, pp. 294, 300).
[59] See for example Marino de Bonis' relation of the mission in 1617 (ibid., pp. 295–6).
[60] Molnár, *Katolikus missziók*, pp. 287–99.
[61] Szini to Kašić, 30 June 1613 (Balázs et al. *Jezsuita Missziók*, 1, p. 132).
[62] Relation of the state of the Christians subjected to the Great Turk by Marino de Bonis, 1617 (ibid., 2, p. 299).

De Bonis, admittedly hardly an impartial witness, insisted that it was the holiness of life, superior grasp of doctrine, charity, and modesty of his colleagues, and the manner in which they converted so many heretics, while working tirelessly and selflessly for others, which was at the root of Bosnian hostility. That which should have edified and cheered the friars, he noted acidly, instead they treated with poisonous hatred. But his observation that the chief motivation for their antagonism was the fear that the people would turn to the Jesuits and abandon the friars seems highly plausible.[63]

From the Bosnian perspective the arrival of Jesuit interlopers evidently seemed to pose a threat to their own historic mission, dating back to their successful confrontation with the medieval Bogomil heresy, to oppose which the province had originally been created. Theirs was a consciousness of historic suffering under Turkish rule borne with patience, where cleaving to the gospel of Christ meant a constant rejection of the easier path of conversion to Islam. In 1632 the Bosnian Franciscan Bishop of Scardona, for instance, encapsulated this sense of historic identity when he noted that the lack of foreign war meant that Turkish oppression of Christians was growing but that local Catholics endured this with good grace 'because they shared in the inheritance of Jesus Christ, promised to them in the Holy Gospel, in which they had been instructed by the fathers of this province since the time of their conversion'. The key role which contributions from outside Bosnia played in facilitating the survival of the order's convents in the region was also of great importance. Deeply rooted in Franciscan spirituality was the sense of sacred immanence. The Bosnian convents were not merely buildings but reservoirs of holiness whose maintenance was made ever more urgent by the creeping tide of Islamicization.[64] Thus two very different senses of Catholic identity, embodying very dissimilar traditions, came into sharp collision with the arrival of the Jesuit missionaries.

The tensions between Ragusans and Bosnians in Belgrade introduced an additional toxic element. In 1633 Pietro Massarechi, the Archbishop of Antivari, who was employed as a papal visitor in the Balkans estimated that a population of roughly 1700 Catholics were resident in Belgrade, of which about 200 were Ragusans and the rest Bosnians.[65] Tensions between the mercantile leadership of these two groupings were considerable and the Ragusan support for the Jesuit mission was an additional reason for Bosnian antagonism, for the services of the Jesuits freed the Ragusans from dependence on Bosnian priests and offered them some clerical protection from spiritual threats. Ready recourse to excommunication was evidently a feature of Bosnian pastoral practice, which was hardly surprising given the lack of any temporal sanctions at the clergy's disposal against recalcitrant members of their flock.[66] Following the Jesuits' arrival this issue erupted when Vukovic denounced one of the Ragusan merchants, who was harbouring a widow in his

---

[63] ibid., pp. 294.

[64] Tommasso Ivkovich to the cardinals of *Propaganda Fide* (Tóth (ed.), *Litterae Missionariorum*, 1, p. 438).

[65] Antal Molnár (ed.), 'Pietro Massarecchi Antivari Érsek és Szendrői Apostoli Adminisztrátor Egyházlátogatási Jelentése a Hódolt Dél-Magyarországról' (1633), *Fons* 2 (1995), 175–219, at 207.

[66] Marino de Bonis's relation of the mission in 1617 (Balázs et al., *Jezsuita Missziók*, 2, pp. 294–5).

house, for public concubinage. Other Ragusans, however, were prepared to testify that the woman was not the merchant's sexual partner. Moreover, she had no other place to go. Vukovic's suggestion that she be sold to the Turks outraged Kašić, who considered the danger of losing the Christian faith among Muslims significantly worse than simple fornication, if this was occurring.

While this incident perhaps highlights a greater Bosnian tolerance for contact with Islam, which to them was an inevitable aspect of life in the Balkans, it seems clear that it also formed part of a complex struggle for power in which both ethnic hostility and the attempt by local clerical forces to maintain authority over secular Catholics played a part. It also pointed up the lack of explicit papal authority at the disposal of the Jesuits, which they saw as the only mechanism to restrain their opponents. Although dispatched with papal approval, the mission was essentially that of the Society of Jesus. Jesuit complaints about the friars thus adumbrated what was to be an ongoing problem for Rome in the Balkans, namely the need to establish a local authority to arbitrate between the various competing Catholic institutions.

The commercial importance of Belgrade made all the Catholic groups at work in the northern Balkans eager to maintain a base there. Given their lack of local contacts, it was particularly important for the Jesuits. The protection afforded by its Ragusan merchants was vital for their mission and Belgrade's position as a hub-site for Ragusan caravans meant that from the city the missionaries could fan out in several directions with relative security.[67] The major routes which the missionaries took were to Timisoara, Karassevó, Pécs, and into Slavonia where they encountered a bewildering array of religious perspectives and a widespread lack of Catholic clergy.

Jesuit interaction with the Orthodox clergy was sharp with mutual hostility. The missionaries bitterly criticized the ignorance of the Orthodox priests and lamented the manner in which the lack of local clergy of their own meant that Catholics often had recourse to them for sacraments. The Jesuits were particularly worried about baptism. They had genuine doubts about whether the Orthodox priests knew enough even to be able to perform the ceremony correctly and in certain cases they re-baptized *ad cautelam*. Even worse was the lack of knowledge, which they ascribed to Orthodox influence, that anyone could baptize in the event of an emergency.[68] In the case of children who died without baptism, in certain areas the local custom was evidently to bring the dead infant to an Orthodox priest for a posthumous ceremony which would allow salvation.[69]

Among the numerous Lutheran, Reformed, and Unitarian populations they encountered similar antagonism but also sometimes possibilities of conversion. Certainly the clergy of these confessions were deeply hostile but, in many of the areas into which they journeyed, the lack of Protestant ministers was almost as acute as that of Catholic priests. Some years later another Jesuit missionary, Marino de Bonis, for instance, when he ventured into the Karassevó region, east of Belgrade

---

[67] Bartolomeo Kašić's relation of the mission, 31 January 1613 (ibid., 1, p. 76); Marino de Bonis's relation of the mission in 1617 (ibid., 2, pp. 288–9).

[68] Bishop of Pristina to Muzio Vitelleschi, 7 February 1619 (ibid., p. 343).

[69] ibid., p. 290.

and south of Timisoara, encountered both Orthodox and Protestant communities who offered to become Catholic if the Jesuits would consent to visit often among them. Similarly, in Slavonia, Protestant villages were prepared to offer conversion to Catholicism if the Jesuits would leave them a priest to act as their teacher. In these cases, the attraction of an educated pastor outweighed questions of denominational affiliation.[70] The community in Karassevó, whom he referred to as 'his new Indies', were enormously isolated and had lacked the services of any educated clergy for decades. De Bonis believed he was the first priest to have reached there in a century. Consequently wherever he went the local population was eager to gain a promise that he would return, particularly, it can be surmised, because the Jesuit was happy to share the primitive local diet and to take the most basic lodgings without looking for any monetary return.

In this region, while many claimed to be Catholics, they were in his opinion closer to pagans. Among those who claimed to be of the faith of Rome, for instance, were people who did not believe in God or in the immortality of the soul.[71] While these, even by Balkan standards, seem to have been exceptionally isolated communities, in many other areas, too, the lack of educated ministry meant that Christian identity effectively existed below the level of confessional differentiation. Bartolomeo Kašić reported of the phenomenon of clergy who serviced different communities, Lutheran, Reformed, and Catholic, tailoring their ministry to the different requirements of their flocks. Similar to other areas of Europe where the proximity of other faiths stimulated the belief that the virtuous of whatever denomination could attain salvation, the Jesuits also encountered resistance to the idea that only within one church was the path to God to be found[72] and they were openly questioned as to how an illiterate population could distinguish the truth between the differing claims of Reformed ministers and Catholic priests. The Jesuit inclination in these circumstances was to emphasize the continuities between their teaching and the ancient religion of the region commemorated in the altars, crosses, and images in the ruined churches which helped to foreground the notion of a glorious Catholic past compared to the miserable present of Turkish subordination.[73]

The readiest acceptance of the missionaries was naturally in those communities which considered themselves Catholics. Some of these were extremely tenacious in their identity as adherents to the ancient Roman faith, although in certain cases this extended to little more than an intense suspicion of religious innovation. Near Bukin, for instance, in the village of Zenta, the missionaries found that most local Catholics were initially reluctant to attend the Jesuits' mass for fear that it was part of an

---

[70] Marino de Bonis' brief relation of the state of the Christians subjected to the great Turk (ibid., p. 299); on other missions radiating out from Pécs, the Jesuits encountered Catholics who went to the preaching of Reformed ministers but who declared their willingness to abandon this mode of procedure if a preaching priesthood was made available to them: see Marino de Bonis's relation of the mission in 1617 (ibid., p. 293).

[71] Balázs et al., *Jezsuita Missziók*, 2, pp. 368, 293.

[72] Bartolomeo Kašić's relation of the mission, 31 January 1613 (ibid., 1, p. 73); Stuart B. Schwartz, *All can be saved: Religious Tolerance and Salvation in the Iberian Atlantic World* (New Haven and London: Yale University Press, 2008).

[73] Balázs et al., *Jezsuita Missziók*, 2, p. 293.

attempt to Protestantize them.[74] To the Jesuits this was proof of divine providence that a population unable even to make the sign of the cross, let alone recite an Our Father or a *Credo*, should have such an instinct to protect themselves from perversion.[75]

It was in Slavonia and Szerémség between the rivers Drava, Sava, and the Danube that the Jesuits encountered the largest Catholic population. They reported huge crowds at their sermons with up to 15,000 coming to attend so that the priests had to preach up to six times in one morning. So large was the confluence of people that the local Turkish authorities began to invite the missionaries to preach in their localities, as the opportunities to make money from the provision of food and services to the visiting crowds was considerable. Here, as everywhere else where the Jesuits penetrated, the extreme dearth of priests in the area over many years resulted in the missionaries offering confession to people who had not frequented this sacrament for decades, which effectively committed them to spending extended periods doing little or nothing else.[76]

This however marked an improvement, from their perspective, on the area around Timisoara where the population showed a marked reluctance to make confessions, with adults insisting that, never having confessed as children, they could not now be expected to do so. Concerned about this critical deficiency, the Jesuit tactic in this regard was apparently to lead individuals apart as if to examine merely the knowledge of prayers and from there to move to the commandments to see which had been broken. This then put them into a position to say that the bulk of the confession had already been made and that little remained beyond the declaration of repentance, a strategy which apparently worked effectively. As elsewhere in the Balkans, in Slavonia the Catholic population had taken on the mores of other Christian denominations in terms of divorce and this was an area where the missionaries laboured intensely to convince married couples to return to their original spouses. Papal enthusiasm for the Jesuit mission was so great that even when it began to run into difficulties of personnel the new general of the Society, Muzio Vitelleschi, could not bring himself to wind it up but instead worked to locate new missionaries to take part.[77]

In addition to their concrete missionary work, the Jesuits made suggestions to Rome concerning the macro framework necessary to support evangelical activity. In 1613 Kašić returned to Rome and over the following winter he produced a variety of memorials concerning what was needed. In these he highlighted the appalling dearth of priests for an area which he estimated contained a population of half a million souls, and also the need to create episcopal structures of authority dependent neither on the Habsburg kingdom of Hungary nor on the Bosnian Franciscans. His recommendation was for an archbishopric to be created in Sirmia with its seat in Belgrade and four suffragan bishoprics in Pécs, Pozsega, Mohács, and Timisoara, all of which were to depend directly on the Holy See rather than on any intermediary

---

[74] Marino de Bonis to Marino Gondala, 8 May 1619 (ibid., p. 350).
[75] ibid.
[76] Brief relation of Marino de Bonis, (ibid., p. 299).
[77] Muzio Vitelleschi to Ferdinand Alber, 7 October 1617 (ibid., p. 276).

power. Matkovic, for whom he constantly expressed support, should be one of these bishops. Rome should provide ten to twelve missionaries and pay their expenses for three years. In the meantime, a major educational commitment was also needed with schools to be supported in Belgrade, Pécs, and with a higher level institution in Ragusa where a seminary should also be set up. In addition the Illyrian college at Ancona was to be re-established. The most radical of Kašić's suggestions was for a papal nunciature at Istanbul. Experience had taught him that mission success was only possible with local Turkish support but that this was potentially feasible. Matkovic's successes as a private individual in gaining privileges in Istanbul indicated the scope of what might be achieved. Kašić was undoubtedly convinced that favours acquired through diplomacy in Istanbul would greatly assist the prospect of the conversion of the other Christian denominational groups in the Balkans. He argued that while the papacy had expended vast resources in supporting war against the Ottomans, France, Venice, and Ragusa had used their good relations with the Supreme Porte to advance the cause of Balkan Catholicism more significantly.[78]

The Jesuit advocacy of an active policy of conciliation with Turkish power is of considerable interest. Another of the Jesuit mission, István Szini, at this time also began to develop a relationship with the influential Turkish ambassador to the Emperor, Gaspar Gratianis, which further indicated the possibilities of a less confrontational relationship with Turkish power. However, the notion of official Roman diplomatic representation in Istanbul flew in the face of the anti-Ottoman identity which remained central to the post-Tridentine papacy. Kašić's argument that a fraction of the resources used in supporting Clement's war against the Turks, if invested in educational resources, could reap significant dividends was also not without validity. The Irish experience of the seventeenth century points up for instance the extraordinary importance of continental colleges in sustaining Catholicism. But the papacy was to find greater difficulty in locating the necessary money for educational purposes than Clement had in supporting the Habsburg war. Kašić's memorials, however, did help to foreground the problems relating to the organization of Catholic missionary activity in territory claimed by the Habsburg monarchy of Hungary. Hungarian bishops nominated to the historic sees of the Turkish-dominated area had little possibility of acting in their dioceses and showed relatively little inclination to do so. Under Clement VIII, however, the papacy had been eager to see the filling of Hungarian sees, even from the area under Turkish control, on the grounds that it ensured reliable Catholic votes in the Hungarian Diet and in negotiations with royal authority[79] and this remained a concern also for his successors.

The attempt to provide the requisite pastoral care for the Turkish-dominated area without creating excessive tension either with the Habsburg kings of Hungary or with the Bosnian Franciscans, was to preoccupy Rome for the following decades. In 1612 the potential difficulties in this regard became apparent when Rome was

---

[78] Bartolomeo Kašić's memorial of 1613 to the Pope (ibid., 1, pp. 186–8), Molnár, *Katolikus missziók*, pp. 177–9.
[79] Instructions to Cesare Speciano, 5 May 1592 (*Die Hauptinstrucktionen Clemens' VIII.*, pp. 53–79, at 58).

faced with a problem concerning the see of Bosnia, to which it had regularly supplied bishops over the previous century while also, and presumably inadvertently,
confirming (different) royal nominees to the same diocese. This contradiction
came to light when the existing papal Bishop requested a coadjutor at the same
time as the royal candidate, Thomas Balásfy, sought papal confirmation. The Curia
therefore sidestepped the issue by appointing Antun Matić to the see of Scardona,
over which the throne of Hungary had no feudal pretensions, and gave him rights
as an Apostolic Visitor in Bosnia. Similarly, in 1618 the advice of the Jesuits was
followed with the nomination of their preferred candidate, Petar Katić, as the
Bishop of Prizren with his seat in Belgrade. The see of Prizren had never pertained
to the Hungarian kingdom (although Belgrade had) and thus a case could be sustained that this did not represent interference with Habsburg rights.[80]

However, a clash soon developed. Katić in company with the Jesuit, Marino
de Bonis, Matkovic and another priest mounted a concerted programme of visitation and evangelization along the banks of the Drava river where significant
numbers of Croat-speaking Protestants were located. Lively clashes ensued, particularly as the missionaries laid claim to several churches on the grounds that
they had been originally built by Catholics. However, Katić's attempts to extend
his episcopal visitations to the Catholic community at Pécs led to a conflict with
a Hungarian Jesuit, János Cserneky, who was acting as the procurator of the
Hungarian Bishop of Pécs and to whom he looked for protection from the missionary prelate.

The last decades of the sixteenth century and the early part of the seventeenth
thus witnessed an increasing Roman interest in the Catholicism of the Balkans
which resulted in a growing body of knowledge and some missionary activity that
brought Jesuits into areas that had lacked clerical ministration for many decades.
However, Jesuit activity was circumscribed by the paucity of the numbers of the
missionaries, their dependence on Ragusan support and the outright hostility of
the Bosnian Franciscans to their activity.

Coherent support for the missions in the Balkans, as elsewhere, was also impeded
by the lack of a central Roman institution. In 1622, however, the newly elected
Pope Gregory XV successfully initiated the *Congregatio de Propaganda Fide*. In
contrast with the previous Clementine organization of the same name, this quickly
attained institutional solidity not least because of the manner in which it rapidly
acquired financial resources, through the papal assignment of the duties on *annelli
cardinalizi*, donations, bequests from its cardinal members and continent-wide
collections. While the congregation was very much the initiative of the Ludovisi
Pope, both his successors Maffeo Barberini (Urban VIII) and Gianbattista Pamfili
(Innocent X) were active cardinal members of *Propaganda Fide* and this helped to
give it institutional continuity.[81] Its first secretary, Francesco Ingoli, was also a
figure of pivotal importance. He was a trusted advisor to the Cardinal-nephew of
Gregory XV, Ludovico Ludovisi, and he both attended and presented political

[80] Molnár, *Katolikus missziók*, p. 190.   [81] Tóth, *Relationes Missionariorum*, p. 88.

arguments at the short-lived Accademia dei Virtuosi over which Ludovisi presided.[82] Although he was to acquire posthumous infamy for his involvement in the two trials of Galileo, whom he knew personally, and his anti-Copernician treatise of 1616, Ingoli was also centrally preoccupied with pastoral practice, publishing *De Parochis et eorum Officio* in 1622, and enjoyed a high reputation for his meticulous grasp of ceremonial procedure and protocol.[83] As secretary he was to combine zeal for the missionary project, to which he was devoted, with meticulous organizational practice. Personally comfortable in six languages, Italian, Latin, French, Spanish, Greek, and Arabic, he canvassed information from all possible sources and strove consistently to improve and regularize missionary procedures. While the cardinals of the congregation were responsible for its decisions, Ingoli's control of the order of business and his expertise and knowledge meant that his opinions were of extreme importance and his advice was generally followed.[84]

While the reach of the new congregation extended over the entire globe, the significance of the European heartland of Christendom was indicated in the geographical division of the world into thirteen areas, eight of which were in Europe. Each of these was entrusted to one of the cardinal members of the congregation. The papal nunciatures were the vital node of communication between the central apparatus and the missionary territories, each of which came under the oversight of a nuncio or equivalent authority. By the end of 1622 when the nunciature at Graz was wound up, Rome maintained nuncios in four Italian centres—Venice, Naples, Florence, and Turin—as well as in Vienna, Cologne, Madrid, Paris, Brussels, Warsaw, and Lucerne, while three prelates with equivalent authority operated as Collector in Portugal, Inquisitor in Malta, and Vice-Legate in Avignon. The nuncios played an important intermediary role with the local hierarchies of the various Catholic states, having responsibility, for instance, in chivvying them to make reports to the congregation concerning the need for missionary personnel and the current state of mission activity in their dioceses.[85] They also provided critical support for *Propaganda's* missionaries in terms of organizing payment, assistance with accommodation and in their journeys, and in maintaining contact with the congregation.[86] The territory of the Balkans initially came under the supervision of three separate authorities. Royal Hungary, Transylvania, Carinthia, Styria, Wallachia, and Moldavia were entrusted to the nuncio at the Imperial court, although later Moldova moved into the sphere of competence of the nuncio to Poland, while Wallachia gravitated towards the vicar

[82] Maria Rosa, 'The "World's theatre": the court of Rome and politics in the first half of the seventeenth century' in Gianvittorio Signorotto and Maria Antonietta Visceglia (eds), *Court and Politics in Papal Rome, 1492–1700* (Cambridge: Cambridge University Press, 2002), pp. 78–98, at 84.

[83] Francesco Ingoli, *De Parochis et Eorum Officio* (Bologna, 1622); Josef Metzler, 'Francesco Ingoli der erste Sekretär der Kongregation (1578–1649)' in Metzler, *Congregationis de Propaganda Fide Memoria Rerum*, 1, pp. 197–42, at 200–4.

[84] Metzler, 'Francesco Ingoli', pp. 201–11; Tóth, *Relationes Missionariorum*, p. 90.

[85] Instructions for Giovanni Battista Lancellotti, 14 December 1622 (Klaus Jaitner (ed.), *Die Hauptinstrucktionen Gregors XV für di Nuntien und Gesandten an den Europäischen Fürstenhöfen 1621–1623* (two vols, Tübingen: Max Niemeyer Verlag, 1997), 2, pp. 897–923, at 899–900).

[86] Giovanni Pizzorusso, '"Per servizio della Sacra Congregazione de Propaganda Fide": i nunzi apostolic e le mission tra centralità romana e chiesa universal (1622–1660)', *Cheiron* 15/30 (1998), 201–27; Molnár, *Katolikus missziók*, pp. 200–1.

of the (exiled in Rome) Latin patriarch of Constantinople, who also exercised over-sight over Thrace, Macedonia, Bulgarian, Serbia, and the area around Istanbul. Within the congregation, Cardinal Hohenzollern-Sigmaringen was entrusted with the German nuncio's territories while the future Pope, Maffeo Barberini, took responsibility for the southern Balkans. Dalmatia, Croatia, Bosnia, Slavonia, Albania, and the Greek islands were allotted to the responsibility of the nuncio in Venice, and Cardinal Pietro Valerio, the only Venetian member of the congrega-tion, was not surprisingly appointed to oversee this area.[87]

Widespread enthusiasm was evident throughout the Catholic world at the foun-dation of a Roman centre for the propagation of faith although in the long run Catholic states, despite the congregation's avowed intention to exercise no temporal jurisdiction, proved reluctant to allow the papacy the free hand to which it aspired in the direction of missions throughout the world. While this has been particularly noted with regard to the Iberian monarchies in the New World, in the Balkans the Habsburg kings of Hungary also came to mount significant jurisdictional oppos-ition to the congregation's activities in terms of the appointment of bishops.[88] Fun-damental to the working of the new congregation was a bifurcate conception of the world, somewhat cognate to the Muslim notion of *Dar al-Islam* and *Dar al-Harb*, as divided between *terrae Sedis Apostolicae*, effectively the territory of Catholic powers, where the normal Catholic hierarchy functioned, and *terrae missionis* which fell under *Propaganda Fide*'s jurisdiction.[89] In the latter Rome worked to create al-ternative structures of authority, grouping missionaries into apostolic praefectures, and appointing individuals to the dignities, in ascending order of importance, of *delegatus apostolicus*, *administrator apostolicus*, or *vicarious apostolicus*.[90]

Upon its creation, the new congregation actively canvassed information. One natural source of data was the titular Hungarian bishops of Turkish-occupied sees who conveniently congregated for the national diet in Sopron from May to August 1622. The nuncio to the Emperor, Carlo Caraffa, therefore invited the Hungarian hierarchy's opinions concerning the propagation of Catholicism, particularly in the Turkish portions of their dioceses. The most dynamic figure in seventeenth-century Hungarian Catholic reform, the Archbishop of Esztergom, Péter Pázmány, prepared a response on his own behalf and that of several colleagues. The substance of Pázmány's report was that the situation for Hungarian Catholicism, whether in Royal Hungary, Transylvania or the Turkish-occupied territory, was singularly diffi-cult. Everywhere there was a profound dearth of priests—in Turkish Hungary he estimated the number of secular priests at perhaps twenty, supplemented by a

[87] István György Tóth, 'A Propaganda megalapítása és Magyarország (1622)', *Történelmi Szemle* 42: 1–2 (2000), 19–68, at 40–1.

[88] Lee, 'La actividad de la Sagrada Congregación', pp. 356–7; Josef Metzler, 'Foundation of the Congregation "de Propaganda Fide" by Gregory XV' in Metzler, *Congregationis de Propaganda Fide Memoria Rerum*, 1, pp. 79–111, at 103–7.

[89] Ireland represented something of an anomaly within this schema because it contained an illegal but functioning resident hierarchy under the congregation's authority: see Tadhg Ó hAnnracháin, *Catholic Reformation in Ireland: The Mission of Rinuccini, 1645–49* (Oxford: Oxford University Press, 2002), pp. 41–68.

[90] Molnár, *Katolikus missziók*, pp. 202–3.

handful of Jesuits in Pécs and Franciscans at Gyöngyös. Outside the Szekler area, Catholicism in Transylvania was practically moribund while the lack of priests even in Royal Hungary meant that the bishops had to tolerate many inadequate individuals and clerical concubinage was rife. For Pázmány the key to reform was the provision of educational establishments to nurture a new, disciplined priesthood which he believed offered the promise of a major renewal of the Catholic faith in all three areas of Hungary, and consequently he saw the role of the new congregation primarily as the provision of monetary support for this programme. When pressed further by the papal nuncio, one of Pázmány's colleagues, the Archbishop of Kalocsa, admitted that he did not even know what religion was professed by the inhabitants of his diocese and his ignorance was certainly not unique within the hierarchy.

For the next two years, with a complete lack of success, the new congregation attempted to have the Hungarian bishops take up residence in their bishoprics. This was in line with the thrust of its policy elsewhere: even such a seasoned Roman resident and eminent theologian as Peter Lombard, the Archbishop of Armagh, came under sharp criticism for his failure to take up residence in his diocese. The most which was achieved, however, was the decision by a number of the Hungarian hierarchy to appoint or to dispatch representatives to their dioceses. At the same time, information from Matkovic emphasized the manner in which the areas under Turkish rule could not be assisted by the bishops of Royal Hungary, who did not wish to go there and who would be treated as spies by the Turks even if they did.[91] Caraffa's advice echoed this assessment. Despite belief in Rome that the Treaty of Vienna of 1615 theoretically conferred protection, the Hungarian bishops were not prepared to risk their lives in Turkish territory and Royal Hungary lacked the clerical manpower even to minister to its own population, let alone to provide missionaries for the Turkish-occupied south. Moreover, the titular bishops of the sees in Turkish territory lacked the resources to support a significant number of missionaries while the local inhabitants were too poor to sustain them. Consequently, the congregation was gradually forced to realize that no major missionary drive could be mounted from Royal Hungary.[92] The interaction, however, was another milestone in the developing jurisdictional conflict between Rome and the Habsburg monarchy concerning Turkish territory as it sharpened the attention of both the congregation and the Hungarian bishops on the status of the area.

The bishops of Ragusa were also put under pressure to take up residence in their dioceses and, although unwilling, in 1623 the bishops of Alessi and Scutari as well as the abbot of Bacs left Ragusa for the territories of which they held titles. In an effort to gain further information about the Balkans, Pietro Massarecchi was dispatched as Apostolic Visitor to investigate Serbia, Bosnia, Bulgaria, and Turkish Hungary, and to determine the size of the Catholic population, the languages and customs in the various areas, the number and character of the priests, and the evangelical strategy to be followed in the conversion of the area's non-Catholics. Although

---

[91] Tóth, 'A Propaganda megalapítása', pp. 43–6. For details of Pázmány's own extraordinary efforts in this regard see Chapter 3.
[92] Molnár, *Katolikus missziók*, pp. 211–12.

he went to Bulgaria, where he reported the existence of some 8000 Catholics and the general impossibility of making conversions among the Orthodox population, he did not feel the need to visit Serbia, partly because of the lack of funds which hampered his entire journey, but principally since he knew the area well and informed the congregation that it contained in the region of 20,000 Catholics. He estimated the Catholic population in Turkish Hungary at about 300,000 and that of Bosnia at a similar number but since his chief area of visitation was merely in the southern part of what had once been the Croatian and Hungarian lands of the throne of St Stephen, these figures were clearly highly unreliable. His most important information concerned the enormous dearth of priests in the area. While little could be hoped for in terms of the Orthodox population, the provision of enthusiastic, linguistically competent and educated clerical personnel would not only provide ministration to the deprived Catholic communities but also promise dividends in terms of converting the area's Protestants. In this regard he suggested that the Turkish authorities could be bribed to expel Protestant preachers which would facilitate this project.

Although it balked at providing money for bribes, *Propaganda* tried to implement Masserecchi's recommendations but this resulted in a series of conflicts which the congregation then tried to adjust, often on the basis of inadequate information. In 1624 Massarecchi's notion of three missionary bishoprics was accepted. Stiga Marini, a Bulgarian Franciscan, was appointed to Sofia, Massarecchi himself was appointed to the see of Prizen with responsibility for Serbia. Most problematically, Albert Rengjic, a Ragusan Franciscan, was appointed to the see of Sirmia but with a basis of operations in Belgrade with the responsibility of oversight over southern Hungary. This marked an acceptance by Rome that the titular bishops of Turkish Hungary would never take up residence and they hoped therefore to have Rengjic accepted as apostolic administrator in their stead. The move, however, was greeted with uneasiness by the Hungarian bishops. The Bosnian Franciscan province was equally unhappy. Essentially, Massarecchi recommended that the Bosnian Franciscan Bishop, Toma Ivković, who enjoyed the title of Scardona, should confine his activities to Bosnia itself but this would threaten the province's control of the relatively lucrative parishes between the Drava and the Sava. The Bishop of Scardona, therefore, claiming also the fictive episcopacy of Diacovo, simply invaded the territory supposedly given to his rival, confirming priests in parishes and administering confirmation widely, insinuating that Rengjic was not a true bishop and securing a permission from the Turkish authorities that he was to be only Catholic bishop in the area, by which he effectively confined his rival to the much poorer eastern parishes. There Rengjic was eventually unable to sustain himself and left the area. *Propaganda* first unsuccessfully tried to restrain Ivković but then, despite Rengjic's complaints, it more or less tolerated this land grab as Ingoli was aware of the pastoral importance of the Bosnian Franciscans.[93] By 1627, for instance, Ivković was

    [93] Archivio Storico 'De Propaganda Fide', SOCG, 56, fos 212–214v; Archivio Storico 'De Propaganda Fide', SOCG, 386, fos 174r–177v; Archivio Storico 'De Propaganda Fide', SOCG, 56, fos 222r–223v; Archivio Storico 'De Propaganda Fide', SOCG, 67, fos 262r–263v.

claiming to have confirmed 17,000 people.[94] Among *Propaganda Fide's* less helpful suggestions was that Rengjic might apply to the nuncio in Vienna and to the Archbishop of Esztergom for funds to assist in providing pastoral care in the poverty-stricken part of his diocese. This was wildly unrealistic for Rengjic had little chance of secure communication with either and would run a not inconsiderable risk if such letters came to the attention of the Turkish authorities.[95]

Ingoli's appreciation of the pastoral role performed by the Bosnian Franciscans in the Balkans was also evidently one of the reasons why *Propaganda Fide* tended to ignore their violation of Ragusan rights over the chapel in Belgrade but then watched with horror as both sides appealed to the Turkish authorities. Eventually this helped to precipitate Pietro Massarecchi's second intervention. He was appointed as apostolic administrator of Turkish Hungary and Bishop of Szendro and was to divide his time between Serbia and the north, centred on Belgrade. Massarecchi's reports were extremely critical of the Bosnia Franciscans. He suggested, as he had done in his previous visitation, that the jurisdiction of the Bosnian-based bishop should be confined to Bosnia itself, that they should be sharply forbidden to appeal to the Turkish authorities in any ecclesiastical matter, and that their faculties should be examined closely. Massarecchi's visitation was intensely unwelcome to the Bosnian Franciscans who justifiably regarded the Apostolic visitor as a danger to their lucrative pastoral positions outside Bosnian borders.[96]

Both in their threats against him and in his reports of their past behaviour, his visitation highlighted the phenomenon of Catholic denunciation of other Catholics to the Turkish authorities. There were a number of grounds on which this could operate. Turkish hostility to papal and Habsburg power meant that it was relatively easy to whip up suspicions concerning individuals with authority derived from outside the borders of the Ottoman empire. Massarecchi, for instance, menaced with denunciation by the Bosnians on this ground and in fear of his life tried to hide his identity as a bishop and apostolic visitor by travelling in the guise of a chaplain to Ragusan merchants. The Bosnians also made use of this tactic against Jesuit missionaries, circulating rumours that they were papal spies and/or taking resources from Ottoman domains for papal use. Another tactic which they utilized in Belgrade concerned the law on church buildings. Ordinances prohibiting the building of fresh churches, or the extension of existing ones, existed within the empire, although repair and maintenance of existing structures was permitted. In Belgrade, the Bosnian Franciscans seem to have insinuated that the Jesuit residence represented a new chapel in the hope that it would be confiscated and then sold at an affordable price which would allow them, at a stroke, to drive the Jesuits out of Belgrade while acquiring their chapel. The Ragusans were apparently denounced for having extended their chapel which Massarecchi considered particularly villainous since this had been done in the interests of accommodating the much more numerous Bosnian population at services.

[94] Archivio Storico 'De Propaganda Fide', SOCG, 146, f. 218r.
[95] Archivio Storico 'De Propaganda Fide', SOCG, 67, fos 270r–273v.
[96] Molnár, *Katolikus missziók*, pp. 268–80.

Despite Massarecchi's outrage, the activities of the Bosnian Franciscans conform to the behaviour of many other groups within contemporary Europe who naturally sought to invoke secular against papal authority, when it suited their purposes. The closest counterpart to this behaviour is possibly in Ireland during the 1630s which also witnessed the phenomenon of Catholic denunciation of co-religionists to non-Catholic authorities. In Ireland, the chief victims of this behaviour were the papally-appointed bishops whose attempts to discipline recalcitrant clergy in their dioceses led them to being brought before the secular courts, on the accusation of their priests, for the crime of having exercised a Roman-derived jurisdiction.[97] While the Bosnians, as a native Balkan group with legitimate privileges from the Supreme Porte among whom leadership credentials, as noted previously, were increasingly defined by the possession of good contacts with the Turks, were the most frequent practitioners of this mode of denunciation, it was not unique to them. In Pécs the expelled Jesuit, János Cserneky, returning to the city as the representative of the bishops of Pécs and Veszprém, invoked the secular authorities against his former order in an attempt to gain control of their property. In the quarrel over the Belgrade chapel the Ragusan colony also had recourse to the Turkish law courts.[98]

The difficulty of acquiring precise information and the manner in which dissatisfied parties could turn to the Turkish authorities thus imposed significant limitations on *Propaganda Fide*'s ability to direct operations in the Balkans. An additional complicating factor was the increasing interest of the Habsburg kingdom in nomination to Balkan sees. The need to treat this issue with caution was heightened by the claims of the Hungarian monarch to the right to appoint bishops on the basis of royal authority *in spiritualibus* as well as *in temporalibus* and as a corollary that bishops in Hungary could exercise functions without confirmation by the Pope.[99] This right, it was claimed, derived from a privilege accorded to Saint Stephen, the founder of the Christian kingdom. The issue had already begun to surface in the sixteenth century when the Clementine pontificate sharply instructed its nuncio to resist Habsburg pretensions in this regard, and to stand by the regulations concerning the appointment of bishops introduced by Gregory XIV in 1591, but it continued to rumble throughout the period under review.[100] After 1624, *Propaganda Fide* had more or less come to accept that bishops nominated by the Habsburg king of Hungary to Turkish-occupied sees would never take up residence in the midst of their flocks. While prepared to tolerate this practice because of the strengthening of the Catholic presence in the critical magnate order of the Hungarian Diet, the

---

[97] Because Irish anti-Catholic laws were far less stringent than in England, priests had less to fear from secular authorities who generally turned a blind eye to their activities. Indeed by the 1640s, the royal Lord Lieutenant, the Marquis of Ormond, was convinced that the act of saying mass did not in itself place a priest outside the law. The exercise of papal jurisdiction, however, was regarded with far greater hostility by the Protestant government: Ó hAnnracháin, *Catholic Reformation*, Chapter 2.

[98] Molnár, *Katolikus missziók*, pp. 260–1.

[99] In this regard see Chapter 3.

[100] Instructions for Cardinal Ludovico Madruzzo, 4 March 1591 (*Die Hauptinstrucktionen Clemens' VIII.*, I, pp. 246–55, at 253–4): Pong Lee, 'La actividad de la Sagrada Congregación', p. 394.

congregation believed that the actual ecclesiastical government of the area under Turkish control should be left to apostolic administrators appointed from Rome. The Hungarian episcopacy, however, due in no small part to the efforts of Pázmány to remodel it as an effective tool of Catholic reformation, demonstrated an increasing interest in the territory under Turkish control and were deeply unwilling to surrender any feudal rights. Indeed they urged their monarch to assert his jurisdiction even over sees currently within Ragusan and Venetian territory. Difficulties of protocol and representation in Rome complicated matters still further so that from 1633 very few royal nominations to Hungarian bishoprics received confirmation in Rome.[101] This accentuated *Propaganda's* determination not to be impeded by the jurisdictional claims of the Hungarian throne. Rome thus tended to apply two qualifications to its respect for Hungarian claims. First, in a fashion analogous to its attitude to the Iberian *padronado*, it drew a distinction between territories which were actually under the control of the Emperor, as King of Hungary, and lands over which he merely claimed jurisdiction.[102] Second, Rome privileged the jurisdictional claims of bishops who had received papal confirmation over those who merely enjoyed royal nomination. This did not preclude a measure of cooperation.

This issue also contributed to the tensions which developed between Italian missionaries, which *Propaganda* proved eager to dispatch into Royal Hungary and Transylvania, and the native hierarchy in Hungary. In 1629 Vincenzo Pinieri da Montefiascone, an Italian conventual Franciscan, began a mission in Zemplén, in the area of Hungary which had been ceded to Gábor Bethlen in the Peace of Nikolsburg, but which after his death returned to Habsburg control. After the cessation of the activity of the original friars, Rome sought to reinvigorate this mission. Benedict Radzinski was appointed as Mission prefect and in 1634 four Italians arrived as missionaries on the doorstep of the Archbishop of Esztergom, Cardinal Péter Pázmány. The Cardinal made efforts to accommodate these, keeping one, Bonaventura da Genova, in his own entourage, and sending the other three to prominent Catholic nobles, György Melith, the widow of the former palatine Sigismund Forgách, Kata Pálffy, then resident with the Bishop of Eger, and one of the most important Transylvanian Catholic lords, Sigismond Kornis, presumably on the grounds that with these Latin communication would be possible.[103] Pázmány, however, apparently then wrote to Rome that Italian missionaries were not needed in Royal Hungary.[104] Consequently, he was not amused when the following year another eight Italian conventual Franciscans arrived with missionary faculties seeking to know where he wished to employ them. Rather brusquely the Cardinal informed them that he would willingly accept fifty priests who were linguistically competent to function in Hungary but

---

[101] Péter Tusor, 'Az 1639. Évi nagyszombati Püspökkari Konferencia: A magyar klérus és a római Kúria kapcsolatainak válsága és reformja', *Századok* 134 (2000), 431–59.

[102] Pong Lee, 'La actividad de la Sagrada Congregación', pp. 376–84.

[103] Bonaventura da Genova to Francesco Ingoli, 11 October 1634 (Tóth, *Litterae Missionariorum*, pp. 507–8); Benedict Radzinski to the cardinals of *Propaganda Fide*, 29 April 1635 (ibid., pp. 558–9).

[104] Angelo Petricca da Sonnino to Francesco Ingoli, 7 July 1635 (ibid., p. 609).

that he had hardly been able to place the previous four and would do nothing for any further Roman missionaries.[105] The original Roman plan had been to send ten missionaries in this group and it is a measure of the gulf between the native Hungarian and Roman conception of the area's religious needs that Ingoli had urged the leaders of the group to recruit an extra member to replace one friar who had become too lame to travel. In the event, one of the Italian lay brothers who was added to the party in the course of their journey did not even know any Latin and so was doubly useless in Hungary.[106]

Pázmány's cold reception was undoubtedly a considerable shock to the two leaders of the Italian Franciscans, the designated provincial for Transylvania, Francesco Antonio da San Felice, and his equivalent for Hungary, Angelo Petricca da Sonnino. Their mission had aroused considerable evangelical zeal in Italy with many friars petitioning them to be allowed to join the party, although, in another demonstration of how the local desire to hold on to the best personnel could trump missionary enthusiasm, they were not given permission to recruit friars holding positions of authority in Italian convents.[107] They were also given access to important pulpits in northern Italy which allowed them to raise funds to defray the cost of their journey to Hungary. Both leaders also demonstrated considerable ardour for their task. Their missionary imperative reflected a belief that their own salvation was tied up in their commitment to the gospel and that without sharing in tribulations they could not expect to enjoy the heavenly crown of their labours.[108] Although they showed no evidence of any success, they evinced a desire to learn Hungarian in order to function more successfully. They were also prepared to contemplate martyrdom, although this did not include allowing themselves to be killed in a casual way by the enemies of their faith without any gain. Thus, despite their desire to enter into Transylvania, the warning that they would be intercepted on the border, castrated and then either killed or flung back, was enough to persuade them not to make an attempt without adequate support.

Rebuffed by Pázmány, both leaders tried to find an alternative niche in Hungary. Angelo Petricca first tried to set up an advanced school where he would teach philosophy and theology with the support of Pázmány's archiepiscopal rival in Kalocsa. But in order to accomplish this he needed to recruit Hungarian-speakers to do the actual teaching of children, while he would offer recompense by teaching the teachers. However, it rapidly became evident that there was little point in setting up a rival institution with little funding in rivalry to Pázmány's own newly-founded university in Nagyszombat. Ultimately the mission leaders set out in return for Italy, sending letters ahead asking for new employment in Constantinople. However, this met with furious response from Ingoli who ordered them back to Hungary and urged for letters of reproach to be written to

[105] Bonaventura da Genova to the cardinals of *Propaganda Fide*, 2 June 1635 (ibid., pp. 584–6); Francesco Antonio da San Felice to Francesco Ingoli, 5 June 1635 (ibid., pp. 587–9).
[106] Bonaventura da Genova to Francesco Ingoli, 2 June 1635 (ibid., p. 603).
[107] Francesco Antonio da San Felice to Francesco Ingoli, 16 December 1634 (ibid., pp. 522–3).
[108] Francesco Antonio da San Felice to Francesco Ingoli, 31 March 1635 (ibid., p. 543); the biblical text on which this was founded was Romans, 5, 3–4.

Pázmány and other Hungarian bishops about their coldness to the missionaries of the congregation.[109]

The inability of Italian missionaries to communicate with the local population in their native languages was evidently the principal reason for the lack of enthusiasm for their presence, which clearly was not confined to Pázmány but was also demonstrated by his Episcopal colleagues in Eger and by the titular Bishop of Transylvania. The more intelligent of the Italian missionaries themselves also clearly came to appreciate the importance of linguistic ability and looked to support local priests with the congregation because of the impact they could make.[110] The lack of native languages certainly limited the ability of Italian missionaries to make conversions. György Lippay, for instance, in the 1660s complained that he could not recall a single instance of conversion by Italian missionaries during his two decades as Archbishop of Esztergom.[111] However, this was certainly not the Italians' own perception. Vincenzo Pineri da Montefiascone, for instance, claimed to have converted 370 people in the course of a ministry of three years.[112] It can be noted that the use of Latin by Italian missionaries did not entirely confine their communicative range to a tiny highly-educated elite. Proficiency in Latin in the area, as in Poland, was evidently more widespread than in contemporary England, for instance.[113] Moreover, the conversion of nobles, with whom communication in Latin was possible, was generally the key to drawing much of the population of their territories in their wake.[114] Bonaventura da Genova, the Italian whom Pázmany chose to keep in his own entourage, and whom he then dispatched on mission work, reported hearing a significant number of confessions in Latin, some of which were evidently made by Protestants.[115] It can be noted, too, despite his brusque reaction to the arrival of additional Italians in 1635, that Pázmány sufficiently valued da Genova's services as to refuse to release him into the service of the Archbishop of Kalocsa.[116] Interpreters were also used for both preaching and the hearing of confessions. While this was hardly ideal, Hungary was desperately short of priests.

In the same time-frame as the Italians were receiving a cold shoulder, the Bishop of Eger was looking for permission to ordain two young men beneath canonical age because of his urgent need of their priestly services.[117] It seems possible that

---

[109] See the decision in Ingoli's hand in response to the letter of Bonaventura da Genova to Ingoli, 2 May 1636 (Archivio Storico 'De Propaganda Fide', SOCG 78, f. 200v).

[110] Pietro Vallonica da Sant'Angelo to Francsco Ingoli, 27 May 1635 (Tóth, *Litterae Missionariorum*, pp. 581–3).

[111] György Lippay to Giulio Spinola, 17 September 1665 (Tóth, *Relationes Missionariorum*, p. 342).

[112] Vincenzo Pineri da Montefiascone to the cardinals of *Propaganda Fide* (ibid., pp. 58–9).

[113] ibid., pp. 9–20.

[114] See for example Pietro Vallonica da Sant'Angelo, 27 May 1635 (Tóth, *Litterae Missionariorum*. pp. 581–3).

[115] Bonaventura da Genova to Cardinal Antonio Barberini, 15 April 1635 (ibid., pp. 545–6); Leone da Modica, in a letter to the cardinals of *Propaganda Fide*, 28 November 1634 (ibid., pp. 515–16), also reported hearing confessions, holding private disputes, and preaching in Latin.

[116] Bonaventura da Genova to Francesco Ingoli, 20 May 1635 (ibid., p. 573); he also praised him to third parties as a good priest and preacher in Italian: see Basilio d'Aire to Francesco Ingoli, 9 June 1635 (ibid., pp. 594–5).

[117] Francesco Cosmi da Mogliano to Francesco Ingoli, 22 May 1635 (Archivio Storico 'De Propaganda Fide', SOCG, 77, f. 202 rv).

one of the reasons for the discrepancy between Italian estimation of their impact in conversions and the local clergy's lack of respect for their activities related to a difference in what was being measured. The local population's perception of denominational affiliation was probably less acute than that of foreign missionaries. Consequently many were evidently prepared to take confession when it became available from Catholic priests, including Italian missionaries, for whom this represented successful reconciliation of lost souls to the church. However, those confessed did not necessarily thereafter avoid Protestant worship. Bonaventura da Genova in the 1630s reported that he was offering confession to many Protestants but was unable to give absolution to numerous others, who had already been reconciled to the church, but who had once again reverted to heresy.[118] Native Hungarians may thus have disregarded the impact of the Italians' 'conversions' because it did not result in a change of denominational affiliation.

In several other respects, too, local Hungarian Catholics may also have felt that the Italians created more trouble than they were worth. While missionary zeal was a significant factor in recruiting workers for the mission, many were clearly also lured by the promise which was made to them that they would receive a doctorate on the conclusion of three years' missionary work. The highly critical György Lippay considered this was the chief motive for their recruitment.[119] Moreover, the Italians who did manage to find a niche rapidly became aware that they needed to behave with extraordinary circumspection.[120] The caricature of friars as lewd and prone to the sins of the flesh, strongly refreshed by Protestant hostility, had obviously sunk deeply into the local culture and thus the slightest lapse was seized upon in a manner which would not have occasioned comment in Italy. Some of the missionary friars clearly created a very bad impression.[121] Polish friars of various orders, unaccustomed to Hungarian wine, seem to have created some particularly riotous scenes. Even ostensibly innocent events were seized upon. When two ancient friars offered an escort on a journey to two nuns, for instance, this immediately became the subject of Protestant innuendo.

The missionaries were frequently blind to local political nuances as they sought to repossess alienated property from Protestants or even influential Catholics such as the palatine of Hungary, Miklos Eszterházy, and what local Catholics saw as political realism they castigated as a lack of zeal. Overt confrontations with Protestants, such as Angelo Petricca da Sonnino proudly reported to Rome in 1636, may also have been counter-productive, creating local tensions without any long-term benefit.[122] Resentment of foreigners also contributed with rumours circulating that

---

[118] Bonaventura da Genova to Cardinal Antonio Barberini, 15 April 1635 (Tóth, *Litterae Missionariorum*, pp. 545–6).

[119] Tóth, *Relationes Missionariorum*, p. 12.

[120] Bonaventura da Genova to Francesco Ingoli, 2 June 1635 (Tóth, *Litterae Missionariorum*, pp. 603–4).

[121] Francesco Cosmi da Mogliano to Francesco Ingoli, 12 May 1635 (ibid., pp. 564–5).

[122] Angelo Petricca da Sonnino to Francesco Ingoli, 4 January 1636 (ibid., pp. 699–700); it is indicative that the Bishop of Nyitra's attitude towards the missionaries seems to have cooled markedly in the wake of these disputations although his anger may also have been provoked by their alms-seeking.

Italian mendicants were coming to Hungary merely to raise money.[123] In the 1660s, György Lippay accused Italian missionaries of collecting chalices, other ecclesiastical equipment, and money in their convents and then transmitting it outside the country.[124] Evidently, the issues between the Hungarian hierarchy and Rome relating to the lack of papal confirmation of Hungarian episcopal titles also apparently contributed to local episcopal hostility. By and large, therefore, it can be suggested that *Propaganda Fide*'s attempts to recruit Italian missionaries to operate in the northern zone in territories where local Hungarian bishops were already attempting to create a new church organization betrayed a certain naivety and were largely unhelpful.

In the 1640s Pázmány's successor as Archbishop of Esztergom, Imre Lósy, was prepared to allow an Italian Franciscan, Giacomo Buoncarpi, to operate in Turkish-occupied Hungary as apostolic delegate and administrator, although to soothe Hungarian sensibilities he was given the titular see of Himeria in Mesopotamia rather than a Balkan title. However, this cooperation came with the caveat that he did nothing to infringe on the rights of Hungarian bishops and his activity soon resulted in clashes with the Hungarian Bishop of Pécs, who considered him an intrusion on his own ecclesiastical arrangements for the oversight of his diocese through delegation to the local Jesuits. For two years, however, Buoncarpi enthusiastically journeyed within Turkish Hungary, giving confirmation to 11,000 people before the outbreak of war between the Habsburgs and Transylvania, and suspicions about his political involvements, forced him to return to Ragusa.[125]

Buoncarpi's brief sojourn, however, pointed up a number of problems relating to Roman mission organization. In contrast to the numerous Italian missionaries which *Propaganda Fide* employed, particularly in Upper Hungary during this period, many of whom signed up for missionary service principally to avail of the reward of a doctorate after three years' service and whose linguistic incompetences limited their effectiveness, Buoncarpi made strenuous efforts to learn Czech, German and after his appointment to Himeria, Croatian, and did not look for swift return to Italy. At the same time, nevertheless, his appointment made clear the dearth of suitable local candidates for the post which pointed up the manner in which Rome had largely failed to generate any notable native priesthood in the previous decade and a half. Rome's major project in this respect was the re-foundation of the Illyrian college in Loreto in 1627 which assigned eight places for the education of students from the Turkish European territories. While graduates from this academy did begin to appear in the Balkans from the early 1630s their numbers were too few to make any decisive difference, particularly as not all those originating from Turkish territory opted to return. The major source of priests remained the Bosnian Franciscan province but like the Jesuit missionaries, bishops such as Rengjic and Massarecchi, and secular priests such as Matkovic, before him, these were precisely the group with whom Buoncarpi had the most significant problems.[126]

[123] Francesco Antonio da San Felice to Francesco Ingoli, 19 May 1635 (ibid., pp. 570–1).
[124] György Lippay to Giulio Spinola, 17 September 1665 (Tóth, *Relationes Missionariorum*, p. 342).
[125] Molnár, *Katolikus missziók*, 317–25.
[126] ibid., p. 350.

From *Propaganda Fide*'s point of view, the Bosnian Franciscans could not be ignored, particularly because, in addition to a poorly educated and turbulent cadre educated within their own convents, they also sent a significant cohort of their best students to Italy for education in Franciscan institutions.[127] Many of these were supported at *Propaganda Fide*'s expense and the congregation looked to make use of them in a missionary context. This however helped to create a reaction within the province as more intransigent elements resented what they saw as Roman interference and wished to maintain the province's customary character. Realizing that Rome tended to appoint Bosnian bishops from the group within the order most amenable to Roman control, the more intransigent faction looked to Vienna in search of royal nominations, thus involving themselves in the jurisdictional clash between Rome and the Hungarian kingdom. The congregation then came under enormous pressure to accede to the elevation of Bosnian friars as bishops, despite reservations about their suitability, and the experience of a series of apostolic visitors who had looked to restrain the Bosnians from imposing their convent-based model of pastoral care in other areas of the Balkans. Ultimately, however, *Propaganda Fide* had few alternatives. Neither the Roman nor the Austrian province of the Society of Jesus was prepared to commit significant resources and the educational infrastructure was incapable of generating sufficient secular priests. Therefore, the congregation was forced to work with the Bosnian province with the consolation that from the 1640s the faction within the order which had enjoyed Italian education and which was less hostile to Roman control was becoming increasingly influential. Symbolic of this shift was the fact that by the middle of the century all of the missionary bishops at work in the Turkish Balkans were drawn from the ranks of the Bosnian Franciscans.[128]

The Balkans during the period under review saw significant manifestations of the missionary impulse of post-Tridentine Catholicism. There can be little doubt concerning the genuine mission commitment both of many operatives in the field, such as Kašić, Marino de Bonis, Matkovic, and Pietro Massarecchi, as well as significant figures in the central apparatus in Rome, most notably Ingoli. Nor should the difficulties of mission organization in the Balkans be under-estimated. In addition to the problems presented by Turkish authority and the existence of large and often hostile Orthodox and Protestant populations, the Catholic communities of the Balkans were themselves divided by ethnic and linguistic barriers and rivalries and suffered from a persistent lack of priests, with the exception of a number of key reservoirs, most notably Bosnia. Moreover, the adaptation of Catholic ecclesiastical structures to the contours of Ottoman power generated significant obstacles to the acceptance of aspects of the new Catholic culture of post-Tridentine Europe. The overwhelming poverty of the area was another factor. Missionaries needed money in order to be able to travel in a highly dangerous environment and frequently the Catholic communities which they visited lacked the resources to offer any meaningful stipend. While missionary zeal could go some distance in compensating for

[127] ibid., pp. 350–3.   [128] ibid., pp. 360–5.

this, even the most dedicated of individuals necessarily had to request not insignificant sums, particularly because the profound dearth of native clergy made it impossible for them to concentrate on merely one locality. Jurisdictional claims by the Habsburg monarchy of Hungary further complicated the situation, particularly for the congregation of *Propaganda Fide*. Nor was reliable information necessarily easy to obtain. Knowledge of the ecclesiastical boundaries prior to the Turkish conquest, which Rome necessarily could not ignore, was often scanty and sometimes non-existent. Monitoring the conflicts which arose between different Catholic factions was not undemanding either.

It should also be remembered that provision of sacraments was a critical aspect of Catholic missionary endeavour. The ability of Italian missionaries, for instance, to either instruct the faithful or to act as vehicles for the conversion of other Christian denominations was clearly compromised by their lack of proficiency in the spoken vernaculars of the areas into which *Propaganda Fide* sent them. Nonetheless, they were capable of administering valid sacraments which, from the perspective both of the congregation and its missionaries, and of the Catholics of the area, was a factor of prime importance. Despite their derogatory comments about linguistic competence, even Pázmány and the Hungarian bishops made use of some of the better missionaries from Italy and attempted to deploy them in the most effective way possible. It should also be borne in mind that the Balkans represented just one field among many throughout the world vying for the congregation's attention and resources.

Yet, notwithstanding these factors, the limitations of what Roman missionary policy and in particular *Propaganda Fide* managed to achieve are also striking. Most tellingly, only a small fraction of the funds expended on war against the Turks under Clement VIII was subsequently directed to the subvention of missionary activity in the Balkans. Critically, the resources necessary to create educational institutions capable of generating a self-sustaining priesthood, educated within the Balkans, were not made available. Urban VIII refounded the Collegio Illirico in Loreto in 1627 and this period also saw papal support for Magyar and Croat educational institutions in the Habsburg domains but together these were insufficient to counter the lack of priests available in the Habsburg-controlled areas, let alone provide a springboard in the Turkish Balkans. In contrast to Ireland, for instance, where an adequate network of colleges did come into existence, a lack of native priests continued to characterize Balkan Catholicism in general. *Propaganda Fide* did not of course create the Irish network of colleges, indeed it is noteworthy that the congregation paid more attention to the relatively minor Scottish mission by Irish Franciscans than to any other Irish issue during the 1620s, a telling indication of the manner in which the heroic narratives of preaching the gospel in hostile environments could prove more exciting than the more prosaic task of ministering to the existing faithful. Nevertheless the efforts and pleas of the Irish Catholic community with the papacy and Catholic powers of the continent successfully generated enough educational establishments to create a sufficiently robust educated clerical elite. By contrast, the poverty of the Balkans and the minority status of the Catholic communities there meant that the native populations of the area would have required a far more significant Roman input in the educational sphere to be successful. Despite Ingoli's avowed interest in the creation of native priesthoods in mission areas, this did not happen because the area did not attract massive investment.

The disparity between the amount of money made available for war in the Balkans during the Clementine pontificate and the amount expended on mission and educational activity during the period under review is made even more pointed when papal advice to Spain concerning the Netherlands is taken into consideration. In the 1590s Rome viewed with increasing concern the parlous financial condition of the universities of Louvain and Douai because of a war which 'stops public revenues and converts for the use of soldiers that which should serve for the support of pastors'.[129] The King of Spain, therefore, was to be urged to invest in an educational infrastructure which would facilitate the maintenance of Dutch Catholicism. Not only would this protect the interests of religion but it would act in the long-term interest of Spain by increasing the fidelity and loyalty of the population to their legitimate monarch. The King was asked to consider 'the not less and for many reasons more secure fruit which he will derive from a small expense which he will make in nourishing these good seeds and in increasing them continually than from the great treasures which are spent in maintaining armies and fleets'.[130]

Yet, as the example of the Balkans demonstrates, the papacy itself during the period under review was constantly fascinated by the prospects of spectacular gains for the Catholic religion through the support of war. This is evident even in the pontificate of Gregory XV, the founder of the congregation of *Propaganda Fide*. The Pope's efforts in this respect were lauded in Rome and, other than the shared Bolognan heritage with his former patron, Gregory XIII, the missionary reputation of the Gregorian name probably represented one of the reasons for his choice of papal title. Nevertheless, it should be noted that between February 1621 and August 1623 Gregory XV provided the Emperor and the Catholic League with subsidies which easily topped half a million scudi.[131] He also sanctioned a collection of tithes and extensive sale of valuables by the French clergy in 1621 to help finance Louis XIII's campaign against the Huguenots.[132] It can be argued that these monies ultimately reaped a significant benefit in terms of re-Catholicization in Bohemia and France yet the contrast with the money made available for the mission activity with which this pontificate is most commonly associated in the same timeframe is particularly stark. The Pope initially endowed *Propaganda Fide* with 3000 scudi per annum from the *Camera Apostolica*. Within a year, extra papal largesse and contributions from other sources in Rome had raised its annual income

[129] 'fa cessare l'entrate publiche et convertire in uso de' soldati quell che doveria servire di nutrimento a pastori': Instructions to Camillo Caetani, 20 September 1592 (*Die Hauptinstrucktionen Clemens' VIII.*, 1, p. 85).

[130] 'che non minor frutto et per molte cause più sicuro caverà da una poca spesa, che ella faccia in nutrire quei buoni semi et in accrescerli continuamente, che dalli gran thesori che si spendono in mantenere gli eserciti et l'armate' (ibid.).

[131] *Die Hauptinstrucktionen Gregors XV*, 2, pp. 608–9, fn. 16.

[132] ibid., p. 551, fn. 31.

to 5600 scudi,[133] perhaps two percent of the contributions made to the German war, and about a third of the almost incidental subsidy provided to Poland for its anti-Turkish defences.[134] While the Pope also made extraordinary donations to the congregation amounting to 23,000 ducats in November and December 1622, these can be set into context with his largesse towards the Cardinal-nephew, Ludovico Ludovisi, who within four months of the papal election had been endowed with an annual income of *circa* 80,000 scudi and who in 1622 was able to purchase the duchy of Zagarola for close to one million scudi, and who also acquired three other splendid properties both within and outside the eternal city.[135]

Ludovico Ludovisi evidently shared the missionary vision of the Pope, insisting that it was recognized in Rome that the greatest need which the church had in those areas where it was in conflict with Protestantism was clerical workers, for which schools and seminaries were necessary. However, finding the money for such endeavours was, the Cardinal-nephew admitted, enormously difficult. It could only be done by the slow and painful union of benefices, by bequests and donations.[136] The massive commitment of monthly expenditure which Sixtus V made for papal soldiers in France and which Clement VIII, Paul V, and Gregory XV made to the Habsburgs and their allies operated according to a different set of rules and expectations.[137] Even in Ireland, arguably the great success-story of *Propaganda Fide* in Europe, it can be noted that the 110,000 scudi which Innocent X sent as war subsidies to the Confederate Catholics dwarfed any papal contributions for educational purposes, despite the dire financial state of many of the Irish continental colleges which maintained the nervous system of the island's Catholicism intact.[138] In the Balkans, in the period under review in this book, the saving of 200 scudi in the dispatch of a bishop was a factor of genuine importance to the congregation of *Propaganda Fide* and there were extraordinary failures to support the education of genuinely worthy candidates from the area, down to Innocent X's refusal to endow an extra college place for the education of natives of the region in Italy.[139]

The mission impulse was a vital influence within Early Modern Catholicism and in the period under review in this book the papacy undoubtedly took an increasing interest in this subject. Through the creation of *Propaganda Fide* Rome developed an institution which could at least assemble, collate and compare information from the enormously varied territories of the area understood as *terrae missionis*.

---

[133] Lettera, che fu scritta à tutti li Arcivescovi e vescovi della christianità, 18 February 1623 (Archivio Storico 'De Propaganda Fide', Lett. Volgari 2, fos 57r–58r).

[134] *Die Hauptinstrucktionen Gregors XV*, 2, p. 750, fn. 15.

[135] Ludwig Von Pastor (trans. Ernest Graf), *The History of the Popes from the Close of the Middle Ages 27* (London: Kegan Paul, Trench, Trubner & Co., 1938), pp. 54–60.

[136] Instructions to GianBatista Lancellotti, 14 December 1622 (Thaddaeus Fitych (ed.), *Acta Nuntiaturae Poloniae Tomus XXII Volumen 1 Ioannes Baptista Lancellotti (1622–27)* (Cracoviae: Academia Scientiarum et Litterarum Polona, 2000), pp. 28–49, at 31–2).

[137] Similarly the 20,000 scudi which Clement VIII contributed to Sigismund Vasa for his journey to take the crown of Sweden far exceeded the sums spent in mission activity during the same period in that kingdom, despite avowed curial interest in this topic: Instructions for Bartolomeo Powinski, 27 July 1593 (*Die Hauptinstrucktionen Clemens' VIII.*, 1, pp. 134–43, at 136–7).

[138] In this regard see Ó hAnnracháin, *Catholic Reformation in Ireland*, esp. Chapters 2, and 4–6.

[139] Molnár, *Katolikus missziók*, p. 335.

The new congregation provided a more stable platform for the papacy's attempts to regulate and direct regular missionary orders, who represented the chief incubator of Catholic missionary activity. This was most evident in its relations with the various families of friars rather than with the Society of Jesus, which maintained an aloofness from the congregation. But, as the case-study of the Balkans indicates, significant limitations, both financial and conceptual, also restricted and constrained Catholic missionary activity. As a mission church, Early Modern Catholicism arguably failed in the Balkan peninsula. By the end of the period under review, the most significant mode of contact between the centre of the Catholic world and the Christian population of the region continued to be mediated by the Bosnian Franciscan province and neither Roman-directed missionaries nor local Italian-educated priests had made a transformative impact. While there were many reasons for this development, of not insignificant importance was the fact that Early Modern Catholicism was not merely, and arguably not even primarily, a mission faith but rather a complex weave of motivations and considerations in which missionary activity was often only of secondary importance.

6

Conclusion—Centre and Peripheries

In terms of the historiography of Catholic Europe, the end-date of the current study is of course far more conventional than the point at which it began. 1648 traditionally refers primarily to the Peace of Westphalia which undeniably marked a *caesura* in terms of fixing the confessional boundaries of the continent. In the previous six decades papal policy had been animated by a sense that the confessional boundaries of Europe could be altered dramatically in favour of Catholicism with the ultimate objective of the reunification of most of the continent under the aegis of the church of Rome. Consequently, throughout the period under review, a consistent series of attempts was made to encourage Catholic governments and monarchs both to adopt internal measures to restrict Protestantism and to engage in war in the interest of the church of Rome. By the middle of the seventeenth century the grounds for optimism in this regard had become far more exiguous.

Clement VIII's experience as papal legate in the genuinely confessionally-mixed society of Poland had helped to sharpen his appreciation of the potential import-ance of monarchical power in inculcating re-Catholicization.[1] In 1601, the new nuncio to France, Innocenzo del Bufalo, was urged to bring the Pope's Polish ex-perience to Henri IV's attention as a template for handling French Huguenots. Key in this regard was the denial of offices to those who were not Catholics. In Poland the result of such exclusion was seen to have been conversion either of those denied magisterial positions or of others who desired to replace them. Supple-menting this was a conscious policy of honouring and supporting those who did convert to the Catholic faith.[2]

Such behaviour could lead to the favouring of the personally unworthy in the interests of a greater good. In a sense, the Clementine decision to absolve Henri IV, despite definite doubts about the King's personal convictions, was influenced by the number of French souls for whom this might lead to salvation. This could be repli-cated at a lower level of magistracy too. The colourful case of Count Alexander Koniecpolski in the 1620s in Poland provides a telling demonstration of how

---

[1] Wieslaw Müller, 'Structure administrative des diocèses catholiques latins en Pologne du xvie au xviiie siècle' in Marian Rechowicz et al. (eds), *Millénaire du Catholicisme en Pologne* (Lublin: The Scientific Society of the Catholic University in Lublin, 1969), pp. 105–9, at 105 estimates that about half the population of the Polish Lithuanian commonwealth in the second half of the sixteenth century were adherents of the church of Rome.

[2] Instructions for Innocenzo del Bufalo, July 1601 (Bernard Barbiche, *Correspondance du nonce en France Innocenzo del Bufalo évêque de camerino (1601–1604)* (Rome and Paris: Presses de l'Université Grégorienne/Editions E. de Boccard, 1964), pp. 143–4).

considerations of the spiritual ramifications of cases for others could take precedence over precise details of justice. In 1623 the details of Koniecpolski's case were brought to the attention of the papal nuncio. He had previously attacked the convent of St Agnetis Stradomiae in the diocese of the Cracow, and taken away by force and married one Sophia Dembinska. Her sister Dorothea accompanied them, apparently willingly. Sophia died leaving a child and the count then married Dorothea and had other children for her. For this he was eventually proscribed in the Diet. The goods of his wife, which entailed control over many villages and castles and rich revenues, then came into the hands of John Ciechanski, a Calvinist. For Koniecpolski to regain these possessions he required a dispensation for his marriage to Dorothea. Interestingly, the papal nuncio, Lancellotti, who referred the matter to Rome, together with the Bishop of Cracow and the Archbishop of Gniezno, favoured granting the dispensation on the grounds that allowing them to remain in Ciechanski's hands represented a great danger to the parishes in question and to their souls:

> because falling into the hands of a heretical lord and having these, as is customary in this kingdom, authority over the lives of vassals, either through force or through their spontaneous will, he will induce them to change Religion, it being commonly seen that subjects and vassals follow the religion of their lords.[3]

While deploring the count's excesses he believed that Koniecpolski's efforts to reconcile himself with the church were attracting sympathy and he did not believe that it would set an unduly bad example. Moreover, if it was not granted then his children too would lose the opportunity to regain their inheritance.[4] Issues of the count's personal guilt were effectively entirely marginalized in this discussion by wider considerations of spiritual utility.

By the 1620s Poland was seen as a particular field of triumph for zealous application of Catholic monarchical pressure. Upon Sigismund's accession much of the population had been Protestants of various hues but, principally by filling magisterial vacancies with Catholics and by directing honours and offices towards his co-religionists, the King was seen to have effected a revolution.[5] Not dissimilar tactics were followed in the same time-frame by the Habsburg kings of Hungary although there the monarch's freedom of action was more circumscribed. Nevertheless similar mechanisms of blandishment towards the magnate order to convert to Catholicism, and the attendant knock-on effect which this had on their dependents, operated in the Hungarian process of re-Catholicization.[6]

---

[3] 'perch'andando in mano di Signore heretico, et havendo questi, come è solito in questo Regno, autorità sopra la vita de'Vassalli, o per forza, o di spontanea volontá, li indurrà a mutar Religione, vedendosi communemente che li Suddite e Vassali seguitano la fede e Religione de'padroni': Lancellotti to Cardinal John Garziae Millino, Vicar of Rome, 23 June 1623 (Thaddaeus Fitych (ed.), *Acta Nuntiaturae Poloniae Tomus XXII Volumen 1 Ioannes Baptista Lancellotti (1622–27)* (Cracoviae: Academia Scientiarum et Litterarum Polona, 2000), pp. 161–2).

[4] ibid.

[5] Instructions to Mario Filonardi, 19 July 1635 (Theresia Chynczewska-Hennel (ed.), *Acta Nuntiaturae Poloniae Tomus XXV Volumen 1 Marius Filonardi (1635–43)* (Cracoviae: Academia Scientiarum et Litterarum Polona, 2003), pp. 21–2). ·

[6] Peter Schimert, 'Péter Pázmány and the Reconstitution of the Catholic Aristocracy in Habsburg Hungary, 1600–1650' (PhD thesis, University of North Carolina, Chapel Hill, 1989), *passim*.

If the deployment of 'soft' monarchical power on behalf of the revival of the Catholic religion in areas of Europe where Protestantism had gained a substantial foothold was the least which was expected of the continent's Catholic princes, more extreme measures were considered highly desirable if the political situation permitted. The Inquisitorial culture of the Italian and Iberian peninsulae, where not only heretical activity but heretical belief could be confronted, coerced and punished, represented the desirable norm. Thus Clement VIII bitterly reproached the Edict of Nantes to the French ecclesiastical leadership in Rome as the 'most cursed that could be imagined... by which liberty of conscience was permitted to everybody, which was the worst thing in the world'.[7] Henri IV's son and heir, Louis XIII, rapidly acquired the reputation of a pious monarch and his campaigns against French Huguenots in the 1620s were enthusiastically supported in Rome, although his willingness to respect the religious terms of the Edict of Nantes while repressing Huguenot military power continued to disappoint.[8] Overall, however, even if from a papal perspective the Peace of Alès of 1629 represented a less than perfect culmination of the French monarchy's struggle against the Huguenot state within a state, Louis's military victories against his Protestant subjects were greatly appreciated.

The Spanish portion of the Habsburg dynasty had been reliably committed to the struggle with heresy since the sixteenth century. Its Austrian wing had been perceived as less zealous in Rome under Rudolf II and Matthias but following the election of Ferdinand II it too was led by a highly-committed and militant Catholic. As analysed in Chapter 3, it was under Ferdinand that policies similar to those which papal diplomacy would have liked to see implemented in France were trialled first in Styria and then in other portions of the Austrian hereditary lands, culminating in the re-Catholicization of Bohemia following the Habsburg victory at the Battle of the White Mountain.[9] Despite the quarrels which ignited between the pontificate of Urban VIII and Emperor Ferdinand II over the issue of Jesuit dominance in Catholic renewal in the country, particularly in terms of the university question in Prague, Bohemia can be seen as representing a fusion of two currents of anti-Protestant activity favoured by Rome during the period under review, namely aggressive internal repression of Protestantism and the attempt to mobilize Catholic powers for conflict with their Protestant counterparts.

As noted in Chapter 3, the extension of the Styrian model of Catholicization to Bohemia depended first on the successful reconquest of the kingdom from Fredrick

---

[7] 'le plus maudit que se pouvoit imaginer...per lequel Edict liberté de conscience estoit permise à tout chacun qui est la pire chose du monde': Arnold d'Ossat to Henri IV, 28 March 1599 (*Lettres de l'Illustrissime et Révérendissime Cardinal d'Ossat, éveque de Bayeux au roy Henry le Grand et à Monsieur Villeroy* (Paris, 1627), book 5, p. 34).

[8] Robert Bireley, *The Jesuits and the Thirty Years War: Kings, Courts and Confessors* (Cambridge: Cambridge University Press, 2003), pp. 49–52.

[9] Regina Pörtner, *The Counter-Reformation in Central Europe: Styria 1580–1630* (Oxford: Clarendon Press, 2001); Howard Louthan, *Converting Bohemia: Force and Persuasion in the Catholic Reformation* (Cambridge: Cambridge University Press, 2009); Olivier Chaline, *La Reconquête Catholiique de L'Europe Centrale xvie–xviie siècle* (Paris: Les Éditions du Cerf, 1998).

of Pfalz. This was an enterprise which was supported with enormous enthusiasm in Rome in the last years of Paul V's pontificate and with even greater commitment by Gregory XV. The level of papal subsidies for the Emperor and the Catholic League under Paul V from the summer of 1618 down to the beginning of 1621 bordered on a quarter of a million scudi. Gregory XV was even more lavish in his support and his financial contributions to the Catholic League and Imperial war effort easily topped half a million scudi in the course of slightly more than two years.[10] With victory obtained and the Bohemian population convicted of rebellion, the way was open to 'constrain them with force to abandon their impiety', although it was also recognized that political considerations would temper the full implementation of repression and that educative and evangelical endeavours were of critical importance.[11]

A significant contributory factor to this papal largesse was the sense of possibility which was engendered by the evidently providential overturning of the threatened Protestant majority in the Imperial electoral college through the defeat of the Winter King. These years can be seen as the high point of Catholic confessional optimism. At this time, the refreshed piety of the French royal house, added to the conflict between the King and the Queen-mother and internal preoccupation with the Huguenot state within a state, all ensured that France did not follow a well-worn diplomatic strategy of support for German Protestant princes against Habsburg imperial power. Frederick was not recognized as King of Bohemia in Paris, and French diplomacy exerted itself on the Emperor's behalf in Constantinople. Louis XIII, under vigorous pressure from his confessor, even offered military aid to the house of Austria, although, hardly surprisingly, no troops were eventually sent.[12]

At the outset of his incumbency of the throne of St Peter, therefore, the European situation allowed Gregory XV to dream that 'during his Pontificate he will see the glory of God and the Catholic religion amplified'.[13] At this point Italy and Spain appeared in an eminently satisfactory condition. In France Louis XIII's piety gave grounds for optimism that he would commit himself to the 'heroic enterprise' of crushing the Huguenots.[14] Thus the opportunity for aggressive Catholic action in the rest of Europe was apparent. In Germany victory seemed at hand: all that was required was Spanish perseverance in order to ensure the permanent maintenance of the Imperial title in Catholic hands. This was of symbolic as well as material importance from a Roman perspective. As the nuncio to the Emperor was informed:

The Catholic church has now lived for one hundred years in perpetual danger of seeing in Germany a non-Catholic Emperor and as if to forecast with the end of the

---

[10] Klaus Jaitner (ed.), *Die Hauptinstrucktionen Gregors XV für di Nuntien und Gesandten an den Europäischen Fürstenhöfen 1621–1623* (two vols, Tübingen: Max Niemeyer Verlag, 1997), 2, pp. 608–9, fn. 16.

[11] 'Constringerli con la forza a lasciare la loro empietà': Instructions for Carlo Carafa, 12 April 1621 (ibid., pp. 620, 621–4).

[12] Bireley, *Kings, Courts and Confessors*, p. 47.

[13] 'vedrà nel suo Pontificato amplificata la religione cattolica e la Gloria di Dio': Instructions for Alessandro del Sangro, 5 April 1621 (*Die Hauptinstrucktionen Gregors XV*, 2, p. 577).

[14] 'heroica impresa': ibid.

Roman Empire the end of the world or to be forced at least to sustain against the heretics the doctrines of the fathers in a manner different to that in which up to the present they have been interpreted.[15]

The symbolic importance of the Imperial title as one of the twin poles anchoring the notion of a united *Republica Christiana* was supplemented by the manner in which the House of Austria was seen to stand as a bulwark between Italy and the threat of hostile and heretical German attack. The sack of Rome in 1527 continued to resonate in the Italian imagination and in the previous two decades the internecine strife within the Habsburg dynasty had seemed to open the door to Protestant aspirations to overthrow the papal citadel.[16] The sudden reversal of fortune, therefore, following the White Mountain was thrown into even sharper relief.

In 1621, from a papal perspective, the lapsing of the Dutch truce with Spain could not have fallen at a more opportune time. Rome ardently opposed any idea of renewing the truce because a better occasion to defeat the Dutch would never present itself, as a result of their internal religious divisions, the failing health of Prince Maurice and the prospect of internal conflict within the house of Nassau and the jealousy of the predominance of Holland in Zeeland and Frisia. Catholic victory in Germany restricted the possibility of assistance to the Dutch from that quarter and, if Louis XIII's hoped-for campaigns against the Huguenots ensued, as they did, then the Dutch could expect no aid from their co-religionists in France. The German crisis had, in addition, revealed the limits of the English King's ambition to protect his own daughter's husband, let alone the European Protestant interest. On the other hand, the renewal of the truce risked losing the fruits of the German victory and would mean that the destiny of the new Christian populations of the extra-European world would remain in danger from Dutch naval power and expansion. If Catholic victory over the Dutch could be added to the triumphs in Germany then this would permanently alter the balance of power in the north and might well induce the various heretical sects in control of the northern states to consider their position in the face of Catholic preponderance and incline them to reconciliation with the dominant religion. At the very least, their capacity to oppress their Catholic populations would be restricted. In this regard, the proposed Spanish–English match seemed to open the way for a substantial moderation of the pressure on Catholics in the Stuart dominions.[17] In a cognate

[15] 'la chiesa cattolica è vissuta già cento anni fa in perpetuo pericolo di vedere nella Germania un imperatore non suo e quasi di pronosticare con la fine dell-Imperio Romano la fin del mondo o di dovere almeno sostentare contra gli heretici le dottrine de'padri in diversa maniera da quell anche insino al presente si sono interpretati.': Instructions for Carlo Carafa, 12 April 1621 (ibid., p. 614).

[16] ibid., p. 606.

[17] Instructions for Alessandro del Sangro, 5 April 1621 (ibid., 2, pp. 577–81); while the English and Scottish Catholic populations had shrunk to such minority status that the Stuart matrimonial project made relatively little difference to their overall numbers, in Ireland recent research has indicated the importance of the plans for the marriage of Charles to a Catholic princess, ultimately fulfilled in his wedding to Henrietta-Maria, in ameliorating pressure on Irish Catholicism: see in particular Brian Mac Cuarta, *Catholic Revival in the North of Ireland 1603–41* (Dublin: Four Courts Press, 2007), pp. 94, 100–1.

fashion, too, Rome hoped to make use of negotiations for a truce between Poland and Sweden to secure free exercise of their religion for Swedish Catholics.[18]

Similarly to the struggle against the Turks analysed in Chapter 4, the providential context in which the conflict with European Protestantism was perceived was of importance. As was also evident in the Turkish struggle, the sense of divine intervention in the course of human events could accentuate both currents of optimism and pessimism. The recrudescence of Austrian Habsburg power under Ferdinand, after the long weakening of Italy's northern bulwark during the fraternal rivalry of Rudolf and Mathias, heightened the sense that divine intervention might be at hand to effect some glorious transformation in Europe's fortunes. But later in the year, in the face of an anticipated Turkish invasion of Poland and the destruction of Germany's eastern shield, extreme anxiety began to colour the perception of events. The prospective fate of Hungary and Germany was coloured by the historical parallel of what had occurred in the Balkans when God:

> had wished for a most just vengeance for the sins of the Greeks, schismatics and perpetual enemies of the Latin name and of the Roman Pontiff, that they should have themselves called the Turks into Europe … so we see the heretics of those nominated provinces, … loving more the Turkish barbaric infidelity than Catholic piety, have confederated with the Ottoman and they invite and call him with great prayers and at the price of gold and gifts into their lands; and so that they should be above us they count it as a glory to be in servitude to him and what is to be waited for if not that they should soon remain his prey, his slaves and his triumph.[19]

This was a fearsome prospect for Catholic Europe:

> for that reason the peril of the Catholics and their terror grows in proportion to that fact that, restricted now to a small part of Europe, they come to be surrounded by the armies of the Turks and the heretics equally, no longer divided among themselves but in an obstinate conspiracy disposed to our destruction.[20]

Subsequent Polish victories removed this immediate threat although, in a further demonstration of the often extreme oscillations between hope and despair which the providential understanding of events could promote, the Polish decision to

---

[18] Instructions for GianBatista Lancellotti, 14 December 1622 (Fitych, *Acta Nuntiaturae Poloniae Tomus XXII*, p. 35).

[19] 'Ha volute per giustissima vendetta delle colpe de'Greci sciasmatici e perpetui nimici del nome latino e del romano pontefice ch'essi medesimi habbiano chiamati i Turchi in Europa … così veggiamo hoggi gli heretici delle nominate provincie … amando più la barbera infedeltà turchescha che la pietà cattolica, si sono confederati con l'Ottomano e l'invitano e chiamano a gran prieghi et a prezzo d'oro e di donativi in casa loro; e purché a noi sopra stieno, contano per gloria l'essergli in servitù e che si vuol dunque aspettare se non che debbano in brieve remanere sua preda, suoi schiavi e suo trionfo?': Third Instruction for Giuseppe Acquaviva, 16 October 1621 (*Die Hauptinstrucktionen Gregors XV*, 2, p. 800).

[20] 'Per la qual cagione tanto più si augmenta il pericolo de' Cattolici e cresce negli animi loro il terrore quanto che, restretti hoggi mai in piccolo parte di Europa, vengono circondati dall'armi de'Turchi e degli heretici egualmente non più fra di loro divisi ma con ostinata congiura disposti allo sterminio nostro': ibid., pp. 800–1.

accept a truce with the Turks then came to be viewed as a lost opportunity to finally destroy Ottoman power in Europe.[21]

The symmetry between the fall of England into heresy through the rejection of one Spanish princess and its potential recovery through the marriage of the *Infanta* to the Prince of Wales was also scrutinized in Rome as part of a potential divine plan for the salvation of a realm once so devoted to the Holy See. In another striking demonstration of the manner in which the sense of a decipherable divine pattern coloured contemporary Roman understanding of events, Pope Gregory XV was inclined to support this match because of the evident linkage between his own choice of papal name and the importance of previous Pope Gregories in the Catholic history of England, dating back to the role of Pope Gregory the Great in the initial conversion of the Anglo-Saxons. So in proportion to the fact that:

> through the not obscure signs of Divine Providence which operating on high offers us also in accidental things some hope of the future, it is made to come to mind that, if the name of Gregory has always been fortunate and happy for England, in the first conversion to the Holy Faith and for the following benefits which England has received from Gregorian popes, it should... through the work of his Holiness begin to recover its damaged health and true Christian felicity.[22]

The glorious Catholicity of Italy itself, which it owed first to a divine election that had chosen it initially to shoulder the temporal and then the spiritual rule of the world, and then to the particular care devoted to it by the popes, was also understood in deeply providential terms.[23] This helped to reinforce the conviction that proximity in practice to Italian modes of behaviour and understanding was integral to the resistance to heresy.

Again in a fashion similar to the understanding of the Ottoman threat, the metaphorical and conceptual constructions through which heresy was perceived helped to reinforce the sense of possibility of sudden and profound transformations in the confessional geography of Europe. The dominant metaphor used within Catholic parlance for the affliction of heresy within the body of the church was that of disease. At the onset of the Gregorian pontificate, for instance, the empire was perceived in Rome as having been being infected historically by Hussite heresy:

> The sickness, although grave, but light in respect of other heresies, was not feared as a great thing nor was that province swift to drive it out or purge itself of its vicious

---

[21] Instructions for GianBatista Lancellotti, 14 December 1622 (Fitych, *Acta Nuntiaturae Poloniae Tomus XXII*, pp. 44–7).

[22] 'Per gl'inditii non oscuri della Divina Providenza che altamente operando ci porge anche nelle cose accidentali alcuna speranza del futuro, ci fa correre all mente che , se'l nome di Gregorio è per la primiera conversione alla santa fede per li seguenti beneficii che dai pontefici Gregorii ha l'Inghilterra recevuti, l'è stato sempre fausto e felice, habbia... per opera di S. B.ne da incominciare ricuperare la smarrita salute et la vera felicità Christiana.': Instructions for Innocenzo de' Massimi, 12 April 1623 (*Die Hauptinstrucktionen Gregors XV*, 2, pp. 959–71, at 962).

[23] Instructions for Tobia Corona, 16 July 1621 (ibid., pp. 741–60, at 743); GianBattista Rinuccini, *Della Dignita et Offitio de i Vescovi: Discorsi Quaranta di Monsignor Gio. Battista Rinuccini, Arcivescovo e Prencipe di Fermo* (two vols, Roma, 1651), 2, pp. 100, 218.

humours. Whence God permitted that afterwards the proud pestilence which Luther began in it should infect all of Germany.[24]

Sicknesses could be long and wasting and, of course, sometimes mortal. But they could also be recovered from, sometimes with miraculous speed, particularly if divine intervention was successfully implored. In conceptual terms, of key importance was the manner in which Protestantism was integrated into a particular historical pattern of heresy which had afflicted the church from its early years. Heresies within this formulation came in many different forms but were always essentially the same. Nor, as the history of ancient heresies seemed to indicate, were they fated to last, although their withering away did not guarantee that new forms would not emerge.[25] The dominance of this understanding of heresy made it entirely logical that rather than rooting themselves within Europe the various Protestant churches, naturally understood as sects rather than true churches, might in fact be subject to swift transformation and overthrow. Such hopes, which were active throughout the period under review, however, gradually receded in the course of the 1630s and received a shattering setback in the following decade, culminating in the Peace of Westphalia.

The peace of 1648 was of direct and crucial importance to several of the societies on which this study has focused. Within the Czech crown lands and in Austria Westphalia was of central significance in terms of copper-fastening the religious revolution which had occurred over the previous decades. In particular, it represented the final disillusionment of the numerous Austrian and Czech exiles who had clung to the hope of return to the lands from which they had been forced by the refusal of conversion, and for the many who had reluctantly opted to convert and who now saw no possibility of retracting that choice. In the Netherlands, too, the ending of the long war with Spain ensured that the prospect of a Catholic revival through the force of Spanish arms was no longer a realistic hope.

For other regions on the periphery of Europe the end of the 1640s also marked an important watershed in matters entirely unrelated to the peace in Germany. In Poland, the Chmielnicki rebellion of 1648 ushered in a period of profound political instability which marked the later part of the century off from the period of Catholic consolidation under Sigismund Vasa and Ladislaw IV. In Ireland the last months of 1648 witnessed the negotiations which finally dissolved the Confederate Catholic state in January 1649 and confirmed that, rather than any attempt at creating an independent polity based on religion, the chief Catholic leadership of the island aligned instead with the Protestant Stuart monarchy. This made inevitable the parliamentarian invasion of Ireland in 1649 which fundamentally altered the social, political, and economic configuration of the island, laying the basis of

---

[24] 'Il morbo, quantunque grave, ma in reguardo dell'altre heresie leggiere, non si temè gran fatto né fu presta quella provincia a cacciarlo o purgarsi de' suoi vitiosi humori. Onde permise Iddio che dapoi la fiera pestilenza che le attaccò Lutero tutta la Germania infettasse': Instructions for Carlo Carafa, 12 April 1621 (*Die Hauptinstrucktionen Gregors XV*, p. 605).

[25] See for instance Rinuccini, *Della Dignita et Offitio de i Vescovi*, 1, p. 77; this concept also underpins the writings of the great Hungarian controversialist, Péter Pázmány: see Péter Pázmány, *Hodoegus. Igazságra vezérlő Kalauz* (Nagyszombat, 1637).

what became a secure Protestant ascendancy and a Catholic ethno-religious identity in the majority of the population, which emphasized tropes of dispossession, persecution, and resentment of the established church. The character of the Catholic elite in Ireland was fundamentally altered by the conquest which began at the end of the 1640s. From a position where Catholics owned a significant majority of the land of the island, including the most fertile areas of the richest provinces of Leinster and Munster, a massive Protestant dominance in landholding developed. Equally crucially the patriciates of the Catholic towns were largely liquidated and what had been the economic nerve centres of the Confederate Catholic proto-state were transformed into bastions of the Protestant interest. For English Catholics too the collapse of the royalist cause in which they had invested heavily marked something of a watershed, bringing to an end the type of court Catholicism which had flourished in Caroline England and ensuring that the type of reintegration of Catholicism into the mainstream of the English political and social elite, which influential members of the community had long aspired to, was not going to take place. In the Balkans, also, the long thirty-nine-year reign of Mehmed IV which commenced in 1648 represented a break with the policies of his predecessors as Sultan in terms of the zeal which he was to show in the conversion of Jews and Christians within his domains to Islam, and this period was to see the intensification of important processes of Islamicization in Albania.[26]

In the peripheral societies of Catholic Europe with which this study has principally been concerned, adherence to the church of Rome by no means corresponded to one single model. In certain areas it was a proscribed creed, open to varying degrees of persecution. In others, such as Ireland, while technically prohibited, the sheer critical mass of the Catholic population offered a high degree of immunity from attempts at religious conversion. In Poland and Hungary in East-Central Europe, Catholicism was a religion of the monarch but in societies which recognized the religious rights of other denominations. In Austria and Bohemia, it became a religion of coercion which, in contrast to the Mediterranean societies of Italy and the Iberian peninsula, moved to deploy repressive policies, not merely against relatively small minorities, but against very large segments of the Christian population. In much of the Balkans, Catholicism was a minority creed whose adherents looked with genuine hunger to the West for the provision of educated clerical personnel who could act as authoritative intermediaries with the sacred. In Bosnia and Albania, it retained more significant redoubts and in the former, in particular, it had become entwined around the institution of the Franciscan province which cherished an identity based on a historic continuity with the medieval past which accommodated itself only with difficulty to newer norms arising from the post-Tridentine revival.

A consistent feature of the Catholicism investigated on the margins of Catholic Europe concerns the role of the social elite in sustaining the various communities.

[26] David Do Paço, ' "La demeure de la paix"? Conflits, religions et sociétés en Europe ottoman, 1453–1683' in Wolfgang Kaiser (ed.), *L'Europe en conflits: Les affrontements religieux et la genèse de l'Europe moderne vers 1500 vers 1650* (Rennes: Presses Universitaires de Rennes, 2008), pp. 267–86, at 273; Lino Sciarra, 'L'Islam in Albania', *Oriente Moderno* new series 15 (1996), 1–77, at 1–5.

In the Western fringe, the continued adherence to the religion of substantial portions of the urban and noble populations to Catholicism was of critical importance. In England, indeed, with the exception of certain scattered geographical pockets, it was only among the social elite that Catholicism remained as a religion of even a recognizable minority in the seventeenth century. Different factors probably operated across this region. In England it seems possible that the strength of the Catholic identity which existed on Elizabeth's accession was an important factor. However, it was only the wealthiest sections of English society which had the resources to counteract the appropriation of the ecclesiastical life of the traditional parish by the state church. Something similar may have operated in the Netherlands. In Ireland, on the other hand, the much more massive attachment of the leadership cadres of both the Old English and Gaelic communities to Catholicism would seem largely to have been determined by the failure of the state to incentivize their conversion. Instead, processes of plantation, political discrimination and economic migration delivered a hostile New English population into the island, which materially disrupted the nature of relationships between the state and the pre-existing elites. In East-Central Europe, as investigated in Chapter 3, a consistent feature of the resurgence of Catholicism was the re-engagement with, and conversion to, the church of Rome of the region's nobles. Here the opposite of the Irish case would appear to have obtained. In this region there were clear incentives to adhere to Catholicism in terms of monarchical favour and access to office, and in Bohemia and Austria in terms of the maintenance of property and residence. As a religion also Catholicism offered advantages in terms of social stability, its practices establishing strong ritual bridges to the mass of population which confirmed the superiority of the societal elite. In addition, the growing intellectual diversity of the different variants of Protestantism in the region and their inability to establish common ground probably enhanced Catholicism's attractions as a confession of doctrinal stability. The refinement of Catholic polemic, emphasizing Rome's unique qualifications as a visible historical church and concentrating heavy fire on the innovations and divisions of the creeds which had emerged from the Reformation, and their providential responsibility for the contemporary disasters of the region, was probably another factor. The evolution of a formidable Catholic educational network throughout Central Europe evidently figured prominently in the movement of elite conversion as Jesuit schools in particular proved attractive to non-Catholic families because of the quality of the instruction provided.

Another constant feature of the Catholicism on the periphery which has been highlighted was the significant role played by women in its maintenance and propagation and in devotional activities. To some extent this could relate to the societal spaces which Catholicism occupied. In Ireland, Britain and Holland, the lack of an established church structure paradoxically may have given women greater freedom. Because the possibility of a separate Catholic ecclesiastical sphere was curtailed in these societies, Catholic practice was driven back into the domestic arena from which women could not easily be excluded. In East-Central Europe on the other hand the unsettled military conditions could make the church attractive as a source of stability, perhaps particularly for widows who otherwise might struggle to maintain familial inheritances in a society such as Early Modern Hungary or in parts of the Polish/Lithuanian commonwealth.

But in seeking such structural reasons for female involvement in Catholicism the actual religious attractions of the confession should not be discounted. In this of course Early Modern Catholicism was not unique. Strong female engagement with various forms of Christianity had been noted across many different eras and societies.[27] The suffering Christ pouring out his bodily fluids for the service and redemption of others arguably possessed a biological resonance for women which Early Modern Catholicism with its Christocentric devotions was capable of mobilizing at least as well as any other contemporary Christian grouping.[28] The devotion to the Infant of Prague, on the other hand, which became so important in the movement of renewal in the Czech crown lands, linked Catholic worship to strong maternal attachments. Again the figure of the Virgin Mary carried particular resonances in an Early Modern society racked by war and disease where so many women were forced to face at least the prospect and often the actuality of the loss of children and found in the Madonna figure an image of comfort and greater meaning.

The gulf between Rome and the marginal Catholicisms of Europe could undoubtedly be significant. In 1645 a memorial was framed concerning the delay in securing papal recognition of György Lippay as Archbishop of Esztergom. Central to this were the activities of Lippay's curial agent, an Italian official. This document outlined the necessary steps which had to be taken to have a cathedral church or monastery filled. In the first place, so that the relevant cardinal-protector could propose the candidate in the Consistory it was necessary to furnish him with a 'processo formato' concerning the quality of the proposed prelate and the state of the vacant church. Once the Cardinal-Protector's auditor had checked that all the requisite information was available he drew together a compendium which was reduced to a memorial and then sent that along with the *processo* to the Cardinal-Protector for signature. These were then returned to the agent of the prelate seeking appointment who was required to have the *processo* signed by three other cardinals, who should be heads of orders. The signed memorial had to be given to the Pope's auditor with additional copies for every cardinal who would be present at the consistory. This would allow the consistory to fill the church which necessarily was done over two sittings with *preconizatione* at the first followed by *propositione* at the second.

In the case of Lippay, the prelate's agent gave the relevant cardinal-protector's auditor, Guglielmo Motmanno, the 'processo' which had already been completed before the nuncio in Vienna. On 8 September a memorial was sent to the Pope's auditor, Monsignor Cherubino. Motmanno then went to see Cardinal Colonna, who was replacing Cardinal Harrach as protector of the hereditary lands of the House of Austria, who duly signed both *processo* and memorial. The agent of the

---

[27] Tony Walter and Grace Davie, 'The religiosity of women in the modern West', *The British Journal of Sociology* 49 (1998), 640–60; Rodney Stark, 'Reconstructing the rise of Christianity: the role of women', *Sociology of Religion* 56 (1995), 229–44.

[28] Elizabeth Weiss Ozorak, 'The power, but not the glory: how women empower themselves through religion', *Journal for the Scientific Study of Religion* 35 (1996), 17–29, at 25–6.

Hungarian bishops then secured the signatures of the three necessary cardinals and forwarded what he believed were the necessary documents to the Pope's auditor. On 18 September Colonna, however, was unable to put Lippay forward for *preconizatione* because the agent had omitted to supply the correct memorial. In October the business was further delayed because Colonna was absent from court. It was finally accomplished in November and December.[29]

While trivial in nature and merely involving a delay of some months in the expedition of ecclesiastical business, this incident does offer some insight into the gulf which could exist between the periphery of the Catholic world and its centre at Rome. Rome operated according to its own rules and with its own bureaucratic procedures which provided, among other things, comfortable occupation for Italian curial functionaries. For such men, the business of the church was the day-to-day activity of the Curia, with its essentially Italian character. This was a very different universe to the contingent and threatened Catholicism of Esztergom, or Amsterdam, or Dublin, or even Vienna. By the 1640s the sack of Rome was not in the living memory of a single person in the Eternal City. At the apex of the governmental structure, it is true, were individuals who had served outside Rome as nuncios. But while postings to Paris in the case of Maffeo Barberini, and Madrid in the case of the Pamfili Pope, probably opened new horizons, in these capitals they were still operating within the context of massive Catholic power. Only Clement VIII of the pontiffs under consideration in this study had any personal engagement with the often threatened and contingent Catholicism of the European periphery.

Nor was the disconnect between Rome and the margins of Europe always trivial. In 1646, Dionysio Massari, the auditor of the nuncio to the Confederate Catholics of Ireland, was dispatched back to Rome to plead with the pontiff for additional aid to the embattled Catholic proto-state. Massari came bearing news of victories won with the assistance of papal gold and captured Covenanter standards which ingratiated him to Innocent X. He was granted extraordinary marks of favour which he evidently knew well how to exploit. When walking with the Pope and asked what had disturbed him most in Ireland he responded that so many churches and altars had been overthrown there and the two Italians evidently shed tears together over the unhappy Catholics of the island. The result of Massari's charm was the commitment to extend further financial aid to the Confederates. News of the failure to capture Dublin darkened the Pope's mood considerably and only the fact that he had publicly committed to furnish the additional aid ultimately forced him to fulfil his promise.[30] By 1648 the prospects for the Confederate Catholics were extremely bleak. Urged on by the papal nuncio they had rejected a treaty with the royalist party largely because it offered major concessions to secular Catholics but did not provide for the institutional position of the Roman church in the island. But the bold strategy of seeking to establish Catholicism as effectively the established religion on the island was undone by a series of military disasters. In April

---

[29] See the 1645 memorial 'Per intendere il fatto successo nell'ultima spedizione Consistoriale dell'Arcivescovato di Strigonia' (Magyar Országos Levéltár, Litterae Roma Exaratae, A29, 23).
[30] Archivio Storico 'De Propaganda Fide', *Miscellaneae Varie*, Vol. 9, 268–94.

1648, therefore, two prominent confederates, Nicholas Plunkett and the Bishop of Ferns, Nicholas French, arrived in Rome seeking two principal objectives: renewed financial aid and a papal decision on the terms that might be considered acceptable for a peace with the royalist party. Although the nuncio had tried to coach them on the best way of dealing with the Curia in Rome, the Irish envoys were forced to kick their heels for months. Finally towards the end of July they penned a particularly frustrated memorial to Cardinal Pancirolo, the Pope's chief minister:

Most eminent lord

Because the most grave business of Your Eminence does not allow him in the manner of his customary kindness to us to give us audience, we supplicate that he should wish to read on our behalf these lines in which the perturbed thoughts of our minds offer our conclusions. In the first place we intrepidly assert: if any people of the earth anywhere had merited the grace and aid of the Apostolic See on account of the profusion of their blood and the sacrifice of fortune for religion, the Irish have. We have poured the sighs, prayers, spirits of this people prostrate at the feet of his Holiness, humbly requesting his decision both in the matter of religion and also aid against the fury of the most evil enemy, who have pledged their very souls to destroy and overthrow together with the people whatever can be considered sacred from the face of the earth. Behold, having spent three whole months in the city, to so many supplications we have not had any response from his His Holiness. We do not relate further the sad state of most noble men who having lost their fortunes for piety's sake spend bitter days unsuitable to their illustrious lineage. But it would be a crime to be silent about our fear concerning the ruin of all sacred things in that people. But this evil is absolutely to be feared if the Apostolic See does not apply opportune aid. Because if by lack of such aid the Catholic people should be permitted not only to be flagellated but destroyed and the churches of God desecrated and the veneration of God trampled underfoot and the very and most august sacrament of the Eucharist violently to be taken from the altars, finally whatever is holy to be defiled, all Christendom, if it has not arrived at a hard heart will mourn and sigh for such a noble destroyed member of the Catholic flock, purpled and dripping with its blood. But whatever ecclesiastics shall survive in the island, their condition will be more intolerable than the fate of thieves, robbers, traitors, homicides or whatever most evil men. In brief, we must leave the city. Thus orders the hard necessity of the dearest Patria which can suffer neither delay nor law. This also is expedient lest our further delay in Rome, in the place of consolation, should become the cause of ruin to the Irish. It will be easy to divine what kind and how bitter a mutation of matters and thoughts in Ireland, how prostrated and abjected the bishops and all good ecclesiastics will be, who most closely joined to the most illustrious Rinuccini [the papal nuncio] acted the work of God, when they will see us, who also have not merited badly for piety, with subsidies from Rome despaired of, empty, sad, and almost scorned and ejected from the city. We commend their matter and cause to God. But we humbly implore Your Eminence, because you are the principal minister at the side of the most holy father, furthermore we conjure in the love and name of the crucified Jesus (whose cause we prosecute for the souls which he redeemed with his blood) that he should open most freely this hard condition of the Irish to the most holy Father. Because if the present opportunity of helping religion in the kingdom is lost, we do not hope to recover it during his reign. But if God should permit that the universal father should not discern here and now to help his sons we will say as the suffering Maccabees: we suffer this for our sins. Furthermore with our full hearts we will pray that the God of Justice thundering over contrite Ireland should shine forth in Rome the God of mercy and that the Roman people will not feel as the Irish the wrath of the flagellating God. Let God keep Your Eminence safe, whose hand we kiss.[31]

It can be noted that this memorial proved prescient. Within five years up to twenty per cent of the Irish population had perished in the course of a savage war of conquest. The institutional structures of the Catholic church were in tatters with over one thousand priests killed or driven into exile and a hierarchy of twenty-seven resident bishops reduced to one old and infirm prelate kept alive on sips of whiskey in rural Ulster. A massive expropriation of Catholic property also ensued.[32] But the passion and despair of the Irish envoys cut no ice in Rome. The Pamfili papacy was not prepared to invest as much in Irish Catholicism as in the nuptials of the Pope's nephew and would not give any hostages to fortune in terms of validating a peace between Catholic and heretical interests. The envoys were blandly informed:

[31] 'Eminentissime Domine, Cum non patiantur gravissima Eminentiae Vestrae negotia pro solita in nos humanitate audientiam praebere, supplicamus ut velit patienter lineas has perlegere, in quibus pro nobis perorant perturbae animarum nostrarum cogitationes. In primis intrepide asserimus: si ullus uspiam terrarum populus fortunarum jactura atque proprii cruoris profusione pro religione a Sancta Sede Apostolica gratiam atque auxilia promeruit, promeruit Ibernicus. Hujus nos populi suspiria, preces, animas, tanquam aquam effundimus, provoluti ad pedes Suae Sanctitatis, humillime effla-gitando ipsius tam sententiam in negotio religionis, quam auxilia contra furorem sceleratissimi hostis, qui juravit ipsas animas de facie terrae delere, et una cum populo quicquid sacrum censeri potest, evertere. Ecce tamen consumptis in urbe mensibus tribus, ad tot supplicationes non habuimus ullum Suae Sanctitatis responsum. Non proponimus amplius tristem nobilissimorum virorum statum, qui, amissis fortunis propter pietatem amaros ducunt dies male cohaerentes cum eorum praeclara prosapia. Metum autem nostrum de sacrorum onmium, in illa gente, ruina silere nefas esset. Id tamen mali omnino timeri debet, si non impertiatur Sedes Apostolica subsidia opportuna. Quod si talium sub-sidiorum carentia non tantum flagellari sed perimi permittatur Catholicus populus, atque ecclesiae Dei violenter pollui, Dei veneratio conculcari, ipsum augustissimum Eucharistiae Sacramentum altari-bus violenter abripi, demum quicquid sanctum est spurcari, Christianitas universa, si ad durum cor non pervenerit, planget et ingemiscet propter sublatum tam nobile gregis Catholicis membrum san-guine suo madens atque purpuratum. Si qui autem in ea insula ecclesiastici supervixerint, erit eorum conditio intolerabilior sorte furum, latronum, homicidarum, perduellium, et quorumvis sceleratissi-morum hominum. Brevissime nobis exeundum est urbe. Ita jubet dura charissimae patriae necessitas, quae nec legem nec mora pati scit. Hoc etiam expedit ne nostra ulterior Romae mora, loco solatii, veniat Ibernis causa ruinae. Facile erit divinare qualis erit, et quam amara rerum et cogitationum in Ibernia mutatio, quam prostrate et abjecti Episcopi atque omnes boni ecclesiastici, qui Illustrissimo Rinuccino arctissime conjuncti opus Dei egerunt, quando videbunt nos, etiam de pietate non male meritos, desperatis Roma subsidiis, vacuos, tristes, et quasi spretos et ex Urbe ejectos. Commendamus Deo rem et causam suam. Vestram autem Eminentiam, cum sit Minister principalis ad latus Sanctis-simi Patris, humillime obtestamur, etiam conjuramus in amore et nomine Jesu Crucifixi (cujus causam prosequimur pro animabus, quas suo sanguine redemit) ut hanc duram Ibernorum conditionem Beatissimo Patri liberrime aperiat. Si enim elabatur praesens in eo Regno religionem juvandi opportu-nitas, non speramus recuperandam ipso regnante. Quod si permittat Deus ut non decernat universalis pater suos hic et nunc filios juvando, dicemus cum tribulatis Machabaeis: Nos pro peccatis nostris haec patimur. Etiam ex toto corde precabimur ut Deus justitiae tonans super contrita Ibernia affulgeat Romae Deus misericordiae, et non persentiscat populus Romanus, sicuti modo Ibernicus, flagellantis Dei iras. Deus incolumem servet suam Eminentiam, cui manus exosculamur': Nicholas French and Nicholas Plunkett to Cardinal Pancirolo, 27 July 1648 (Stanislaus Kavanagh, (ed.), *Commentarius Rinuccianus, de sedis apostolicae legatione ad foederatos Hiberniae catholicos per annos 1645–9* (six vols, Dublin: Irish Manuscripts Commission, 1932–49), 3, pp. 405–6.
[32] Patrick Corish, 'The Cromwellian Regime, 1650–60' in T.W. Moody, F.X. Martin, and F.J. Byrne (eds), *A New History of Ireland III* (Oxford: Oxford University Press, 1976), pp. 375–86.

Concerning a peace to be contracted between Catholics and heretics, the Apostolic See is accustomed to do nothing to approve the same, and it will be led by the good hope that the said envoys and all other Catholics of Ireland in all their actions will aim for the greater advantage and utility of the Catholic religion.[33]

Such a position was useless to the envoys and it is hardly surprising that on their return to Ireland they abandoned their former patron, the nuncio Rinuccini, and helped to broker a peace with the royalist party in Ireland which neither he nor his superiors could accept.[34]

For the Irish envoys, the visit to Rome was evidently an eye-opening experience and a deep disappointment. In this and in other letters which they produced in the same period a sense not merely of anger but of betrayal and disillusionment is clearly evident. Yet if the memorial of Nicholas Plunkett and Nicholas French offers witness to the gulf which could separate Rome from the utterly different conditions on the margins of Catholic Europe, it testifies also to the passionate sense of attachment to Rome which also coexisted. In some respects the relationship with Rome was more intensely cherished on the periphery of Catholic Europe than in its more secure heartlands. Ironically, also it was on the margins of Europe, in Ireland and the Netherlands in particular, that Rome acquired the greatest freedom of action in terms of ecclesiastical action, substantially free from the interference of secular interests in the creation of structures of authority.

Roman policy on the periphery of Europe was by no means uniformly successful. As the example of the Confederate Catholics of Ireland demonstrates, the type of concessions and elasticity which would have made the lives and politics of Catholics forced to live under the aegis of a non-Catholic power easier could be very hard to gain from Rome. Similarly, the rigidity of the Tridentine identity which evolved in the period under review stunted the horizons of what was possible to accomplish in the East. The Union of Brest, for instance, was largely a failure, not least because of the ungenerous terms which were on offer in Rome to the practitioners of the Greek rite. In the Balkans, as was demonstrated in Chapters 4 and 5, the championing of military confrontation with Ottoman power was the most significant Roman policy in the period under review. Bartolomeo Kašić's imaginative suggestions concerning the possibility of creating leverage for Balkan Catholics by diplomatic representation in Istanbul aroused little interest. More pertinently, despite the development of *Propaganda Fide*, Rome failed to provide the educational resources to maintain the redoubts of Catholicism in the Balkans let alone to expand them. In this regard, the sheer scale of expenditure which the papacy was prepared to countenance in military endeavours against Islamic and Protestant power throws into relief the rather exiguous sums which were provided for educational and missionary purposes.

---

[33] 'Sedem Apostolicam quoties de pace inter Catholicos et haereticos contrahenda agitur, solere nullas in ea re partes agere ad eam approbandam, seque bona duci spe futurum ut iidem oratores atque omnes Iberniae Catholici in cunctis eorum actionibus collinent in majorem religionis Catholicae profectum et utilitatem' (Kavanagh, *Commentarius Rinuccianus*, 3, p. 409).

[34] Patrick Corish, 'Bishop Nicholas French and the Second Ormond Peace, 1648–9', *Irish Historical Studies* 6 (1948), 83–100.

As noted in Chapter 2, Catholics who lived in confessionally-mixed societies naturally often developed more differentiated understandings of heresy. Indeed the problem could lie in convincing Catholics of the inevitable damnation of those outside the salvific vessel which the Roman church represented. As Péter Pázmány sorrowfully noted in Hungary there were many Catholics who dared to question the church's certainty concerning the damnation of heretics and followers of other religions who lived virtuous lives. In Ireland by the end of his tenure the nuncio, GianBattista Rinuccini, was frankly amazed at the distinctions which his political Catholic opponents were prepared to make between various Protestant positions, and in particular loyal supporters of the King and his church 'as if respect for the King alone could qualify heresies or purge the contagion which falsities inflict on souls'.[35] Yet if a figure such as Rinuccini represented a figure deeply unwilling to consider gradations in religious difference from Rome, other papal ministers were not always so inflexible. Particularly during the Ludovisi papacy, a realization that certain Protestant sects were worse than others helped shape attitudes towards Europe north of the Alps. In Bohemia a distinction could be drawn between Hussites, with whom, similar to the adherents of the Orthodox church, the possibility of eventual union and assimilation seemed to exist and radical sects such as the Adamites, Anabaptists, and Pikardists. In Germany, too, it was recognized that the difficulty of 'purging the evil humours' could not be accomplished all at once for fear of creating a savage backlash.[36] Thus, there, excessive force should be eschewed and instead with 'the gentle ardour and ardent kindness that the Holy Spirit is accustomed to love in his affairs' policy should be implemented.[37] Similarly in Hungary it was acknowledged that, given the evils of the current situation, tolerance of the Augustan Confession would not represent the worst possible outcome, since it was seen to diverge less from Catholicism than more radical sects.[38] It is noteworthy that in this distinction between Hussites and even Lutherans, on the one hand, with whom more gentle and long-term projects of assimilation might be considered, and radical Protestant sects which had to be opposed more violently, the Reformed churches were seen firmly in the latter camp. This was evident not merely in the attitude towards Central Europe but in France where the opportunity to 'annihilate the Huguenots' was eagerly coveted[39] and in the Gregorian attempts to create a diplomatic interface between Savoy and France which would allow for the conquest of Geneva where 'the worst masters...Calvin and Bèze...had poured out the proudest and most mortal poison that any heretic or heresiarch had ever given rise to'.[40]

---

[35] 'Come se il solo rispetto del Re qualificasse l'eresie o purgasse il contagio, che portano all'anime le falsità...': Rinuccini's relation to the Pope, 1649 (G. A. Aiazzi, *Nunziatura in Irlanda di Monsignor Gio. Baptista Rinuccini arcivescovo di Fermo negli anni 1645 à 1649* (Florence, 1844), p. 432).

[36] 'purgar gli humori peccanti': Instructions for Carlo Carafa, 12 April 1621 (*Die Hauptinstrucktionen Gregors XV*, p. 624).

[37] 'l'ardor soave e la piacevolezza ardente che suole amare nell'opere sue lo Spirito Santo' (ibid.).

[38] ibid., pp. 624–5.

[39] 'annichilare gli Ugonotti': Instructions for Ottavio Corsini, 4 April 1621 (ibid., p. 554).

[40] 'Calvino et Bezio...pessimi maestri...hanno versato il più fiero e mortale veleno che da niuno heretic o da heresiarca sia mai uscito': Instructions for Tobia Coran, 16 July 1621 (ibid., pp. 741–60,

Despite the highly Italocentric nature of the Early Modern papacy, a certain breadth of vision could exist in Rome. The foundation of *Propaganda Fide*, and the fact that, as with its Clementine predecessor, its membership included an array of the most important cardinals in Rome, testified to the desire to learn more concerning the vast world outside the limited borders of the European Catholic heartland. This extended to the very apex of the ecclesiastical system. Paul V, for instance, took an intense interest in the relations of Jesuit missionaries from the Balkans and Innocent X was similarly eager to hear the results of his investment of papal gold in Ireland. The huge, and costly, system of *nunziature* was not merely a practical and bureaucratic instrument but was also embedded in a philosophical sense of responsibility. As Ludovico Ludovisi instructed the nuncio to Poland in 1622, in the course of outlining the vast nature of the commonwealth and the many varied responsibilities pertaining to a nuncio and the great talents the position required:

> It is a great work of human virtue to direct peoples wisely and to judge rightly their cases and controversies and to be for them not only director and judge, but joining ecclesiastical and secular power, to exercise paternally the incomparable office of bishop and pastor of souls.[41]

A fundamental aspect of this responsibility, of course, was to bring the religious practices and beliefs of different societies into as close a concord with contemporary Roman models as possible. As the nuncio in Ireland in the 1640s, Rinuccini, reported to his superiors concerning the 'primitive and persecuted' nature of the Irish church:

> I am confident, if we have a little peace, to shape them so much to my way that they will take and conserve the Roman style.[42]

Such a vision of religious uniformity within the Catholic world also nestled within a wider providential hope both for the destruction of Ottoman power and for the rolling back of the effects of the Reformation. For both of these ends the papacy was prepared to commit significant financial resources and immense diplomatic efforts. But the triumph of Tridentine norms which it aspired to accomplish was not seen as extrinsic to these attempts to reintegrate and expand the *Republica Christiana* against its exterior enemies. Rather it would facilitate their accomplishment in two ways: first by the creation of Catholic societies which would recognize their duties and religious responsibilities; and, second, by appeasing the wrath of God with the sinfulness of his people and, therefore, redirecting his ire against the

---

at 744); in this regard see also the sheer level of spleen towards Calvinism in the Instructions for Fabrizio Verospi, 13 January 1622 (ibid., pp. 831–2).

[41] 'Egli è grand'opera dell'humana virtù il reggere savviament popoli e'l giudicare con dirittura le liti e controversie loro, e l'esserne non solamente rettore e giudice, ma la podestà del secolo con l'ecclesiastica congiongendo, l'esercitare paternamente l'ufficio incomparabile di Vescovo e di pastore di anime': Instructions to Giovanni Lancellotti, 14 December 1622 (Fitych, *Acta Nuntiaturae Poloniae Tomus XXII*, p. 30).

[42] 'Una chiesa primitiva e perseguitata'; 'mi basta l'animo, se averemo un poco di pace, di formarli tanto a mio modo, che pighleranno e conserveranno lo stilo Romano': Rinuccini to Pamfili, 30 December 1646 (Aiazzi, *Nunziatura in Irlanda*, p. 187).

enemies of true religion. Papal interaction with the wider world of Catholic Europe during the period under review was thus both wide ranging and simultaneously narrow in its focus. A genuine sense of responsibility for the world outside Italian borders, extending even to an area like Ireland which in immediate geopolitical terms was of little significance, coexisted with a religious vision which placed great value on a rather narrow interpretation of doctrinal and disciplinary norms derived from Trent and which tended to measure value in terms of proximity to the contemporary orthodoxies of Rome.

Yet on the margins of Europe, as indeed in societies such as Italy or Spain, Early Modern Catholicism was always more capacious than the narrow orthodoxies of its Roman leadership. Bosnian Franciscans and Polish Dominicans refused to accept the superiority of Jesuits at work in their territories and continued to articulate a proud sense of their own Catholic identity which drew heavily from their medieval inheritances. Old English Catholics in Ireland effectively banished the papal nuncio from the island's shores in the late 1640s and in the Netherlands *kloppen* seized upon the unusual conditions of the *Missio Hollandica* to explore possibilities of female agency. Despite the anomalous conditions in which they operated compared to contemporary Italy, these communities on the margins of Europe were highly active in elaborating a sense of their own Catholic identity, adapted to the peculiar contours of their own situations. It is true, too, that despite the strong criticisms of other variants of Catholicism which could be levied by Italian nuncios, a consistent current of pragmatism ran through the exercise of Roman leadership. Reform of the regular orders of Poland, Ireland or Bosnia was certainly seen as highly desirable but the efforts to accomplish it were often quite conciliatory, seeking to exploit internal currents of reform rather than attempting to impose solutions harshly. In a cognate fashion, despite the frustration of papal representatives in attempting to construct anti-Islamic and anti-Protestant coalitions of Catholic states, a strong adaptation to the limits of the possible obtained in the exercise of Roman diplomacy. Moreover, despite the strong currents of Italo-centricism which distinguished the Roman conception of religious orthodoxy and best practice, a respect for the hardships which the marginal Catholicisms of the continent had to confront was by no means absent. As Rinuccini, deeply moved by the expressions of loyalty of the people of Galway, noted in 1649, it was possible for the centre to learn also from the periphery:

> Perhaps the most distant country of Christendom in reverence of the Supreme Pontiff, and in the defence of his ministers will serve as a standard for its nearer adherents; and to understand the subjection of the faithful to its head, it will be necessary that the peoples nourished in the light of truth should go to discover a climate where one never sees the sun.[43]

---

[43] 'Forse il più lontano paese della Cristianità nell adorazione del Sommo Pontificato, e nella difesa dei suoi ministri servirà di norma alle comittele dei più vicini; e per intendere la soggezione dei fedeli al suo capo, bisognerà che i popoli nutriti nella luce del vero vadano a trovare un clima dove non si vede mai sole': Rinuccini's relation to the Pope, 1649 (Aiazzi, *Nunziatura in Irlanda*, p. 433).

Bibliography

MANUSCRIPT SOURCES

Hungary
Budapest
Magyar Országos Levéltár
Litterae Roma Exaratae, A29.
Magyar Kancelláriai Levéltár, Litterae Archiepiscoporum 1589–1710, A30.
Magyar Kancelláriai Levéltár, Litterae Capitolorum, Capitulum Jauriense 1632–1741, A31.
Magyar Kancelláriai Levéltár, Litterae Palatinorum 1614–1765, A21.

Italy
Fermo
Archivio Arcivescovile di Fermo
iii C/13—'Instruttione pratica per la cura episcopale di Monsignor Gio. Battista Rinuccini, Arcivescove di Fermo'.
Synodus Civitatis et Dioc. Firmane—Decrees of synod of 1628.

Milan
Archivio Storico Comunale di Milano
Biblioteca Trivulziana, cod. n. 1958.
Biblioteca Trivulziana, cod. n. 1963.
Biblioteca Trivulziana, cod. n. 1964.

Rome
Archivio Segreto Vaticano
Acta Miscellanea, 97.
Acta Vicecancellarii S.R.E., 17.
Epistulae ad Principi, 51, 53.
Lettere di Cardinali, Vols 12–14.
Lettere di Vescovi e Prelati, Vols 16, 23, 24, 25, 27, 29, 30, 31, 32, 33, 35.
Lettere di Vescovi e Principi, Vol. 29.
Particolari, Vols 17, 24.

Archivio Storico 'De Propaganda Fide'
Acta Sacrae Congregationis, 4, 6.
Fondo di Vienna, 14, 39.
Lettere Latine, Vol. 9.
Lettere Volgari, Vols 2, 7, 22.
Miscellaneae Varie, Vol. 9.
Scritture Originali Referite nelle Congregazioni Generali, Vols 14, 56, 67, 78, 89, 140, 141, 142, 143, 145, 146, 294, 295, 337, 386.

Scritture riferite nei Congressi, 1.
Visite, 10.

Archivio della congregazione per le cause dei Santi
Decreta Liturgica, 1622–6.

Biblioteca Apostolica Vaticana
Barberini Latini Mss, 3631, 4729, 4886, 4994, 5253, 5653, 5678, 6485, 6583, 6827, 8223, 8238, 8649, 8651, 8653, 8655.
Nunziatura d'Inghilterra, 8.

Ireland
Dublin
UCD Archives, Franciscan manuscripts
D II, D III, D IV.

National Library of Ireland
Ms. 7–12.
Ms. 345.

Trinity College
Mss 846.
http:<//1641.tcd.ie/deposition.php?depID=820011r009>.

Britain
London

British Library
Egerton Mss 917.
Harleian Mss 4551.

The National Archives
SP/63/182/47 (consulted on microfilm in Trinity College Dublin).

France
Paris

Archives du Ministère des Affaires Étrangeres
Correspondence Politique (Rome), 90, 91, 92.

Bibliothèque Nationale
Fonds Français, 4168, 4169, 4170.

Spain
Simancas

Archivio General (consulted on microfilm in National Library of Ireland)
Negoc. de Roma, 1613–99.

PRINTED PRIMARY SOURCES

A.C., *True Relations of Sundry Conferences had between certain Protestant doctours and a Iesuit called M. Fisher* (St Omer: English College Press, 1626).

Aiazzi, G., *Nunziatura in Irlanda di Monsignor Gio. Baptista Rinuccini arcivescovo di Fermo negli anni 1645 à 1649* (Florence, 1844).

Androtius, Fulvius, *Certain Devout Considerations of Frequenting the Blessed Sacrament with sundrie other precepts and rule of direction composed for the benefit of such as seek to attaine to the perfection of virtue* (Douai, 1606).

Aringhi, Paolo, *Memorie istoriche della vita del venerabile servo di Dio Pier Francesco Scarampi* (Roma, 1744).

Atkinson, Ernest George (ed.), *Calendar of the State Papers relating to Ireland Elizabeth I, 1599 April–1600 February* (London: Public Record Office, 1899).

Balász, Mihály (ed.), *Szántó (Arator) István S.J., Confutatio Alcorani* (Szeged: Scriptum KFT, 1990).

Balász, Mihály, Fricsy, Ádam, Lukács, László, and Monok, István (eds), *Erdélyi és Hódóltsági Jezsuita Missziók* (two vols, Szeged: Scriptum KFT, 1990).

Balduinus, Friedrich, *Phosphorus Veri Catholicismi: Devia Papatus, & viam regiam ad Ecclesiam vere Catholicam & Apostolicam fideliter monstrans, facemque praelucens legentibus Hodegum Petri Pazmanni olim Jesuitae, nunc Cardinalis Ecclesiae Romano-Papisticae* (Wittenberg, 1626).

Barbiche, Bernard (ed.), *Correspondance du nonce en France Innocenzo del Bufalo évéque de camerino (1601–1604)* (Rome: Presses de l'Université Grégorienne/Editions E. de Boccard, Paris, 1964).

Bentivoglio, Guido, *Memorie del cardinal Guido Bentivoglio con correzioni e variant dell'edizione d'Amsterdam del 1648* (Milan: G. Daelli, 1844).

Bilinski, Adelbertus (ed.), *Acta Nuntiaturae Poloniae Tomus XVXIII Volumen 1 Honoratus Visconti* (Rome: Institutum Historicum Polonicum Romae, 1996).

Blet, Pierre (ed.), *Correspondance du Nonce en France Ranuccio Scotti (1639–41)* (Paris and Rome: E. de Boccard, 1965).

Brady, W. Maziere (ed.), *State papers concerning the Irish church in the time of Queen Elizabeth* (London: Longmans, Green, Reader & Dyer, 1868).

Brewer, J.S. and Bullen, W. (eds), *Calendar of Carew Papers in the Lambeth Palace Library* (London: Kraus-Thomson, 1873).

Bunny, Edmund, *A Booke of Christian Exercise, Appertayning to Resolution... and Accompanied Now with a Treatise Tending to Pacification* (London, 1584).

Caraman, Philip (ed.), *John Gerard, the autobiography of an Elizabethan* (London: Longmans, Green, 1951).

Chynczewska-Hennel, Theresia (ed.), *Acta Nuntiaturae Poloniae Tomus XXV Marius Filonardi (1635–43) Volumen 1* (Cracoviae: Academia Scientiarum et Litterarum Polona, 2003).

Corish, Patrick, 'Two Reports on the Catholic Church in Ireland in the Early Seventeenth Century', *Archivium Hibernicum* 22 (1959), 140–62.

D'Ossat, Arnold, *Lettres de l'Illustrissime et Révérendissime Cardinal d'Ossat, éveque de Bayeux au roy Henry le Grand et à Monsieur Villeroy* (Paris, 1627).

De Leda, G. (ed.), *La Legazione di Roma di Paolo Paruto 1592–95: Monumenti storici publicati dalla R. Deputazione Veneta di storia di patria* (three vols, Venice, 1886–7).

Fejér, Georgius (ed.), *Jurium ac Libertatum Religionis et Ecclesiae Catholicae in Regno Hungariae Partibus adnexis Codicillus Diplomaticus* (Buda: Typis Regiae Scientiarum Universitatis Hungaricae, 1847).

Bibliography

Fitych, Thaddaeus (ed.), *Acta Nuntiaturae Poloniae Tomus XXII Volumen 1 Ioannes Baptista Lancellotti (1622–27)* (Cracoviae: Academia Scientiarum et Litterarum Polona, 2000).

Gilbert, J.T. (ed.), *The history of the Irish confederation and war in Ireland, 1641–1649: containing a narrative of affairs of Ireland... with correspondence and documents of the confederation... with contemporary personal statements, memoirs, etc.* (seven vols, Dublin: 1882–91).

Hajnal, István (ed.), *Esterházy Miklós Nádor Iratai I. Kormányzattörténeti Iratok: Az 1642 Évi Meghiúsult Országgyűlés Időszaka (1640 December–1643 Március)* (Budapest: Esterházy Pál Herceg Kiadása, 1930).

Hanuy, Ferenc (ed.), *Pázmány Péter összegyujtött levelei* (two vols: Budapest, 1910–12).

Hosius, Stanislaus, *Confessio catholicae fidei Christiana* (Antwerp, 1561).

Ingoli, Francesco, *De Parochis et Eorum Officio* (Bologna, 1622).

Jaitner, Klaus (ed.), *Die Hauptinstruktionen Clemens' VIII. für die Nuntien und Legaten an den europäischen Fürstenhöfen, 1592–1605* (two vols, Tübingen: Max Niemayer Verlag, 1984).

Jaitner, Klaus (ed.), *Die Hauptinstrucktionen Gregors XV für di Nuntien und Gesandten an den Europäischen Fürstenhöfen 1621–1623* (two vols, Tübingen: Max Niemeyer Verlag, 1997).

Jennings, Brendan, 'Miscellaneous documents II 1625–40', *Archivium Hibernicum* 14 (1949), no. 9.

Jennings, Brendan (ed.), *Wadding Papers* (Dublin: Irish Manuscripts Commission, 1953).

Juvencius, Josephus, *Historiae Societatis Jesu pars quinta.Tomus Posterior Ab anno Christi MDXVI ad MDCXVI* (Roma, 1710).

Kavanagh, Stanislaus (ed.), *Commentarius Rinuccinianus, de sedis apostolicae legatione ad foederatos Hiberniae catholicos per annos 1645–49* (six vols, Dublin: Irish Manuscripts Commission, 1932–49).

Lukács, Ladislaus (ed.), *Monumenta Paedegogica Societatis Iesu 6: Collectanea de ratione studiorum Societatis Iesu* (Rome: Monumenta Historica Societatis Iesu, 1986).

Pázmány, Péter, *Hodoegus. Igazságra vezérlő Kalauz* (Nagyszombat, 1637).

Pázmány, Péter, *Felelet Magyari István Sárvári Prédikátornak as Ország Romlása Okairul Írt Könyvére*, ed. Emil Hargittay (Budapest: Universitas, 2000).

Rinuccini, G.B., *Il Cappuccino Scozzese* (Roma: per il moneta, 1645).

Rinuccini, G.B., *Della Dignita et Offitio de i Vescovi: Discorsi Quaranta di Monsignor Gio. Battista Rinuccini, Arcivescovo e Prencipe di Fermo* (two vols, Roma, 1651).

Sacrosancti et Oecumenici Concilii Tridentini Paulo III, Iulio III, et Pio IV.PP.MM. Celebrati Canones et Decreta (Brussels, 1688).

Shuckburgh, E. (ed.), *Two biographies of William Bedell, Bishop of Kilmore: with a selection of his letters and an unpublished treatise* (Cambridge: Cambridge University Press, 1902).

Szelestei, László (ed.), *Naplók és útleírások a 16–18 századból* (Budapest: Universitas Könyvkiadó, 1998).

Szögi, László (ed.), *Régi Magyar Egyetemek Emlékezete: Memoria Universitatum et Scholarum Maiorum Regni Hungariae 1367–1777* (Budapest: Eötvös Loránd Tudományegyetem, 1995).

Tárnóc Márton, *Pázmány Péter prédikációi* (Budapest: Szépirodalmi Könyvkiadó, 1987).

Theiner, Augustin (ed.), *Vetera Monumenta Slavorum Meridionalium* (two vols, Rome and Zagreb, 1863–75).

Tóth, István György (ed.), *Relationes Missionariorum de Hungaria et Transilvania (1627–1707)* (Rome and Budapest: Biblioteca Academiae Hungariae, 1994).

Tóth, István György (ed.), *Litterae Missionariorum de Hungaria et Transilvania (1572–1717)* (two vols, Roma and Budapest: Biblioteca Academiae Hungariae, 2002).

Tygielski, Adalbertus, *Acta Nuntiaturae Poloniae Tomus XVIII Volumen 1 Franciscus Simon-etta 21 VI 1606–30 IX 1607* (Rome: Institutum Historicum Polonicum Romae, 1990).

Veress, Andreas (ed.), *Epistolae et Acta P. Alfonsi Carrillii S. J., 1591–1618: Monumenta Hungariae Historicaa Diplomataria 32* (Budapest: Magyar Tudományos Akadémia, 1906).

Veress, Andreas, *Epistolae et Acta Jesuitarum Transylvaniae Temporibus Principum Báthory (1571–1613)* (Budapest: Athenaeum, 1911).

Veress, Andreas, *Argenti iratai 1603–1623* (Szeged: József Attila Tudományegyetem Bölcsészettudományi Kara, 1983).

Veress, Andreas, *Relationses Nuntiorum apostolicorum in Transsilvaniam Missorum a Clemente VIII, 1592–1600): Monumenta Vaticana Historiam Regni Hungariae Illustrantia* (2nd edn, Budapest: Metem, 2001).

SECONDARY SOURCES

Ágoston, Gábor, *Guns for the Sultan: Military Power and the Weapons Industry in the Ottoman Empire* (Cambridge and New York: Cambridge University Press, 2005).

Alberigo, Guiseppe, 'Studi e problem relative all'applicazione del concilio di Trento in Italia', *Rivista Storica Italiana* 70 (1958), 239–98.

Alberigo, Guiseppe, *Lo sviluppo della dottrina sui poteri nella Chiesa universale. Momenti essenziali tra il XVI e il XIX secolo* (Rome: Herder, 1964).

Alberigo, Guiseppe, 'The Council of Trent', in John O'Malley (ed.), *Catholicism in Early Modern History: A Guide to Research* (St. Louis: Centre for Reformation Research, 1988), pp. 213–21.

Alberigo, Guiseppe, 'From the Council of Trent to "Tridentinism"', in Raymond Bulman and Frederick Parella (eds), *From Trent to Vatican II: Historical and Theological Investigations* (Oxford: Oxford University Press, 2006), pp. 19–38.

Arblaster, Paul, 'The Southern Netherlands Connection: networks of support and patronage', in Benjamin Kaplan, Bob Moore, Henk Van Nierop, and Judith Pollmann (eds), *Catholic Communities in Protestant States: Britain and the Netherlands c. 1570–1720* (Manchester: Manchester University Press, 2009), pp. 123–38.

Armstrong, Robert and Ó hAnnracháin, Tadhg, 'Alternative Establishments? Insular Catholicism and Presbyterianism', in Robert Armstrong and Tadhg Ó hAnnracháin (eds), *Insular Christianity: Alternative models of the church in Britain and Ireland c. 1570–c.1700* (Manchester: Manchester University Press, 2013), pp. 1–27.

Armstrong, Robert and Ó hAnnracháin, Tadhg (eds), *Insular Christianity: Alternative models of the church in Britain and Ireland c. 1570–c.1700* (Manchester: Manchester University Press, 2013).

Arrizabalaga, Jon, 'Poor Relief in Counter-Reformation Castile: An Overview', in Ole Peter Grell, Andrew Cunningham, and Jon Arrizabalaga (eds), *Health Care and Poor Relief in Counter-Reformation Europe* (London and New York: Routledge, 1999), pp. 151–76.

Aveling, Hugh, *Northern Catholics: the Catholic recusants of the North Riding of Yorkshire* (London: Geoffrey Chapman, 1966).

Aveling, Hugh, *The handle and the axe: the Catholic recusants in England from Reformation to Emancipation* (London: Blond and Briggs, 1976).

Bahlke, Joackim, Bömelburg, Hans-Jürgen, and Kersken, Norbert (eds), *Ständefreiheit und Staatsgestaltung in Ostmitteleuropa: Übernationale Gemeinsamkeiten in der politischen Kultur vom 16–18. Jahrhundert* (Leipzig: De Gruyter, 1996).

Bahlke, Joackim, Lambrecht, Karen, and Maner, Hans-Christian (eds), *Konfessionelle Pluralität als Herausforderung: Koexistenz und Konflikt in Spätmittelalter und Frühen Neuzeit. Winfried Eberhard zum 65. Geburtstag* (Leipzig: Leipziger Universitätsverlag, 2006).

Barnard, T.C., 'Conclusion: Settling and Unsettling Ireland: The Cromwellian and Williamite Revolutions', in Jane Ohlmeyer (ed.), *Ireland from Independence to Occupation, 1641–60* (Cambridge: Cambridge University Press, 1995), pp. 265–91.

Barnard, T.C., '"Parlour entertainment in an evening?" histories of the 1640s', in Micheál Ó Siochrú (ed.), *Kingdom in Crisis* (Dublin: Four Courts Press, 2001).

Barnard, T.C., *A New Anatomy of Ireland: The Irish Protestants, 1649–1770* (New Haven and London: Yale University Press, 2003).

Barta, László, 'Adatok a Kalauzra Adott Wittenbergi Válasz Készítéséhez', in Emil Hargittay (ed.), *Pázmány Péter és kora* (Piliscsaba: PPKE BTK, 2001), pp. 268–73.

Becker, Rotraud, *Nuntiaturen des Malesta Baglioni, des Ciriaco Rocci und des Mario Filonardi* (Tübingen: Max Niemeyer, 2004).

Berger, Peter, Davie, Grace, and Fokas, Effie, *Religious America, Secular Europe? A Theme and Variation* (Aldershot: Ashgate, 2008).

Bergerhausen, Hans-Wolfgang, 'Die "Verneuerte Landesordnung" in Böhmen 1627: ein Grunddokument des habsburgischen Absolutismus', *Historische Zeitschrift* 271 (2001), 327–52.

Bergin, Joseph, 'The Crown, the Papacy and the Reform of the Old Orders in Early Seventeenth Century France', *Journal of Ecclesiastical History* 33 (1982), 234–55.

Bergin, Joseph, 'The Counter-Reformation Church and its Bishops', *Past & Present* 165 (1999), 30–73.

Bergin, Joseph, *Church, Society and Religious Change in France 1580–1730* (Yale: Yale University Press, 2009).

Bireley, Robert, *Religion and Politics in the Age of the Counter Reformation: Emperor Ferdinand II, William Lamormaini, S.J. and the Formation of Imperial Policy* (Chapel Hill: University of North Carolina Press, 1981).

Bireley, Robert, 'The Thirty Years' War as Germany's Religious War', in K. Repgen (ed.), *Krieg und Politik 1618–1648* (Munich: Oldenbourg, 1988), pp. 85–106.

Bireley, Robert, 'Ferdinand II: Founder of the Habsburg Monarchy', in R.J.W. Evans and T.V. Thomas (eds), *Crown, Church and Estates: Central European Politics in the Sixteenth and Seventeenth Centuries* (London and New York: Palgrave Macmillan, 1991), pp. 232–40.

Bireley, Robert, *The Refashioning of European Catholicism: A Reassessment of the Counter Reformation* (Washington D.C.: The Catholic University of America Press, 1999).

Bireley, Robert, *The Jesuits and the Thirty Years War: Kings, Courts and Confessors* (Cambridge: Cambridge University Press, 2003).

Bitskey, István, *Hitvitak tüzében* (Budapest: Gondolat, 1978).

Bitskey, István, 'Pázmány Péter és a Római Collegium Germanicum Hungaricum', in I. Bitskey and A. Tamás (eds), *A Debreceni Kossuth Lajos Tudományegyetem Magyar Irodalomtörténeti Intézetének Közleményei*, XXIII (Debrecen: Debrecen University Press, 1985), pp. 29–40.

Bitskey, István, 'The Collegium Germanicum Hungaricum in Rome and the Beginning of the Counter Reformation in Hungary', in R.J.W. Evans and T.V. Thomas (eds), *Crown, Church and Estates: Central European Politics in the Sixteenth and Seventeenth Centuries* (London and New York: Palgrave Macmillan, 1991), pp. 110–22.

Bossy, John, *The English Catholic community 1570–1850* (London: Darton, Longman and Todd, 1975).

Boudens, Robrecht, 'Présence de la Congrégation dans l'histoire religieuse des Provinces-Unies des Pays-Bas', in Josef Metzler (ed.), *Sacrae Congregationis de Propaganda Fide Memoria Rerum (350 anni a servizio della missioni 1622–1972)* (three vols, Rome, Freiburg, Vienna: Herder, 1971–6), 1, pp. 93–110.

Bowen, Lloyd, 'The Battle of Britain: History and Reformation in Early Modern Wales', in Tadhg Ó hAnnracháin and Robert Armstrong (eds), *Christianities in the Early Modern Celtic World* (Basingstoke: Palgrave Macmillan, 2014), pp. 135–50.

Bray, Massimo, 'L'arcivescovo, il viceré, il fedelissimo popolo', *Nuova Rivista Storica* 74 (1990), 313–15.

Broderick, James, *The Life and Work of Blessed Robert Francis Cardinal Bellarmine, 1542–1621* (two vols, London: Burns, Oates & Washbourne, 1928).

Burke, Peter, 'How to be a Counter-Reformation Saint', in *idem, The Historical Anthropology of Early Modern Italy* (Cambridge: Cambridge University Press, 1987), pp. 48–62.

Canny, Nicholas, *Making Ireland British* (Oxford: Oxford University Press, 2002).

Capucci, Martino, 'Caratteri e Fortune di un cappucino scozzese', *Studi Secenteschi* 20 (1979), 43–88.

Caracciolo, Alberto and Caravale, Mario, *Lo Stato pontificio da Martino V a Pio IX* (Torino: UTET Università, 1978).

Cardinale, Igino, *Le Saint-Siège et la Diplomatie* (Paris: Desclee, 1962).

Carlsmith, Christopher, 'Struggling towards success: Jesuit education in Italy, 1540–1600', *History of Education Quarterly* 42 (2002), 215–46.

Carrafiello, Michael, 'English Catholicism and the Jesuit Mission of 1580–81', *Historical Journal* 37 (1994), 761–74.

Cartledge, Bryan, *The Will to Survive: A History of Hungary* (London: Timewell Press, 2006).

Catalano, Gaetano and Martino, Federico (eds.), *Potestà civile e autorità spirituale in Italia nei secoli della riforma e controriforma* (Milano: Giuffrè, 1984).

Cavazza, Silvano (ed.), *Controriforma e monarchia assoluta nelle province Austriache: Gli Asburgo, l'Europa Centrale e Gorizia all'epoca della Guerra dei Trent'Anni* (Gorizia: Istituto di storia sociale e religiosa, 1997).

Cavazza, Silvano, 'Religione, cultura e società nelle province austriache. Un bilancio storiografico', in Silvano Cavazza (ed.), *Controriforma e monarchia assoluta nelle province Austriache: Gli Asburgo, l'Europa Centrale e Gorizia all'epoca della Guerra dei Trent'Anni* (Gorizia: Istituto di storia sociale e religiosa, 1997), pp. 109–24.

Chaline, Olivier, *La Reconquête Catholique de L'Europe Centrale XVIe–XVIIe siècle* (Paris: Les Editions du Cerf, 1998).

Chaline, Olivier, 'Frontières Religieuses: La Bohême après la Montagne Blanche', in Eszter Andor and István György Tóth (eds), *Frontiers of Faith: Religious Exchange and the Constitution of Religious Identities 1400–1750* (Budapest: Central European University European Science Foundation, 2001), pp. 55–65.

Chiocchetta, Pietro, 'La S. Congregazione e gli Itali-Greci in Italia', in Josef Metzler (ed.), *Sacrae Congregationis de Propaganda Fide Memoria Rerum (350 anni a servizio della missioni 1622–1972)* (three vols, Rome, Freiburg, Vienna: Herder, 1971–6), 1, pp. 3–23.

Clark, Peter (ed.), *The European Crisis of the 1590s* (London: George Allen and Unwin, 1985).

Clarke, Aidan, *The Old English in Ireland, 1625–42* (London: Macgibbon and Kee, 1966).

Clarke, Aidan, 'Varieties of Uniformity: The First Century of the Church of Ireland', in W.J. Sheils and Diana Wood (eds), *The Churches, Ireland and the Irish: Studies in Church History* 25 (1989), 105–22.

Cochrane, Eric, 'Caesar Baronius and the Counter-Reformation', *Catholic Historical Review* 66 (1980), 53–8.

Collinson, Patrick, *The Birthpangs of Protestant England: Religious and Cultural Change in the Sixteenth and Seventeenth Centuries* (London: Macmillan, 1988).

Collinson, Patrick, 'Comment on Eamon Duffy's Neale Lecture and the Colloquium', in Nicholas Tyacke (ed.), *England's Long Reformation 1500–1800* (London: University College London Press, 1998), pp. 71–86.

Connelly, John Patrick, 'Antonio Possevino's Plan for World Evangelization', *The Catholic Historical Review* 74:2 (1988), 179–98.

Coreth, Anna, *Pietas Austriaca. Österreichische Frömmigkeit in Barock* (Vienna: Verlag für Geschichte und Politik, 1982).

Corish, Patrick, 'Bishop Nicholas French and the Second Ormond Peace, 1648–9', *Irish Historical Studies* 6 (1948), 83–100.

Corish, Patrick, 'The Cromwellian Regime, 1650–60', in T.W. Moody, F.X. Martin, and F.J. Byrne (eds), *A New History of Ireland III* (Oxford: Oxford University Press, 1976), pp. 375–86.

Corish, Patrick, *The Catholic Community in the Seventeenth and Eighteenth Centuries* (Dublin: Helicon Press, 1981).

Corish, Patrick, *The Irish Catholic Experience: a historical survey* (Dublin: Gill and Macmillan, 1985).

Corish, Patrick, 'Women and Religious Practice', in Margaret MacCurtain and Mary O'Dowd (eds), *Women in Early Modern Ireland* (Edinburgh: Edinburgh University Press, 1991), pp. 212–20.

Cregan, Donal, 'The Social and Cultural Background of a Counter-Reformation Episcopate, 1618–60', in Art Cosgrove and Donal MacCartney (eds), *Studies in Irish history presented to R. Dudley Edwards* (Dublin: University College Dublin, 1979), pp. 85–117.

Cunningham, Bernadette, 'John Colgan as historian', in Raymond Gillespie and Ruairí Ó hUiginn (eds), *Irish Europe 1600–1650: Writing and Learning* (Dublin: Four Courts Press, 2013), pp. 121–34.

Czaika, Otfried, 'La Scandinavie', in Wolfgang Kaiser (ed.), *L'Europe en conflits: Les affrontments religieux et la genèse de l'Europe modern vers 1500–vers 1650* (Rennes: Presses Universitaires de Rennes, 2008), pp. 137–68.

Dawson, Jane, 'Calvinism and the Gaidhealtachd in Scotland', in Andrew Pettegree, Alastair Duke, and Gillian Lewis (eds), *Calvinism in Europe 1540–1620* (Cambridge: Cambridge University Press, 1994), pp. 231–53.

de Maio, Romeo, 'Introduzione: Bellarmino e la Controriforma', in Romeo de Maio, Agostino Borromeo, Luigi Gulia, Georg Lutz, and Aldo Mazzacane (eds), *Bellarmino e la Controriforma* (Sora: Centro di Studi Sorani Vincenzo Patriarca, 1990), pp. xxi–xxiv.

de Mooi, Charles, 'Second-class yet self-confident: Catholics in the Dutch Generality Lands', in Benjamin Kaplan, Bob Moore, Henk Van Nierop, and Judith Pollmann (eds), *Catholic Communities in Protestant States: Britain and the Netherlands c. 1570–1720* (Manchester: Manchester University Press, 2009), pp. 156–67.

de Waele, Michel, 'Autorité, Legitimité, Fidelité: le Languedoc Ligueur et la reconnaissance d'Henri IV', *Revue d'histoire modern et contemporaine* 53:2 (2006), 5–34.

Delumeau, Jean, *Catholicism between Luther and Voltaire* (London: Burns & Oats, 1977).

Delumeau, Jean, *Le péché et la peur: La culpabilisation en Occident (Xiiie–XViiie siècles)* (Paris: Librarie Arthème Fayard, 1983).

Deslandres, Dominique, *Croire et faire croire: Les missions française au xviie siècle* (Paris: Fayard, 2003).

Ditchfield, Simon, 'How not to be Counter-Reformation Saint: The Attempted Canonization of Pope Gregory X, 1622–5', *Papers of the British School at Rome* 60 (1992), 379–422.

Ditchfield, Simon, *Liturgy, Sanctity and History in Tridentine Italy: Pietro Maria Campi and the Preservation of the Particular* (Cambridge, 1995).

Ditchfield, Simon, 'Sanctity in Early Modern Italy', *Journal of Ecclesiastical History* 47 (1996), 98–112.

Ditchfield, Simon, 'Of Missions and Models: The Jesuit Enterprise (1540–1773) Reassessed in Recent Literature', *Catholic Historical Review* 93 (2007), 325–43.

Ditchfield, Simon, 'Tridentine Worship and the Cult of Saints', in R. Po-Chia Hsia (ed.), *The Cambridge History of Christianity: Reform and Expansion* 6 (Cambridge: Cambridge University Press, 2007), pp. 201–24.

Ditchfield, Simon, 'Thinking with Saints: Sanctity and Society in the Early Modern World', *Critical Inquiry* 33 (2009), 552–84.

Dmitriev, Mikhail V., 'Western Christianity and Eastern Orthodoxy', in R. Po-Chia Hsia (ed.), *The Cambridge History of Christianity: Reform and Expansion*, 6 (Cambridge: Cambridge University Press, 2007), pp. 321–42.

Dmitriev, Mikhail V., 'Conflict and Concord in Early Modern Poland: Catholics and Orthodox at the Union of Brest', in Howard Louthan, Gary B. Cohen, and Franz A. J. Szabo (eds), *Diversity and Dissent: Negotiating Religious Difference in Central Europe, 1500–1800* (New York and Oxford: Berghahn Books, 2011), pp. 114–36.

Do Paço, David, '"La demeure de la paix"? Conflits, religions et sociétés en Europe ottoman, 1453–1683' in Wolfagng Kaiser (ed.), *L'Europe en conflits: Les affrontements religieux et la genèse de l'Europe moderne vers 1500 vers 1650* (Rennes: Presses Universitaires de Rennes, 2008), pp. 267–86.

Dolan, Frances, 'Gender and the "Lost" Spaces of Catholicism', *Journal of Interdisciplinary History* 32 (2002), 641–65.

Dolinar, France Martin, 'La cultura controriformistica nell'Austria interna: i Gesuiti a Graz e Lubiana', in Silvano Cavazza (ed.), *Controriforma e monarchia assoluta nelle province Austriache: Gli Asburgo, l'Europa Centrale e Gorizia all'epoca della Guerra dei Trent'Anni* (Gorizia: Istituto di storia sociale e religiosa, 1997), pp. 99–107.

Dompnier, Bernard, 'La France du premier XVIIe siècle et la frontiers de la Mission', *Melanges de l'École Française de Rome: Italie et Méditerranée* 109 (1997), 621–52.

Doran, Susan, 'Religion and politics at the Court of Elizabeth: the Habsburg marriage negotiations of 1559–1567', *English Historical Review* 104 (1989), 908–26.

Duffy, Eamon, 'The English Secular Clergy and the Counter-Reformation', *Journal of Ecclesiastical History* 34 (1983), 214–30.

Duffy, Eamon, 'The Long Reformation: Catholicism, Protestantism and the multitude', in Nicholas Tyacke (ed.), *England's Long Reformation 1500–1800* (London: University College London Press, 1998), pp. 33–70.

Duffy, Eamon, *The Voices of Morebath: Reformation and Rebellion in an English Village* (New Haven and London: Yale University Press, 2003).

Duffy, Eamon, *Fires of Faith: Catholic England under Mary Tudor* (New Haven and London: Yale University Press, 2009).

Duhamelle, Christophe, *L'Héritage Collectif: La Noblesse d'Église rhénane, 17e et 18e siècle* (Paris: Éditions de l'École des Hautes Études en Sciences Sociales, 1998).

Durkan, J., 'Early letter of John Brown, Minim and report to *Propaganda Fide*, 1623, by Scots Minims', *Innes Review* 52 (2001), 75–6.

Eberhard, Winfried, 'Die deutsche Reformation in Böhmen 1520–1620', in Hans Rothe (ed.), *Deutsche in den böhmischen Ländern* (Cologne: Böhlau, 1992), pp. 103–23.

Edelmayer, Friedrich, 'La Nobilità Austriaca nella prima metà del Seicento', in Silvano Cavazza (ed.), *Controriforma e monarchia assoluta nelle province Austriache: Gli Asburgo, l'Europa Centrale e Gorizia all'epoca della Guerra dei Trent'Anni* (Gorizia: Istituto di storia sociale e religiosa, 1997), pp. 61–70.

Edwards, David, 'A haven of popery: English catholic migration to Ireland in the age of plantations', in Alan Ford and John McCafferty (eds.), *The origins of sectarianism in early modern Ireland* (Cambridge: Cambridge University Press, 2005), pp. 95–126.

Elbel, Martin, 'The Making of a Perfect Friar', in Jaroslav Miller and László Kontler (eds), *Friars, Nobles and Burghers—Sermons, Images and Prints: Studies of Culture and Society in Early-Modern Europe in memoriam István György Tóth* (Budapest: Central European University Press, 2010), pp. 149–78.

Ellis, Steven, 'Economic Problems of the Church: why the Reformation failed in Ireland', *Journal of Ecclesiastical History* 41 (1990), 239–65.

Ellis, Steven, *Ireland in the age of the Tudors 1447–1603: English expansion and the end of Gaelic Rule* (London: Longman, 1998).

Evans, R.J.W., *The making of the Habsburg Monarchy 1550–1700* (3rd impression, Oxford: Clarendon Press, 1991).

Evans, R.J.W. and Thomas, T.V. (eds), *Crown, Church and Estates: Central European Politics in the Sixteenth and Seventeenth Centuries* (London and New York: Palgrave Macmillan, 1991).

Fattori, Maria Teresa, *Clemente VIII e il Sacro Collegio, 1592–1605: Meccanismi istituzionali e accentramento di governo* (Stuttgart: Hiersemann, 2004).

Feldkamp, M., 'Das Breve "Zelo Domus Dei" vom 26 November 1648', *Archivium Historiae Pontificae* 31 (1993), 293–305.

Finlayson, Michael, *Historians, Puritanism and the English Revolution* (Toronto: University of Toronto Press, 1983).

Finnegan, David, 'The influence of the Irish Catholic clergy in shaping the religious and political allegiances of Irish Catholics, 1603–41', in Robert Armstrong and Tadhg Ó hAnnracháin (eds), *Insular Christianity: Alternative models of the Church in Britain and Ireland, c. 1570–1700* (Manchester: Manchester University Press, 2013), pp. 107–28.

Ford, Alan, *The Protestant Reformation in Ireland, 1590–1641* (2nd edition, Dublin: Four Courts Press, 1997).

Fragnito, Gigliola, *Church, Censorship and Culture in Early Modern Italy* (Cambridge: Cambridge University Press, 2001).

Fragnito, Gigliola, *Proibito Capire: La Chiesa e il volgare nella prima età moderna* (Bologna: Società Editrice il Mulino, 2005).

Fraknói, Vilmos, *A Magyar Királyválasztások Története* (Máriabesnyő—Gödöllő: Attraktor Kft., 2005).

Freiberg, Jack, 'The Lateran Patronage of Gregory XIII and the Holy Year 1575', *Zeitschrift für Kunstgeschichte* 54 (1991), 66–87.

Frijhoff, Willem 'Shifting identities in hostile settings: towards a comparison of the Catholic communities in early modern Britain and the Northern Netherlands', in Benjamin Kaplan, Bob Moore, Henk Van Nierop, and Judith Pollmann (eds), *Catholic Communities in Protestant States: Britain and the Netherlands c. 1570–1720* (Manchester: Manchester University Press, 2009), pp. 1–17.

Frost, Robert 'Union as process: Confused sovereignty and the Polish-Lithuanian Commonwealth, 1500–1795', in Micheál Ó Siochrú and Andrew Mackillop (eds), *Forging the State: European State Formation and the Anglo-Scottish Union of 1707* (Dundee: Dundee University Press, 2009), pp. 69–92.

Galeota, Gustavo, 'Genesi, Sviluppo e fortuna delle *Controversiae* di Roberto Bellarmino', in Romeo de Maio, Agostino Borromeo, Luigi Gulia, Georg Lutz, and Aldo Mazzacane (eds), *Bellarmino e la Controriforma* (Sora: Centro di Studi Sorani Vincenzo Patriarca, 1990), pp. 3–48.

Gandy, M., 'Ordinary Catholics in mid-17th century London' in Marie Rowlands (ed.), *English Catholics of parish and town* (London: Catholic Record Society, 1999), pp. 153–77.

Gentilcore, David, 'Methods and Approaches in the Social History of the Counter-Reformation in Italy', *Social History* 17 (1992), 73–98.

Giannini, Massimo Carlo, 'Note sul problema del controllo politico degli Ordini religiosi nell'Italia della prima metà del seicento' in C.J. Hernando Sánchez (ed.), *Roma y España. Un crisol de la cultura europea en la Edad Moderna* (Madrid: SEACEX, 2007), pp. 551–76.

Giblin, Cathaldus, (ed.), *Irish Franciscan Mission to Scotland, 1619–46* (Dublin: Assisi Press, 1964).

Gillespie, Raymond and Ó hUiginn, Ruairí (eds), *Irish Europe 1600–1650: Writing and Learning* (Dublin: Four Courts Press, 2013).

Gorski, Karol, 'L'histoire de la spiritualité polonaise', in Marian Rechowicz (ed.), *Millénaire du Catholicisme en Pologne* (Lublin: The Scientific Society of the Catholic University in Lublin, 1969), pp. 281–354.

Gregory, Jeremy, 'The making of a Protestant nation: "success" and "failure" in England's Long Reformation', in Nicholas Tyacke (ed.), *England's Long Reformation 1500–1800* (London: University College London Press, 1998), pp. 307–33.

Gudziak, Borys, *Crisis and Reform: The Kyivan Metropolitanate, the Patriarchate of Constantinople and the Genesis of the Union of Brest* (Cambridge, MA: Harvard University Press, 1998).

Gürkan, Emre Safa, 'The Centre and the Frontier: Ottoman Cooperation with the North African Corsairs in the Sixteenth Century', *Turkish Historical Review* 1 (2010), 125–63.

Haigh, Christopher, 'From Monopoly to Minority: Catholicism in Early Modern England', *Transactions of the Royal Historical Society* fifth series 31 (1981), 129–47.

Haigh, Christopher, 'Revisionism, the Reformation and the History of English Catholicism', *Journal of Ecclesiastical History* 36 (1985), 394–405.

Haigh, Christopher, *The Plain Man's Pathways to Heaven: Kinds of Christianity in Post-Reformation England, 1570–1640* (Oxford: Oxford University Press, 2007).

Hargittay, Emil (ed.), *Pázmány Péter és kora* (Piliscsaba: PPKE BTK, 2001).

Harris, Steven J., 'Transposing the Merton Thesis: Apostolic Spirituality and the Establishment of the Jesuit Scientific Tradition', *Science in Context* 3 (1989), 29–65.

Harris, Steven J., 'Confession Building, Long-Distance Networks and the Organization of Jesuit Science', *Early Science and Medicine* 1 (1996), 287–318.

Harris, Steven J., 'Mapping Jesuit Science: The Role of Travel in the Geography of Knowledge', in Gauvin Alexander Balley, Steven J. Harris, John O'Malley, and T. Frank Kennedy (eds), *The Jesuits: Cultures, Sciences and the Arts, 1540–1773* (Toronto: University of Toronto Press, 1999), pp. 212–40.

Hefner, Robert, 'Multiple Modernities: Christianity, Islam and Hinduism in a Globalizing Age', *Annual Review of Anthropology* 27 (1998), 83–104.

Hermann, Christian, *L'Eglise d'Espagne sous le patronage Royal (1476–1834)* (Madrid: Casa del Velásquez, 1988).

Hibbard, Caroline, 'Early Stuart Catholicism: revisions and re-revisions', *Journal of Modern History* 52 (1980), 1–34.

Hill, J.E.C., 'Puritans and the "Dark Corners of the Land"', *Transactions of the Royal Historical Society* fifth series 13 (1963), 77–102.

Hilton, J.A., 'The Catholic poor: Vagabonds and paupers 1580–1780', in Marie Rowlands (ed.), *English Catholics of parish and town* (London: Catholic Record Society, 1999), pp. 115–28.

Hroch, Miroslav and Barteček, Ivo, 'Die Böhmische frage im Dreissigjährigen Krieg', *Historische Zeitschrift Beihefte* new series 26 (1998), 447–60.

Ingegneri, Gabriele, 'L'opera dei Cappuccini nell'Europa centro-orientale', in Silvano Cavazza (ed.), *Controriforma e monarchia assoluta nelle province Austriache: Gli Asburgo, l'Europa Centrale e Gorizia all'epoca della Guerra dei Trent'Anni* (Gorizia: Istituto di storia sociale e religiosa, 1997), pp. 90–9.

Jacqueline, Bernard, 'Missions en France', in Josef Metzler (ed.), *Sacrae Congregationis de Propaganda Fide Memoria Rerum (350 anni a servizio della missioni 1622–1972)* (three vols, Rome, Freiburg, Vienna: Herder, 1971–6), 1, pp. 111–48.

Jeffries, Henry, *The Irish Church and the Tudor Reformations* (Dublin: Four Courts Press, 2010).

Jenkins, Philip, 'The Anglican Church and the unity of Britain: the Welsh experience, 1560–1714', in Steven Ellis and Sarah Barber (eds), *Conquest and Union: Fashioning a British state 1485–1725* (Harlow: Longman, 1995), pp. 115–38.

Jobert, Ambroise, *De Luther à Mohila: La Pologne dans la crise de la chrétienté, 1517–1648* (Paris: Institut d'Études Slaves, 1974).

Kaiser Wolfgang (ed.), *L'Europe en conflits: Les affrontments religieux et la genèse de l'Europe modern vers 1500–vers 1650* (Rennes: Presses Universitaires de Rennes, 2008).

Kamen, Henry, 'Toleration and Dissent in Sixteenth-Century Spain: The Alternative Tradition', *Sixteenth-Century Journal* 19 (1988), 3–23.

Kamen, Henry, *The Phoenix and the flame: Catalonia and the Counter Reformation* (New Haven and London: Yale University Press, 1993).

Kaplan, Benjamin, '"Remnants of the Papal Yoke": Apathy and Opposition in the Dutch Reformation', *Sixteenth Century Journal* 25 (1994), 653–69.

Kaplan, Benjamin and Moore, Bob, Van Nierop, Henk, and Pollmann, Judith (eds), *Catholic Communities in Protestant States: Britain and the Netherlands c. 1570–1720* (Manchester: Manchester University Press, 2009).

Kaplan, Benjamin and Pollmann, Judith, 'Conclusion: Catholic minorities in Protestant states, Britain and the Netherlands, c. 1570–1720', in Benjamin Kaplan, Bob Moore, Henk Van Nierop, and Judith Pollmann (eds), *Catholic Communities in Protestant States: Britain and the Netherlands c. 1570–1720* (Manchester: Manchester University Press, 2009), pp. 249–64.

Kearney, Hugh, 'Ecclesiastical Politics and the Counter-Reformation in Ireland, 1618–48', *Journal of Ecclesiastical History* 11 (1960), 202–12.

Kearney, Hugh, *Strafford in Ireland: A study in absolutism* (2nd edition, Cambridge: Cambridge University Press, 1989).

Kesselring, K.J., *The Northern Rebellion of 1569* (Basingstoke: Palgrave Macmillan, 2010).

Kilroy, Phil, 'Women and the Reformation', in Margaret MacCurtain and Mary O'Dowd (eds), *Women in Early Modern Ireland* (Edinburgh: Edinburgh University Press, 1991), pp. 179–96.

Kirk, James, *Patterns of Reform: Continuity and Change in the Reformation Kirk* (Edinburgh: T. & T. Clark, 1989).

Kloczowski, Jerzy, 'Some Remarks on the Social and Religious History of Sixteenth-Century Poland', in Samuel Fiszman (ed.), *The Polish Renaissance in its European Context* (Bloomington and Indianapolis: Indiana University Press, 1988), pp. 96–110.

Knoll, Paul, 'Religious Toleration in Sixteenth Century Poland: Political Realities and Social Constraints', in Howard Louthan, Gary B. Cohen, and Franz A. J. Szabo (eds), *Diversity and Dissent: Negotiating Religious Difference in Central Europe, 1500–1800* (New York and Oxford: Berghahn Books, 2011), pp. 30–52.

Kooi, Christine, 'Popish Impudence: The Perseverance of the Roman Catholic Faithful in Calvinist Holland, 1572–1620', *Sixteenth Century Journal* 26 (1995), 75–85.

Kooi, Christine, '*Sub Jugo Haereticorum*: Minority Catholicism in Early Modern Europe', in Kathleen Comerford and Hilman Pabel (eds), *Early Modern Catholicism. Essays in Honour of John W. O'Malley, S. J.* (Toronto: University of Toronto Press, 2001), pp. 147–62.

Kortepeter, C.M., 'Ġāzī Girāy II, Khan of the Crimea, and Ottoman Policy in Eastern Europe and the Caucasus, 1588–94', *The Slavonic and East European Review* 44:102 (1966), 139–6.

Kowalski, Waldemar, 'From the Land of Diverse Sects to National Religion: Converts to Catholicism and Reformed Franciscans in Early Modern Poland', *Church History* 70 (2001), 482–526.

Kowalski, Waldemar, 'Change in Continuity: Post-Tridentine Rural and Township Parish Life in the Cracow Diocese', *Sixteenth Century Journal* 35 (2004), 689–715.

Krasenbrink, Josef, *Die Congregatio Germanica und die katholische Reform in Deutschland nach dem Tridentinum* (Münster: Aschendorff, 1972).

Krokar, James, 'New means to an old end: Early modern maps in the service of an anti-Ottoman Crusade', *Imago Mundi* 60:1 (2008), 23–38.

Liptai, Ervin (ed.) *Magyarország Hadtörténete* (two volumes, Budapest: Zrínyi Katonai Kiadó, 1984).

Litak, Stanislaus, 'La paroisse du XVIe au XVIIIe siècle' in Marian Rechowicz (ed.), *Millénaire du Catholicisme en Pologne* (Lublin: The Scientific Society of the Catholic University in Lublin, 1969), pp. 109–19.

Loserth, J., 'Die Steirische Religionspazifikation und di Fälschung des Vizekanzlers Dr. Wolfgang Schranz', *Jahrbuck der Gesellschaft für die Geschichte des Protestantismus in Österreich* 48 (1927), 1–57.

Lotz-Heumann, Ute, 'Confessionalisation in Ireland: periodisation and character, 1534–1649', in Alan Ford and John McCafferty (eds.), *The origins of sectarianism in early modern Ireland* (Cambridge: Cambridge University Press, 2005), pp. 24–53.

Louthan, Howard, *Converting Bohemia: Force and Persuasion in the Catholic Reformation* (Cambridge: Cambridge University Press, 2009).

Louthan, Howard, Cohen, Gary B., and Szabo, Franz A. J. (eds), *Diversity and Dissent: Negotiating Religious Difference in Central Europe, 1500–1800* (New York and Oxford: Berghahn Books, 2011).

Luria, Keith P., *Sacred Boundaries, Religious Co-existence and Conflict in Early-Modern France* (Washington D.C.: Catholic University of America Press, 2005).

Lyons, Mary Ann, 'St Anthony's College Louvain: Gaelic texts and articulating Irish identity, 1607–40', in Raymond Gillespie and Ruairí Ó hUiginn (eds), *Irish Europe 1600–1650: Writing and Learning* (Dublin: Four Courts Press, 2013), pp. 21–43.

Mac Craith, Mícheál, 'The political and religious thought of Florence Conry and Hugh McCaughwell', in Alan Ford and John McCafferty (eds.), *The origins of sectarianism in early modern Ireland* (Cambridge: Cambridge University Press, 2005), pp. 183–202.

Mac Craith, Mícheál, 'Collegium S. Antonii Lovanii, quod Collegium est unicum remedium ad conservandam Provinciam', in Edel Bhreathnach, Joseph MacMahon, and John McCafferty (eds), *The Irish Franciscans, 1534–1990* (Dublin: Four Courts Press, 2009), pp. 233–59.

Mac Cuarta, Brian, *Catholic Revival in the North of Ireland, 1603–41* (Dublin: Four Courts Press, 2007).

MacCurtain, Margaret, 'Women, education and learning in early modern Ireland', in Margaret MacCurtain and Mary O'Dowd (eds), *Women in Early Modern Ireland* (Edinburgh: Edinburgh University Press, 1991), pp. 160–78.

MacHardy, Karin J., 'The Rise of Absolutism and Noble Rebellion in Early Modern Habsburg Austria, 1570–1620', *Comparative Studies in Society and History* 34 (1992), 407–38.

MacHardy, Karin J., 'Cultural Capital, Noble Identities and Family Strategies in Early Modern Habsburg Austria, 1579–1620', *Past & Present* 163 (1999), 36–75.

Macinnes, Alan, 'Catholic recusancy and the penal laws, 1603–1707', *Records of the Scottish Church History Society* 23 (1987), 27–63.

Mączak, Antoni, 'The Structure of Power in the Commonwealth of the Sixteenth and Seventeenth Centuries', in J.K. Fedorowicz, Maria Bogucka, and Henryk Samsonowicz (eds), *A Republic of Nobles: Studies in Polish History to 1864* (Cambridge: Cambridge University Press, 1982), pp. 109–34.

Majorana, Bernadette, 'Une pastorale spectaculaire: Missions et missionnaires jésuites en Italie (XVIe-XVIIIe siècle)', *Annales, Histoire, Sciences Sociales* 57 (2002), 297–320.

Makkai, László, Mócsy, András, and Szász, Zoltán (eds), *Erdély Története* (three vols, Budapest: Akadémiai Kiadó, 1986).

Maltby, Judith, *Prayer Book and People in Elizabethan and Early Stuart England* (Cambridge: Cambridge University Press, 1998).

Mancia, Anita, 'La Controversia con i Protestanti ed i programme degli studi teologici nella Compagnia di Gesù (1547–1599), *Archivium Historicum Societatis Iesu* 54 (1985), 1–43.

Mant, Richard, *History of the Church of Ireland, from the Reformation to the Revolution* (London: J.W. Parker, 1840).

Martin, Lynn, 'Papal Policy and European Conflict, 1559–1572', *Sixteenth Century Journal* 11:2 (1980), 35–48.

Martin, Lynn, 'Vocational Crises and the Crisis in Vocations among Jesuits in France during the Sixteenth Century', *Catholic Historical Review* 72 (1986), 201–21.

Mat'a, Petr, 'Der Adel aus den böhmischen Landern am Kaiserhof 1620–1720: Versuch eine falsche Frage richtig zu lösen', in Václav Bůžek and Pavel Král (eds), *Šlechta v habsburské monarchii a císařský dvur, České Budějovice Opera historica* 10 (2003), pp. 191–203.

Mat'a, Petr, 'Vorkonfessionelles, überkonfessionelles, transkonfessionelles Christentum: Prolegomena zu einer Untersuchung der Konfessionalität des böhmischen und mährischen Hochadels zwischen Hussitismus und Zwangskatholisierung', in Joachim Bahlcke, Karen Lambrecht, and Hans-Christian Maner (eds), *Konfessionelle Pluralität als Herausforderung: Koexistenz und Konflikt in Spätmittelalter und Frühen Neuzeit. Winfried Eberhard zum 65. Geburtstag* (Leipzig: Leipziger Universitätsverlag, 2006), pp. 307–31.

Mat'a, Petr, 'Constructing and Crossing Confessional Boundaries: The High Nobility and the Reformation of Bohemia', in Howard Louthan, Gary B. Cohen, and Franz A.J. Szabo (eds), *Diversity and Dissent: Negotiating Religious Difference in Central Europe, 1500–1800* (New York and Oxford: Berghahn Books, 2011), pp. 10–29.

Mazzone, Umberto, 'I dibattiti tridentini: techniche di assemblea e di controllo', in Paolo Prodi and Wolfgang Reinhard (eds), *Il Concilio di Trento e il moderno: Annali dell'Istituto Storico Italo-Germanico Quaderno 45* (Bologna: Il Mulino, 1996), pp. 101–36.

McCoog, Thomas M., '"Replant the uprooted trunk of the tree of faith": the Society of Jesus and the continental colleges for religious exiles', in Robert Armstrong and Tadhg Ó hAnnracháin (eds), *Insular Christianity: Alternative models of the church in Britain and Ireland c. 1570–c.1700* (Manchester: Manchester University Press, 2013), pp. 28–48.

McCormack, Anthony, *The Earldom of Desmond, 1463–1583: The Decline and Crisis of a Feudal Lordship* (Dublin: Four Courts Press, 2005).

McCullough, Diarmaid, 'Putting the English Reformation on the map', *Transactions of the Royal Historical Society* 15 (2005), 75–95.

McGrath, Patrick, 'Elizabethan Catholicism: a reconsideration', *Journal of Ecclesiastical History* 35 (1984), 414–28.

Metzler, Josef, 'Foundation of the Congregation "de Propaganda Fide" by Gregory XV', in Josef Metzler (ed.), *Sacrae Congregationis de Propaganda Fide Memoria Rerum (350 anni a servizio della missioni 1622–1972)* (three vols, Rome, Freiburg, Vienna: Herder, 1971–6), pp. 79–111.

Metzler, Josef, 'Francesco Ingoli der erste Sekretär der Kongregation (1578–1649)', in Josef Metzler (ed.), *Sacrae Congregationis de Propaganda Fide Memoria Rerum (350 anni a servizio della missioni 1622–1972)* (three vols, Rome, Freiburg, Vienna: Herder, 1971–6), pp. 197–42.

Metzler, Josef, (ed.), *Sacrae Congregationis de Propaganda Fide Memoria Rerum (350 anni a servizio della missioni 1622–1972)* (three vols, Rome, Freiburg, Vienna: Herder, 1971–6).

Miller, James, 'The Origins of Polish Arianism', *Sixteenth Century Journal* 16 (1985), 229–56.

Milton, Anthony, 'A Qualified Intolerance: the Limits and Ambiguities of Early Stuart Anti-Catholicism', in A. Marotti (ed.), *Catholicism and Anti-Catholicism in Early Modern English Texts* (London: St Martin's Press, 1999), pp. 85–115.

Molnár, Antal, 'Pietro Massarecchi Antivari Érsek és Szendrői Apostoli Adminisztrátor Egyházlátogatási Jelentése a Hódólt Dél-Magyarországról (1633)', *Fons* 2 (1995), 175–219.

Molnár, Antal, 'A kalocsai érsekség a XVII századi püspöki processzusok tanúvallomásainak tükrében', in Zsuzsanna J. Újvári (ed.), *Ezredforduló—századforduló—hetvenedik évforduló. Ünnepi tanulmányok Zimányi Vera tiszteletére* (Piliscsaba: PPKE, 2001), pp. 140–63.

Molnár, Antal, 'A horvát és magyar katolikus Biblia-fordítás és a romai inkvizízió', *Magyar Könyvszemle* 118 (2002), 24–37.

Molnár, Antal, *Katolikus missziók a hódolt Magyarországon I 1572–1647* (Budapest: Balassi Kiadó, 2002).

Morey, A., *The Catholic Subjects of Elizabeth I* (London: George Allen and Unwin, 1978).

Müller, Wieslaw, 'Structure administrative des dioceses catholiques latins en Pologne du xvie au xviiie siècle', in Marian Rechowicz (ed.), *Millénaire du Catholicisme en Pologne* (Lublin: The Scientific Society of the Catholic University in Lublin, 1969), pp. 105–9.

Mullett, Michael, '"So they become contemptible": clergy and laity in a mission territory', in Benjamin Kaplan, Bob Moore, Henk Van Nierop, and Judith Pollmann (eds), *Catholic Communities in Protestant States: Britain and the Netherlands c. 1570–1720* (Manchester: Manchester University Press, 2009), pp. 33–47.

Murdock, Graeme, 'Un espace-carrefour: l'Europe centrale', in Wolfgang Kaiser (ed.), *L'Europe en conflits: les Affrontements religieux et la genèse de l'Europe modern vers 1500–vers 1650* (Rennes: Presses Universitaires de Rennes, 2008), pp. 221–38.

Murphey, Rhoads, *Ottoman Warfare, 1500–1700* (New Brunswick, N.J.: Rutgers University Press, 1999).

Murray, James, 'The diocese of Dublin in the sixteenth century: clerical opposition and the failure of the Reformation', in James Kelly and Daire Keogh (eds), *History of the Catholic Diocese of Dublin* (Dublin: Four Courts Press, 2000), pp. 92–111.

Murray, James, *Enforcing the English Reformation in Ireland: clerical resistance and political conflict in the Diocese of Dublin, 1534–1590* (Cambridge: Cambridge University Press, 2009).

Murray, James and Brady, Ciaran, 'Sir Henry Sidney and the Reformation in Ireland', in Elizabethanne Boran and Crawford Gribben (eds), *Enforcing Reformation in Ireland and Scotland, 1550–1700* (Aldershot: Ashgate Publishing, 2006), pp. 14–39.

Nešev, Georgi, 'La propaganda catholique dans les terres bulgares au XVIIe siècle et le développement historique du Sud-Est européen', *Bulgarian Historical Review* 3 (1975), 43–52.

Newman, P.R., 'Roman Catholic Royalists: papist commanders under Charles I and Charles II', *Recusant History* 15 (1981), 396–405.

Nicholls, Kenneth, 'The other massacre: English killings of Irish, 1641–2', in David Edwards, Pádraig Lenihan, and Clodagh Tait (eds), *Age of Atrocity: Violence and Political Conflict in Early Modern Ireland* (Dublin: Four Courts Press, 2007) pp. 176–91.

Nicholls, Mark, 'Strategy and Motivation in the Gunpowder Plot', *Historical Journal* 50 (2007), 787–807.

Niederkorn, Jan Paul, *Die europäischen Mächte und der 'Lange Turkenkrieg' Kaiser Rudolfs. II (1593–1606)* (Vienna:Verlag der österreichischen Akademie der Wissenschaften, 1993).

Norelli, Enrico, 'The authority attributed to the early church in the *Centuries of Magdeburg* and the *Ecclesiastical Annals* of Caesar Baronius', in Irena Backus (ed.), *The Reception of the Church Fathers in the West from the Carolingians to the Maurists* (two vols, Leiden, New York, Köln: Brill, 1997), 2, pp. 745–74.

Noyes, Ruth, 'On the Fringes of Centre: Disputed Hagiographic Imagery and the Crisis over the *Beati Moderni* in Rome c. 1600', *Renaissance Quarterly* 64:3 (Fall 2011), 800–46.

Nussdorfer, Laurie, 'The Vacant See: Ritual and Protest in Early Modern Rome', *Sixteenth Century Journal* 18 (1987), 173–89.

O'Banion, Patrick, 'Only the king can do it: Adaptability and Flexibility in Crusade Ideology in Sixteenth-Century Spain', *Church History* 81:3 (2012), 552–74.

Ó Buachalla, Breandán, '*Annála Ríoghachta Éireann* is *Foras Feasa ar Éirinn*: An Comhthéacs Comhaimseartha', *Studia Hibernica* 22–3 (1982–3), 59–105.

Ó Buachalla, Breandán, 'Na Stíobhartaigh agus an t-aos léinn: Cing Seamas', *Proceedings of the Royal Irish Academy* 83 (1983), section C, 81–134.

O'Connell, Marvin, *Thomas Stapleton and the Counter Reformation* (New Haven and London: Yale University Press, 1964).

O'Connor, Thomas, 'Hugh O'Neill: free spirit, religious chameleon or ardent Catholic?', in Hiram Morgan (ed.), *The Battle of Kinsale* (Bray: Wordwell, 2004), pp. 59–72.

Ó hAnnracháin, Tadhg, 'Vatican diplomacy and the mission of Rinuccini to Ireland', *Archivium Hibernicum* 47 (1993), 78–88.

Ó hAnnracháin, Tadhg, *Catholic Reformation in Ireland: The Mission of Rinuccini, 1645–49* (Oxford: Oxford University Press, 2002).

Ó hAnnracháin, Tadhg, 'Theory in the Absence of Fact: Irish Women and the Catholic Reformation', in Christine Meek (ed.), *Pawns or Players: Studies on Medieval and Early Modern Women* (Dublin: Four Courts Press, 2003), pp. 141–54.

Ó hAnnracháin, Tadhg, 'Conflicting loyalties, conflicted rebels: Political and religious allegiance among the Confederate Catholics of Ireland', *English Historical Review* 119 (2004), 851–72.

Ó hAnnracháin, Tadhg, 'The consolidation of Irish Catholicism within a hostile Imperial framework: A comparative study of Early Modern Hungary and Ireland', in Hilary Carey (ed.), *Empires of Religion* (Basingstoke: Palgrave Macmillan, 2008), pp. 25–42.

Ó hAnnracháin, Tadhg, 'Guerre de religion ou guerre ethnique? les conflits religieux en Irlande 1500–1650', *Revue Historique* 647 (2009), 65–97.

Ó hAnnracháin, Tadhg, 'The Maintenance of Habsburg Rule in Early Modern Hungary', in Micheál Ó Siochrú and Andrew Mackillop (eds), *Forging the State. European State Formation and the Anglo-Scottish Union of 1707* (Dundee: Dundee University Press, 2009), pp. 87–100.

Ó hAnnracháin, Tadhg, 'The Miraculous Mathematics of the World: Proving the existence of God in Cardinal Péter Pázmány's *Kalauz*', *Studies in Church History* 46 (2010), 248–59.

Ó hAnnracháin, Tadhg, 'Bridging the Ethnic Divide: Creating a Catholic Identity in Early Modern Ireland', in Rita Librandi and Maria D'Anzi (eds), *Lingua e testi delle riforme cattoliche in Europa e nelle Americhe* (Cesati, Firenze, 2013), pp. 265–79.

Ó hAnnracháin, Tadhg, 'Introduction: Religious Acculturation and Affiliation in Early Modern Gaelic Scotland, Gaelic Ireland, Wales and Cornwall', in Tadhg Ó hAnnracháin and Robert Armstrong (eds), *Christianities in the Early Modern Celtic World* (Basingstoke: Palgrave Macmillan, 2014), pp. 1–16.

Ó hAnnracháin, Tadhg, 'Plantation, 1580–1641', in Alvin Jackson (ed.), *The Oxford Handbook of Modern Irish History* (Oxford: Oxford University Press, 2014), pp. 291–315.

Ó hAnnracháin, Tadhg, 'The Bishop's Role in Two Non-Catholic States: the Cases of Ireland and Turkish Hungary Considered', *Church History and Religious Culture* 95 (2015).

Ó hAnnracháin, Tadhg and Armstrong, Robert, 'An alternative establishment: the evolution of the Irish Catholic hierarchy, 1600–49', in Robert Armstrong and Tadhg Ó hAnnracháin (eds), *Insular Christianity: Alternative models of the Church in Britain and Ireland, c. 1570–1700* (Manchester: Manchester University Press, 2013), pp. 190–206.

Ó hAnnracháin, Tadhg and Armstrong, Robert, (eds), *Celtic Christianities in the early modern world* (Basingstoke: Palgrave, 2014).

Ó hAnnracháin, Tadhg and Armstrong, Robert, 'The Bishop's Role in Two Non-Catholic States: the Cases of Ireland and Turkish Hungary Considered', in Jan Wim Buisman, Marjet Derks and Peter Raedts (eds), *Sacred Authority or Personal Charisma? Religious Leadership in Europe, 1100–2000* (Leiden/Boston: Brill, forthcoming 2015).

O'Malley, John, *Trent and All That: Renaming Catholicism in the Early Modern Era* (Cambridge, MA: Harvard University Press, 2000).

Ó Riain, Pádraig, 'The Louvain Achievement II: Hagiography', in Edel Bhreathnach, Joseph MacMahon, and John McCafferty (eds), *The Irish Franciscans, 1534–1990* (Dublin, Four Courts Press, 2009), pp. 189–200.

Obirek, Stanislaw, 'Jesuits in Poland and Eastern Europe', in Thomas Worcester (ed.), *The Cambridge Companion to the Jesuits* (Cambridge: Cambridge University Press, 2008), pp. 136–50.

Oborni, Teréz, *Erdély Fejedelmi* (Budapest: Pannonica Kiadó, 2002).

Ogilvie, Sheilagh, 'Germany and the General Crisis', *Historical Journal* 35 (1992), 417–41.

Ogilvie, Sheilagh, '"So that every subject knows how to behave": Social Disciplining in Early Modern Bohemia', *Comparative Studies in Society and History* 48 (2006), 38–78.

Ohlmeyer, Jane, *Making Ireland English: The Irish Aristocracy in the Seventeenth Century* (New Haven: Yale University Press, 2012).

Olson, Katharine, '"Slow and cold in the true service of God": Popular Beliefs and Practices, Conformity, and Reformation in Wales, c. 1530–1600', in Tadhg Ó hAnnracháin and Robert Armstrong (eds), *Celtic Christianities in the early modern world* (Basingstoke: Palgrave, 2014), pp. 92–110.

Őry, Miklós and Szabó, Ferenc, 'Pázmány Péter (1570–1637)', in Miklós Őry, Ferenc Szabó, and Péter Vass (eds), *Pázmány Péter Válogatás Műveiből* (Budapest: Szent István Társulat Az Apostoli Szentszék Könyvkiadója, 1983), pp. 48–53.

Palmitessa, James R., 'The Prague Uprising of 1611: Property, Politics and Catholic Renewal in the Early years of Habsburg Rule', *Central European History* 31 (1998), 299–328.

Pánek, Jaroslav, 'The Religious Question and the Political System in Bohemia before and after the Battle of the White Mountain', in R.J.W. Evans and T.V. Thomas (eds), *Crown, Church and Estates: Central European Politics in the Sixteenth and Seventeenth Centuries* (London and New York: Palgrave Macmillan, 1991), pp. 129–48.

Parish, Richard, *Catholic Particularity in Seventeenth Century French Writing* (Oxford: Oxford University Press, 2011).

Parker, Charles H., 'Paying for the Privilege: The Management of Public Order and Religious Pluralism in two Early Modern Societies', *Journal of World History* 17 (2006), 267–96.

Parker, Charles H., *Faith on the Margins: Catholics and Catholicism in the Dutch Golden Age* (Cambridge, MA and London: Harvard University Press, 2008).

Parker, Charles H., 'Cooperative confessionalisation: lay-clerical collaboration in Dutch Catholic communities during the Golden Age', in Benjamin Kaplan, Bob Moore, Henk Van Nierop, and Judith Pollmann (eds), *Catholic Communities in Protestant States: Britain and the Netherlands c. 1570–1720* (Manchester: Manchester University Press, 2009), pp. 18–32.

Parker, Geoffrey, *The Dutch Revolt* (Ithaca, NY: Cornell University Press, 1977).

Parker, Geoffrey and Smith, L.M., 'Introduction', in Geoffrey Parker and L.M. Smith (eds), *Europe and the General Crisis* (London and New York: Routledge, 1997), pp. 1–31.

Partner, Peter, 'Papal Financial Policy in the Renaissance and the Counter-Reformation', *Past & Present* 88 (1980), 17–62.

Patrouch, Joseph F., 'Who pays for building the Rectory? Religious Conflicts in the Upper Austrian parish of Dietach, 1540–82', *Sixteenth Century Journal* 26 (1995), 297–310.

Pavone, Sabina, *I Gesuiti: dalle origini alle soppressione, 1540–1773* (Rome and Bari: Editori Laterza, 2004).

Pawlikowska-Butterwick, Wioletta, 'A "Foreign" Elite? The Territorial Origins of the Canons and Prelates of the Cathedral Chapter of Vilna in the second half of the Sixteenth Century', *The Slavonic and East European Review* 92:1 (January, 2014), 44–80.

Perrone, Sean T., 'The Procurator General of the Castilian Assembly of the Clergy, 1592–1741', *Catholic Historical Review* 91 (2005), 26–59.

Péter, Katalin, *Esterházy Miklós* (Budapest: Gondolat, 1985).

Pizzorusso, Giovanni '"Per servizio della Sacra Congregazione de Propaganda Fide": i nunzi apostolici e le missioni tra centralità romana e chiesa universal (1622–1660)', *Cheiron* 15/30 (1998), 201–27.

Po-chia Hsia, R., *The World of Catholic Renewal, 1540–1770* (Cambridge: Cambridge University Press, 1998).

Po-chia Hsia, R., *The Cambridge History of Christianity: Reform and Expansion* (Cambridge: Cambridge University Press, 2007).

Pollmann, Judith, 'Countering the Reformation in France and the Netherlands: Clerical Leadership and Catholic Violence 1560–85', *Past & Present* 190 (2006), 83–120.

Polman, Pontien, *L'élément historique dans la controverse religieuse du XVIe siècle* (Gembloux: J. Duculot, 1932).

Pörtner, Regina, *The Counter-Reformation in Central Europe: Styria 1580–1630* (Oxford: Clarendon Press, 2001).

Poutrin, Isabelle, 'Cas de conscience et affaires d'État: le ministère du confesseur royal en Espagne sous Philippe III', *Revue d'histoire moderne et contemporaine* 53 (2006), 7–28.

Prodi, Paolo, *Il sovrano pontefice* (Bologna: Il Mulino, 1982).

Questier, Michael, 'Arminianism, Catholicism and Puritanism in England during the 1630s', *Historical Journal* 49 (2006), 53–78.

Questier, Michael, *Catholicism and community in early modern England: politics, aristocratic patronage and religion, c. 1550–1640* (Cambridge: Cambridge University Press, 2006).

Rainer, Johann, 'L'assolutismo politico e confessionale in Austria nei secoli XVI e XVII', in Silvano Cavazza (ed.), *Controriforma e monarchia assoluta nelle province Austriache: Gli Asburgo, l'Europa Centrale e Gorizia all'epoca della Guerra dei Trent'Anni* (Gorizia: Istituto di storia sociale e religiosa, 1997), pp. 11–28.

Rebel, Hermann, 'The Rural Subject Population of Upper Austria' (PhD dissertation, University of California, Berkeley, 1976).

Reddaway, W.F., Penson, J. H., Halecki, O., and Dyboski, R. (eds), *The Cambridge History of Poland from the origins to Sobieski (To 1696)* (Cambridge: Cambridge University Press, 1950).

Reinhard, Wolfgang, 'Il Concilio di Trento e la modernizzazione della Chiesa' in Paolo Prodi and Wolfgang Reinhard (eds), *Il concilio di Trento e il moderno* (Bologna: Il Mulino, 1996), pp. 27–53.

Richgels, Robert, 'The Pattern of Controversy in a Counter-Reformation Classic: the *Controversies* of Robert Bellarmine', *Sixteenth Century Journal* 11:2 (1980), 3–15.

Roberts, Peter, 'Tudor Wales, National Identity and the British Inheritance', in P. Roberts and B. Bradshaw (eds), *British Consciousness and Identity: The Making of Britain, 1533–1707* (Cambridge: Cambridge University Press, 1998), pp. 8–42.

Robinson, Philip, *The Plantation of Ulster: British Settlement in an Irish Landscape 1600–1670* (2nd edition, Belfast: Ulster Historical Foundation, 1994).

Roden, Marie-Louise, 'Cardinal Decio Azzolino and Papal Nepotism', *Archivium Historiae Pontificae* 34 (1996), 127–57.

Rosa, Maria, 'The "World's theatre": the court of Rome and politics in the first half of the seventeenth century', in Gianvittorio Signorotto and Maria Antonietta Visceglia (eds), *Court and Politics in Papal Rome, 1492–1700* (Cambridge: Cambridge University Press, 2002), pp. 78–98.

Rothe, Hans (ed.), *Deutsche in den böhmischen Ländern* (Cologne: Böhlau, 1992).

Rothenberg, G.E., 'Christan Insurrections in Turkish Dalmatia, 1580–1596', *The Slavonic and East European Review* 40:94 (1961), 136–47.

Rowlands, Marie, 'Hidden people: Catholic Commoners 1558–1625', in Marie Rowlands (ed.), *English Catholics of parish and town* (London: Catholic Record Society, 1999), pp. 10–35.

Russell, Conrad, *Parliaments and English Politics, 1621–29* (London and Oxford: Clarendon Press, 1979).

Ryan, Salvador, '"New wine in old bottles": implementing Trent in early modern Ireland', in Thomas Herron and Michael Potterton (eds), *Ireland in the Renaissance, c.1540–1660* (Dublin: Four Courts Press, 2007), pp. 122–37.

Ryrie, Alec, *The Age of Reformation: The Tudor and Stewart Realms 1485–1603* (Harlow: Pearson Longman, 2009).

Sample Wilson, Christie, *Beyond Belief: Surviving the Revocation of the Edict of Nantes in France* (Bethlehem, Penn.: Lehigh University Press, 2011).

Sanchez, Magdalena, 'A House Divided: Spain, Austria and the Bohemian and Hungarian Successions', *Sixteenth Century Journal* 25:4 (1994), 887–903.

Schilling, Heinz, *Early Modern European Civilization and its Political and Cultural Dynamism: The Menahem Stern Jerusalem Lectures* (Hanover and London: University Press of New England, 2008).

Schimert, Péter, 'Péter Pázmány and the reconstitution of the Catholic Aristocracy in Habsburg Hungary, 1600–1650' (unpublished PhD dissertation, University of North Carolina, Chapel Hill, 1989).

Schwartz, Stuart B., *All can be saved: Religious Tolerance and Salvation in the Iberian Atlantic World* (New Haven and London: Yale University Press, 2008).

Sciarra, Lino, 'L'Islam in Albania', *Oriente Moderno* new series 15 (1996), 1–77.

Selwyn, Jennifer, *A Paradise Inhabited by Devils: The Jesuits' Civilizing Mission in Early Modern Naples* (Aldershot: Ashgate, 2004).

Senyk, Sophia, 'The Union of Brest: An Evaluation' in B. Groen (ed.), *Four Hundred Years: Union of Brest 1596–1996* (Leuven: Peeters Publishing House, 1998), pp. 1–16.

Setton, Kenneth, *Venice, Austria and the Turks in the Seventeenth Century* (Philadelphia: The American Philosophical Society, 1991).

Sheehan, Anthony, 'The Recusancy Revolt of 1603: A reinterpretation', *Archivium Hibernicum* 38 (1983), 3–13.

Sheils, William, '"Getting on" and "getting along" in parish and town: Catholics and their neighbours in England', in Benjamin Kaplan, Bob Moore, Henk Van Nierop, and Judith Pollmann (eds), *Catholic Communities in Protestant States: Britain and the Netherlands c. 1570–1720* (Manchester: Manchester University Press, 2009), pp. 67–83.

Shell, Alison, *Catholicism, Controversy and the English Literary Imagination 1558–1660* (Cambridge: Cambridge University Press, 1999).

Signorotto, Gianvittorio, 'The *Squadrone Volante:* "Independent" Cardinals and European Politics in the Second Half of the Seventeenth Century', in Gianvittorio Signorotto and Maria Antonietta Visceglia (eds), *Court and Politics in Papal Rome, 1492–1700* (Cambridge: Cambridge University Press, 2002), pp. 177–211.

Slaski, Jan, 'Bellarmino e la letteratura della controriforma in Polonia', in Romeo de Maio, Agostino Borromeo, Luigi Gulia, Georg Lutz, and Aldo Mazzacane (eds), *Bellarmino e la Controriforma* (Sora: Centro di Studi Sorani Vincenzo Patriarca, 1990), pp. 521–30.

Spaans, Jo, 'Catholicism and Resistance to the Reformation in the Netherlands', in Philip Benedict, Guido Marnef, Henk Van Nierop, and Marc Venard (eds), *Reformation, Revolution and Civil War in France and the Netherlands 1555–1585* (Amsterdam: Royal Netherlands Academy of Arts and Sciences, 1999), pp. 149–63.

Springer, Elisabeth, 'Kaiser Rudolf II, Papst Clemens VIII und die bosnischen Christen: Taten und Untaten des Cavaliere Francesco Antonio Bertucci in kaiserlichen Diensten in den Jahren 1594 bis 1602', *Mitteilungen des Österreichischen Staatsarchiv* 33 (1980), 77–105.

Spurlock, R. Scott, 'The Laity and the Structure of the Catholic Church in early modern Scotland', in Robert Armstrong and Tadhg Ó hAnnracháin (eds), *Insular Christianity: Alternative models of the church in Britain and Ireland c. 1570–c.1700* (Manchester: Manchester University Press, 2013), pp. 231–51.

Stark, Rodney, 'Reconstructing the rise of Christianity: the role of women', *Sociology of Religion* 56 (1995), 229–44.

Stolarski, Piotr, *Friars on the Frontier: Catholic Renewal and the Dominican Order in Southeastern Poland, 1594–1648* (Farnham: Ashgate, 2010).

Sturmberger, Hans, *Adam Graff Herberstorff: Herrschaft und Freiheit im konfessionellen Zeitalter* (Vienna: Verlag für Geschichte und Politik, 1976).

Sutter Fichtner, Paula, 'Dynastic Marriage in Sixteenth-Century Habsburg Diplomacy and Statecraft: An Interdisciplinary approach', *The American Historical Review* 81:2 (1976), 243–65.

Svatoš, Martin, 'Zur Mehrsprachigkeit der Literatur in den böhmischen Ländern des 17. und 18. Jahrhunderts', *Wiener slavistisches Jahrbuch* 46 (2000), 33–42.

Szabó, Ferenc, *A Teológus Pázmány: A grazi 'theologica scholastica' Pázmány művében* (Roma: Metem, 1990).

Szakály, Ferenc, 'The Hungarian-Croatian border defense system and its collapse', in János Bak and Béla K. Király (eds), *From Hunyadi to Rákóczi: War and Society in Late Medieval and Early Modern Hungary* (Brooklyn, NY: Social Science Monographs, Brooklyn College Press, 1982).

Szechi, Daniel, 'Defending the True Faith: Kirk, state and Catholic missioners in Scotland, 1653–1755', *Catholic Historical Review* 82 (1996), 397–411.

Tallon, Alain, *La France et Le Concile de Trente (1518–1563)* (Paris: Diffusions de Boccard, 1997).

Tapié, Victor L., *The Rise and Fall of the Habsburg Monarchy* (London: Pall Mall Press, 1971).

Tatarenko, Laurent, 'La Naissance de l'Union de Brest: La Curie romaine et le tournant de l'année 1595', *Cahiers du Monde russe* 46: 1/2 (2005), 345–54.

Tatarenko, Laurent, 'Pluriconfessionnalité et politique de tolerance: le cas de la Pologne' in Wolfgang Kaiser (ed.) *L'Europe en conflits: les Affrontements religieux et la genèse de l'Europe modern vers 1500–vers 1650* (Rennes: Presses Universitaires de Rennes, 2008), pp. 239–66.

Taunton, Nina and Hart, Valerie, '*King Lear*, King James and the gunpowder treason of 1605', *Renaissance Studies* 17 (2003), 695–715.

Tazbir, Janusz, *A State Without Stakes: Polish Religious Toleration in the Sixteenth and Seventeenth Centuries* (Wzdawniczy: Panstwowy Instytut, 1973).

Thils, Gustave, *Les Notes de l'Église dans l'apologétique catholique depuis la réforme* (Gembloux: J. Duculot, 1937).

Ting Pong Lee, Ignacio, 'La actividad de la Sagrada Congregación frente al Regio Padronado' in Josef Metzler (ed.), *Sacrae Congregationis de Propaganda Fide Memoria Rerum (350 anni a servizio della missioni 1622–1972)* (three vols, Rome, Freiburg, Vienna: Herder, 1971–6), pp. 353–438.

Toifl, Leopold and Leitgeb, Hildegaard, *Die Türkeneinfälle in der Steiermark und in Kärnten vom 15. Bis zum 17. Jahrhundert* (Vienna: Bundesverlag, 1991).

Tollet, Daniel, 'Cohabitation, concurrence et conversion dans la confederation Polono-Lithuanienne au tournant des xvie et xviie siècles', in Eszter Andor and István György Tóth (eds), *Frontiers of Faith: Religious Exchange and the Constitution of Religious Identities 1400–1750* (Budapest: Central European University European Science Foundation, 2001), pp. 67–78.

Tusor, Péter, 'Az 1639. Évi nagyszombati Püspökkari Konferencia: A magyar klérus és a római Kúria kapcsolatainak válsága és reformja', *Századok* 134 (2000), 431–59.

Tóth, István György, 'Between Islam and Catholicism: Bosnian Franciscan Missionaries in Turkish Hungary, 1584–1716', *The Catholic Historical Review* 89 (2003), 409–33.

Tóth, István György, 'Old and New Faith in Hungary, Turkish Hungary, and Transylvania' in R. Po-chia Hsia (ed.), *A Companion to the Reformation World* (Oxford: Blackwell Publishing, 2004), pp. 205–22.

Tóth, István György, *Politique et religion dans la Hongrie du XVIIe siècle: Lettres des missionnaires de la Propaganda Fide* (Paris: Honoré Champion, 2004).

Tóth, István György, 'A Propaganda megalapítása és Magyarország (1622)', *Történelmi Szemle* 42: 1–2 (2000), 19–68.

Tóth, István György (ed.), *A Concise History of Hungary: The History of Hungary from the Early Middle Ages to the Present* (Budapest: Corvina, 2005).

Tutino, Stefania, *Law and Conscience: Catholicism in Early Modern England, 1570–1625* (Ashgate: Aldershot, 2007).

Urban, Wincenty, 'L'oeuvre des missions de l'église catholique en pologne', in Marian Rechowicz (ed.), *Millénaire du Catholicisme en Pologne* (Lublin: The Scientific Society of the Catholic University in Lublin, 1969), pp. 357–409.

Válka, Josef, 'Die "Politiques": Konfessionelle Orientierung und politische Landesinteressen in Böhmen und Mähren (bis 1630)', in Joackim Bahlke, Hans-Jürgen Bömelburg, and Norbert Kersken (eds), *Ständefreiheit und Staatsgestaltung in Ostmitteleuropa: Übernationale Gemeinsamkeiten in der politischen Kultur vom 16–18. Jahrhundert* (Leipzig: De Gruyter, 1996), pp. 229–41.

Van Eck, Xander, 'Paintings for clandestine Catholic churches in the Republic: typically Dutch', in Benjamin Kaplan, Bob Moore, Henk Van Nierop, and Judith Pollmann (eds), *Catholic Communities in Protestant States: Britain and the Netherlands c. 1570–1720* (Manchester: Manchester University Press, 2009), pp. 216–29.

Van Horn Melton, James, 'The nobility in the Bohemian and Austrian lands, 1620–1780', in H.M. Scott (ed.), *The European Nobilities* (two vols, New York: Longman, 1995), 2, pp. 105–11.

Večeva, Ekaterina, 'L'église catholique et le peuple bulgare (XVIIe-XVIIIe siècle)', *Bulgarian Historical Review* 11 (1983), 65–84.

Visceglia, Maria Antonietta, *La Città Rituale: Roma e le sue cerimonie in età moderna* (Rome: Viella, 2002).

Vodipivec, Peter, 'Reformation and Counter-Reformation in Inner Austria', in Eszter Andor and István György Tóth (eds), *Frontiers of Faith: Religious Exchange and the Constitution of Religious Identities 1400–1750* (Budapest: Central European University European Science Foundation, 2001), pp. 203–12.

Von Pastor, Ludwig (trans. Ernest Graf), *The History of the Popes from the Close of the Middle Ages 27* (London: Kegan Paul, Trench, Trubner & Co., 1938).

Walker, Claire, 'Prayer, patronage and political conspiracy: English nuns and the Restoration', *Historical Journal* 43 (2000), 1–23.

Walker, Claire, 'Priests, nuns, presses and prayer: the Southern Netherlands and the contours of English Catholicism', in Benjamin Kaplan, Bob Moore, Henk Van Nierop, and Judith Pollmann (eds), *Catholic Communities in Protestant States: Britain and the Netherlands c. 1570–1720* (Manchester: Manchester University Press, 2009), pp. 139–55.

Walsh, T.J., *The Irish Continental College Movement: The Colleges at Bordeaux, Toulouse, and Lille* (Dublin and Cork: Golden Eagle Books, 1973).

Walsham, Alexandra, *Church Papists: Catholicism, conformity and confessional polemic in early modern England* (Woodbridge: Boydell Press, 1993).

Walsham, Alexandra, '"Domme Preachers"? Post-Reformation English catholicism and the culture of print', *Past & Present* 168 (2000), 72–123.

Walsham, Alexandra, 'Translating Trent? English Catholicism and the Counter Reformation', *Historical Research* 78 (2005), 288–310.

Walter, Tony and Davie, Grace, 'The religiosity of women in the modern West', *The British Journal of Sociology* 49 (1998), 640–60.

Weaver, Andrew H., 'Music in the Service of Counter-Reformation Politics: The Immaculate Conception at the Habsburg Court of Ferdinand III (1637–57)', *Music and Letters* 87 (2006), 361–78, at 363–5.

Weiss Ozorak, Elizabeth, 'The power, but not the glory: how women empower themselves through religion', *Journal for the Scientific Study of Religion* 35 (1996), 17–29.

Williams, Glanmor, *Welsh Reformation Essays* (Cardiff: University of Wales Press, 1967).

Williams, Glanmor, *Recovery, reorientation and Reformation: Wales c. 1415–1642* (Oxford: Oxford University Press, 1987).

Williams, Glanmor, *Renewal and Reformation: Wales c. 1415–1642* (Oxford: Oxford University Press, 1993).

Wilson, P.H., 'The Causes of the Thirty Years War', *English Historical Review* 123 (2008), 554–86.

Winkelbauer, Thomas, *Fürst und Fürstendiener: Gundaker von Liechtenstein, ein österreichischer Aristokrat des konfessionellen Zeitalters* (Vienna: Oldenbourg Verlag, 1999).

Wright, A.D., *The Counter-Reformation: Catholic Europe and the non-Christian world* (London: Weidenfeld and Nicolson, 1982).

Wright, A.D., 'Bellarmine, Baronius and Federico Borromeo', in Romeo de Maio, Agostino Borromeo, Luigi Gulia, Georg Lutz, and Aldo Mazzacane (eds), *Bellarmino e la Controriforma* (Sora: Centro di Studi Sorani Vincenzo Patriarca, 1990), pp. 325–70.

Wright, A.D., *The Early Modern Papacy: From the Council of Trent to the French Revolution, 1564–1789* (Harlow: Longman, 2000).

Wright, A.D., *The Divisions of French Catholicism, 1629–45: The Parting of the Ways* (Farnham: Ashgate, 2011).

Yates, Frances A., *Astraea: The Imperial Theme in the Sixteenth Century* (London: Pimlico).

Zdeněk, David, 'Lutherans, Utraquists and the Bohemian Confession of 1575', *Church History* 68 (1999), 294–336.

Zen, Stefano, 'Bellarmino e Baronio', in Romeo de Maio, Agostino Borromeo, Luigi Gulia, Georg Lutz, and Aldo Mazzacane (eds), *Bellarmino e la Controriforma* (Sora: Centro di Studi Sorani Vincenzo Patriarca, 1990), pp. 279–321.

Index

Accademia dei Virtuosi 197
Acquaviva, Claudio, general of the Society of
  Jesus 18–19, 186–8
Act of Uniformity, Ireland (1560) 11, 45
Adamites 228
Adrian (Pope) 44
Adriatic littoral 150
Agan (Jesuit College) 178
Ahmed I (1590–1617), Ottoman sultan 186
Albania 146, 148, 183, 198, 221
  Catholics 168, 180, 183
  Orthodox 183
Alberigo, Guiseppe 3
Albert of Brandenburg-Ansbach, grand
  master of the Teutonic knights 76
Aldobrandini, Cinzio
  (Cardinal-nephew) 21, 157
Aldobrandini, Giovanni Francesco, papal
  general 149, 159, 162, 167
Aldobrandini, Ippolitio (see Clement VIII)
Aldobrandini, Pietro (Cardinal-nephew) 21
Alessi, Bishop of 199
Allegretti, Giovanni Francesco 147
Alps 1, 228
Alsolindvar 186
Alt, Salome 102
Alvinczi, Péter 130
Amalteo, Attila, papal nuncio to
  Transylvania 154
Americas 43, 142, 198
Amsterdam 60–1, 224
Anabaptists 25, 110–11, 228
Angelo, Friar 147
Anglicanism 8, 118
Anglo-Norman invasion of Ireland 44
Anglo-Saxon conversion to Christianity 219
Anna (Anne) of Denmark, Queen of Scots,
  England and Ireland 41
Annales Ecclesiastici 22, 26
Annals of the Four Masters 68
Anti-Islamic wars 140, 144, 147,
  168, 230
Antiquarianism 113
Anti-Trinitarianism 25, 77, 82
Anti-Unitarianism 81
Apostolic Constitutions 6
Aquitaine 178
Ardfert and Aghadoe diocese 53
Armenians 76
  church 186
Arminians 61
Arsengo, Girolamo 141

Asia 142
Atlantic archipelago (Britain and Ireland) 7, 29,
  55, 69
Augustinian Order 106
Aulic Council 105
Austria (*Erblande*/Inner Austria) 8, 18, 27, 36,
  78, 97–8, 101, 103, 105–9, 112, 114–16,
  119, 131, 173, 220–2
  Austrians 149
  Catholic clergy 101–2
  Estates 98–101, 106, 122, 155
  nobility 98, 101, 105, 107–9
  peasant revolt 104, 108, 135
  Protestantism 99–101, 104–5, 107
  re-Catholicization 99–101, 104–5, 107, 135
  see also Habsburg dynasty
Avignon 197

Balásfy, Thomas 196
Balaton, Lake 184
Balduinus, Friedrich 131
Balkan Peninsula 7–8, 16, 27, 39, 144, 147,
  150, 152, 159, 168–9, 218, 221, 227
  Apostolic visitations 141
  Catholic population 177, 194, 208–9
  Christian population 16, 27–8, 141–2,
    146–7, 149, 154, 170, 185
  Northern Balkans 173–212
  Orthodox population 208
  Ottoman zone 141, 177, 179
Baltic 18
Bánffy, Kristóf 186
Bar, archbishopric 180, 183
Barlow, Ambrose 37
Baronius, Cesare 21–4, 26, 79
Baroque devotion 106
Basiliens of the congregation of the Holy
  Trinity 89
Basta, George 166
Báthory, Andrew 154
Báthory, Balthasar 154
Báthory, Cardinal Andrew 154, 163–7, 171
Báthory dynasty 14, 154
Báthory, Sigismund, Prince of Transylvania
  142–4, 147, 153–7, 159–66, 170–2
Báthory, Stephen 154
Báthory, Stephen (Stefan), King of
  Poland-Lithuania (1576–86) 82, 84, 96,
  154, 156
Batthyány, Adám 123
Bavaria 105
Béarn 178

Index

261

partium 121
patriots 124
Protestant nobility 122–3
re-Catholicization 119, 126, 128, 134, 142, 214
Royal Hungary 119–21, 128, 133–4, 153, 159, 167, 170, 177, 184, 186, 197–9, 203
Turkish conquest 125–7, 143, 180–1, 184
Turkish zone 185–6, 195, 198–202, 207
wars in 16, 119, 121, 148, 152, 154, 162, 228
Hussites 75, 109–10, 219, 228
Hussite mass, 112

Iberian Peninsula 67, 221
Iconoclasm 60
Idolatry 126–7, 130
Ignatian spirituality 97
Il Cappucino Scozzeze 32
Illésházy, István 119
Illyrian College (Loreto) 207, 209
Illyrian College (Rome) 147
Imitation of Christ 129
Immaculate Conception (doctrine) 106, 114
Imperial Army 148, 158, 161–2, 216
Imperial Court 156, 158, 161, 163–4, 166, 171, 197
Imperial Diet 143, 155
Imperial Electoral College 216
In Coena Domini (Papal Bull) 145
Ingoli, Francesco 196–7, 201, 204, 208, 210
Ingolstadt 22, 24, 30
Jesuit University 100
Innocent X, Pope (1644–54/5) 7, 196, 211, 224–5, 229
Gianbattista Pamfili 196
and Irish and English Catholics 31
Pamfili papacy 9, 224, 226–7
Inquisition 72–3, 120, 215
Ireland 10–11, 27–33, 36, 38, 41, 43–60, 63, 67–70, 72, 94, 107, 117, 132, 175, 177, 179, 202, 209, 211, 220–2, 229–30
anti-Protestantism 56
Catholic episcopate 52–3, 55, 70, 179, 202, 226
Catholic reformation 51–2, 58–9
English government in 50–2, 57, 59, 107
English military intervention 46, 48–9, 70, 220–1
Irish language 51, 59, 117, 175
Irish mercenaries in Spanish service 49
Irish parliament 11, 45, 51, 57, 117
kingdom of Ireland (1541) 44
medieval church 44–5, 48, 68
national identity 59, 68, 70, 117, 221
New English settlers in 47, 50, 56–7, 117, 132, 222
papal donation 30, 44
papal military intervention 12, 49

Protestant ascendancy 221
Protestant boroughs 51, 221
Protestant (established) church 11–13, 48, 50–1, 54, 59, 69, 107, 132
Protestant community 50–1, 55–6, 67, 69–70, 117
Protestant episcopate 11, 45, 51
rebellions 11, 49, 54
Royalists 56–7, 67, 224–5, 227–8
sectarian violence 56–7
Spanish military intervention 13, 49
trading links with continent 48
traditional elites 49–50, 52–3, 221
Irish Catholics 30, 43, 179, 209, 221, 224–5, 228
clergy 55, 179, 202
denunciation to authorities 202
education abroad 12, 14, 47, 49, 53, 58, 74
erosion of ethnic differences 57–9, 69, 221
Irish Colleges 14, 53, 209
(*see also* Salamanca, Louvain)
irredentism 56–7, 221
massive property confiscations 226
repression 96
urban elite almost liquidated 221
Irish Franciscans 70
mission to Gaelic Scotland 43, 177, 209
Observants 48, 177
Third Order Regular 48
Isabella Clara Eugenia (1566–1633), daughter of Philip II, Infanta of Spain, ruler of the Spanish Netherlands 9, 65, 139, 151
Islamic world 139–40
Islamicization 96, 136, 140, 142, 168, 180, 183, 185, 221
Istanbul (Constantinople) 140–1, 147, 152, 160, 172, 186, 188, 195, 198, 204, 216
exiled Latin patriarch 198
Isteni Igazságra Vezérlö Kalauz (*Guide to the Divine Truth*) 130
Italians 103, 146, 181
missionaries in Hungary 129, 142, 180, 203–7, 209
population in Austria 109
princes 144, 146, 149
Italy 8, 20, 26–7, 32, 67, 72–3, 117, 140, 143–4, 145, 149–50, 158–9, 174, 177–8, 182–3, 204, 208, 211–12, 216–17, 219, 221, 230
Ivkovič, Toma, Bishop of Scardona 200–1

Jagiellonian dynasty 82, 96
James I, King of England, Scotland and Ireland (1603–25)
James VI of Scotland (1567–1625) 30, 38, 40, 50, 52–3
outbreak of Thirty Years Wa 217
Jansenism 70, 176
Japan 30